D1385331

Birding Nebraska

Jon Farrar

NEBRASKAland Magazine

Volume 82, Number 1, January-February 2004
Published monthly except for combined January-February and August-September issues by
the Nebraska Game and Parks Commission, 2200 N. 33rd Street, Lincoln, NE 68503.
Copyright 2004 by the Nebraska Game and Parks Commission, all rights reserved.

ISSN: 0028-1964
ISBN: 0-9727806-0-2
Periodicals postage paid at Lincoln, Nebraska.
POSTMASTER: Send all address changes to NEBRASKAland Magazine,
P.O. Box 30370, Lincoln, NE 68503-0370.

Cover: Emblems of Nebraska's prairie avifauna, long-billed curlews can be found on western grasslands. Photo by Jon Farrar.
Inside Front Cover: Eastern screech-owls are at the western edge of their range in western Nebraska. Photo by Bob Grier.

CONTENTS

White-throated sparrows are common migrants in eastern Nebraska and some winter in the southeast.

INTRODUCTION

"NOW WHY IS IT that we have so many birds in Nebraska? I do not like to be referring to that old worn-out subject of the location of Nebraska, the variation in surface configuration of the state, the difference in altitude of different sections, and so on, but I can hardly avoid speaking of these points here. Every one of you upon looking at that map of Nebraska can see that it is located centrally between the floor and the ceiling; just about such a position has Nebraska with reference to the rest of the states."

These "worn-out" words were spoken by University

Five species of hummingbirds have been reported in Nebraska, of which two are classified as accidental. The ruby-throated hummingbird (above) is the most common, especially in the east where it is an occasional nester.

of Nebraska zoologist Lawrence Bruner at the first meeting of the Nebraska Ornithologists' Union (NOU) in December 1899. Words conveying the same meaning, supported by substantially more evidence, are still written and spoken today.

The first step in understanding Nebraska's bird life is to understand the state's geographical position on the continent. The geographic center of the contiguous United States is in north-central Kansas, and the geographic center of the North American continent is

in north-central North Dakota. Nebraska sells no postcards with either of those claims, but birds do not live in geographers' musty workbooks. Nebraska and neighboring states are the middle of the continent, and that alone accounts for a varied avifauna. While Nebraska may not be in the precise continental middle, it is in the center of the Great Plains – an enormous grassland that in its primal state rivaled the African Serengeti for wildlife abundance. Nebraska is large – more than 77,000 square miles – with diverse physiographic regions.

The second step in understanding Nebraska's variety of bird species is to recognize the state's range of bird habitats. It is in Nebraska that western coniferous forests meet eastern deciduous forests, and southern and northern grasslands merge. Nebraska is at the center of the great migration flyway spanning the Western Hemisphere, a highway in the sky along which many species pass in uncountable numbers twice each year as they travel between wintering and nesting grounds. Nebraska is on the southern edge of the nesting grounds for northern-breeding species and on the northern edge for southern-breeding species. Add the unique Sandhills region – fully one-quarter of the state, and as pristine an expanse of grassland as can be found on the continent – and the internationally important Rainwater Basin and Platte River complex in south-central Nebraska, and Nebraska becomes a darn good birding state. Nebraska is at the avian crossroads of the continent. On that count Nebraska could sell a few postcards.

Most states claim unique or exceptional avifauna of one sort or another. That is why birders travel from state to state – to see new species. In terms of number of species documented, Nebraska is about average. Of 1,049 known bird species in the lower 48 states, 447 are currently recognized by NOU as setting foot or flying over Nebraska. Of those, about half are regular or occasional breeders. Large states bordering subtropical regions or oceans support far more avian variety – Florida has 680 documented bird species, California 646 and Texas 628. Compared to its neighbors, Nebraska is in the middle – Oklahoma, Kansas and Colorado report a few more species, the Dakotas, Minnesota, Montana and Wyoming a few less.

Before Euroamerican settlement, eastern deciduous forests pioneered onto the Great Plains grasslands, hugging riverbottoms and valley bluffs where they were protected from wildfires and sheltered from the desiccating summer sun. From the west, coniferous forests ventured eastward along the Niobrara River and on rugged Panhandle escarpments. Between these forests was a vast grassland – tallgrass prairie in the east, shortgrass plains in the west and a blend of the two as mixed-grass prairie in the middle of the state. And there were wetlands – streams gathering into larger rivers coursing easterly to the Missouri River and their floodplains filled with oxbows and backwaters; shallow pools and ponds that filled with rainwater in south-central Nebraska; clear-watered lakes and marshes fed by groundwater in the Sandhills to the north. Between the Kansas and South Dakota state lines there was a ladder of wetlands – traditional staging and resting areas for migrating birds on twice-a-year travels.

First and foremost, though, Nebraska was a grassland state, and that largely explains why more bird species are not found here. Before Euroamerican settlement less than three percent of Nebraska's surface area was covered by woodlands. That percentage is about the same today but the distribution of woodlands in the state has changed. Those woodlands, however, are home to 48 percent of the state's breeding avifauna. More than 95 percent of the rest of the state was blanketed with grasslands – roughly one-third tallgrass prairie, one-third Sandhills prairie and one-third shortgrass and mixed-grass prairie. University of Nebraska ornithologist Paul Johnsgard calculated that Nebraska's grassland supported only about 30 breeding bird species or 15 percent of the state's avifauna. He attributes the paucity of grassland species to the fact that the Great Plains grassland was late developing compared to North American forests, and the full diversity of species that might one day have evolved here was never realized. Johnsgard also noted grasslands lack the structural complexity and habitat diversity of woodlands and woodland edge. Natural grasslands, especially large expanses, are rare in North America today. So it is not surprising that it is the grassland birds – greater prairie-chickens, upland sandpipers or Henslow's sparrows – that many birders travel to Nebraska to see.

Before settlement, and still today, wetlands were less than one percent of Nebraska's land surface, but they are incredibly rich in bird life. Like Nebraska's grasslands, they have changed in character. While natural wetlands in the Sandhills, Rainwater Basin and river floodplains have declined significantly, large reservoirs for flood control and irrigation have increased surface water in the state. Acre for acre, reservoirs do not support the abundance of bird life found in a marsh or shallow lake, especially during the breeding season, but they do account for species not formerly found in Nebraska. By Johnsgard's computations, wetlands, principally natural wetlands, are used by about 30 percent of the state's species during the breeding season.

While Nebraska is not the wild land it once was, the birds still come, albeit in diminished abundance. Some species are no longer found in Nebraska. Two – the Carolina parakeet and the passenger pigeon – are extinct. Some vanished for decades and have since returned. Other species that historically were not here have come. The list of Nebraska birds yesterday, today and tomorrow is a snapshot in time. It is ever changing.

Birding Nebraska is not an identification guide. Many excellent identification guides are available, and some are listed in the recommended reading section. Rather, this is a guide to where to find birds in Nebraska, and it provides an overview of the state's avifauna, its history and study.

We hope even expert Nebraska birders – those from whose collective knowledge much of the information for these pages was drawn – will find new tidbits of lore and natural history. People who watch birds in Nebraska are a diverse lot: Those from distant states and countries who come here to find species not found where they live; birders from one part of Nebraska who occasionally travel to other regions of the state in search of birds; and birders who seldom stray far from home, content to find old friends in the woodlands, grasslands and wetlands where they live. We hope all will find something of value in this special issue.

Recommended birding destinations are at the core of this special issue. Though derived from many sources, most are recommendations from some of the state's best birders and wildlife managers, and from *The Nebraska Bird Review,* the official publication of the Nebraska Ornithologists' Union. Today much is known about Nebraska's bird life. Some is recorded in books, some in scientific monographs, and much in 70 years of *The Nebraska Bird Review.* A wealth of information, though, resides in the memories of living birders, written by hand on note cards and entered into their computer hard drives. We have used all these sources in fashioning this, an overview of Nebraska bird life. Many people contributed their time and knowledge to this issue, and their assistance is noted in the acknowledgements in the appendix. In preparing this guide we attempted to simplify technical information so it can be easily understood, while not compromising accuracy. Some birders will want additional information, and some excellent sources are listed in the appendix. Several books about Nebraska's birds have been published in the past five years. They are a warehouse of information and should be acquired by serious birders while still in print.

The story of Nebraska's bird life, and of the men and women who have studied it, is rich. The pages that follow tell stories of the loss of wild lands and the accompanying losses of avifaunal heritage. But these pages also tell stories of hope for the future. Never in this state and nation has there been such concern for the preservation of wild creatures, and commitment to protect what remains and to bring back some of what once was so abundant. Because of the perseverance of thousands of bird watchers – both professionals and amateurs – spanning two centuries, we know more of Nebraska's rich bird life today than ever before. So, let our journey through time and across the state begin. The birds are on the move and we need to start finding them. ∎

EARLY BIRD STUDY

THE STUDY OF BIRDS in what is now Nebraska began long before Lewis and Clark scratched notes with quill pens in morocco-bound notebooks. The daily lives of American Indians were intricately interwoven with the plants and animals around them. To Indians, the comings and goings of birds were surely as important signs of changing seasons as the position of the sun or stars in the sky. Birds told Indians many things: Of the nearness of water, the approach of danger, and the presence of plant and animal foods. The Pawnee believed magpies told the nearness of bison. Eagles, hawks, woodpeckers and

Birds played an important role in the daily lives of American Indians, and feathers were often used as adornments. Karl Bodmer painted the northern **Great Plains Mandan Indians** *shown here in 1833.*

owls were sacred and honored birds among many Great Plains tribes. The Indians' study of birds was neither abstract nor scientific, it was practical and spiritual.

For Native Americans, birds and their eggs were food, their plumage ornamentation for lodges, clothing and ceremonies. The Sioux name for the April moon translates as "when geese lay their eggs," an observation probably more utilitarian than merely marking the passage of time. The name of their July moon related

to the molting time of geese – a time when adults and still flightless juveniles could be easily captured. The feathers of some species were highly valued. The red-feathered head of a pileated woodpecker was the equal of a quality bison robe to tribes north of that woodpecker's range. Eagle, owl and turkey feathers have been identified as ornamental objects of the Omaha tribe. Feathers were the fletching for arrows and ornamentation for quivers. Sacred bundles and war bundles containing bird skins or feathers were believed to impart the strengths and attributes of the species to the man.

Alice C. Fletcher and Francis La Flesche in the *Twenty-Seventh Annual Report of the Bureau of American Ethnology, 1905-1906,* described two Omaha tribe ceremonial pipe stems fashioned from ash and richly decorated: "The stem was feathered, like an arrow, from the wing of the golden eagle. Around the mouthpiece was a band of iridescent feathers from the neck of the duck; midway the length was a ruff of owl feathers; over the bowl end were stretched the head, neck, and breast of the mallard duck . . . From each stem depended a fan-like arrangement of feathers from the tail of the golden eagle, held together and bound to the stem by two buckskin thongs; the end, which hung from the fan-shaped appendage, was tipped with a downy eagle feather. One of these fan-shaped feather arrangements was composed of ten feathers from the tail of a mature golden eagle. These were dark and mottled in appearance and were fastened to the blue stem; this pipe represented the feminine element. The other stem, which was painted green, had its appendage of seven feathers from the tail of a young golden eagle. The lower part of these feathers is white; the tips only are dark. These were the feathers worn by men as a mark of war honors and this pipe symbolized the masculine forces." Another article used with the two ceremonial pipes was a whistle fashioned from the wing bone of an eagle.

Fletcher and La Flesche wrote "the association of birds with the powers of the air is very ancient." Some species were thought "in close relation with the storm and the storm cloud, the abode of Thunder, the god of war. The flight of the birds brought them near the god and they were regarded as his special messengers." The Omahas believed that because birds had command of the sky they observed all that occurred on the Earth below, they watched the warrior in battle. Swallows that flew "before the coming tempest were regarded as heralds of the approaching god." Birds of prey were associated with the destruction caused by storms, crows and other carrion feeders were believed to haunt "the places where the dead lay" and were considered allies of the "devastating forces of the god of war."

Fletcher and La Flesche listed 56 birds recognized by the Omaha tribe, although exactly which species their names referred to is in some instances conjectural. In other cases there can be little doubt as to the species. The Omaha name for the American bittern translates as "looks up at the sky," a reference to the bittern's habit of freezing with bill pointed skyward when alarmed or threatened. A distinction was made between the "big curlew" and a smaller curlew, perhaps the Eskimo curlew. Blue-winged teal, mallards ("green neck") and wood ducks ("summer duck" or "the crying duck") were named. Five hawks were named, as were five owls, including the barred, horned, screech and snowy. Only one thrush was named but three woodpeckers, suggesting the importance of that family in Omaha mythology and ceremony. The Omaha name for hummingbird translates as "butterfly bird." While the list of Nebraska bird species numbers well over 400 today, many people would be pressed to name 56 or know nearly as much about them as did the Omaha tribe.

Birds were prominent in American Indian stories and myths. To the Omahas, the eagle was a bird of tireless strength, the owl a symbol of the night and death, the woodpecker of the day and life. Similarly, to the Pawnee, the eagle was "chief of the day," the owl "chief of the night," and the duck "chief of the water." In a twist of irony, considering the low esteem in which the crow is generally held today, the crow figured prominently in the Omaha tribe's creation mythology. Waterfowl and raptors were of great importance to the Omahas. They made few distinctions among the small songbirds.

Among the Teton Sioux, the owl was a sacred bird. "The owl moves at night when men are asleep," Frances Densmore wrote in *Mandan and Hidatsa Music*, a Bureau of American Ethnology bulletin published in 1923. "The medicine-man gets his power through dreams at night and believes that his dream is clear, like the owl's sight. So he promises that he will never harm an owl. If he did so, his power would leave him. For this reason some medicine-men wear owl feathers. The medicine-man also regards the owl as having very soft, gentle ways, and when he begins to treat sick persons he is supposed to treat them very gently."

Densmore also wrote that by honoring the crow, the Crow Owners Society of the Teton Sioux believed their arrows would "fly swift and straight as the crow." Among the Lakotas, small birds – swallows and black-capped chickadees – could be messengers from the gods. The Pawnee believed the blue jay carried prayers and sacrifices to the sky gods, and that meadowlarks and bluebirds were messengers. The tiny wren was honored by the Pawnee as a creature of humility, revealing to all that no matter how small and insignificant, one can be "cheerful and happy." The feathers of cranes were of sacred importance to the Pawnee who occupied the Loup and Platte rivers

"We need another wiser and perhaps more mystical concept of animals. Remote from universal nature, and living by complicated artifice, man in civilization surveys the creature through the glass of his knowledge and sees thereby a feather magnified and the whole image in distortion. We patronize them for their incompleteness, for their tragic fate of having taken form so far below ourselves. And therein we err, and greatly err. For the animal shall not be measured by man. In a world older and more complete than ours they move finished and complete, gifted with extensions of the senses we have lost or never attained, living by voices we shall never hear. They are not brethren, they are not underlings; they are other nations, caught with ourselves in the net of life and time, fellow prisoners of the splendor and travail of the earth."

– Henry Beston,
The Outermost House, 1947

Tab. 48.

INDIANISCHE GERÄTHSCHAFTEN UND WAFFEN. USTENSILES ET ARMES INDIENS.

INDIAN UTENSILS AND ARMS.

Feathers were used for utilitarian purposes such as fletching for arrows but also lavishly employed as ornaments for ceremonial objects. Many species of birds were assigned special importance such as swallows, which the Lakota believed could be messengers from the gods. Eagle feathers were prized because the bird symbolized the god of war. Karl Bodmer painted the objects of Northern Plains tribes above.

in Nebraska.

Because many Indian tribes translated the character and nature of some bird species into human characteristics, bird names frequently became Indian names. Some species were revered, the displays of others imitated. Unfortunately, little of the ties between birds and American Indians, other than artifacts, was preserved. Among tribes whose spoken languages endured long enough to pass into written history, it is evident that tribes had specific names for bird species. Perhaps no people since have held the birds of the Great Plains in such esteem.

Early Exploration of the Plains

Francisco Vasquez Coronado and his 30 Spanish horsemen might have ventured as far north as Nebraska in 1541; certainly they traversed Kansas. Upon his return to Mexico, Coronado reported his findings to the King of Spain, describing the region, mentioning pronghorns, "lobo" wolves, prairie dogs and jackrabbits, but not one word about bird life they encountered. By the 1670s French trappers and traders

were spreading across the Great Plains from the northeast, not in search of gold as were the Spaniards, but for the pelts of beavers and other furbearers. The first confirmed incursion into Nebraska by Spaniards from the south was led by Lt. Col. Pedro De Villasur, who traveled as far as the Platte River in 1720. The Spaniards had a skirmish with the Pawnee, and retreated south. In 1739, Pierre and Paul Mallet and six French companions journeyed from St. Louis, up the Missouri River to the Otoe villages at the mouth of the Platte, and farther north probably to what is today Dixon County. Then, they traveled overland southwest to a river they named the "Plate," the Platte River of today, south across the Republican River and ultimately to the Spanish city of Santa Fe. None of the French trappers, traders and explorers left a written word of the birds they encountered. Their business was commerce, and birds had no value.

In 1762, Louis XV of France ceded the Province of Louisiana, including most of the northern Great Plains and present-day Nebraska, to Charles III of Spain. For 38 years Louisiana remained a Spanish province, but no one came to study the birds. At the close of the

18th century, James Mackay, a Scotsman working for a Spanish trading company in St. Louis – the Commercial Company for the Discovery of Nations of the Upper Missouri – explored northern and northeastern Nebraska. Late in 1795 he was part of a party sent up the Missouri River to establish commerce with the natives. After overwintering along the Missouri River in present-day Dakota County, he proceeded west along what one day would be the northern border of Nebraska, crossed the Niobrara River in eastern Cherry County, then turned south into the northern Sandhills lake country and looped back to the Missouri River. Mackay passed through country surely rife with summer bird life but he made no notes. Bird study remained the realm of the Sioux, the Pawnee, the Otoe and the Ponca.

Two hundred years ago, in the spring of 1804, Meriwether Lewis and William Clark, as instructed by President Thomas Jefferson, began their historic exploration of America west of the Missouri. Only four years earlier, France had reacquired control of the vast Louisiana territory. On May 2, 1803, diplomats signed a treaty in Paris transferring the Louisiana territory from France to the United States, all 828,000 square miles, for $15 million. Even before the treaty was signed, Jefferson had laid plans for an expedition to reconnoiter the American West. While Jefferson was as interested in commercial exploitation of the mid-continent, as had been the French and Spanish, he was also naturally curious about unknown regions and had a keen interest in the natural world. Among Jefferson's instructions to Lewis and Clark was to observe "the animals of the country generally & especially those not known in the U.S., the remains and accounts of any which may [be] deemed rare or extinct."

Lewis and Clark left St. Louis on May 14, 1804. On July 11 they reached land that 63 years later would become Nebraska, and made camp on a large sandy island colonized by willows at the mouth of the Big Nemaha River southeast of present-day Rulo in Richardson County. On September 7, where the Missouri River turned north into present-day South Dakota, the expedition left Nebraska behind. If the formal study of Nebraska birds has a beginning, it was during those two summer months.

During their time along Nebraska's eastern coast, Lewis and Clark described surprisingly few species of birds, about 20, in their journals, certainly far fewer than they saw. Still, they did admirably well considering no one in the party was a trained naturalist, and that the expedition was daily executing numerable assignments for President Jefferson – mapping uncharted territory, negotiating with and studying Native American tribes – while struggling to move their keelboat upstream in the debris-filled Missouri River. Lewis and Clark recorded 556 miles of Nebraska shoreline, 171 miles more than is present today, an understandable measure of the effect of channelization, impounding and confining the Missouri River, and a suggestion of the incomprehensible loss of wild lands

and wildlife that occurred during the past 100 years.

After the acquisition of the Louisiana territory, and the historic expedition of Lewis and Clark, exploration of the Great Plains became more frequent, and naturalists often accompanied later expeditions. Through their observations and writings, knowledge of Nebraska's bird life grew.

The Englishman John Bradbury, accompanied by botanist and ornithologist Thomas Nuttall, traveled up the Missouri River from St. Louis to present-day Washington County, Nebraska, in 1811, and Bradbury traveled overland with fur traders to an Otoe village in present-day Thurston County. Curiously, it was Bradbury, not Nuttall, who made notes about the birds of the Missouri River. Bradbury noted vultures, albeit obliquely, in what is now Otoe County, writing that the fur traders shot two wapiti [elk], "but they were so lean that we left them for the vultures." Nebraska ornithologist Myron Swenk, writing in *The Nebraska Bird*

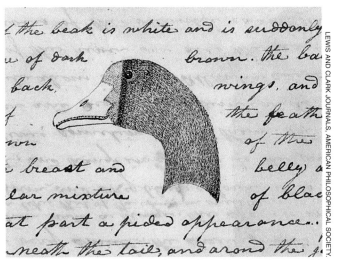

Meriwether Lewis frequently embellished his descriptions with sketches of species the Corps of Discovery expedition encountered. In 1806 he rendered this drawing of the greater white-fronted goose.

Review in the mid-1930s, assumed these vultures were turkey vultures, a species still common along the Missouri River bluffs. Bradbury noted the shooting of "prairie hens" in present-day Washington or Burt County, a species Swenk determined to be ruffed rouse; and the collection of "a bird of the genus recurvirostra," probably an American avocet in present-day Otoe County. Bradbury also related he encountered passenger pigeons about 25 miles south of the current Nebraska-Kansas state line, but he made no mention of the species in Nebraska.

Henry M. Brackenridge, who traveled up the Missouri with fur traders later in 1811 to join Nuttall and Bradbury before continuing upstream, recorded in May 1811 in the present Nemaha County that he "Killed some pigeons," an almost certain reference to passenger pigeons.

Usually, early-day naturalists and gadfly adventurers received safe passage through the Louisiana territory during the early-1800s by traveling with fur traders, who were armed and usually on good terms with native tribes. In 1812, Robert Stuart accompanied traders of the American Fur Company, the Astorians, who traveled from the mouth of the Columbia River eastward across the Rocky Mountains, crossing through the South Pass, and reaching the upper waters of the Platte River where they made winter camp. Driven from their camp by Arapahos, they fled east, arriving in present-day Nebraska the day before Christmas. Stalled by heavy snow, the party retreated to a winter camp near the present location of Torrington, Wyoming, where they remained until March 20, 1813, before resuming their journey down the Platte, reaching the mouth of Salt Creek on April 18. Stuart's narrative contains the earliest references to swans and curlews in Nebraska. In commenting on the birds Stuart reported, Swenk make no attempt to determine if the swans the party saw in present Garden, Keith, Buffalo, Phelps, and Kearney counties were tundra or trumpeter swans. Either species could have been present. Several swans were shot for food, and Stuart noted the roots of arrowhead, a common aquatic plant, were found in the crops of two shot in Kearney County.

Like earlier chroniclers, Stuart made no species distinctions when noting ducks or geese. Near the end of March, in eastern Garden County and western Keith County, Stuart and his companions encountered "an endless variety of Ducks" on swampy land along the North Platte River, and on April 1 a "quantity of wild

Fowl" north of the present-day city of North Platte. Three miles west of the present site of Keystone, Stuart flushed "five Pheasants or as they are called in this Country Prairie Hens," which Swenk assumed to be greater prairie-chickens although sharp-tailed grouse seem more likely. "Kurlews" and "Oldfield Larks" (the latter Swenk assumed to be western meadowlarks) were sighted south of present-day Shelton. One of Stuart's most useful observations was of a wild turkey killed in present-day Butler County and his comment that it was "the first we have seen," suggesting the western-most edge of the species and woodlands of any consequence along the Platte at that time. Farther downstream on the Platte and along the Missouri River he noted, "Turkeys are to be found in the greatest plenty." As with American Indians before them, and sportsmen after them, those who wrote of Nebraska's bird life in the early and mid-1800s were most likely to remark on birds large enough to make a meal.

Swelling Bird Notes

In 1819, naturalist Thomas Say traveled with the Major Stephen H. Long expedition up the Missouri River. The expedition wintered at Engineer's Cantonment just above present-day Omaha and the group remained there until June of the following year. Say's record of birds was the most complete and accurate accounting of Nebraska species to that time. He listed 145 bird species while camped on the Missouri River, including the Carolina parakeet and passenger pigeon. He made the first accepted, scientific description of the orange-crowned warbler. On the Iowa side of the river he collected a specimen of the long-billed dowitcher, the type specimen for that species. After leaving the Missouri River, the expedition journeyed west to the Rocky Mountains. Near Pawnee villages on the Platte River close to its confluence with the lower Loup River, Say collected the type specimen for the yellow-headed blackbird. A burrowing owl specimen taken at the same time once was the type specimen for the North American subspecies of burrowing owls, a distinction that now belongs to California. Also near the mouth of the Loup, Say recorded a marbled godwit with young, a breeding record for Nebraska not repeated until 1990 in Dawes County. There have been unconfirmed breeding reports in Sheridan County in recent years.

Even a casual birder today might have assembled lengthier and more accurate bird lists than naturalists who traversed the state during the early-1800s. In *Birds of Nebraska*, published in 2001, Roger Sharpe, Ross Silcock and Joel Jorgensen addressed that issue, writing: ". . . suspect identifications are commonplace among 19th century observers, leaving one to question historical geographic distributions of some species or the observational skills of observers or both. It should be noted, however, that some of these naturalists had limited experience in the American West and were often foreign-born and educated. Thus their familiarity

ROD NABHOLZ

*The **yellow warbler** is a common migrant and breeder statewide. The species usually nests in thickets and brush, especially in willows, along streams. Making a squeak often lures them from thickets.*

Red-shouldered hawks are rare migrants, winter visitors and breeders in eastern Nebraska. Fontenelle Forest Nature Center near Omaha is the only consistent nesting location in the state. Nest are most usually on wooded upland slopes near wetlands.

with the regional avifauna was limited, and they were also hampered by the absence of suitable reference works and field optics." There were no Peterson or Sibley field guides in 1804, not even Frank Chapman's *Bird-Life* illustrated with scant black-and-white drawings by Ernest Seton Thompson. When Lewis and Clark passed up the Missouri River, numbers of plump shorebirds scurrying about on sandbars were "small species of Kildee."

The authors of *Birds of Nebraska* remarked that one of the best natural history accounts of the region in the 19th century was the product of the travels of German explorer Prince Alexander Philipp Maximilian von Wied. Maximilian was intensely interested in observing and documenting the American West before it was settled. Accompanying him were Swiss artist Karl Bodmer and taxidermist David Dreidopple. The Bodmer paintings now in the Joslyn Art Museum's permanent collection in Omaha are a vivid impression of Nebraska and the Great Plains of that time.

Maximilian's party traveled up the Missouri River by steamboat in the spring of 1833, passing along what would become Nebraska's border during the first two weeks of May. After ascending the river to Fort Mackenzie in Montana, where they wintered, the party passed quickly down the Missouri River the following spring. While the expedition's brush with Nebraska was brief, their documentation of the native fauna and flora was significant. About 60 species were observed, collected or sketched in Nebraska, among them: eastern towhee, scarlet tanager, red-bellied woodpecker, northern flicker, common yellowthroat, northern cardinal, great crested flycatcher, yellow-breasted chat, house wren, American redstart, yellow warbler, eastern kingbird, purple martin, red-winged blackbird, mourning dove, whip-poor-will, passenger pigeon, greater prairie-chicken, long-billed curlew, upland sandpiper, swallow-tailed kite, pelican, wood duck and a host of herons, ducks, sparrows, finches, cuckoos and thrushes not identified by species.

While most of the bird species observed on the Maximilian expedition can still be found along the Missouri River today, some have vanished forever, such as the Carolina parakeet and passenger pigeon. Others, like the bald eagle, Canada goose and wild turkey, vanished but returned to their native haunts in

Historically, **woodlands along the Missouri River** *were restricted to the floodplain and ravines in the bluffs as shown in George Catlin's 1832 painting, "Blackbird's Grave," of what is now Thurston County. Prairie fires prevented woody plants from colonizing the bluff tops. Today, Missouri River bluffs are heavily wooded and eastern deciduous bird species are more abundant.*

recent times, often through reintroduction programs.

There were other expeditions in the early-1800s – Duke Paul Wilhelm along the Elkhorn in 1823, Zebulon Pike along the Republican River in 1829, John Kirk Townsend along the Platte in 1834, John C. Fremont up the Platte River and Lodgepole Creek in 1842 and others. Each left little more than sketchy descriptions of the landscape and precious few words about birds or other animal life. Townsend did, however, collect and describe two species along the Platte River in western Nebraska – the lark bunting and the chestnut-collared longspur – which were new to science and became type specimens for the species.

John James Audubon

In the spring of 1843, a naturalist whose life was largely devoted to the study of birds passed by what would be Nebraska on the Missouri River. From May 6 to about May 24, John James Audubon, traveling with companions John Bell, Edward Harris and Isaac Sprague (all of whom would have a bird species bearing their names) traveled the Missouri along Nebraska's east coast. Audubon's magnum opus, *The Birds of America,* had been published five years earlier, and his mission on the Missouri was sketching and studying mammals for his new work, *The Viviparous Quadrupeds of North America.*

But the painter did not neglect bird life. Audubon and Harris made notes on 150 species they observed and collected. "Notably absent today, however, are such species as the Carolina parakeet, pileated woodpecker, swallow-tailed kite, and common raven," Sharpe, Silcock and Jorgensen wrote in 2001. Since their book was published, the pileated woodpecker has returned to Missouri River woodlands and nested for several years in the Fontenelle Forest Nature Center south of Omaha. Audubon mentioned nesting bald eagles near Rulo, caged magpies at Fort Atkinson that had been trapped in the vicinity during the previous winter, and nesting Canada geese throughout the Nebraska portion of the trip.

The Harris's sparrow was first collected from the Missouri River woodlands. Because he thought the bird was a finch, Audubon named it *Fringilla harrisii* in honor of his friend and financial supporter, Edward Harris. Harris's name remains attached to the species' common name but is not part of the scientific name today, *Zonotrichia querula*. Similarly, a small vireo was collected by John Bell in present-day Dixon County and subsequently named Bell's vireo, *Vireo bellii*.

Bell's vireo, Harris's sparrow and the western meadowlark were all first described in Nebraska on Audubon's expedition, but the type specimens for those three species are all from birds collected later in other states. While some of the names applied to species reflect the knowledge and taxonomy of birds at that time – green-backed swallows, black-headed gulls, clay-colored buntings, Henslow's buntings, red-winged starling – the species to which they refer are obvious. While at the abandoned Fort Atkinson, Audubon saw

*Early explorers encountered large flocks of **American white pelicans** on the Missouri River. Lewis and Clark noted more than 5,000 flying over sandbars. John James Audubon painted the pelican shown.*

yellow-headed blackbirds for the first time and collected several for study.

Collecting specimens for study, often in numbers seeming to exceed the need, was a common practice of 19th century naturalists. Audubon was no exception and occasionally commented in his notes on the table qualities of unexpected species. On May 15, 1843, on the Nebraska side of the river near present-day Sioux City, the party discovered a heronry, almost certainly great blue herons. They shot four herons and a raven that had come to feed on eggs while the nests were unprotected. Before leaving the shoreline, the party noted a difference in the song of the meadowlarks. "We saw Meadow Larks whose songs and single notes are quite different from those of the Eastern States," Audubon wrote. "We have not been able to kill one to decide if new or not."

As instructive as the bird notes assembled on the Audubon expedition are, the descriptions of the Missouri River Valley before it was transformed by settlement and agriculture are an even more precious record. As the party traveled upstream the heavily wooded floodplain and valley bluffs thinned. Above the mouth of the Platte River they noted extensive floodplain prairie. Because of the absence of timber

Red-bellied woodpeckers are common residents in eastern Nebraska deciduous forests. During the 20th century, as woodlands spread westward along the Republican, Platte, Loup and Niobrara rivers the red-bellied woodpecker has extended its range.

ROD NABHOLZ

close to the river, they resorted to burning driftwood for fuel. Along the stretch that defines present-day northeastern Nebraska they saw grassland mammals – wolves, mule deer, elk and bison carcasses floating downstream. At the mouth of the James River below present-day Yankton, they sighted their first chestnut-collared longspurs and lark buntings, rare species in eastern Nebraska today. On the river bordering present-day Cedar County, the party saw northern harriers, common nighthawks, red-headed woodpeckers and purple martins nesting in woodpecker holes in large cottonwood trees. They no longer saw Carolina parakeets and ruffed grouse, which were common on the wooded lower Missouri River Valley. Barn swallows had replaced rough-winged swallows. Finally, observers were making distinctions between closely related species.

In *Birds of Nebraska*, the authors comment on one other important expedition in Nebraska during the 19th century, that of F.V. Hayden, a geologist for the U.S. Geological Survey who made several trips into Nebraska as part of Gouverneur Kemble Warren's expeditions during the 1850s. It was Warren who labeled much of western Nebraska as "irreclaimable"

desert and described the Sandhills as "exceedingly solitary, silent, and desolate, and depressing to one's spirits." Because he penetrated the Nebraska interior, Hayden's records could have been valuable in documenting the state's bird life and other aspects of natural history. One report listed 191 bird species but "unfortunately, most of the species accounts are very general and do not clearly identify a species," Sharpe, Silcock and Jorgensen noted. In Nebraska, Hayden wrote descriptions of birds not previously described – the vesper sparrow in Blaine County and the piping plover on the lower Loup River.

Some accounts are both intriguing and puzzling. One was the description of large numbers of sandhill cranes south of the Platte River and west of present-day Columbus by Lieutenant James Henry Carleton while on a military expedition to meet with the Pawnee in 1844. "These birds are very large, and as an article of food are said to be very delicious," Carleton wrote. "They have a very loud and peculiarly discordant note." He wrote of "a great many antelopes and sand hill cranes." Before settlement, sandhill cranes regularly staged during migration, principally in the spring, in the lower Platte River Valley and migrated along the Missouri River, but Carleton observed the birds in late-August, a month before the first vanguard of sandhill cranes moves south through Nebraska today. Their presence in large numbers does not suggest breeding birds unless the Platte Valley was a staging area for birds nesting not far to the northwest. If any one description of the early-day bird life of Nebraska could be hoped for, it might be of the cranes, ducks, geese and other waterbirds gathered on the Platte River during spring migration. While hundreds of thousands of settlers passed up the river in the mid-1800s, spring migration was complete by the time they trailed along the Platte.

A huge void in the ornithological history of Nebraska exists because few early expeditions were accompanied by naturalists, and even when they were, disappointingly little information was recorded and few specimens taken. Bird notes of untrained travelers left even more to be desired. For example, in 1844 Carleton described birds seen along the Blue River in southeastern Nebraska as "paroquets, grouse, partridges, black-birds, prairie-hawks, whip-'o'wills, larks, plovers and swallows."

Most of the expeditions from this period were government sponsored. Surveying the land and its potential for development, and improving relations or fashioning treaties with indigenous people, were foremost in their instructions. Most of what is known of the state's bird life before 1860 is known only for the Missouri River Valley, and even that is scant. From the 1860s to 1900, some of the best bird records are from hunters, relating not only the abundance of various species but also the variety. Nature study was a popular avocation in the last half of the 19th century, and because many sportsmen of the time were prosperous and educated, they frequently wrote of bird species other than those they shot for sport. ∎

Nebraska Birds of Lewis and Clark

Paul Johnsgard, in his recent book, Lewis and Clark on the Great Plains – A Natural History, *calculated that Lewis and Clark reported about 20 bird species along Nebraska's eastern shore, the number varying with how liberally the reader interprets the bird names given. Some, including frequent references to "ducks," were poorly described or names were applied preventing identification to species. And, some distribution assumptions must be made, for example, that eagles reported by the expedition in northeastern Nebraska were probably bald eagles.*

Other bird species first named or described on the expedition beyond Nebraska's present-day borders are found in the state and might have been observed. Johnsgard wrote that Lewis and Clark described four Great Plains birds – the greater sage-grouse, common poorwill, McCown's longspur and Lewis's woodpecker – for the first time. Additionally, two least tern specimens were carefully described and measured. Johnsgard said there can be no doubt that Lewis and Clark discovered these five species of birds, at minimum, while they were on the Great Plains. Other authorities have credited the expedition with discovering even more species.

ERIC FOWLER

Piping plovers still nest on Missouri River sandbars.

American bittern – Captain Clark mentioned the "Indian hen" was found along the Missouri River as far upstream as the mouth of the Little Sioux River east of Tekamah.

American White Pelican – A flock of several hundred were observed resting on a sandbar in present-day Burt or Thurston County. One of the birds was shot. Sergeant Ordway noted in his journal that the specimen "had a bag under his neck and bill which held five gallons of water." More than 5,000 were reported on or flying over the sandbars.

Black-bellied Plover - Myron Swenk, an early-day University of Nebraska zoologist, believed that "plovers" reported by Clark on August 15, 1804, in what is now Dakota County were either migrating black-bellied plovers or American golden plovers. Johnsgard speculated that the migration time was more consistent with black-bellied plovers.

Canada Goose – Geese were encountered on the Missouri River from Richardson County on the south to Boyd County on the north and Ordway reported "large

flocks" at the mouth of the Niobrara River. A molting adult female and nearly full-grown goslings were killed for food along the shore of the Missouri River in Richardson County, suggesting the species nested along the river.

Carolina Parakeet – Clark reported this now-extinct "parotqueet" along the Missouri River as far upstream as Omaha.

Cliff Swallow – Apparently common along the Nebraska border, cliff swallows were reported nesting on cliffs and rock outcrops.

Great Blue Heron – Large numbers were reported above Blackbird Hill in present-day Thurston County. On August 30, while camped in western Cedar County, "a blue crane flying over attempted to light on the mast of our boat. One of the men caught it and gave it to one of the [Yankton Sioux] Indians," Ordway reported.

Great Egret – A specimen was shot in early-August at Fort Calhoun, Washington County. Great egrets do not nest in Nebraska but disperse north and west from southern and eastern breeding grounds.

Greater Prairie-Chicken – Captain Clark reported these "Prairie fowl" as common as far north as present-day Cedar County. Clark wrote that above the James River, downstream from present-day Yankton, "the Sharpe tailed Grows commence," a reference to sharp-tailed grouse.

Interior Least Tern – A specimen was shot in Washington County. Johnsgard noted that Lewis carefully described the specimen and he rightfully deserved credit for discovering the species. The species was officially described and accepted in 1843 from a West Indies specimen.

Piping Plover – Captain Clark described a "small species of Kildee" on the Missouri River as far upstream as Burt County. Johnsgard speculates that the small plovers were probably piping plovers.

Red-tailed Hawk – Citing the opinion of Myron Swenk, Johnsgard wrote that the hawks noted along eastern Thurston and Burt counties were probably of this species.

Red-winged Blackbird – Clark noted large numbers of a "black bird" on the Missouri River opposite Dixon County. Gary Moulton, author of the 13-volume Journals of the Lewis and Clark Expedition, *has suggested that by late-August this species would be forming into large migratory flocks.*

Ruffed Grouse – While at camp south of Council Bluffs, members of the expedition killed "several grous" on the Iowa side of the river. At that time, ruffed grouse were undoubtedly found on the Nebraska side of the river as well.

Whimbrel or Eskimo Curlew – A shorebird called the "Jack Curloo" was reported along the Nebraska border. Whimbrels, Johnsgard noted, were earlier called Hudsonian curlews. Johnsgard doubted that the birds were whimbrels because their fall migration occurs mainly along the Atlantic Coast.

Whip-poor-will – Captain Clark noted the calling of whip-poor-wills in early-September near present-day Blair.

Wild Turkey – Wild turkeys were killed by the expedition as it passed by present-day Washington, Knox, Boyd and either Burt or Douglas counties.

A CENTURY OF BIRD STUDY

THE SECOND WAVE OF NATURALISTS to study Nebraska's bird life arrived soon after the University of Nebraska was founded in 1869. In 1875, Samuel Aughey became the university's first chair of natural history, and as part of his responsibilities the first state ornithologist. A minister by training, Aughey wrote prolifically of the state's geology, geography, fauna and flora. His tenure was a wobbly first step toward a scientific study of birds in Nebraska. In *The Nebraska Bird Review,* former University of Nebraska at Omaha ornithologist Roger Sharpe wrote in 1993, "Aughey's

*A 1901 Frank Shoemaker photo captures **Isadore S. Trostler** photographing a least bittern nest at Carter Lake north of Omaha. The "head gear is because of mosquitoes," Shoemaker wrote on the margin of the glass-plate negative.*

works, early and potentially important, unfortunately have left subsequent scientists and readers with many questions about their accuracy and authenticity." While at the university, colleagues criticized Aughey for fabricating plant records, and that might have been the reason he was asked to resign in 1883. Sharpe suggested that Aughey compiled the state's first bird list more on speculation than with records or specimens.

While Aughey's work was questionable science, it should be viewed in the context of the times and his circumstance. The University of Nebraska was established as a land-grant college, emphasizing the advancement of agriculture in the fledgling state. Not surprisingly, much of Aughey's bird work centered on

the beneficial attributes of insect-eating birds to the farmer and rancher. During the 1870s, periodic irruptions of grasshoppers ravished Nebraska croplands and pastures. Of the 252 species on Aughey's first bird list, he asserted that nearly every species preyed on "locusts," as migratory grasshoppers were often called at that time. Sharpe pointed out that Aughey included such unlikely species as eared grebes – an entirely aquatic avian species – the nectar-feeding ruby-throated hummingbird and snowy owls, which only periodically venture into the state during the depth of winter, as being the farmer's friends in controlling grasshoppers and other injurious insects. No doubt there was pressure on Aughey to publish, to make the tie between the state's bird life and agriculture, and to keep funding flowing to the university – circumstances not entirely foreign to the system today. Unfortunately, Aughey's list of Nebraska birds, published in the *1878 Report of the United States Entomological Commission,* found its way into subsequent Nebraska bird lists and other ornithological publications. From this inauspicious beginning, the field of ornithology in Nebraska was launched.

The Bruner Years

The Department of Entomology and Ornithology was established at the University of Nebraska in 1895 under the chairmanship of Lawrence Bruner, arguably the father of Nebraska ornithology. If joint paternity were to be assigned to the birth of the Nebraska Ornithologists' Union (NOU) – the dominant ornithological influence in Nebraska for more than 100 years – the other father would probably be Isadore S. Trostler.

Lawrence Bruner is often considered the father of ornithology in Nebraska.

"In 1894 Dr. Isadore S. Trostler of Omaha sent a notice to the ornithological magazine *Oologist* asking that all persons interested in Nebraska ornithology and oology might submit their names and addresses to him," wrote ornithologist Paul Johnsgard in a souvenir program for NOU's 100-year celebration in May 1999, "From this effort he received about ten replies. He tried to arrange a meeting with those persons with a view to forming a state organization devoted to birds, but failed. He tried again in 1895 and 1896, and failed both years. Again in 1898 he tried to organize a meeting in conjunction with the Trans-Mississippi Exposition, but only managed to visit with a few of his now nearly 25 contacts when they visited the exposition. Finally, in May 1899, he arranged a preliminary organizational meeting with five others. These people were mostly from the Omaha area, but also included M.A. Carriker Jr., of Nebraska City. They decided their group should be called the Nebraska Ornithologists' Association."

They soon learned that only about three months earlier Robert H. Wolcott and Bruner, zoologists at the University of Nebraska, had organized a Nebraska Ornithological Club in Lincoln. The Omaha group then petitioned the Lincoln group to open its membership to the entire state. As a result, in May of 1899, the Lincoln club sent letters around the state, inviting interested people to join. On July 15, 1899, the first meeting was held with 43 people attending to elect officers. The first annual meeting took place in Lincoln on December 16, 1899, with 14 ornithologists and bird students present. The group was renamed the Nebraska Ornithologists' Union and its constitution was ratified with more than 90 active and associate charter members. Bruner was elected president, Trostler vice-president, Wolcott recording secretary and W.D. Hunter corresponding secretary. Hunter and Trostler would soon leave Nebraska, but Bruner and Wolcott would remain at the forefront of Nebraska bird study for several decades.

An entomologist by training, **Robert H. Wolcott** *was a key figure in Nebraska bird study.*

Born in Pennsylvania in 1856, Bruner arrived in Omaha with his family by stagecoach only six months later. The Bruners settled on a farm near Omaha and later relocated near West Point. Even in his youth, Bruner was intensely interested in natural history, especially insects. He mounted more than 1,000 bird and mammal specimens, principally to fund his studies. Having observed the devastating effects of grasshopper invasions in 1873 and 1876, Bruner turned his studies to grasshoppers and related species under Samuel Aughey. During the 1890s, Bruner served with the U.S. Department of Agriculture as state entomologist, and was a member of the University's Department of Entomology and Ornithology. One of his first efforts was to prepare a revised list of Nebraska birds to update Aughey's 1878 list.

"Lawrence Bruner was the spark plug of the N.O.U. in them days," Arthur S. Pearse wrote in 1950. "He was a nice, modest, genial little man. He accumulated a small collection of skins and eggs in his basement rooms at the university." Pearse was one of many

The Nebraska Bird Review

The Nebraska Ornithologists' Union (NOU) published six volumes of proceedings and papers between 1900 and 1915. For nine years, beginning in 1916, Nebraska proceedings and papers were published in the Wilson Bulletin, *which posted on its cover that it was the "Official Organ of the Wilson Ornithological Club and the Nebraska Ornithologists' Union." In 1925, the NOU reinitiated publishing with its mimeographed Letter of Information. Sixty-eight issues totaling 314 pages were printed.*

In 1933 the NOU resumed independent publication with its official journal, The Nebraska Bird Review. *As in selecting a state bird, an inordinate amount of discussion ensued about selecting the journal's name. Incorporating bird names into the title of ornithological publications had a long history and was suggested for the NOU publication – The Prairie Lark, The Killdeer, The Meadowlark, The Chat and others. Another camp in the membership preferred a more formal title, and suggested such titles as the Nebraska Bird Bulletin, Nebraska Bird Quarterly and the N.O.U. Observer. When the discussion ended,* The Nebraska Bird Review *was selected as the title of the new journal. Publication has been continuous since 1933.* The Nebraska Bird Review *has been issued quarterly, except from 1938 through 1948 when it was semi-annual and 1949 when only one issue was published.*

Artwork for the cover of the first issue was a rather hawkish-looking burrowing owl drawn by J.L. Ridgway, brother of well-known ornithologist Robert Ridgway. The drawing had illustrated A.K. Fisher's paper, "Hawks and Owls as Related to the Farmer" *published in the U.S. Department of Agriculture's 1894 Yearbook. The burrowing owl was an appropriate choice because the type specimen of the North American subspecies (*hypugaea*) had been collected near Nebraska's Platte River during the Long Expedition of 1820. Beginning in 1938, George Miksch Sutton's more anatomically correct and charming drawing of the little denizen of prairie dogs' burrows appeared. Henry Baumgarten's drawing of a rather angry looking burrowing owl was on the cover from 1953 through 1968, but in 1969 Sutton's drawing reappeared and has been used since.*

Wilson Tout and other birders view a cliff swallow nesting colony on the North Platte River south of Oshkosh in the summer of 1910. In 1934 Tout organized the North Platte Bird Club, later renamed the **Tout Bird Club.** *The club disbanded in 1997.*

students of zoology at the university in the late-1800s and early-1900s and he would leave his own mark on the scientific world. A native of Crete and charter member of the NOU, Pearse received his doctoral degree in zoology at Harvard. He traveled widely and at the time of his death was emeritus professor of zoology at Duke University.

In 1899, when the NOU organized, Wolcott was completing his fourth year at the University of Nebraska and was an adjunct professor in the zoology department. A native of Illinois, Wolcott had earned a Bachelor of Law, Bachelor of Science and Doctor of Medicine at the University of Michigan before coming to Nebraska, not to practice medicine but to study and teach biology. He had published scientific papers in ornithology before coming to Nebraska. While his entomological interests were broad, he specialized in the study of mites, a field in which he became nationally recognized. In 1905 he became a full professor at the university and served as acting dean of the newly organized College of Medicine. In 1915 he became chairman of the Zoology Department, a position he held until his death in 1934.

Wolcott strove constantly to improve the accuracy and documentation of bird records, and proposed a system for estimating and standardizing the language used to describe a species's abundance. He encouraged thorough reports of sightings and urged that a records committee review and pass rigorous scientific judgment on the veracity of reports. In 1901 he presented a paper naming species that might have been erroneously listed as occurring in the state, noted doubtful records, and suggested species for which better documentation was needed.

"We live in a state in which, more than in almost any other, the greatest possible care must be taken in regard to the making of records," Wolcott wrote in the *Second Annual Proceedings*. "Our faunal position is such that within our borders is a remarkable mingling of species from different faunal regions; here the eastern and western subspecies meet; here is a transition from the smaller, shorter-tailed and darker eastern forms to the larger, longer-tails and paler birds characteristic of the plains. And when we turn to the books we are met by the, to us, meaningless 'West to the edge of the Great Plains,' or 'From the Plains to the Pacific.' We must settle ourselves the problems which we see facing us."

The Zoology Boys

There were many fledgling ornithologists at the university in the 1890s and early-1900s who would leave their mark on the sciences in Nebraska and beyond. Among them were the Hunter brothers.

Walter Hunter taught entomology at the university and later became an entomologist with the U.S. Department of Agriculture in Washington, D.C. His younger brother, Joseph S. Hunter, joined the university staff in 1898 when taxidermy courses were added to the Department of Entomology and Ornithology. He was one of the more accomplished field workers in the department and was adept at collecting specimens. Joseph Hunter moved to Berkeley, California, in 1901, where he worked in economic ornithology at the University of California.

Wilson Tout, a charter member of the NOU at age 18, recalled the early days of ornithology in Nebraska on the occasion of the 50th anniversary of the NOU with a story about Joseph Hunter. Upon returning from a field trip to woodlands along Salt Creek near Roca south of Lincoln, Hunter reported to professor Bruner and others gathered in the laboratory that he had just shot a Carolina wren, a species that had only been reported twice in the state, both times in Richardson County, and at that time had never been collected. Hunter explained that the wren was coming out of a cavity in a tree and it had fallen back into it when shot so he could not collect the specimen.

Tout wrote, "The boys all gave him the razz. Professor Bruner suggested that he take them to the place and they would cut off the limb and get the specimen. He agreed but was not enthusiastic about it. After a three-mile walk he pointed out the hole in a dead limb. With an axe they soon cut away the outside wood and they took from the hole the lifeless body of a Carolina wren, the first record for the state. No one ever doubted the word of J.S. Hunter after that."

In 1900, M.A. Carriker assumed an assistantship in ornithology. Merritt Cary, who came to the department to study mammals, made significant contributions in ornithology, too. Myron Swenk joined the university teaching staff as an adjunct professor in the Department of Zoology in 1899. Unlike so many of Bruner's students, Swenk remained at the university, ultimately stepping into Bruner's shoes and becoming the driving force of the NOU in the early-1900s. These young men were Bruner's "Corps of Discovery," his "boys," and they accompanied him on many field expeditions as well as conducting their own field research.

Another figure in Nebraska ornithology during the early-1900s was Frank H. Shoemaker, who began his study of birds on Child's Point in Omaha, now part of Fontenelle Forest and Gifford Point Wildlife Management Area.

Throughout his life, Shoemaker eked out a meager living, first working in the Union Pacific office in Omaha, and later in life by doing photography at the University of Nebraska in Lincoln and for the College of Medicine. Shoemaker often accompanied early zoologists on extended field expeditions. He was accomplished with the camera, and his photographs are probably the best visual record of bird life and bird study in Nebraska from the early-1900s.

With so many enthusiastic workers in the field, the

Publisher and editor of the Lincoln County Tribune, ***Wilson Tout*** *was an avid birdwatcher and mentor for scores of young bird students. He also trapped and banded birds.*

knowledge of the state's bird life grew rapidly. In 1896, Bruner published *A List of Nebraska Birds,* a compilation of his own observations combined with reports of others. It included 415 species and subspecies and 225 breeding species and subspecies. Not surprisingly, Bruner incorporated many of Aughey's unverified records. Aughey had been, after all, Bruner's instructor and mentor at the university. In the first years of the 20th century, Bruner led or organized field trips to the Pine Ridge region to collect insects, birds and mammals. Those were the golden years of university field research, when natural science was conducted by men traveling by horse-drawn wagon into Nebraska's little-studied regions.

In May 1900, for example, Bruner, Cary, Joseph Hunter and J.C. Crawford traveled to the Pine Ridge region to study animal life. In those days studying meant collecting of both specimens and egg sets. The expedition camped in Monroe Canyon (Gilbert-Baker Wildlife Management Area today) for two weeks. They collected a black-headed grosbeak, a loggerhead shrike, the western race of the yellow-rumped warbler, a common yellowthroat, a yellow-breasted chat, a rock wren, house wren, the western race of white-breasted

Nature study, and birdwatching in particular, was immensely popular during the early years of the 1900s.

nuthatch and Swainson's thrush specimens. Crawford reported the party also collected full egg sets of a sharp-shinned hawk, American kestrel, chipping sparrow and hairy woodpecker. Eggs of Krider's red-tailed hawk (a pale-colored prairie race) and white-throated swift were not secured because, as Crawford reported, "We could not get at them." Two Townsend's solitaire nests were found, one containing no eggs, "the set having been collected by a bullsnake, which was killed near there," Crawford reported. Examination of the snake's stomach revealed four "badly incubated and broken eggs."

Determined to learn more of the avifauna of the Pine Ridge, Bruner organized a party the next spring to camp in Monroe Canyon for two months – a luxury few ornithologists, professional or amateur, have been allowed in recent times. In 1902, Bruner led a biological survey of the lower Niobrara River, starting at the bridge north of Bassett and ending at the river's mouth, traveling by flatboat and canoe. In 1905 and 1906, Bruner again led research parties on collecting expeditions to the Pine Ridge.

In 1904, Bruner, Wolcott and Swenk published *A Preliminary Review of the Birds of Nebraska*, which included identification keys and the occurrence documentation for 338 species. The 1904 list was reviewed critically to correct undocumented reports included in Bruner's 1896 list. It was a heady time for

naturalists at the university. Every field expedition revealed new records, and often, new species for the state. Bird lists and species distribution were less speculative than they had been in Aughey's time, and a bird did not have to be the farmer's friend to be worth studying.

Scarce Bird Students

Almost from the beginning, attracting enough members and funds through dues was a problem for the Nebraska Ornithologists' Union. In 1900, there were 55 members – 40 active members with full privileges, and 15 associate members who received publications but did not have voting rights. Annual dues were $1.

The early volumes of the *Proceedings* proved to be of a quality, content and cost beyond the means of the NOU. After Volume III in 1902, publication was suspended for six years. In 1904, members voted to raise dues to $2 for active members and $1 for associate members. That year a majority of members defeated an amendment to accept members from outside of Nebraska, saying "our identity as a Nebraska organization ought not to be lost."

In 1908, the NOU prepared and printed a field checklist of Nebraska birds. The list included 404 species and subspecies divided into three groups

– 276 "commoner eastern species," 50 "commoner western species" and 78 "rare or accidental species." Knowledge of western Nebraska birds remained scant, mostly gleaned from forays by university zoologists into the Sandhills and Pine Ridge regions in the late-1800s and early-1900s. Most NOU members and observers lived in eastern counties. A cooperative spring bird migration report published in 1925 illustrates the concentration of bird students in eastern Nebraska. Reports came from Omaha, Lincoln, Fairbury, Superior, Red Cloud and Hastings, cities, except Red Cloud, with active birding clubs. At Red Cloud, dedicated bird observers such as J.M. Bates and Charles S. Ludlow provided information. In 1926, for example, Ludlow conducted nesting bird surveys on his 60-acre farm, locating 91 nesting pairs of 38 species.

By the mid-1910s, the NOU seemed to be losing momentum. Some of the university's best field workers left the state for better positions and new students of the same caliber did not replace them. Professors Lawrence Bruner, Robert Wolcott and Myron Swenk were probably increasingly occupied with other responsibilities.

The early volumes of the *Proceedings* had, in part, been as good as they were because several members published observations and information gathered over many years and from earlier expeditions throughout Nebraska. Papers presented at the annual meetings became more casual and less meaty.

From 1903 through 1914, the formerly annual *Proceedings* were combined into three slender volumes, principally a record of NOU meetings and business. A "permanent educational committee" was appointed to encourage bird study clubs in public schools, an effort that largely failed. Annual meetings and field days were held each spring, most often in Lincoln or Omaha, but also at Hastings, Peru, Weeping Water and Superior. Sponsored by a local birding club, the meetings were usually held in early-May to coincide with spring migration. Several birding clubs were active in Nebraska during the 1910s and 1920s – the Bruner Bird Club of Lincoln, the Nature Department of the Women's Club of Superior, the Nebraska Audubon Society of Omaha, the Omaha Nature Study Club, and the Brooking Bird Club of Hastings.

At the 16th annual meeting in May 1915, the NOU voted to form an affiliation with the Wilson Ornithological Club, and the *Wilson Bulletin* became the official NOU organ. It was an admission that the NOU could not carry on publication of notes. Of the $2 annual dues, $1.50 went to the Wilson Ornithological Club. Swenk, the NOU secretary-treasurer, wrote in 1916 that by merging with the Wilson club NOU was "entering a new era of usefulness," while acknowledging in the same message to members that "the Nebraska Ornithologists' Union is not one-half as large as it should be in a state like Nebraska, with its remarkable bird fauna and great general interest in bird study." The high hopes at the NOU organizational meeting in 1899 had not been realized, but neither had they been abandoned.

The Swenk Years

By 1918, Lawrence Bruner's vigor was diminishing. He was 62 years old, and he asked to be replaced as chairman of the Department of Entomology. The following year he moved to California, where he died in 1937. He left behind a framework around which the study of Nebraska birds would continue, and numerous students who would make their names

University of Nebraska professor **Myron Swenk** *was a key figure in Nebraska ornithology.*

in natural sciences in Nebraska and beyond. M.A. Carriker, for example, went on to become one of the most prolific collectors of tropical birds in Central and South America for several national museums. John T. Zimmer, Bruner's student in the 1910s, worked in entomology for the U.S. Department of Agriculture in Lincoln during the early-1900s, often combining entomological fieldwork with bird study. He was a regular contributor to bird study in Nebraska before leaving to become assistant curator in the Department of Birds of the Field Museum of Natural History in Chicago, assistant curator of birds at the American Museum of Natural History in New York under F.M. Chapman, and editor of the *Auk,* the scientific publication of the American Ornithologists' Union. He was awarded the Brewster medal, the highest award of the American Ornithologists' Union, in 1952.

The quality and far-reaching influence of University of Nebraska botanists at the end of the 19th century and in early decades of the 20th century – Charles Bessey, Roscoe Pound, Frederick Clements, John Weaver and Raymond Pool – is rightfully pointed to with pride. Often neglected, however, are the achievements of the students of zoologists Bruner, Wolcott and Swenk.

There were many parallels between Swenk's early years and those of his mentor, Bruner, perhaps in part explaining their affinity for one another despite the 27 years difference in their ages. Swenk's family moved to Beatrice from Illinois in 1885, when he was about two years old. In 1901 the family moved to Lincoln. Like Bruner, Swenk was intensely interested in nature as a boy, collecting his first ornithological specimen, an orange-crowned warbler, when he was 15 years old. He became a charter member of the NOU while still in high school. Swenk was Bruner's student at the university where he earned a master's degree in 1908, and later served as an assistant professor.

In 1919 Swenk replaced Bruner as chairman of the Department of Entomology. Swenk was the glue that bound the NOU together for 40 years, especially during the Depression of the late-1920s and 1930s when the young organization often seemed on the

The 1901 Proceedings of the Nebraska Ornithologists' Union *included Frank Shoemaker photos of a **ruby-throated hummingbird** on its nest near Bellevue. The nest was covered with "sea-green lichens" bound with "a mesh of spider webs."*

brink of vanishing.

From 1925 through 1932, the periodic publication of the NOU was a modest mimeographed *Letter of Information,* which began as one page but grew to as many as 14 pages in the early-1930s. It was issued about 10 times annually. Most reports came from birding clubs. The heyday of university scientific fieldwork in the 1890s and opening decade of the 1900s was over. From the 1920s to the present, amateur ornithologists would gather most Nebraska bird information. This introduced a thorny problem: Who were the reporters who reliably identified species and who did not?

Through the 1920s, apparently all reports were published in *Letter of Information* with only occasional comments relating to their accuracy by Swenk as the editor. At the second annual meeting in 1901, a set of criteria for accepting records was adopted, and a permanent records committee was selected to review reports at the third annual meeting in 1902, principally for rare species or species reported outside of their expected range or season. Little was ever heard from the committee. Perhaps it was deterred from its mission by the fear of offending reporters in the small and usually struggling organization. Updated lists of Nebraska birds were published in 1945, 1958 and 1971, and reports were subjected to increasing scrutiny, but a functioning records committee was not established until 1986.

A small number of amateur and professional bird students were at the core of the NOU, but during the Depression of the 1930s the organization faltered for lack of members. In 1928, a year before the stock market crash, NOU had 94 members, an all-time high. Membership fell to 62 in 1931, and then to 43 active members in 1932. When dues were reduced from $2

a year to $1 in 1933, NOU rebounded to 79 members.

In 1932, despite its declining membership, NOU suspended publication of its mimeographed *Letter of Information* and replaced it with a printed, quarterly, magazine-format journal, *The Nebraska Bird Review,* which has been published since without interruption. Because NOU's membership was too small to support its often-ambitious agenda, funding was a nagging problem.

During the late-1800s and early-1900s, nature study had been immensely popular at all levels of society. World War I, drought, Depression and another world war diverted attention from the woods and wetlands. Not until the rise of environmentalism and the swelling popularity of outdoor pursuits beyond hunting and fishing in the 1960s would it return. The NOU survived the 1930s, and late in that decade listed 120 active members on its roll, including three charter members – A.L. Haecker, Wilson Tout and Swenk.

Amateur Ornithologists

While university zoologists led the quest for knowledge in the early-1900s, they were only at the head of a phalanx of enthusiastic bird students. Across the state, on farms, in small towns and in Nebraska's largest cities, farmers, businessmen and housewives studied birds, relishing opportunities to share their sightings and to hear the reports of others. Some were sportsmen, like Cyrus Black of Kearney, who once took great pains to kill birds, including bald eagles, for mounting and display. From the 1920s into the 1940s, he became a regular reporter of whooping cranes along the Platte River, and his records constitute essentially all that is known about that rare species in Nebraska during those decades.

Among those making significant contributions documenting Nebraska's bird life in the early-1900s was John M. Bates, an Episcopal minister born in Connecticut. Bates came to Omaha in the mid-1880s, and because of a bad cough was soon assigned work in western Nebraska. Bates traveled regularly from Valentine to Neligh and Rushville, his "outstations in the mission field," and always made time to observe birds.

At the first annual meeting of the NOU in 1899, Bates presented a paper enumerating his bird records from north-central Nebraska, including a list of birds of the Long Pine area assembled by "a lad in Long Pine High School, Will Smith," who Bates noted had become interested in bird study "partly, I trust, though my influence." After a brief tour of duty in Custer County in 1903, Bates was stationed at Red Cloud in Webster County where he made extensive bird observations.

In 1934 *The Nebraska Bird Review* published a Bates's paper – "Twenty-One Years of Bird Study at Red Cloud" – in which he modestly stated his ornithological activities "have been directed more toward creating an interest in birds on the part of others than in a search for new or rare bird forms for the state."

Nebraska's State Bird

In July 1925, Myron H. Swenk, secretary-treasurer of the Nebraska Ornithologists' Union (NOU), received a resolution from the Jefferson County Girls Camp signed by 38 girls requesting that the Nature Study Department of the Fairbury Women's' Club ask the NOU to initiate in a campaign to select a state bird. So the quest for a Nebraska state bird began.

Prominent NOU member John M. Bates immediately suggested the western meadowlark because: "He is here early and late, and always on the job catching cutworms and grasshoppers and singing in November as if it were spring." A.M. Brooking of Hastings proposed the burrowing owl, arguing, "We should have something the other states do not all have." And there was Mrs. Addison E. Sheldon, the pragmatist, wondering about the desirability of having a state bird at all, who asked, "What purpose would be subserved by such a selection?" A committee was appointed to take the matter under consideration.

In July 1926, the committee reported it was not prepared to "inaugurate and actively further a movement to have the Nebraska Legislature designate a state bird," but when the time came, it unanimously favored the western meadowlark.

In October 1927, the National Chairman of the Division of Wild Life of the General Federation of Women's Clubs announced a national campaign to encourage all states to select a state bird. Elizabeth Hoefer, chairman of the Nebraska chapter, suggested the robin, catbird, brown thrasher, meadowlark or bobwhite, and urged Nebraska to select a species not already chosen by another state.

She narrowed her suggestions to the catbird or bobwhite, noting that even though the bobwhite was nearly extinct in the state, the object of naming a state bird was to "lead to the protection of the chosen bird." The NOU chose not to act immediately on the matter but subsequently mailed a ballot to members to vote for their preference for a state bird. Twenty-eight members voted for the western meadowlark, three opposed, and the NOU threw its support behind the western meadowlark as the official state bird.

At the October 1928 Nebraska Federation of Women's Clubs convention in Kearney, a resolution passed that "a bird typical of the prairies and abundant in all parts of the state be chosen by this convention assembled and the result combined with the vote of the school children of the state and interested societies to be presented to the next session of the State Legislature for acceptance." A list of five species was prepared – western meadowlark, robin, bobwhite, brown thrasher and house wren. The meadowlark was chosen.

At the request of the Conservation Department of the Nebraska Federation of Women's' Clubs, a bill was introduced in the 1929 legislative session, and subsequently passed, declaring the western meadowlark the official state bird of Nebraska. Governor Adam McMullen signed the bill on March 22, 1929. Kansas, Montana, North Dakota, Oregon and Wyoming also chose the western meadowlark as their state bird.

BUB BLAKE

The western meadowlark became Nebraska's official state bird March 22, 1929.

Birding Clubs

Myron Swenk died in 1941, leaving the NOU and Nebraska ornithology without professional leadership. There would not be another ornithologist on the University of Nebraska staff until Paul Johnsgard came in 1961. Swenk had been at the center of bird study in Nebraska for over 40 years, served as editor of the *Letter of Information* and *The Nebraska Bird Review,* and held NOU offices continuously since 1903. The NOU did not falter after Swenk's death, but it did change in character. How much of the change should be attributed to the loss of university leadership, and how much simply was a reflection of the times is conjecture.

Birding clubs organized in the early-1900s assumed more prominence in the 1930s, 1940s and 1950s. In the 1933 volume of *The Nebraska Bird Review,* Mrs. H.F. Hole, a member of the Fairbury club, explained its beginnings: "The Nature Study Department of the Fairbury Women's Club is really a continuation of the Art Department of that Club. For a number of years the Art Department studied the old masters and world famous pictures, and also visited art galleries and exhibits whenever opportunity offered. In 1916, when

the Department had reached modern art and living artists, it decided to turn to the beautiful in Nature, and began the study of bird life. We were woefully ignorant of birds, but very enthusiastic, and entered into the new study whole-heartedly. We each bought copies of Reed's *Bird Guide* and Chapman's *Bird Life,* along with the set of fifty-two Audubon Society Leaflets, and started our bird study along the same plans that we had used in studying art."

Women were often at the forefront of bird study during the early-1900s. As in Fairbury, the Superior Bird Club was organized in 1922 as a department within the Superior Women's Club. The Brooking Bird Club of Hastings began as a bird study class in 1920 under the sponsorship of the YWCA with A.M. Brooking as the teacher. The class became so popular that in 1923 the club formally organized. In addition to birdwatching, the club carried out projects establishing bird sanctuaries, held lectures, conducted a Christmas census and sponsored an annual field day during which the best birdhouses were judged.

The Omaha Nature Study Club organized in 1926 to replace the faltering Omaha Audubon Society, which had been formed about 1910, largely under the leadership of Solon R. Towne and L.O. Horsky. A number of other birding clubs were active during the 1930s – the Bruner Nature Club of Lincoln, the Ingleside Club of David City and the Grand Island Bird Club. By the mid-1940s, the Inez Houghton Audubon Society, later renamed the Audubon Society of Chadron, had organized and the University Place Bird Club in Lincoln had replaced the Lincoln Bird Club as the only bird club in the capital city. By the 1950s the Nature Lovers Club had organized in Scottsbluff and there was a birding club in Long Pine. Some birding clubs had brief histories, vanishing as the number of interested members dwindled, such as the Nebraska City Ornithological Association, of which M.A. Carriker was a member as a boy before 1900.

Other bird clubs prospered for decades, such as the North Platte Bird Club organized under the leadership of Tout, who was superintendent of schools in North Platte. In 1920 he purchased the *Lincoln County Tribune* and became the paper's editor. Born in Sutton, Tout attended the University of Nebraska and became acquainted with Lawrence Bruner. In his book, *Lincoln County Birds,* published in 1947, Tout wrote that he arrived in Lincoln County June 1, 1907: "I recorded two birds the first day I was here and have been making records continuously ever since." Tout and nine others met on April 7, 1934, to form the North Platte Bird Club, which was later renamed the Tout Bird Club. Tout died in 1951 but the bird club bearing

First published in 1897, Frank Chapman's **Bird-Life,** *with black-and-white illustrations by Ernest Seton Thompson, was the standard text for bird study and identification for several decades. Until recently, most bird identification guides were either for eastern or western regions, leaving Nebraska birders in between in a gray zone.*

his name continued until 1997.

While bird study advanced by large strides during the first half of the 20th century, ornithology was not in the forefront of scientific study in the state by the middle of the century. Of the 23 accredited colleges in the state in 1950, only six offered courses in ornithology – the University of Nebraska, Union College, Hastings College, Doane College, Concordia Teachers College and the Kearney State Teachers College. Half of those institutions offered an ornithology course only in alternating years. Thirteen Nebraska institutions of higher education had bird collections. The University of Nebraska had about 3,000 specimens, and the other schools had less than 500, five with 100 or fewer.

R. Allyn Moser of Omaha and William Rapp of Crete were prominent leaders in the NOU in the middle of the 20th century. Moser, an Omaha physician and an assistant dean at the University of Nebraska College of Medicine, joined the NOU in 1935. He served as president in 1943, treasurer in 1944 and president from 1946 through 1948. Moser was active in several national ornithological organizations. He published papers on piping plovers, juncos and glaucous gulls, and collaborated in publishing several checklists of Nebraska birds. In 1940, Moser and F.W. Haecker privately published the *Pocket Check-List of Nebraska Birds.* In 1945, Moser, Haecker and Jane Swenk published the *Check-list of the Birds of Nebraska.* The last previous annotated checklist, *The Birds and Mammals of Nebraska* by Myron Swenk, had been published in the *Nebraska Blue Book* in 1920. Swenk's list included 431 "native species and subspecies." Moser and Haecker's 1940 checklist included 457 "forms" of birds in Nebraska. The 1945 checklist included 388 species and 85 additional races.

Moser's most important contributions to bird study in Nebraska might have been behind the scenes and usually without acknowledgement – influencing old members to be more active, recruiting new members and dipping into his own pocket to publish *The Nebraska Bird Review.* He also brought lectures and national ornithological meetings to Nebraska. The Nebraska Bird Review was nearly $500 in debt and several months behind in publication in 1948 when Moser convinced Rapp to serve as editor, a position he held through 1954. In his remembrance of Moser at his death in 1961, Rapp recalled that Moser gave him a blank check in 1948 to cover the cost of the next issue of *The Nebraska Bird Review.*

In the midst of WWII, Moser told Nebraska birders it was not unpatriotic to continue their study of birds. He wrote in *The Nebraska Bird Review,* "If we occasionally follow the song of a bird, watch one in flight, or make notes on any of their life habits, we are not detracting from the war effort. We, on the contrary are given renewed and stronger faith, courage and hope to carry on for the future."

Bird study found its way into state government in the 1940s. Before that time, the state's primary interest had been issuing hunting licenses for game birds and enforcing the Migratory Bird Treaty Act of 1918 and state statutes. In the 1940s a new breed of biologist was hired by the state game agency. It was a renaissance of a sort, mimicking the bloom of ornithologists at the university in the early-1900s. As with those at the university earlier, most of these biologists would leave the state to distinguish themselves elsewhere.

The 1940s and 1950s saw not only the first stirrings of wildlife management in the state, but the heyday of field research. Research studies were conducted not just for short-term and practical considerations, but for pure science, the need to better understand all Nebraska wildlife. In 1937, Congress passed the Federal Aid in Wildlife Restoration Act, better known as the Pittman-Robertson Act, establishing an excise tax on sporting firearms and ammunition. The proceeds of those taxes are divided among state conservation agencies to do wildlife conservation work. For the first time, Nebraska's game department had the funds to do more than stock fish and enforce game laws.

One of the first biologists hired by the Commission was Levi Mohler, who grew up in Chase County. His master's thesis study was on prairie-chickens in southwestern Nebraska. The Commission hired Mohler in 1941, and others like him – H. Elliott McClure, Henry Sather, Knox Jones, George Schildman, Dave Damon, John Wampole, Edson Fichter, and John Mathisen – after World War II. Many of those young men had just completed college on the GI bill. Nearly all eventually left Nebraska, some to complete advanced degrees and many to teach in prominent colleges and universities. While in Nebraska, they studied everything – not just game animals. These young biologists explored the most remote corners of the state, often traveling in a panel van that served as mobile laboratory, kitchen and bedroom. Their findings about the food habits of coyotes and owls, and about muskrat populations in Sandhills marshes were published in national wildlife journals.

They also studied birds – both game birds and nongame birds. Their reports, frequently published in *The Nebraska Bird Review,* included everything from observations of nesting long-billed curlews, to reports of Lewis's woodpeckers, to the return of wood ducks in the 1950s, to sandhill crane counts, to summaries of birds observed in the Sandhills, to the unexpected appearance of pinyon jays in eastern counties and raptor surveys in the Panhandle. It was during this time that Rainwater Basin wetlands and their disappearance were first studied, documented and an acquisition program initiated to protect some of the wetlands remaining. One of the Commission's biologists, Edson Fichter, served as co-editor of *The Nebraska Bird Review* in the mid-1940s.

DOUG CARROLL

Until the 1970s, migrating sandhill cranes on the Platte River each March attracted little attention beyond birders in that region. By the 1980s, **crane watching** *had become immensely popular, attracting thousands of birders from across the state and beyond to view the natural spectacle.*

A New State Bird?

Ask a birder from another state about the bird life of Nebraska, and he or she will probably first mention sandhill cranes. Oddly, migrating sandhill cranes attracted little attention in Nebraska before the 1970s, and sporadic reports in NOU publications were usually of small gatherings, not the massive flocks found along the Platte River in March today. One of the best reporters was Cyrus Black at Kearney. Another was Levi Mohler, who estimated the largest gathering of cranes he observed at 6,000 birds. Counts of sandhill cranes along the Platte before 1950 were small – 40,000 being the most reported.

In the 1950s, Nebraska's cranes entered the national spotlight. The July 1954 issue of *The Nebraska Bird Review* published a note recounting a visit by *Life Magazine* photographer Alfred Eisenstaedt to the Platte River to photograph sandhill cranes the previous March. NOU secretary Doris Gates drove a pickup and Eisenstaedt rode in the back, laden with camera equipment, as they tried to approach the cranes closely enough to photograph. Eisenstaedt finally complained, "They won't dance. You see, that is my problem!" Abandoning his hope for images of dancing cranes, Eisenstaedt asked Gates to run at a flock to flush them so he could get a spectacular photo. That March, Lawrence Walkinshaw, the North American authority on cranes, had been in the same area studying sandhill cranes. A photo of Nebraska's sandhill cranes in

In 1949, the 50th anniversary of the **Nebraska Ornithologists' Union,** *members gathered in Lincoln for their annual meeting and posed for a group photograph. Front row (from left): William Rapp, unidentified, Wilson Tout, unidentified, R. Allyn Moser, unidentified. Second row, (from left): Jane Swenk, Mrs. A.M. Brooking, Mrs. Glen Chapman, Mrs. A.H. Jones, unidentified, George Blinco, Mrs. A.M. Jones, Harold Benckessor. Third row, (from left): Edson Fichter, Levi Mohler, W.E. Eigsti, Allegra Collister, Florence Patton, Mrs. George Blinco, unidentified, Doris Gates, Carol Kinch, Mrs. Herman Chapman. Back row, left to right: unidentified, Adrian Fox, unidentified, Bud Pritchard, David Damon, unidentified, unidentified, unidentified.*

Life Magazine and an international crane researcher on the central Platte River might have sparked an interest in watching birds in Nebraska, but it did not. The time was not right. The frenzy of interest in sandhill cranes staging on the Platte River was 20 years in the future.

Credit the discovery of Platte River cranes to the controversy surrounding the proposed mid-state dam project on the central Platte River during the early-1970s, or to Roger Tory Peterson's crowning of the central Platte in March as "one of the dozen birding hotspots in the nation." The attention lavished on sandhill cranes caused a rebirth of bird study in Nebraska. Birdwatching became an acceptable outdoor pursuit. And, if it was acceptable behavior to watch cranes, it was all right to sniff around a patch of sagebrush in Dundy County for a Cassin's sparrow, too.

Today, the central Platte River is awash with birdwatchers in March, and the sandhill crane phenomenon is estimated to infuse as much as $25 to $53 million into the Nebraska economy annually. Could Lawrence Bruner, who was compelled to justify the role of birds by their importance to agriculture, imagine sandhill cranes on the license plates of every passenger vehicle in Nebraska?

Nebraska's identity as a bird study state grew in 1961 with the arrival of Paul Johnsgard at the

University of Nebraska. A native of southeastern North Dakota, Johnsgard's doctoral research at Cornell University under Charles Sibley was an ecological and evolutionary approach to the comparative behavior of mallards, black ducks, Mexican ducks and Florida ducks. He did post-doctoral study at the Wildfowl Trust in Slimbridge, England, studying the courtship of 133 species of waterfowl. That research led to a book, *Handbook of Waterfowl Behavior*, published by Cornell University Press in 1965. It remains the definitive work on waterfowl courtship.

In the spring of 1962, Roger Sharpe, Johnsgard's first graduate student, introduced him to the Platte River and its cranes. Since that day, the river and its cranes have been recurring topics of Johnsgard's writing. The presence of Johnsgard, an ornithologist of international reputation, in Nebraska for more than 40 years has played a significant role in promoting Nebraska bird study by infusing an enthusiasm for birds in students and a wider audience through his writing.

The emergence of nongame wildlife programs in Nebraska and across the nation during the 1970s helped put birds and other wildlife in the public eye, and began to systematically take stock of the nation's fauna and flora. Nebraska's nongame wildlife program began in 1971, funded only from money derived from the sale of hunting licenses. In 1975, the Nebraska Legislature passed the Nongame and Endangered Species Conservation Act, assigning the Commission the authority and responsibility to conserve nongame species and species determined to be endangered or threatened. The Nongame and Endangered Species Conservation Act led to a state threatened and endangered species list, and the legal authority to intervene to protect listed species. Financial aid from general tax revenues helped fund the program. In 1984 the legislature established the State Income Tax Check-off for Nongame Wildlife, enabling taxpayers to contribute all or part of their refund to the program. The Nongame Wildlife Tax Check-off provided $1.6 million from 1984 through 2001, although receipts have been declining in recent years.

Under Nebraska's nongame wildlife program, the state finally took the lead in studying and managing all bird species. One of the program's first bird projects was to document the status and distribution of raptors, especially golden eagles, prairie falcons, ferruginous hawks and merlins. The migration of whooping cranes, the breeding of least terns and piping plovers and the wintering and nesting by bald eagles is monitored and better documented than ever before. Sandhill cranes are surveyed each March, as are migrant shorebirds during spring and fall migrations. Reports of bird mortalities are investigated and documented with the intent of identifying and reducing threats.

To accomplish many nongame bird goals, the Commission and other agencies and organizations have formed partnerships. The endangered peregrine falcon has been established as a breeding species in the state through a partnership with Woodman of the World, Fontenelle Forest, Omaha Audubon and Raptor Recovery Nebraska. In partnership with Raptor Recovery Nebraska, over 300 captive-reared barn owls were released in southeastern Nebraska to re-establish a breeding population.

American kestrel nesting boxes have been installed along Interstate 80 between Omaha and Lincoln with the cooperation of the Nebraska Department of Roads, Sierra Club and Omaha Audubon. The Nebraska Prairie Partners program with the Rocky Mountain Bird Observatory is surveying and monitoring shortgrass prairie bird species in western Nebraska. Bluebirds Across Nebraska has 1,700 members working to increase populations of eastern and mountain bluebirds by building nest boxes and monitoring them during the breeding season.

Partnerships have brought together the Commission and the University of Nebraska to monitor and protect least tern and piping plover nesting grounds, and to promote bird conservation and education through programs like International Migratory Bird Day events. Perhaps the most promising development in recent years has been the formation of the Nebraska Partnership of All-Bird Conservation, a statewide partnership bringing together individuals representing more than 45 diverse organizations and agencies with the common goal of bird conservation.

Return of the Peregrine

Historically, the peregrine falcon was probably only a seasonal visitor to Nebraska, although they may have once nested in the Pine Ridge. University zoologist Lawrence Bruner reported young and old birds in August 1903 in buttes west of Fort Robinson, at what "may have been the nesting site." Peregrines were never abundant. Estimates in the 1930s and 1940s placed the North American population at about 1,500 breeding pairs.

Peregrine populations began to decline in the 1950s when environmentally persistent pesticides, particularly DDT, led to thin egg shells in raptors and declining nesting success. In the 1970s, the American and Arctic peregrine populations were listed as endangered under the Endangered Species Conservation Act of 1969. DDT was banned for most uses in the United States in 1972 but residues of the pesticide persisted.

Efforts to establish the species as breeders in Nebraska began in 1988 when six young birds were hand-raised at the Woodmen Tower in Omaha, an artificial nesting habitat mimicking cliff sites. Birds were also hand-raised at the Mutual of Omaha building. The first nesting occurred at the Woodmen Tower in 1992 when a pair successfully fledged three young. Nesting has taken place at the Woodmen Tower every year since. A banded male released in Omaha began frequenting the state capitol in Lincoln in the early-1990s. In 2003 a pair nested at the capitol, but their eggs did not hatch. The peregrine was upgraded from endangered to threatened on the Nebraska list in 1995 and removed from the federal endangered list in 1999.

Today, outside of re-established breeding areas in Omaha and Lincoln, peregrines are most often reported from the Rainwater Basin, where they follow migrating flocks of shorebirds, which are preferred prey species.

Two peregrine falcons sit on a nesting platform with their eggs atop the Woodman Tower in Omaha.

Bird Study Today

The new era in Nebraska bird study that began in the 1970s bore fruit in the 1990s. Bird study changed, becoming more scientific at the amateur level and more intense. By the end of the 20th century the bar for bird study in Nebraska had been raised. Accuracy in identification was demanded. Distribution needed to be better defined. Little-studied species, races and hybrids needed to be better documented. In the early days, documentation came at the front end of a Marble's Game Getter loaded with birdshot and a properly labeled specimen in a museum tray. Better field guides, better optics, higher standards and more restricted collector permits changed the way birding was done.

The Nebraska Bird Review is a good measure of change in bird study during the past 20 years. Each volume has grown fatter with better bird records as more dedicated observers spend more time in the field. Casual observations and counts continue, but the standards for documented reports of new or rare species, or species out of their range or time of year, became stricter.

Reliable documentation of sightings was not a revolutionary objective in the 1990s. At the second annual NOU meeting in 1901, criteria were defined for recognizing reports in one of three categories: positive, probably and doubtful. Positive reports were based on a specimen or on the observation of an experienced observer, if the species was common in the state. Rare or unexpected species in the state were not accepted without a specimen, regardless of the credentials of the observer. At that meeting, Robert Wolcott presented a paper pleading for better documentation: "These problems must be met and answered in a spirit of scientific accuracy, if our conclusions are to carry weight with those living outside our borders. We must know what we know and record only what we know we know. As a society we must judge kindly, but most critically with the records presented by our members for our consideration."

Documentation of observations no doubt declined along with the practice of taking specimens, and by the middle of the 20th century had become rather casual.

In 1986, the NOU established a records committee to review reports of species not previously reported in Nebraska or rare, and species seen out of their expected range or season. A list of species in need of better documentation was published. That same year, *The Birds of Nebraska: A Critically Evaluated List*, was published by Tanya Bray, Barbara Padelford and Ross Silcock. In the introduction, the authors wrote: "Nebraska has never had a systematic method for evaluating bird records prior to publication, and previous lists of Nebraska birds have generally been published without stated criteria for inclusion." The authors accepted 407 species as documented.

When Paul Johnsgard wrote *Birds of the Great Plains* in 1979, he discovered that of all Great Plains states, Nebraska had the least information on breeding birds. That was largely rectified during the 1980s with fieldwork for *The Nebraska Breeding Bird Atlas*. The atlas project was initiated in 1984 and completed in 1989. The object was not to record the presence of bird species, although that was a by-product, but to document those species breeding in Nebraska and to determine their breeding range. A total of 443, nine-square-mile blocks, totaling less than five percent of the state, were chosen to sample as many types of habitat found in each county as possible. Atlas projects in other states used randomly selected blocks, but Wayne Mollhoff, the Nebraska project coordinator, realized it was more important to sample the best breeding bird habitat because of the large area to be surveyed by a limited number of observers. When the project was finished, 26,000 records had been gathered and observers had logged a total of 5,803 hours looking for nesting birds.

*A bevy of **wildlife biologists** came to the Nebraska Game, Forestation and Parks Commission in the 1940s and 1950s. J. Henry Sather (left) and Knox Jones studied Sandhills wildlife, living in a panel van that served as a mobile laboratory.*

Duck Stamp Artists

The Migratory Bird Conservation Act in 1929 provided for wetland acquisition through the national wildlife refuge system, but the Great Depression eliminated any hopes of federal funding for conservation. In 1934, Jay N. "Ding" Darling was appointed chief of the Bureau of Biological Survey. A nationally known political cartoonist for The Des Moines Register, Darling had frequently turned his talents to scathing cartoons depicting the destruction of the nation's wetlands. Darling was instrumental in conceiving and promoting a way to fund wetland protection. On March 16, 1934, Congress passed and President Franklin D. Roosevelt signed the Migratory Bird Hunting Stamp Act, requiring all waterfowl hunters 16 years or older to buy a duck stamp annually. The revenue generated from stamp sales was earmarked for the purchase or lease of wetlands across the country. The first stamp, designed by Darling, cost $1 and went on sale August 22, 1934. By 2003, more than $600 million has been generated by stamp sales, preserving over five million acres of wetland habitat and paying for many of the more than 540 national wildlife refuges in the United States. Two Nebraska artists have been selected as winners of the duck stamp art competition.

"At 1:45 p.m., Mr. A.M. Brooking passed around a dozen or more watercolor paintings of birds by Claremont Pritchard of Juniata, Adams County, a twenty-year-old lad who has taken quite an interest in birds and painting of them," The Nebraska Bird Review reported in an account of the May 1936 annual meeting of the Nebraska Ornithologists' Union. "These paintings elicited considerable favorable comment."

C.G. "Bud" Pritchard joined the Nebraska Ornithologists' Union in 1948 and his bird art was regularly featured in The Nebraska Bird Review. His wife, Mary (Hanson) Pritchard, a retired professor of zoology at the University of Nebraska-Lincoln, still serves as NOU librarian. From 1949 until 1973, Pritchard was an illustrator for the Nebraska Game and Parks Commission, producing hundreds of wildlife paintings and drawings for a number of publications. He is best remembered as illustrator of the long-running "Notes on Nebraska Fauna" that appeared in NEBRASKAland Magazine and its predecessor, Outdoor Nebraska. An astute bird watcher and avid bird hunter, Pritchard studied birds the old-fashioned way – in the field with pencil and paper. He won second place in the duck stamp competition in 1952 and 1956. His pen-and-ink drawing, as was required at the time, was selected for the 1968-69 Federal Migratory Bird Stamp and translated into color at a federal engraving office. Pritchard's original depiction of hooded mergansers was small to conform to the competition criteria, and he sold it to a collector in Long Island, New York. Later Pritchard did a larger color version of the same birds that was used in Outdoor Nebraska and for prints.

Bud Pritchard's 1968-69 duck stamp, "Hooded Mergansers."

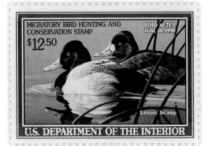

Neal Anderson's 1989-90 duck stamp, "Lesser Scaup."

Neal Anderson's 1994-95 duck stamp, "Red-breasted Merganser."

Several years after Pritchard died, Lincoln artist Neal Anderson began painting wildlife for NEBRASKAland Magazine's "Notes on Nebraska Fauna." Anderson's gouache and acrylic painting of a pair of lesser scaup was selected from a field of 681 entries for the 1989-90 federal duck stamp. Before winning, Anderson had placed in the top 20 finalists of the federal stamp competition four times. His art was used for Nebraska conservation stamps, the first Nebraska Trout Stamp and the Nebraska Wood Duck Stamp. He was selected "Artist of the Year" by Ducks Unlimited in 1984. Anderson won the federal duck stamp competition a second time in 1994-95 with a painting of a pair of red-breasted mergansers.

An average of 48 species was documented per block, ranging from 12 species in shortgrass prairie and wheat farm in Kimball County to 92 in a Sarpy County block with woods and marsh. When the data was compiled, 191 species met all the criteria as a confirmed breeding species. Funding for the project was only $1,200, and volunteers did nearly all the fieldwork. For the first time, Nebraska had a snapshot in time of its breeding avifauna.

At the dawn of the 21st century, bird study in Nebraska has never been stronger, and has never had more dedicated, skilled observers. Membership in the NOU stands at about 260, and the pages of The Nebraska Bird Review are filled with reliable information. A spate of books about Nebraska birds and ecology was published during the past three years in addition to Mollhoff's The Nebraska Breeding Bird Atlas. Among the best are: Birds of Nebraska by Roger Sharpe, Ross Silcock and Joel Jorgensen; Prairie Birds and The Nature of Nebraska by Paul Johnsgard; and Birds of the Untamed West – The History of Birdlife in Nebraska, 1750 to 1875 by James Ducey. Never has there been better information about Nebraska birds.

So much has changed, and yet so little, in 100 years of bird study in Nebraska. Speaking at the first annual meeting of the Nebraska Ornithologists' Union in 1899, Lawrence Bruner addressed a handful of the state's best birders: "We have perhaps fewer workers who are interested in birds in this state than are to be found in some of the neighboring states. Although these workers may be fewer in number, I think there is no doubt that they are more earnest in the work they are doing." ∎

ECOREGIONS AND DESTINATIONS

THE STORY OF NEBRASKA'S BIRD LIFE is the history of the land. The face of the land dictated what species evolved here. How we have reshaped the land dictates what species live here today. Most species now found in the state are remnants of what once was, others have come to what we've made of it.

Birds are specialists. Each species evolved to occupy a narrow niche in the natural world. When those niches vanish, so do the birds living in them. When niches are created, new birds come to occupy them – feral pigeons replace upland sandpipers where grain elevators stand on former prairie land. Birds do not quickly adapt to change. Move a prothonotary warbler from swampland in an eastern forest to mid-continent grasslands and it perishes. Move a man and he will build a sod house rather than a log cabin.

Change is part of the natural system – rivers rage and scour away valley vegetation, wildfires sweep across grasslands consuming everything in their paths. On a greater scale of time, climates change, glaciers advance and retreat, mountains rise and are worn away. While man's hand on the land is not so grand, it has been persistent. In less than 150 years – two human life spans – acre by acre, river by river, grassland by grassland, man has transformed the face of Nebraska and its composition of bird life.

Before the coming of Euroamericans, less than three percent of the state was covered by forests. Deciduous woodlands clung to the Missouri River and the lower reaches of its tributaries. Sparse pine forest found protection from prairie fires on rocky escarpments in the Panhandle and eastward along the northern rim

of the Niobrara River. Between those woodlands were hundreds of miles of grass – grass to the next ridge and beyond, tallgrass prairie in the east, shortgrass plains in the west. Meandering shallow rivers and creeks, lakes, marshes and ephemeral pools dotted the grasslands. Across the land birds were in great variety and abundance.

Man's influence on wildlife in Nebraska can be divided into two periods. The first, extending from the mid-1700s until nearly 1900, was a time of unadulterated and conspicuous exploitation – the taking of what the land produced so abundantly. Vast herds of grazing animals vanished, furbearers were trapped until few remained and birds with table or market value were ruthlessly harvested. Huge flocks of passenger pigeons, Carolina parakeets and Eskimo curlews, once thought to be without limit, vanished.

The second period of exploitation began in the late-1800s and continues today. Although less direct, conspicuous and repugnant than the earlier exploitation, and generally heralded as progress, the methodical destruction or degradation of wildlife habitat has been infinitely more profound in determining which species would prosper, which would decline, and which would vanish.

On the pages that follow, Nebraska is divided into broad regions representing the state's principal ecosystems. Within each, smaller, ecologically distinct regions are identified. James M. Omernik proposed the system used here in 1987. With the collaboration of others, his concept was expanded, detail was added, and in 2001 it was published in map-chart form as *Ecoregions of Nebraska and Kansas*. Geographic regions can be drawn along many criteria: geology, climate, physiography, soils, land-use, hydrology and plant and animal communities. Omernik et al. considered all of these criteria in drafting their map of Nebraska, defining its regions. This system considers what the land once was and what it is today; hence the former tallgrass prairie region of eastern Nebraska becomes the western Corn Belt Plains. We have omitted some technical terminology and details from the *Ecoregions of Nebraska and Kansas* for the sake of organization and reader convenience and to better tell the story of Nebraska's bird life. Two ecoregions that enter Nebraska in the north – the Northwestern Great Plains and the Northwestern Glaciated Plains, are not treated separately because avifauna in those regions is not distinct from larger, adjoining ecoregions.

Within each region, public access sites were selected to represent the avifauna and to provide geographic distribution throughout the region. These sites were selected from recommendations by Nebraska Game and Parks Commission wildlife managers and by compiling records from *The Nebraska Bird Review*, the official publication of the Nebraska Ornithologists' Union. There many other public lands in each region

ROD NABHOLZ

Chestnut-sided warblers are spring and fall migrants, most common in the Missouri River Valley.

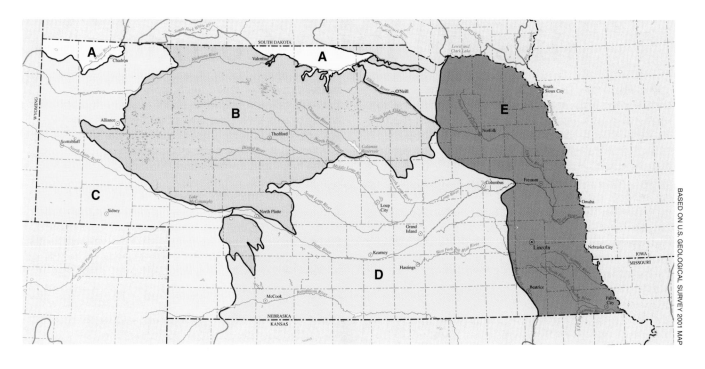

BASED ON U.S. GEOLOGICAL SURVEY 2001 MAP

A **Northwestern Great Plains**
The Missouri River Plateau region of the Great Plains. Semiarid, rolling plains with occasional buttes. Mixed-grass prairie with limited agriculture, principally spring wheat and alfalfa.

B **Nebraska Sandhills**
Grass-stabilized sand dunes with numerous lakes and wetlands. Fragile sandy soils, distinctive Sandhills prairie. Limited agricultural development, sparsely populated, used as rangeland.

C **Western High Plains**
Semiarid climate, nearly level to irregular plains extensively converted to agriculture, principally wheat. Grassed dunes in south. Mixed-grass prairie in the north, shortgrass prairie in the south.

D **Central Great Plains**
Former mixed-grass prairie largely converted to agriculture. Loess soils. Except for Rainwater Basin in south, well drained by streams. Flat to rolling topography.

E **Western Corn Belt Plains**
Former tallgrass prairie almost entirely converted to agriculture. Nearly level to gently rolling, glaciated plains. Deciduous woodlands along streams, particularly in Missouri Valley.

Approximately 69 miles

worthy of a birder's attention, and excellent birding opportunities on private land that often can be accessed with no more than a courteous request. Many sites provide consistently good bird viewing opportunities for the same species year after year. Birds, however, are adept at finding places to suit their immediate needs. One year's birding hotspot might not be the same the following year. This is especially true for wetlands. Birders, like the birds they seek, must search for the best opportunities.

To understand bird life of each region, what it once was and is today, it is essential to understand the nature of land before settlement and how it has changed. In the pages that follow, the story of the land precedes recommendations of birding destinations. While the history of land use is often a tale of sorrow, now it is only history. It is where we have been. The future of wild lands and wildlife is being fashioned today.

The text provides basic information for each recommended destination. For more details about best time of year to view a species, its frequency in Nebraska and whether it is a breeder or a migrant, consult the Checklist of Nebraska Birds beginning on page 152. Precise maps, bird lists and information about facilities

and regulations are often available on the Internet. State wildlife management area destinations are identified as WMAs. These tracts were purchased and are maintained with funds from the sales of hunting licenses and habitat stamps. Except during hunting seasons these areas are lightly used. WMAs are scattered across the state and typically offer some of the best bird habitat in the region. WMAs have parking areas and are open year-round to the public. Birders can contribute to the acquisition and management of WMAs by purchasing annual Nebraska Habitat Stamps.

For a guide to WMAs, state parks and recreation areas, contact the Nebraska Game and Parks Commission, P.O. Box 30370, 2200 North 33rd St., Lincoln, NE 68503, 402-471-0641, outdoornebraska.org. Request a copy of the current *Nebraska Hunt Guide and Public Lands* for a list of wildlife management areas, or a guidebook to state parks and brochures for specific areas. Those publications are also usually available where hunting and fishing licenses are sold. State recreation areas, designated as SRAs, typically have better camping facilities but less wildlife land than WMAs. Park entry permits are required at state parks, and SRAs. No permit is required to enter a WMA. ▪

Missouri River Corridor

IN THE 1700S TRAPPERS COURSED the rivers of what would become Nebraska, harvesting or trading for what grew wild, leaving little evidence of their passage. Military forts and trading posts along the Missouri in the early-1800s were the first Euroamerican settlements. Their inhabitants reshaped the land, cutting trees for construction and firewood. By the mid-1800s, steamboats regularly ascended the Missouri River and more timber fell for firewood. Small settlements grew into towns, then cities, and settlers flowed to the free and fertile land in the West. By the 1840s and 1850s, a torrent of immigrants moved from eastern states to the Pacific coast, and the Nebraska Territory was along the most advantageous route in between.

The densely wooded bluffs of the Missouri River today suggest the valley was always heavily forested, but it was not. In 1819, Edwin James traveled up the Missouri River with the Stephen H. Long expedition to the Rocky Mountains. Of the Missouri River between the mouth of the Platte and present-day Omaha, he wrote: "The bluffs on each side are more elevated and abrupt, and being absolutely naked, rising into conic points, split by innumerable ravines . . . The forests within the valley are of small extent, interspersed with wide meadows." When the Long Expedition selected a site for its winter quarters in late-September 1819, the men chose the western side of the Missouri north of the present-day site of Omaha, where timber and stone were available for construction. "The river is here and there seen meandering in serpentine folds, along its broad valley, chequered with woodlands and prairies, while at a nearer view you look down on an extensive plain interspersed with a few scattered copses or bushes," James wrote of the view from the camp. By the end of the 1870s, after two decades of settlers and travelers hungry for saw lumber on the treeless prairie, the Missouri River woodlands were probably a shadow of what they once had been.

"But they are all gone now, and so has most of the woods, for that matter," Sandy Griswold wrote of the ruffed grouse in his August 27, 1905, *Omaha World-Herald* column. "The timber, even along the turbid Missouri, today scarcely possesses a trait of the primeval forests of forty years ago. The oldest trees have a comparatively youthful appearance, and are pygmies in girth beside the decaying stumps of their giant ancestors. They are not as shagged with moss nor so scaled with lichens. The woods' floor has lost its ancient carpet of ankle-deep moss and the intricate maze of fallen columns in every stage of decay, and in many places look clean swept and everywhere along the singing Elkhorn is gone, many of the species which composed it having quite disappeared as have many of the birds and animals that flourished in the perennial shade of the old wilderness."

During his time in Nebraska, from the late-1880s until his death in 1929, Griswold observed the final years of great game bird abundance in Nebraska and its inevitable decline. By the time he arrived in Omaha, the destruction of Missouri River woodlands had been underway for 30 years or more. In 1905, Griswold wrote that the ruffed grouse had virtually vanished before he arrived in Nebraska in 1886. Griswold knew many of the state's old sportsmen, and in the case of the ruffed grouse, much of his information was surely secondhand. Griswold wrote that ruffed grouse had once been found along portions of the Elkhorn River, Loup River, Niobrara River and Rawhide Creek in addition to the Missouri River.

Gone, too, were the woodcocks that Griswold wrote had been "almost everywhere in the neighborhood" of Omaha before his arrival. In 1905 he wrote the woodcock "is almost as extinct as the [passenger] pigeon. It never has been plentiful since my residence in this part of the country."

ROD NABHOLZ

*The **brown creeper** is a rare resident and migrant, principally in the east. It is an infrequent nesting species.*

Griswold occasionally mentioned that while market hunters principally shot larger game birds, songbirds were not exempt from the gun. Before the sale of wild game was prohibited, and even after, songbirds were found in Omaha meat markets. Griswold also wrote that immigrants were fond of eating small birds.

Market hunting and shooting birds that raided grain fields were instrumental to the disappearance of passenger pigeons and Carolina parakeets, once abundant nearly beyond comprehension, but the destruction of woodlands probably contributed to their disappearance and alone would have rendered the same outcome within a few years. Nebraska was on the western edge of the range of both species. Wild turkeys were common along the Missouri when John James Audubon passed in 1843 and for several decades afterward. By the 1870s turkeys were rare, and were probably gone from the state by 1900.

The loss and degradation of Nebraska's scant deciduous woodlands was only the beginning of land-use changes that would have profound implications

*Before the **Missouri River** was dammed and channelized in the 20th century, it ranged across a floodplain as wide as 20 miles, carving new channels and abandoning old. Today, only the Missouri upstream from Ponca (above) resembles the river of old along Nebraska's border.*

on Missouri Valley bird life. Along with the ruffed grouse and wild turkey, dozens of small bird species at the western edge of their range in Nebraska's eastern deciduous woodlands probably also vanished. "Destroy the thickets and briery spots, and both are unsightly on the well groomed farm, no matter how necessary they are ... [and] what are the gaudy woodpeckers, yellowhammers and sapsuckers to do when you cut away and burn every dead tree, stump and bough," Griswold wrote in 1910.

The woodlands were only one element in a complex natural system. Before the Missouri River was dammed and channelized in the 20th century, it ranged freely between the bluffs across a floodplain as wide as 20 miles, carving new channels and abandoning old with whimsy. Sandbars were everywhere. Some were no more than raw sand where migrating waterfowl roosted and shorebirds fed and nested; others were colonized by patches of willows and annual plants until the Missouri again reclaimed them. Some channels, abandoned and isolated from the river, became sickle-shaped oxbow lakes rife with bird life. Others became chutes filled with sluggish river flow, which were periodically flushed and renewed when the river rose. Shallow wetlands on the floodplain

were fed by groundwater. Like the ancient valleys of the Tigris and Euphrates, the bottomland soils were fertile and deep. The silty leavings of the Missouri River were seemingly created to grow crops.

In the spring of 1905, Griswold and a companion traveled to one of their favorite snipe-hunting grounds south of the present site of Fort Calhoun. They found "the whole vast area . . . as dry as a bone," he wrote. "Huge drains and ditches criss-cross the old grounds in all directions, and while there are a few straggling pools yet remaining, they too will soon disappear, as the system of draining up there is perfect and another year will see the entire expanse under cultivation. The progress and thrift of the agriculturalist is something that the jacksnipe even cannot interfere with it."

A year later, in Burt County, an ambitious drainage project was complete. To drain a four- to five-mile wide strip of fertile bottomland between the bluffs and the Missouri River, a 19-mile long ditch was dredged to carry the waters of Silver, Mud and Tekamah creeks to the Missouri River. Most years these creeks flooded, making farming the fertile bottomland impossible. Scrapers and two steam-powered, floating dredges cut a ditch 60 feet wide at its mouth and 15 feet deep. Reclaiming the wasteland of the Missouri River

Western Corn Belt Plains

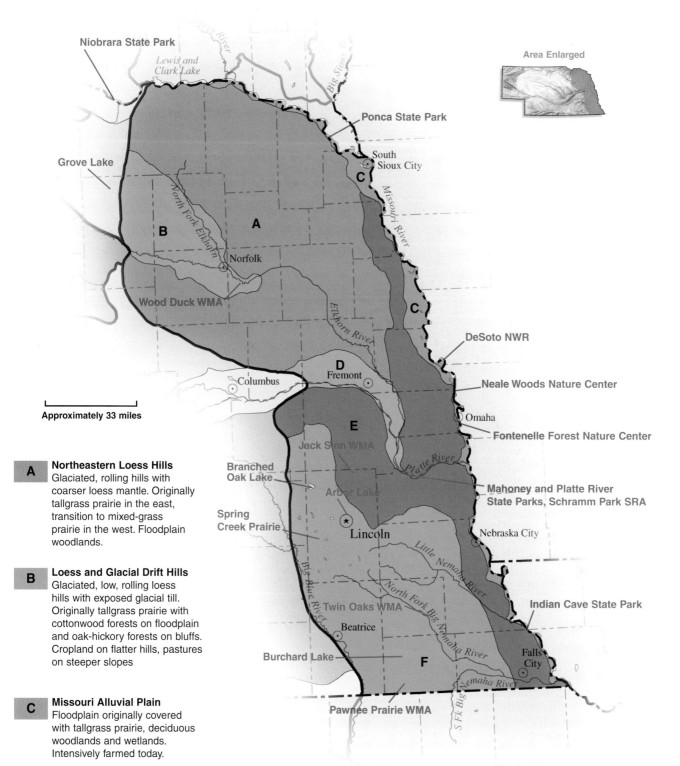

Niobrara State Park

Lewis and Clark Lake

Ponca State Park

Grove Lake

South Sioux City

C

B

A

North Fork Elkhorn

Norfolk

Wood Duck WMA

Missouri River

Elkhorn River

C

DeSoto NWR

D

Fremont

Columbus

Neale Woods Nature Center

Omaha

Fontenelle Forest Nature Center

E

Jack Sinn WMA

Branched Oak Lake

Arbor Lake

Mahoney and Platte River State Parks, Schramm Park SRA

Platte River

Spring Creek Prairie

Lincoln

Nebraska City

Little Nemaha River

Big Blue River

North Fork Big Nemaha River

Twin Oaks WMA

Indian Cave State Park

Beatrice

Burchard Lake

Big Nemaha River

F

Falls City

Pawnee Prairie WMA

S Fk Big Nemaha River

Nemaha River

Area Enlarged

Approximately 33 miles

A **Northeastern Loess Hills**
Glaciated, rolling hills with coarser loess mantle. Originally tallgrass prairie in the east, transition to mixed-grass prairie in the west. Floodplain woodlands.

B **Loess and Glacial Drift Hills**
Glaciated, low, rolling loess hills with exposed glacial till. Originally tallgrass prairie with cottonwood forests on floodplain and oak-hickory forests on bluffs. Cropland on flatter hills, pastures on steeper slopes

C **Missouri Alluvial Plain**
Floodplain originally covered with tallgrass prairie, deciduous woodlands and wetlands. Intensively farmed today.

D **Lower Platte Alluvial Plain**
Flat, alluvial plain originally tallgrass prairie and deciduous woodlands on floodplain and bluffs. Few floodplain wetlands and native grass pastures remain. Intensively farmed.

E **Nebraska/Kansas Loess Hills**
Glaciated, deep, rolling loess-covered hills. Originally tallgrass prairie with floodplain woodlands and scattered oak-hickory forests. Principally cropland today except on steep slopes.

F **Loess and Glacial Drift Hills**
Glaciated, rolling low hills. Originally tallgrass prairie with cottonwood-dominated floodplain forest. Oak-hickory bluff forests. Today cropland on flatter land, pastureland on steeper slopes.

BASED ON U.S. GEOLOGICAL SURVEY 2001 MAP

MICHAEL FORSBERG

*Common migrants and breeders in eastern Nebraska, **green herons** are most often found in woodlands bordering rivers. The species appears to have expanded its range westward as woodlands have established along rivers such as the Platte.*

bottomland was zealously pursued in the early-1900s, especially in northeastern Nebraska where the river shifted east, away from the Nebraska bluffs. In the early-1900s, conversion of wetlands to cropland was largely accomplished by local drainage districts. By the mid-1900s the federal government had taken on the job of taming the river.

Channelization of the Missouri River below Sioux City to maintain a six-foot-deep navigation channel and to prevent flooding began in the 1930s. Additional dredging, diking and bank stabilization work between 1947 and 1965 deepened the channel to nine feet and shortened the river by cutting across meanders. When the work was completed the Missouri River bordering Nebraska was shorter by about 171 miles than it had been in the time of Lewis and Clark. Under the federal flood control act of 1944, the Pick-Sloan Missouri River Basin Program led to the construction of six main stem dams on the Missouri, Gavins Point near Yankton being the farthest downstream. By the mid-1950s, the Missouri no longer burst from its banks to flood farmland and cities, and carried enough water to float commercial barges during the navigation season.

Confining the Missouri River allowed the clearing of floodplain forest for cropland and eliminated sandbars once used by waterbirds. And, as the channel cut

deeper, floodplain wetlands vanished. The chutes dried out as did the oxbows and wetlands. Channelization, dikes and levies confined the river to where man wanted it to be, isolated river bluffs miles from the river, left parts of Nebraska on the Iowa side of the river and parts of Iowa on the Nebraska side. Today, the only stretches of the Missouri River along Nebraska's border resembling a wild river are found between the South Dakota border and Niobrara, and between Gavins Point Dam and Ponca State Park.

One hundred years of reshaping the Missouri River has had a profound effect on the bird life once found there. With the sandbars gone, the abundance of waterfowl, wading birds and shorebirds has significantly diminished. In early-October 1843, as the fall migration of waterfowl was only beginning, Audubon noted, "the Geese and Ducks are abundant beyond description" on the Missouri River. In 1913, Sandy Griswold wrote: "Several years ago I went from Omaha to a point several miles below Bellevue in a rowboat on the Missouri river. That was in the spring and the river and bars between Child's Point and the first bend below Bellevue was literally covered with ducks and geese of all kinds."

Before the mid-1900s, the Missouri was the principal travel lane for geese and ducks in the midcontinent.

But as the river changed, as backwaters, shallow water and sandbars vanished, the number of waterfowl traveling Nebraska's eastern coast began to dwindle. Snow geese increasingly abandoned the Missouri, shifting westward where wetlands and grain fields were more abundant, or they passed over Nebraska's Missouri River, hopping from one wildlife refuge to the next. Piping plovers and least terns, which once found abundant sandbars in the Missouri for nesting, became rare. But those are only the conspicuous species – the ones that were counted. A mitigation of sort was made, not formally or by design, but a trade-off all the same. For the loss of a free-flowing Missouri River and all the bird life it supported, forestland and the species adapted to it became more abundant. The prothonotary warbler, noted in wooded wetlands along the Missouri River by naturalists in the 1800s, apparently vanished when forests were logged, only to return as part of Nebraska's breeding avifauna in recent years. Back, too, is the pileated woodpecker. New species expanded their ranges westward to eastern Nebraska and deciduous woodland species already there became more abundant.

*Extirpated from Nebraska by 1900, the **pileated woodpecker** returned as a nester along the Missouri River in the late-1990s.*

In recent years there has been a glimmer of hope that the Missouri River of old might, in small ways, in a few places, be restored to what it once was, but at a huge cost. At the beginning of the 21st century, oxbows and chutes are being brought back to life, once again connected to the river, and there are efforts to release water from upstream dams to simulate the seasonal rise and fall of the old Missouri River. But, these efforts are embroiled in state rivalry and litigation. Today, public areas where native woodlands and floodplains are protected along the Missouri River – state parks, wildlife lands and federal refuges – are more numerous than ever.

If Lewis and Clark, or even Sandy Griswold, were to return to the Missouri River today it is unlikely they would recognize places they once knew, particularly on the floodplain. They would be amazed that the river was so straight and deep and free of troublesome sandbars. On the bluff tops they would find woodlands or cropland, not native grass scoured free of woody plants by wildfires. In the woodlands, they would encounter familiar birds, species found in the 1800s. Little would they know that many species had vanished and later returned with Nebraska's eastern deciduous forest.

Today, eastern deciduous forest extends along the entire reach of the Missouri River on Nebraska's eastern border. In the extreme southeast, Nebraska's forest most resembles deciduous forests of eastern states. But, only about 80 of the 200 woody species found in the center of the great eastern forests are found in southeastern Nebraska. Those woodlands become less complex along the Missouri River in northeastern Nebraska and the variety and abundance of eastern woodland species also declines from south to north. University of Nebraska ornithologist Paul Johnsgard estimated there are 138 to 140 breeding bird species in the Missouri River Valley south of Omaha, the largest for any region in Nebraska. He lists the red-shouldered hawk, broad-winged hawk, chuck-will's-widow, white-eyed vireo, Carolina wren, summer tanager, Louisiana waterthrush, northern parula and cerulean, prothonotary, Kentucky and yellow-throated warblers as representative of species with southeastern affinities native to the lower Missouri River in Nebraska. No matter where birders look, though, on the floodplain or bluff top, at Indian Cave State Park or Ponca State Park, they will find birds in great variety along the Missouri River. Let the journey begin.

Indian Cave State Park

The first tract of land to create Indian Cave State Park was acquired in 1962. Additions since have brought the park to 3,399 acres, of which 2,386 are wooded. Indian Cave is the southern-most public access to an extensive tract of eastern deciduous forest in Nebraska, and hence it is the most likely location to find birds with ranges principally to the east and south. It has not received the same degree of attention from birders as have Missouri River sites closer to

*When prairie fires still ranged at will across Nebraska, bluff tops along the Missouri River were blanketed with grass. During the last century woodlands expanded from protected ravines and colonized bluff tops at areas such as **Indian Cave State Park** (above).*

Omaha. Spring migration in May is the prime time for viewing the maximum number of species, especially warblers. May is also the best time to view springtime wildflowers. By June the forest canopy has closed off sunlight for wildflowers and the view for birders, but breeding species are still to be found. A species of particular interest that should be looked for year-round, but especially during the breeding season, is the pileated woodpecker. The calls and characteristically large, oblong entrances to nesting cavities of this species were reported at Indian Cave in 1969. At that time, there had only been one other report (at Fort Calhoun in 1952) of the large woodpecker in Nebraska since 1895. They were again reported at Indian Cave in the winter of 2002, and the following May a pair was observed entering apparent nesting cavities. In the spring of 2003 young were observed in a nesting cavity.

Cerulean warblers, summer tanagers, northern parulas, Louisiana waterthrushes, white-eyed vireos, Kentucky and yellow-throated warblers and other species with ranges principally in the southeastern United States have all be reported at Indian Cave. The park is probably the best site in the state to find Acadian flycatchers. It is not uncommon for expert birders to see or hear 100 species in one day during May at Indian Cave. In late winter, listen for the calls of barred owls, which are year-round residents and probably more abundant in Missouri River woodlands in southeastern Nebraska than anywhere in the state. On summer nights, birders will hear the calls of both whip-poor-wills and the less common Chuck-will's-widows, a bird with a range principally to the southeast of Nebraska. Chuck-will's-widows were first reported in Nebraska in 1963, and at Indian Cave three years later. Turkey vultures are always present from late spring into early fall and are probably breeders. Bald eagles nest in bottomland cottonwoods. Another species to watch in the future is the ruffed grouse. Twenty ruffed grouse trapped in Minnesota were released at Indian Cave in 1968 but did not establish.

Indian Cave Bird Sampler

Wood Duck	Swainson's Thrush
Sharp-shinned Hawk	Hermit Thrush
Cooper's Hawk	Wood Thrush
Broad-winged Hawk	Tennessee Warbler
American Woodcock	Orange-crowned Warbler
Black-billed Cuckoo	Nashville Warbler
Yellow-billed Cuckoo	Northern Parula
Barred Owl	Chestnut-sided Warbler
Chuck-will's-widow	Magnolia Warbler
Whip-poor-will	Black-throated Green-Warbler
Ruby-throated Hummingbird	Blackburnian Warbler
Red-bellied Woodpecker	Bay-breasted Warbler
Pileated Woodpecker	Blackpoll Warbler
Olive-sided Flycatcher	Black-and-white Warbler
Eastern Wood-Pewee	American Redstart
Acadian Flycatcher	Prothonotary Warbler
Alder Flycatcher	Ovenbird
Least Flycatcher	Louisiana Waterthrush
Great Crested Flycatcher	Kentucky Warbler
Bell's Vireo	Mourning Warbler
Yellow-throated Vireo	Wilson's Warbler
Blue-headed Vireo	Summer Tanager
Warbling Vireo	Scarlet Tanager
Red-eyed Vireo	Eastern Towhee
Cliff Swallow	Fox Sparrow
Tufted Titmouse	Lincoln's Sparrow
White-breasted Nuthatch	White-throated Sparrow
Carolina Wren	Harris's Sparrow
Ruby-crowned Kinglet	Rose-breasted Grosbeak
Blue-gray Gnatcatcher	Indigo Bunting

In recent years, ruffed grouse have been released in Missouri just across the river and there was a report of two ruffed grouse in southern Nemaha County in 2001.

Paved roads take visitors through the bluffs, but most of the park can be seen only by hiking or on horseback. There are over 20 miles of trails ranging in length from less than a mile to seven miles, providing access to nearly all of the park. A recent bottomland addition includes a Missouri River backwater that is currently being restored. A viewing blind and deck are available.

Although Indian Cave remains less developed than most other state parks, it offers a modern RV campground with full facilities as well as ample areas for group camping and primitive camping. Adirondack shelters and picnic areas are available. Trail rides and heritage programs are offered during summer months. An interpretive log cabin has been built on the site of the mid-1800s St. Deroin community, and an early-day, one-room schoolhouse was reconstructed. A state park entry permit is required.

• Additional Information: From the junction of U.S. Highway 136 and Nebraska Highway 67 near Brownville, go south approximately 9 miles to Nebraska Spur 64E, then east 5 miles to the park. Indian Cave State Park, RR 1 Box 30, Shubert, NE 68437-9801, (402) 883-2575, icavesp@ngpc.state.ne.us.

Fontenelle Forest

Located on the Missouri River bluffs south of Omaha and east of Bellevue, Fontenelle Forest Nature Center had its beginning in 1912. Late that year a group of "Omaha's most public spirited and far-seeing men" gathered to form the Fontenelle Forest Association, recounted Alice Deweese in the April 1964 *The Nebraska Bird Review*. Deweese was the daughter of Solon R. Towne, an early-day proponent of bird study and protection. A.A. Tyler, Harold Gifford, Sr. and Towne were leaders in the effort, and Gifford advanced money to purchase 365 acres of Childs' Point, a peninsula formed by a loop in the Missouri River and a favorite birding destination as early as the late-1800s. The association was chartered in April 1913 and became Nebraska's first private wildlife preserve. The preserve was named for Logan Fontenelle, the son of a French-American fur trader and his Omaha Indian wife. In 1822, the Missouri Fur Company established a trading post within the present-day boundaries of Fontenelle Forest, a settlement that ultimately grew to become the city of Bellevue, Nebraska's oldest settlement. In 2000, the organization's name was changed to the Fontenelle Nature Association.

Fontenelle Forest was founded as, and remains, a privately funded, nonprofit association. Today, it

ROD NABHOLZ

Eastern phoebes are most common in the east, and are breeders in the northeast. They frequently nest under bridges.

encompasses 1,400 acres. The bluffs' loess soils have been deeply cut by erosion, leaving steep slopes. The area is laced with springs flowing year-round along limestone sheets underlying the deep mantle of loess. On the ridges and intervening ravines a unique plant and animal community evolved. At least 40 deciduous tree species are found at Fontenelle. A 45-acre wetland, the Great Marsh, on the bottomland adds plant community diversity and attracts wetland-woodland species not found in the bluffs. In 1964, Secretary of the Interior Stuart J. Udall designated Fontenelle Forest as one of seven notable Natural Historic Landmarks in the United States.

Fontenelle Forest's avifauna has been observed and reported more thoroughly and for a longer period than perhaps any other site in Nebraska. In the past 10 years, 246 species of birds have been reported within the Fontenelle Forest boundaries. More than 100 are potential breeding species. Early- to mid-May is the best time to observe migrating species, but all seasons provide exceptional birding opportunities. Thirty-five species of warblers have been reported at Fontenelle. Acadian flycatchers, yellow-throated vireos, Carolina wrens, scarlet and summer tanagers, Louisiana waterthrushes, and cerulean, prothonotary and Kentucky warblers are all reported at Fontenelle. Until the spring of 2003, when a nesting pair of brown creepers was reported at Neale Woods, Fontenelle Forest was the only documented nesting site of that species in the state. The first documented nesting of yellow-crowned night-herons in Nebraska, a bird with a more southeasterly distribution, was at Fontenelle in 1963. Before 1895, it was presumed pileated woodpeckers occasionally nested along the Missouri River in southeastern Nebraska, but nesting was never confirmed. After several years of scattered reports of pileated woodpeckers in the forest, several birds were sighted in the spring of 1999 and one pair nested, the first documented nesting in Nebraska. A nesting pair has been documented at Fontenelle every year since, except in 2002.

Birders will find excellent access to all parts of the forest via nearly 17 miles of well-maintained hiking trails, including a mile-long, barrier-free boardwalk along which hikers are occasionally at eye-level with birds in the woodland canopy. Nature interpretation and education is at the heart of Fontenelle's mission and trained naturalists staff the recently completed visitor's center. Inquiries at the front desk will usually reward birders new to the area with tips on where to look for particular species. A bird checklist, trail maps, newsletters and other informational aids are available. The center and trails are open daily 8 a.m. to 5 p.m. except on some holidays. The nature center and trails are free to members of the Fontenelle Nature Association, but an admission fee is required from nonmembers.

• Additional Information: South of downtown Omaha, take the U.S. Highway 75 exit from Interstate 80; south on U.S. 75 for 2½ miles to Chandler Rd. exit; turn left (east) on Chandler until it ends at Bellevue Blvd.; turn right on Bellevue Blvd.; Fontenelle Forest is ½ mile ahead on the left. Fontenelle Nature Association, 1111 N. Bellevue Blvd., Bellevue, NE 68005, (402) 731-3140, www.fontenelleforest.org and info@fontenelleforest.org.

• Nearby Birding Destinations: Located immediately east of Fontenelle Forest and occupying the point of

the same peninsula is **Gifford Point Wildlife Management Area.** The 1,300 acres of floodplain forest complements the rugged bluff woodlands of Fontenelle, completing the varied plant and bird communities found from river's edge to bluff top. Interior roads provide access to birders. There are no maintained trails. Look for nesting woodcocks in late spring.

Several Omaha city parks offer passerine migration viewing opportunities and the Papio watershed reservoirs are good sites for waterbirds, especially uncommon gull species. For additional Omaha and eastern Nebraska birding sites, go to the Audubon Society of Omaha Birding Areas web site at http://audubon-omaha.org.

Neale Woods

In 1971, the Fontenelle Nature Association accepted the gift of 120 acres of land north of Omaha on the

Looking at the Parts

Members of some bird families – warblers, flycatchers and vireos – are superficially similar and difficult to identify. Skilled birders mentally narrow the options to arrive at identification by asking themselves questions. What species are expected here? Which of those would be in this particular type of habitat at this time of the year? Still, there may be similar-appearing species left as options. That is when they stop looking at the bird as whole and begin looking for telltale markings.

Both the red-eyed vireo and Bell's vireo shown here can be seen at Indian Cave State Park during spring migration. The red-eyed vireo frequents the deciduous forest and Bell's prefers dense brush. Perhaps the bird in view, though, is where a band of shrubs abuts woodland. It's time to look for details. Some vireos have wing bars, including Bell's vireo. Others, like the red-eyed vireo, do not. The distinguishing dark line through the eye suggests the bird is a red-eyed vireo, and of course, given a good view, the bright red eye confirms the identification. Plumage color, while an important identification aid, is not always reliable because it can vary from bird to bird, with the season and even as the light changes. Expert birders also note subtle differences in song, posture, movements and temperament of a species.

Bell's vireo

Red-eyed vireo

MICHELE ANGLE FARRAR

Fontenelle Forest Bird Sampler

Green Heron
Red-shouldered Hawk
Barred Owl
Whip-poor-will
Ruby-throated
  Hummingbird
Pileated Woodpecker
Yellow-throated Vireo
Blue-headed Vireo
Tree Swallow
Tufted Titmouse
Brown Creeper
Carolina Wren
Winter Wren
Blue-gray Gnatcatcher
Gray-cheeked Thrush
Swainson's Thrush
Hermit Thrush
Wood Thrush
Tennessee Warbler
Nashville Warbler
Northern Parula

Chestnut-sided Warbler
Magnolia Warbler
Black-throated Green-
  Warbler
Yellow-throated Warbler
Bay-breasted Warbler
Blackpoll Warbler
Black-and-white Warbler
American Redstart
Prothonotary Warbler
Northern Waterthrush
Louisiana Waterthrush
Mourning Warbler
Wilson's Warbler
Canada Warbler
Scarlet Tanager
Eastern Towhee
Fox Sparrow
Lincoln's Sparrow
White-throated Sparrow
Rose-breasted Grosbeak
Indigo Bunting

Washington and Douglas county line and named it
Neale Woods. In subsequent years the nature
association added contiguous parcels of land to the
area, which today make Neale Woods 554 acres.
One of those additions probably includes the site of
Fort Lisa, which was situated near Stephen Long's
winter of 1819-20 Engineer Cantonment.

Neale Woods encompasses both bluff and floodplain
forests, nearly a mile of Missouri River frontage and
abuts Rock Creek on the north. Woodlands vary in age
from 30 to 200 years, including 35 tree species – oaks,
hickory and basswood on uplands, maples, sycamores
and cottonwoods on floodplain forests. A prairie
restoration program has created 25 acres of native
grassland and there is a cultivated butterfly garden.
In addition to birding and wildflower opportunities,
Neale Woods offers excellent views of the Missouri
River Valley.

The area's bird checklist includes 190 species, of
which 57 are known or likely breeders. Many of the
species found at Fontenelle Forest can also be found
at Neale Woods. Eighteen trails totaling 9 miles lace
Neale Woods, providing access to birds of all
vegetation zones. There is an observatory and an
interpretive center. As at Fontenelle Forest, nonmembers
pay an entrance fee, and other rules and regulations
are similar.

• Additional Information: In north Omaha, take the
30th St. exit (13) off Interstate 680, turn south on 30th
St., then immediately left (east) on Dick Collins Rd.;
continue ¼ mile to Pershing Drive and turn left
(north); continue 2.7 miles, then turn left onto White
Deer Lane; take the first left onto Edith Marie Ave.;
Neale Woods is ¼ mile ahead. Fontenelle Nature
Association, 1111 N. Bellevue Blvd., Bellevue, NE
68005, (402) 731-3140, www.fontenelleforest.org and
info@fontenelleforest.org.

DeSoto National Wildlife Refuge

The seven-mile-long horseshoe lake that is the
centerpiece of this 7,823-acre federal refuge was once
the main channel of the Missouri River. In 1959, the
Army Corps of Engineers cut a new channel to
straighten the river, isolating an old bend and creating
DeSoto National Wildlife Refuge. The boundary line
between Nebraska and Iowa remained in the center
of the old channel so the land inside the loop technically
remains part of Nebraska even though it is now east
of the new channel. It is likely that Lewis and Clark
camped at this loop in the river in August 1804 after
their historic meeting with Indians at the "council
bluff."

Because of its location in the river's old floodplain,
DeSoto offers birders a different look at the Missouri
River than any other large park or nature preserve
along Nebraska's eastern border. Its primary purpose
as a federal wildlife refuge is to provide habitat for
migrating ducks and geese. It is one of the few places
along the Missouri River bordering Nebraska still used
by migrating snow geese; more than 800,000 stop some
years during the fall migration from Arctic nesting
grounds to wintering grounds in the south. Ducks,
principally mallards, also pause on the lake to rest and

ROD NABHOLZ

*A rare migrant and uncommon breeder, principally along the
Missouri River, the **prothonotary warbler** nests in cavities in
woodlands adjacent to wetlands. Loss of floodplain wetlands
probably contributed to a decline in the species's abundance.*

to feed in nearby grain fields. Only 30 years ago the fall snow goose migration on the Missouri River peaked in late-September and early-October. But, refuges established in the Dakotas now provide geese food and water, and delay their peak push into DeSoto until late-October and early-November. Bald eagles follow the waterfowl migration and peak in numbers at DeSoto in late-November and December and again in early-March. As many as 145 bald eagles have been observed at DeSoto at one time.

While the DeSoto refuge lacks wooded bluffs, it provides birds and birders with a mix of habitats – Missouri River frontage, a large oxbow lake, riparian deciduous woodland, shrub patches, replanted prairie, ponds and small wetlands and cropland. The refuge checklist cites 240 species, of which 81 breed there. An additional 11 species are reported on the refuge as accidental. Waterbirds are well represented, including 10 species of waders, 31 species of shorebirds and 18 species of ducks. The relatively deep waters in the oxbow lake attract diving ducks and mergansers. Grebes, gulls and terns are present in great variety.

In recent years, a variety of rare and accidental waterbird sightings have been reported at DeSoto, including three species of scoters, king eider, long-tailed duck, bean goose and brown pelican. Because of its diverse habitats, the refuge attracts many raptors during migration and winter months, including short-eared and long-eared owls. In 2002 and 2003, bald eagles nested and successfully fledged two young. The diverse terrestrial habitats at DeSoto also attract bird species of shrub and woodland-grassland edge, such as tree and Harris's sparrows, red-headed woodpeckers and migrating woodland birds. More than 20 warbler species have been reported.

There are 12 miles of paved and gravel roads at DeSoto and four trails, each less than a mile, passing through different habitats. One trail is wheelchair accessible. The visitor center offers an excellent view of the oxbow lake, wildlife interpretive displays and an exhibit of artifacts recovered from the steamboat *Bertrand*, which sank in the Missouri in 1865 and was unearthed from the refuge in 1969. A fee is charged to access the refuge, which is open year-round during daylight hours. The visitor's center is open between 9 a.m. and 4:30 p.m., except some holidays.

• Additional information: From Blair drive east 7 miles on U.S. Highway 30, crossing the Missouri River into Iowa to refuge entrance. DeSoto National Wildlife Refuge, 1434 316th Lane, Missouri Valley, IA 51555, (712) 642-4121, e-mail DeSoto@fws.gov, information http://midwest.fws.gov/desoto/

• Nearby Birding Destinations: **Boyer Chute National Wildlife Refuge,** located east of Fort Calhoun, is a satellite refuge of DeSoto NWR. Opened in 1996, Boyer Chute is a conservation partnership to re-establish Missouri River flows through a two-mile abandoned chute. The 3,200-acre area has five miles of trails, two short trails through woodlands and a longer trail passing through grasslands and wetlands. Sedge wrens and Nelson's sharp-tailed sparrows have been

---

DeSoto Bird Sampler

Snow Goose	Red-headed Woodpecker
Ross's Goose	Red-bellied Woodpecker
Canada Goose	Yellow-bellied Sapsucker
Wood Duck	Acadian Flycatcher
Mallard	Willow Flycatcher
American Black Duck	Great Crested Flycatcher
Ring-necked Duck	Warbling Vireo
Lesser Scaup	Red-eyed Vireo
Common Merganser	White-breasted Nuthatch
Common Loon	Brown Creeper
Pied-billed Grebe	Sedge Wren
American White Pelican	Golden-crowned Kinglet
Double-crested Cormorant	Eastern Bluebird
Great Blue Heron	Wood Thrush
Osprey	Gray Catbird
Bald Eagle	Yellow Warbler
Sharp-shinned Hawk	American Redstart
American Coot	Ovenbird
Killdeer	Common Yellowthroat
Greater Yellowlegs	Dickcissel
Spotted Sandpiper	Eastern Towhee
Hudsonian Godwit	Clay-colored Sparrow
American Woodcock	Vesper Sparrow
Ring-billed Gull	Henslow's Sparrow
Black Tern	Harris's Sparrow
Yellow-billed Cuckoo	Yellow-headed Blackbird
Eastern Screech-Owl	Orchard Oriole

sighted at Boyer Chute in recent years, suggesting prairie restoration work there is successful. To reach Boyer Chute from Fort Calhoun, turn east on Madison Street from U.S. Highway 75 and proceed to a T-intersection. Turn right on County Road 34 and proceed approximately 3 miles to refuge's main gate. Information is available through DeSoto NWR or Boyer Chute NWR, P.O. Box 69, Fort Calhoun, NE 68023, (402) 468-4313, e-mail boyerchute@fws.gov, information, http://boyerchute.fws.gov

Ponca State Park

Ponca State Park in Dixon County began in 1934 as 200 acres donated to the state. One hundred and sixty of those acres were purchased with funds raised by "popular subscription," an effort coordinated by Ponca American Legion Post 117. The new park was dedicated on July 31, 1934. Today, Ponca State Park encompasses 1,921 acres of rugged Missouri River bluffs cloaked in hardwood forest and floodplain bottomland. The deciduous forest at Ponca is less complex than those in southeastern Nebraska. Bur oak, basswood, green ash, walnut, hackberry and cottonwood are the dominant tree species since the disappearance of American elms. Although Ponca offers fewer showy spring wildflowers than do sites in southeastern Nebraska, its array includes columbine, blue phlox, Dutchman's breeches, Jack-in-the-pulpit, American ginseng and meadow anemone. Wildflowers with more northerly ranges – Canada white violet, bloodroot and Virginia waterleaf – appear there. Millions of years of geologic history is

Ponca Bird Sampler

Bald Eagle	Cliff Swallow
Cooper's Hawk	Red-breasted Nuthatch
Broad-winged Hawk	Carolina Wren
Wild Turkey	Winter Wren
Piping Plover	Blue-gray Gnatcatcher
Spotted Sandpiper	Swainson's Thrush
Least Tern	Wood Thrush
Black-billed Cuckoo	Gray Catbird
Barred Owl	Cedar Waxwing
Whip-poor-will	Golden-winged Warbler
Ruby-throated	Magnolia Warbler
Hummingbird	American Redstart
Red-bellied Woodpecker	Ovenbird
Great Crested Flycatcher	Scarlet Tanager
Northern Shrike	Eastern Towhee
Eastern Wood-Pewee	Spotted Towhee
Eastern Phoebe	Lark Sparrow
Bell's Vireo	Rose-breasted Grosbeak
Yellow-throated Vireo	Orchard Oriole
Warbling Vireo	Baltimore Oriole
Red-eyed Vireo	Purple Finch
Black-billed Magpie	Pine Siskin

exposed in the bluffs where the Missouri River has carved through beds of loess, limestone, shale and sandstone.

Until recently, Ponca was exclusively a woodland park, but the acquisition of Missouri River floodplain to the north since 2000 has greatly expanded birding opportunities. Many of the same river-associated species found at DeSoto NWR and many woodland species found at Fontenelle Forest are also at Ponca. The park borders a portion of the Missouri River that has not been channelized and resembles the Missouri River of old. Ponca Park is at the southeastern end of the Missouri National Recreational River, a 59-mile long reach protected under the Wild and Scenic River Act of 1978. As in times before the Missouri River was channelized, waterfowl rest and shorebirds and wading birds feed on sandbars. Least terns and piping plovers are again nesting on river sandbars.

Floodplain wetlands attract a variety of wetland species both during migration and the nesting season. Dog-hair stands of cottonwoods and patches of scrubby, weedy sandbars are used by a variety of passerine birds. Look for tree swallows using bluebird nesting boxes, colonies of bank swallows on river banks and a nesting colony of cliff swallows on the limestone cliff at the boat ramp. Periodic high river flows in the future will hopefully again make the floodplain a dynamic and constantly changing environment. Native prairie, including both grasses and forbs, have been seeded on a portion of the floodplain and in the future will expand both the park's species list and birding opportunities. Nearly 300 species are reported at Ponca and the surrounding area, more than 70 of which breed there.

Ponca State Park offers visitors full facilities, including cabins, RV camping pads, showers, a swimming pool, over 70 primitive campsites, group camping areas,

shelter houses and picnic areas. Primitive camping is allowed year-round, other facilities are open from mid-April to mid-November. There are six hiking trails totaling 22 miles. Foot traffic is allowed on the floodplain portion of the park and beginning in 2004 hayrack birding rides will be available. There are several wheelchair-accessible observation decks. Wildlife viewing blinds are scheduled to be added. One of the best places to observe a sample of the park's passerine species is at the feeders at the resource center.

A staff naturalist at Ponca develops enrichment programs, including nature study hikes offered throughout the open season. Bird programs include owl prowls, and eagle and bluebird nest monitoring. Loaner binoculars and field guides are available. A nine-hole golf course is adjacent to the park. The recently completed Missouri National Recreational River Resource and Education Center has interpretive displays and exhibits, a field laboratory and conference rooms.

• Additional Information: Located 2 miles north of Ponca. Follow signs from Nebraska Highway 12 through Ponca to Spur 26E. Ponca State Park, 88090 Spur 26E, Ponca, NE 68770-7096, (402) 755-2284, poncasp@ngpc.state.ne.

ROD NABHOLZ

Barred owls *are year-round residents in extensive tracts of mature deciduous forest and are most common along the Missouri River.*

Niobrara State Park

Closing the Gavins Point Dam gates in 1956 had profound effects on the Missouri River both upstream and downstream. One was the accumulation of sediment at the mouth of the Niobrara River and subsequent rising groundwater at the upper end of Lewis and Clark Lake. The rising water table eventually flooded basements and led to relocating the town of Niobrara in the mid-1970s. In 1987, Niobrara State Park moved from the bottomland at the mouth of the Niobrara River to hills to the west. If there was a benefit to the rising water, it was the creation of marshland habitat on the upper end of Lewis and Clark Lake. A checklist of Cedar and Knox counties compiled by Steve Van Sickle, including birds of the Niobrara State Park area, lists 259 species. As would be expected, many waterbirds are included.

Within its 1,260 acres, Niobrara Park includes many habitats and consequently has a diverse avifauna. Bluff-top grasslands, riparian forest, wet meadows and wetlands attract a variety of bird species. The old park site located on an island near the mouth of the Niobrara River has been allowed to revert to riverine wetlands. Seven miles of roads and more than 14 miles of hiking trails provide ready access to the park. In addition to 19 cabins, the park has a modern RV campground, 10 camping areas, picnic grounds, trail rides and a swimming pool. Cabins, camping sites and other modern park facilities are located on the bluff top with a commanding view of the Missouri River. A lodge is available for conferences and a nine-hole golf course is nearby. Excursions on the unchannelized Missouri River are available through the park office.

• Additional Information: Located 2 miles west of Niobrara on U.S. Hwy 12. Niobrara State Park, 89261 522 Ave., Niobrara, NE 68760-0226, (402) 857-3373, nsp@ngpc.state.ne.us
• Nearby Birding Destinations: Niobrara State Park is an excellent headquarters from which birders can range to other birding destinations. **Bazile Creek Wildlife Management Area** begins at the mouth of the Niobrara River and extends nine miles downstream on the southern side of the Missouri River and Lewis and Clark Lake. To access the river, turn north from Nebraska Highway 12 at the school in Niobrara, drive north to the river, then east on a road paralleling the river. Another access point is the boat ramp about three miles east of Niobrara. A sign on Nebraska Highway 12 marks the turnoff. This site also provides access to woodlands. This 4,900-acre area includes riparian woodlands, open grassland and extensive cattail marsh. Bazile Creek's marshland on the head of Lewis and Clark Lake is so extensive locals call it "Nebraska's Everglades." Summer gatherings of postbreeding great egrets and autumn flocks of great-tailed grackles suggest such a comparison may not stray far. Experienced canoeists might wish to explore the marshy backwaters.

In recent years, **Lewis and Clark Lake** and the tailwaters below Gavins Point Dam have produced sightings of pelagic species either rare or uncommon in Nebraska. Most sightings have occurred from October through December, occasionally into January. Species documented include: Iceland, glaucous, laughing, lesser black-backed, Sabine's, mew, Thayer's and Bonaparte's gulls; black-legged kittiwake; red-necked grebe; Pomarine jaeger; surf scoter; red-breasted merganser; and long-tailed duck. In late-June and early-July 2002, a brown pelican, only the fifth documented record for the state, was photographed below Gavins Point Dam. The dam is also one of the state's best bald eagle viewing areas. Eagles begin arriving with the November migration of waterfowl and some usually remain in the area through the winter into spring migration in March. Lewis and Clark Lake and the wooded bluff land provide year-round, bird-viewing opportunities. Modern cabins, RV facilities, tent camping and other park facilities are available at Lewis and Clark Lake State Recreation Area, located on the south side of the lake west of Gavins Point Dam.

• Additional information: Lewis and Clark SRA, 54731 897 Rd., Crofton, NE 68730-3290, (402) 388-4169, lcsra@ngpc.state.ne.us ∎

Niobrara Bird Sampler

Snow Goose	Belted Kingfisher
Canada Goose	Red-headed Woodpecker
Wood Duck	Northern Flicker
Redhead	Eastern Wood-Pewee
Common Goldeneye	Eastern Phoebe
Common Merganser	Bell's Vireo
Common Loon	Warbling Vireo
American White Pelican	Cliff Swallow
Double-crested Cormorant	White-breasted Nuthatch
American Bittern	Marsh Wren
Great Blue Heron	Ruby-crowned Kinglet
Great Egret	Gray-cheeked Thrush
Snowy Egret	Gray Catbird
Green Heron	Cedar Waxwing
Osprey	Tennessee Warbler
Bald Eagle	Orange-crowned Warbler
Swainson's Hawk	Yellow Warbler
Golden Eagle	Yellow-rumped Warbler
Gray Partridge	Blackpoll Warbler
Virginia Rail	Black-and-white Warbler
Sora	American Redstart
Semipalmated Plover	Common Yellowthroat
Piping Plover	Wilson's Warbler
Greater Yellowlegs	Eastern Towhee
Spotted Sandpiper	Dickcissel
Semipalmated Sandpiper	American Tree Sparrow
Least Sandpiper	Chipping Sparrow
Baird's Sandpiper	Clay-colored Sparrow
Stilt Sandpiper	Savannah Sparrow
Long-billed Dowitcher	Lincoln's Sparrow
Wilson's Phalarope	Harris's Sparrow
Ring-billed Gull	Yellow-headed Blackbird
Least Tern	Great-tailed Grackle
Long-eared Owl	House Finch
Whip-poor-will	Pine Siskin

Tallgrass Prairie

IN THE 30 YEARS following the Civil War, immigrants spilled across Nebraska's tallgrass prairie, buying government land for $1.25 an acre or claiming a quarter section at a time under the Homestead Act of 1862 for nothing more than a promise to live on it and make it productive.

As settlers left the wooded Missouri River Valley behind, they advanced into a treeless country of unimaginable dimensions. Some had seen tallgrass prairie in Ohio, Illinois and Iowa, but never had they encountered such an endless sweep of shoulder-high bluestem and compass plant. Some might have been intimidated, but not for long. By 1900, 85 to 90 percent of the tallgrass prairie in eastern Nebraska had been turned with the plow and was growing crops. Where the terrain was too steep to farm, the settlers fenced the grassland for livestock.

"In 1854 there was not over one square mile of land under cultivation in the territory of Nebraska, but the unsurpassed fertility of the soil and the salubriousness of the climate had begun to attract attention," Joseph Allen Warren wrote in the *Annual Report of the Nebraska State Board of Agriculture for the Year 1909*. "Within the memory of comparatively young men still living in Nebraska, the state has been transformed from a great hunting ground to one of the most prosperous, most productive and best improved agricultural states in the union." Therein is the history of Nebraska's tallgrass prairie and its native bird life.

A year later, *Omaha World-Herald* writer Sandy Griswold described the state's progress from a different perspective: "Every summer I am more and more curious to know how the meadow lark survives, how it succeeds in rearing a brood when year by year the meadows in which it builds are cut closer and closer with clanging mowing machines. Where do the quail find shelter on our highly cultivated and smoothly shorn farms? Then the hungry skunks, minks, weasels and coyotes have their fill of birds where there is no thick cover for them to hide in, and the farm house cats, prowling from field to field and from orchard to orchard, devour every fledgling that they can find. By night these predatory nomads hunt with the other varmints. The farmers' pigs, nosing everywhere, eat up the eggs of all the birds that nest

JON FARRAR

Broad-winged hawks are small woodland hawks, uncommon migrants in eastern Nebraska and rare breeders in the southeastern part of the state.

on the ground. Enlightened farming, the making of productive and neatly shorn estates, the march of the plow, the ditching machine, the underground tile, the patent reaper and mower and thresher, the cats and skunks and minks, winter without shelter, summer without food, and the whole of the time without natural requisites to wild life, is what is driving the birds away. Men's guns and women's hats are hard on birds, but civilized doings are harder still."

The best record of lost or diminished avifauna is of larger birds, most often game birds, but their history is also the history of other grassland bird species. Substitute burrowing owl or Sprague's pipit for the prairie-chicken and the story would be the same.

Before settlement, the greater prairie-chicken's range closely paralleled the distribution of tallgrass prairie. Early in the settlement period, when small crop fields were interspersed in large expanses of grassland, prairie-chickens prospered. They benefited both from an expanded source of winter food and from the disturbance of the previously uniform prairie that introduced diversity. As primitive farming spread westward, prairie-chickens moved with it. During the late-1880s and early-1900s, they extended their range, invading the traditional range of the sharp-tailed grouse.

During those decades, prairie-chickens were incredibly abundant. Market hunters shot and trapped large numbers of prairie-chickens to satisfy the appetites of East Coast markets. In 1877, University of Nebraska entomologist and ornithologist Samuel Aughey attempted to ascertain the number of prairie-chickens sold locally and shipped out-of-state by making inquiries of meat merchants in eastern Nebraska's larger towns. One of 10 Lincoln firms "engaged in the meat business" estimated selling about 19,000 prairie-chickens during a six-week period in the winter of 1875, about half of which "were caught in Lancaster County." Factoring in crude estimates from other counties, Aughey figured the number of prairie-chickens shot or trapped for the market or home use from 30 eastern Nebraska counties in 1874 was about 300,000 birds.

In 1902, Griswold recalled that when he came to Omaha in the mid-1880s, land "west of the court house

Of the estimated 10 million acres of tallgrass prairie once in eastern Nebraska, less than one percent remains and it has been diminished by decades of overgrazing and annual haying. **Spring Creek Prairie** *southwest of Lincoln is one of the largest remaining tracts.*

was little better than unbroken thicket" with all the prairie-chicken shooting a sportsman could want. By 1926, a sighting of eight prairie-chickens near Hastings warranted special mention in a Nebraska Ornithologists' Union publication. As with the ruffed grouse and wild turkey along the Missouri River, the greater prairie-chicken was the most conspicuous bird to decline in abundance in the tallgrass prairie. Like an obituary editor, Griswold chronicled the demise of other grassland game birds as agriculture spread and became more intensive.

The American golden-plover still paused in Nebraska's grasslands in vast numbers during spring migration in the late-1800s. They were less abundant during fall migration. In 1907, Griswold wrote, "But the golden plover is but a dram of the past, notwithstanding the unusual numbers seen this fall, and in a few more years will be extinct." Like the prairie-chicken, plovers found some agricultural benefits, and were not adverse to probing or scratching for insects in fields and agricultural wasteland. "I do not believe that a pair of them today, down in old New York, at Rector's, Sherry's or Shanley's would allow you

much change out of a $5 William," Griswold continued. Hunters killed untold thousands of golden-plovers, but like so many other grassland species, including the Eskimo curlew and upland sandpiper, destruction of essential habitat and other factors played crucial roles in their decline, and in time would have led to the same conclusion without a shot being fired. Often writers alleged that these tallgrass prairie birds were "pushed west," but the reality is these species vanished from where they once were, and their range and abundance was much diminished.

In the years following their legal protection, prairie grouse and shorebirds did not return in the numbers that had once occurred. Across most of eastern Nebraska the tallgrass prairies were gone, and what remained bore no resemblance to native prairie. Once there had been 400,000 square miles of tallgrass prairie in North America, extending from western Indiana to the eastern portions of Kansas, Nebraska and the Dakotas, and south to Oklahoma and Texas. Less than 10 percent remains nationwide today. Of the estimated 10 million acres of tallgrass prairie once found in eastern Nebraska, less than one percent remains, and it

*The **scissor-tailed flycatcher** is a rare breeder in southeastern counties, most common in open grasslands with scattered trees.*

JON FARRAR

woody plants. Gallery forests lined the shorelines of the lower reaches of the Platte, Elkhorn, Blue, Nemaha and Republican rivers, and persisted on islands and deep ravines where they were often protected from prairie fires. And in the grasslands, small woody plants – chokecherry, plum, sumac, buffaloberry, snowberry and poison ivy – gathered. These woody plants, although often short, added a habitat element allowing numerous species of birds to prosper. Similarly, wetlands were the reason dozens of species of birds were found in grasslands. The number of species found today in eastern Nebraska is significantly more than when the land was blanketed with tallgrass prairie because woodlands have expanded westward along streams, and because of man-planted woodlands in cities, farmsteads and shelterbelts.

In recent years, the federally funded Conservation Reserve Program (CRP) has paid landowners to plant native grasses where row crops once grew. To the eye, when the big bluestem, switchgrass and Indiangrass are tall and ripe at the end of summer, these fields suggest tallgrass prairie mostly in that they are treeless and not cropland. When interseeded with legumes and other forbs, they replicate tallgrass prairie, providing some of the habitat that grassland birds require. Several studies have revealed the obvious: There are more summer birds in CRP grasslands than in land planted in row crops. Desirable native grassland birds, such as upland sandpipers, chestnut-collared longspurs, dickcissels, and the grasshopper, field and Savannah sparrows occupy CRP grasslands. Some prairie birds are more abundant than they have been in decades. Prairie-chickens, in a modest way, have reclaimed old territory in southeastern Nebraska, northern harriers glide low in search of unwary voles, and meadowlarks claim springtime territories from the tops of hedge posts. The millions of CRP grassland acres have certainly been a boon to some bird species, but if the history of federal land-retirement programs is also the future, most will be lost when grain prices rise, payments end and grass is again plowed under.

On a small scale, native plant seeds have been gathered and sown on reclaimed prairies, giving them a likeness to native prairie. But native prairies are not easily created. Nearly 300 species of plants have been reported on a tract of native prairie west of Lincoln. In states east of Nebraska, 700 plant species were known to exist in tallgrass prairie. It is often said that once a species is gone it cannot be brought back, and to a degree the same is true of tallgrass prairie. Prairie ecologist John Weaver said it best: "Prairie is much more than land covered with grass. It is slowly evolved, highly complex, centuries old. It approaches the eternal. Once destroyed it can never be replaced by man."

Audubon Spring Creek Prairie

The largest example of public-access tallgrass prairie remaining in Nebraska is Spring Creek Prairie in southwestern Lancaster County. Purchased by the

is much diminished from its former state. What remains is fragmented, a few acres here and there, and no areas large enough to support the full complement of grassland bird life. Twenty- and 40-acre patches of tallgrass prairie are not the same as 1,000 acres of contiguous prairie. And, on the scale by which grasslands were once measured, even 1,000 acres is no more than a remnant.

During the past 25 years, U.S. Geological Survey Breeding Bird Survey data indicate that 20 of 29 grassland bird species adequately surveyed had declining populations. Systematic grassland bird surveys began in the mid-1960s, and while declines before that time are not documented, they were undoubtedly substantial. No other formerly large habitat type in North America has more bird species in decline than does the grassland. While the introduction of woodlands onto grassland areas has increased the number of bird species, the gain has mostly been in generalist species, such as the common grackle, American robin, and brown thrasher, which have plentiful habitat elsewhere and are not in decline. As a state, we have gained in variety but lost much of our native avifauna. Many bird species of concern today are grassland species – the long-billed curlew, upland sandpiper, mountain plover, burrowing owl, greater prairie-chicken, eastern meadowlark, chestnut-collared longspur, lark bunting and the Henslow's, grasshopper and Brewer's sparrows.

Wherever they are found in the world, grasslands do not support the number of bird species found in wooded or wetland habitats. University of Nebraska-Lincoln ornithologist Paul Johnsgard calculated that only about 15 percent of the state's breeding avifauna, about 30 species, are strictly associated with grasslands. He attributed that to grasslands evolving rather late compared to North American forests and that they "have far less three-dimensional structural complexity," hence grasslands provide fewer food sources, and roosting and nesting sites.

The tallgrass prairie, though, was not without

Nebraska branch of the National Audubon Society in 1998, the 610 acres had been owned by the O'Brien family since 1903 and operated as a livestock ranch. The Wachiska Audubon Society purchased sixteen adjoining acres in 2000. Nearly 80 percent of the ranch had been untouched by the plow because of the rock-strewn, steep hills – an ancient glacial moraine. Five birds species on Audubon's watch-list of declining species are found at Spring Creek Prairie – dickcissel, field sparrow, greater prairie-chicken, Bell's vireo and red-headed woodpecker. The area has the full complement of tallgrass prairie habitats – grassland, wetlands, springs, creeks, and gatherings of deciduous woodlands composed of hackberry, American elm, cottonwood and bur oak. Rotational grazing and periodic controlled burns are used to maintain the grassland and discourage the invasion of woody plants. The prairie is used as an outdoor classroom for school groups and there are interpretive, self-guided trails and an educational-interpretive center.

• Additional Information: Spring Creek Prairie is located three miles south of Denton in Lancaster County, immediately south of SW 100th Street and Saltillo Road. The entrance is on the east side of the country road; take the driveway to the ranch house. The prairie is open from 9 a.m. to 5 p.m. weekdays, except for major holidays and some weekends. Call (402) 797-2301 for more information. Admission is free for Audubon members, donations accepted from others. Audubon Spring Creek Prairie, P.O. Box 117, 11700 SW 100th Street, Denton, NE 68339, (402) 797-2301, Nebraska@audubon.org

Pawnee Prairie WMA

With 1,140 acres, Pawnee Prairie is one of the largest wildlife management areas in southeastern Nebraska. Much of its upland is maintained by rotational mowing and periodic controlled burns. There are small tracts of native prairie. Johnson Creek and its intermittent

BUB BLAKE

Bobolinks have declined in abundance as their preferred nesting habitats – native grass and wetland meadows – have vanished.

tributaries on the northern end of the area are densely wooded, providing habitat for woodland and edge bird species. There are small ponds throughout the area, adding a wetland element to the flora and fauna.

Located only two miles from the Kansas border, Pawnee Prairie is a likely location to find northern mockingbirds, scissor-tailed flycatchers, Carolina wrens and other species with southerly distributions. This WMA is an out-of-the-way destination that, while often neglected by birders, offers an excellent opportunity to see a variety of species. Before the appearance of CRP grasslands in the past 20 years, Pawnee Prairie was one of a few sites in southeastern Nebraska with greater prairie-chickens. In recent years, a booming ground on the western end of the area has had about eight or 10 cocks. Flocks of 40 to 50 prairie-chickens can be seen in spring. Display grounds can easily be located in the early morning and late evening by listening for the resonant booming of the cocks. Display begins as early as mid-March, peaks in mid-April and continues into May or later, but with less vigor. There are no permanent viewing blinds but portable blinds are allowed.

The WMA has service roads, but no trails. Massasauga rattlesnakes are present, but the chance of finding one of these rare snakes is remote. Often called swamp rattlers, they are listed as threatened by both the Nebraska Game and Parks Commission and the

Spring Creek Bird Sampler

Great Blue Heron	Common Yellowthroat
Northern Harrier	Eastern Towhee
Greater Prairie-Chicken	Chipping Sparrow
Northern Bobwhite	Field Sparrow
Wild Turkey	Vesper Sparrow
Upland Sandpiper	Savannah Sparrow
Yellow-billed Cuckoo	Grasshopper Sparrow
Red-headed Woodpecker	Henslow's Sparrow
Eastern Kingbird	Le Conte's Sparrow
Bell's Vireo	Swamp Sparrow
Tree Swallow	Harris's Sparrow
Sedge Wren	Rose-breasted Grosbeak
Eastern Bluebird	Dickcissel
Gray Catbird	Bobolink
Northern Mockingbird	Eastern Meadowlark
Brown Thrasher	Western Meadowlark
Sprague's Pipit	Orchard Oriole
Yellow Warbler	Baltimore Oriole

Feather Types

Everyone knows birds are covered with feathers, but not everyone knows not all feathers are the same. Certainly they are of different colors and shapes from one species to another and from different parts of the body of the same bird, but there are five distinct types of feathers found on birds. Contour feathers cover the bird, give them their shape and are the wing feathers that makes flight possible.

A contour feather has a central shaft or quill with a flat vane on either side. In microscopic view the vane is an interlocking network of parallel barbs and barbules, creating a flat surface that is both strong and light. When a bird preens an individual feather by drawing it between its mandibles it is realigning and interlocking the microscopic structures forming the vane. The upper half of a semiplume looks much like a contour feather, but the lower half is fluffy. Semiplumes are usually found under a covering of contour feathers on the sides of the abdomen, but elsewhere as well. They provide bulk to a bird's feather covering and insulation.

Down feathers are fluffy plumes with either poorly developed or absent shafts and barbules lacking hooks. Down is most developed on waterbirds, and is present to a lesser degree on birds such as owls and grouse. Some birds, such as woodpeckers and kingfishers, have few if any down feathers. The function of down feathers is to conserve body heat. Powder down looks like a bedraggled filoplume disintegrating into a talc-like powder. Powder down feathers grow continuously and are never molted. Typically they are found on the breast. The purpose of powder down feathers is not fully understood but birds lacking oil glands, such as wading birds, have more than other birds. Some experts suggest the talc-like material is a substitute for oiling and grooming feathers. Filoplumes are sparsely scattered, hair-like feathers. Their use is not known. They may serve as sensory structures. The bristles found around the mouths of flycatchers, nighthawks and swallows may be modified filoplumes.

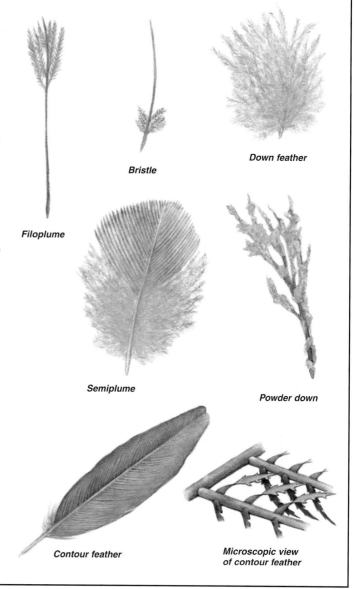

Bristle

Down feather

Filoplume

Semiplume

Powder down

Contour feather

Microscopic view of contour feather

U.S. Fish and Wildlife Service.

• Additional Information: Pawnee Prairie is located seven miles south of Burchard on Nebraska Highway 99, then east 1 mile. There is also access via a county road on the south and east sides of the area.

Burchard Lake WMA

The Southeast Nebraska Sportsman's Club raised seed money to purchase land that became Burchard Lake Wildlife Management Area in 1958. Its 160-acre impoundment lake was completed two years later. The WMA's remaining 400 acres are high-quality tallgrass prairie. The water quality in the lake is excellent, a feature not overlooked by anglers and fish-eating birds. Woodlands are limited but attract migrant passerines and some nesting species. Because Pawnee County has few large bodies of water, Burchard Lake is a magnet for waterbirds. In addition to waterfowl, wading birds and shorebirds, common loons, Neotropic cormorants and little blue herons have been

reported there in recent years. Burchard is one of the best tallgrass prairie sites for upland sandpipers, Henslow's sparrows and sedge wrens.

A high hill between the two arms of the reservoir has long been a prairie-chicken booming ground. Two observation blinds are available on a first-come, first-served basis. Each blind holds about eight adults, and can be accessed with a short walk from the perimeter road. If the blinds are occupied, late-arriving observers should watch the spring courtship display from a distance to avoid frightening grouse on the grounds. The most intense display by the cocks is in early morning although there is also displaying at the end of the day. Courtship display begins in March and continues well into May. Hens visit the ground in mid-April to mate, and the cocks display most vigorously at that time. In recent years, 10 to 12 cocks have been using the ground at one time. Nearby CRP grasslands now also have display ground sites.

Primitive camping is allowed. An interior road provides access to the area, but there are no hiking trails. Burchard Lake is managed as a refuge and the road is closed during the waterfowl hunting season.

• Additional Information: Burchard Lake is three miles east and 1½ miles north of Burchard via county roads in Pawnee County.

Twin Oaks WMA

One hundred and fifty years ago, when southeastern Nebraska was still a tallgrass prairie, eastern deciduous forest pioneered westward from the Missouri River Valley, following drainages and colonizing tracts of rugged terrain that escaped prairie fires. Portions of Twin Oaks Wildlife Management Area in Johnson County were probably such a linear woodland in a sea of grass. Bur oak was a pioneer tree species because its thick, corky bark protected it from prairie fires. Because prairie fires no longer discourage woody plants from establishing in grasslands, other woody species – honey locust, Osage orange, Siberian elm and eastern red cedar – have advanced. Since 1995, the Nebraska Game and Parks Commission has filled the role once performed by wildfire at Twin Oaks, removing undesirable trees and shrubs, restoring the matrix of grassland with islands of woodland.

Today, two tracts totaling 1,120 acres compose Twin Oaks WMA along the North Fork of the Big Nemaha River. The mature bur oak and shagbark hickory forest and shrubby underbrush, hedgerows, grasslands, weedy areas and food plots are migration traps for passerine birds and support year-round resident species. The WMA's grasslands on the area are both native tallgrass prairie and warm-season grasses planted on former cropland.

• Additional Information: Twin Oaks is two miles east and three miles south of Tecumseh in Johnson County.

Nearby Birding Destinations: To reach **Osage WMA** headquarters from Tecumseh, travel north three miles on Nebraska Highway 50, then two miles west on Nebraska Highway 41, and ¾ mile north on a Johnson County road. Two satellite tracts are located south

Sedge wrens are uncommon migrants and rare but regular breeders in eastern counties, principally in wet meadows.

of Nebraska Highway 41. These areas are a mix of deciduous woodlands along drainages, shelterbelts and hedgerows, grasslands and cropland and offer excellent birding opportunities for edge species. **Hickory Ridge WMA,** ½ mile west and 3½ miles south of Vesta, is similar to Twin Oak WMA although smaller at 444 acres. It has 60 acres of timber. The principal birds expected are woodland, woodland-edge and grassland species.

Eastern Saline Wetlands

Salt Creek and its tributaries in Lancaster and Saunders counties rise from buried shales laid down in a vast inland sea 70 to 160 million years ago. These salt-laden waters ooze from springs and seeps, and are wicked to the surface during dry summers and periods of drought. Over thousands of years, salts precipitated out and accumulated in the soil, creating the only extensive saline wetlands in eastern Nebraska. During the past 100 years, that pattern has been altered by draining, channelizing and down-cutting streams. Urban sprawl north and west of Lincoln destroyed many saline wetlands. Today, eastern Nebraska saline wetlands, and the fauna and flora associated with them, are perhaps the rarest ecosystem in the state.

These clay soils with poor aeration and high concentrations of salt are a hostile environment for plants. But, some species adapted over thousands of years of evolution. These plants have names seldom heard in midcontinent: saltwort, sea blite, saltbush, spearscale, seaside heliotrope and saltmarsh aster. The Salt Creek tiger beetle, found in only a handful of sites north of Lincoln, is one of the most endangered insects in North America, their total number estimated to be less than 1,000. Much diminished, too, is the bird life that once frequented these saline wetlands. In the

---

Southeast WMA Bird Sampler

Sharp-shinned Hawk	Gray Catbird
Red-tailed Hawk	Northern Mockingbird
Greater Prairie-Chicken	Orange-crowned Warbler
Upland Sandpiper	Chestnut-sided Warbler
Yellow-billed Cuckoo	Prairie Warbler
Eastern Screech Owl	Eastern Towhee
Long-eared Owl	American Tree Sparrow
Red-bellied Woodpecker	Field Sparrow
Downy Woodpecker	Lark Sparrow
Loggerhead Shrike	Grasshopper Sparrow
Bell's Vireo	Henslow's Sparrow
Tufted Titmouse	Harris's Sparrow
White-breasted Nuthatch	Dickcissel
Carolina Wren	Orchard Oriole
Eastern Bluebird	Baltimore Oriole
Swainson's Thrush	American Goldfinch

early-1900s, the salt lake on the western edge of Lincoln now known as Capitol Beach was a great migration stopover for waterbirds. At the first annual meeting of the Nebraska Ornithologists' Union in 1899, University of Nebraska zoologist J.S. Hunter read a paper, "The Bird Fauna of the Salt Basin, Near Lincoln," in which he listed 89 species of waterbirds observed there. His list included species such as the Caspian tern, American black duck, three species of scoters, tundra swan, whooping crane, American avocet, black-bellied plover, piping plover and ruddy turnstone. Snow geese were listed as common, as they were yet in the 1950s on the Ceresco Flats along Rock Creek to the north during migration.

Jack Sinn WMA

Today, few examples of Nebraska's eastern saline wetland complex remain. The largest is found at Jack Sinn Memorial Wildlife Management Area straddling the Lancaster-Saunders county line south of Ceresco. In the years after Salt Creek was channelized to prevent flooding in Lincoln, the bed of Rock Creek, a tributary that flows through the Sinn area, downcut to adjust its level to Salt Creek. This eliminated the cycle of flooding and evaporation, and the oozing of salt-laden groundwater to the surface, that created and maintained the saline soils and wetlands. In recent years, low-level dikes to impound runoff and construction of weirs on Rock Creek to halt the downcutting are attempts to restore the natural hydrology. While the salt flats south of Ceresco are not the same as they once were, birders will find water and grassland species on Sinn's 832 acres.

With shallow-water marshes returning, snow geese again pause during their March migration, and a diverse assortment of shore and marsh birds follow. Many species linger to nest: Canada geese, mallards, blue-winged teal, sora and Virginia rails, great-tailed grackles, Wilson's snipe, grasshopper sparrows, willow flycatchers, Wilson's phalaropes, American

bitterns, sedge wrens, and bobolinks. During the fall, look for migrating American pipits and Le Conte's, savannah and sharp-tailed sparrows. Northern harriers are common, and in winter, short-eared owls can be found in the grassland. From late-March into May is the best time to see the waterbird migration, and from May into July is the best time to find breeding species. The number of waterbirds depends on the amount of surface water. There are no maintained trails, but county roads offer access to the area's entire length. Bring knee-high boots to fully enjoy this wet area.

• Additional Information: Jack Sinn Memorial WMA is on both sides of U.S. Highway 77 one mile south of Ceresco, extending one mile west and three miles east of the highway.

• Nearby Birding Destinations: **Arbor Lake,** a saline wetland immediately north of Lincoln, was acquired by the city as mitigation for the destruction of a smaller saline wetland filled during the construction of a bypass. Arbor Lake is managed by the Nebraska Game and Parks Commission. A water-control structure re-creates the historical hydrology and salinity levels. The area is open to the public and visitors may use an elevated boardwalk and observation platform. Birding at Arbor Lake ranges between good and mediocre, depending on the alignment of migration and water levels. Most eastern saline wetland species can be expected there when conditions are ideal. Interesting species seen in recent years include Bonaparte's and Franklin's gulls, long-billed dowitchers, American pipits, pectoral sandpipers, ospreys, great-tailed grackles and four sparrow species – Le Conte's, Nelson's sharp-tailed, grasshopper and Lincoln's. A rare insect species, the Salt Creek tiger beetle, and a rare saline plant, saltwort, are found there. The area includes about 50 acres of wetland and 13 acres of grassland.

• Additional Information: Arbor Lake is on the east side of North 27th Street between Arbor Road and Bluff Road.

Branched Oak SRA

Since they were built in the 1960s by the U.S. Army Corps of Engineers, the flood-control reservoirs in the Salt Valley near Lincoln have had a significant effect on bird life and birdwatching. These ten impoundments total 15,039 acres, with 4,438 acres of water. In addition to providing flood control in the Salt Valley, especially to Lincoln, and water-based recreation, the relatively large bodies of water encircled with grasslands and woodlands are magnets for birds and birders. With the exception of Holmes Lake in Lincoln, all are managed by the Nebraska Game and Parks Commission as state recreation areas and wildlife management areas. All are open to the public. A state park permit is required to visit these areas except for WMAs.

The largest Salt Valley reservoir is Branched Oak Lake, completed in 1967, with a pool of 1,800 acres. Located in rolling hill country, some areas in this SRA are native prairie. The best example is the dog trial area on the northern side of the lake's northern arm.

*Common migrants and regular breeders statewide, **spotted sandpipers** are not found in flocks like other shorebirds. They prefer streamsides and the shorelines of lakes and ponds, typically where there is more shoreline vegetation than most sandpipers frequent.*

Native grasses have been planted on former farmland around the lake. In 2002 and 2003, some trees and shrubs planted on uplands as wildlife habitat and invasive species, such eastern red cedar and Russian olive, were removed to re-establish grasslands, primarily to increase the number of pheasants on the area. These habitat changes should also benefit grassland bird species that are in decline. The upper reaches of the two arms are heavily wooded, shallow backwaters. Patches of trees and shrubs fill ravines in grassland areas. The western end of the southern arm is a waterfowl refuge, but it is open to foot traffic.

Branched Oak SRA offers varied birding opportunities for migrant, breeding and resident grassland, woodland and edge species. Look for tree swallows near bluebird nesting boxes. Because the Salt Valley lakes are located in a region with few large bodies of water, these lakes attract waterbirds. In recent years, numerous rarely reported species have been reported at Branched Oak Lake. All four North American loon species have been documented, usually in October and November but occasionally in summer; Caspian terns, usually in May, late-August and September; red-necked grebes in fall; a variety of gull species, including Bonaparte's, glaucous, herring, Iceland, lesser black-backed, mew, Thayer's and California; black-legged kittiwakes, and red-breasted mergansers, greater scaup and all three species of scoters. Snow geese increasingly use all Salt Valley lakes during migration. Flocks of American white pelicans use the lake during migration and as many as 20 bald eagles

might be seen in late winter. Listen for the peenting calls of woodcocks at dawn and dusk in spring in wooded lowlands. During low-water periods, shorebirds are along the shorelines. In addition to expected eastern Nebraska shorebirds, dunlins, ruddy turnstones, buff-breasted sandpipers, red knots and whimbrels have been sighted at Branched Oak.

- Additional Information: Branched Oak SRA is

Branched Oak Bird Sampler

Canada Goose	California Gull
Hooded Merganser	Herring Gull
Common Merganser	Iceland Gull
Red-breasted Merganser	Lesser Black-backed Gull
Ruddy Duck	Glaucous Gull
Red-throated Loon	Caspian Tern
Pacific Loon	Long-eared Owl
Common Loon	Loggerhead Shrike
Yellow-billed Loon	White-breasted Nuthatch
Horned Grebe	Eastern Bluebird
Red-necked Grebe	Eastern Towhee
Clark's Grebe	Field Sparrow
American White Pelican	Grasshopper Sparrow
Whimbrel	Harris's Sparrow
Red Knot	Indigo Bunting
Buff-breasted Sandpiper	Dickcissel
Franklin's Gull	Rusty Blackbird
Bonaparte's Gull	Orchard Oriole
Mew Gull	Baltimore Oriole
Ring-billed Gull	American Goldfinch

located three miles north of Malcolm in northwestern Lancaster County. Consult the current *Nebraska Hunt Guide and Public Hunting Lands* for a list of other nearby WMAs and Salt Valley lakes.

Lower Platte River Parklands

One of the state's best warbler migration viewing areas is **Schramm Park State Recreation Area** – the Nebraska Game and Parks Commission's oldest property. Located on the northern side of the Platte River south of Gretna, Schramm had its beginning in 1879 as the Santee Hatchery, a privately owned fish-rearing station. In 1882 the Nebraska Fish Commission purchased the hatchery and surrounding 54 acres for $1,200, and it became the state's first fish hatchery. The hatchery building, built in 1914, is now the Gretna Fish Hatchery Museum. Fish have not been raised there since 1974, when the springs feeding the ponds ceased to carry enough water. In 1967, E.F. Schramm, a University of Nebraska geology professor, willed an adjoining 277 acres to the Commission and Schramm Park had its beginning. The 12,000-square-foot Ak-Sar-Ben Aquarium and

Outdoor Education Center opened in 1979 and serves as an interpretive center and classroom. Schramm's two 1½-mile trails loop through wooded bluffs above the Platte River.

- Additional Information: From Gretna, drive south 9 miles on Nebraska Highway 31 (from Interstate 80 exit 432, 6 miles south). Schramm Park SRA and Ak-Sar-Ben Aquarium, 21502 W. Hwy. 31, Gretna, NE 68028-7264, (402) 332-3901, akaq@ngpc.state.ne.us

Platte River State Park is south of the Platte River, three miles west of Louisville. Created by the purchase of three adjoining parcels of land, the park opened in 1982 and now includes 418 acres of bluff woodlands. The park has 21 year-round cabins and additional camper-cabins, which are available for use from late-April through October. There are no campsites in the park, but RV facilities and tent camping sites are available at Louisville SRA four miles downstream. Ten miles of hiking trails carry birders through the park's deciduous woodlands. A park permit is required for entry.

- Additional Information: From the junction of Nebraska highways 66 and 50 at Louisville, 2 miles west on Nebraska Highway 66. Platte River State Park,

BUB BLAKE

Before 1900, **wood ducks** *probably nested only along the Missouri River and lower reaches of other eastern rivers. Since the 1960s, the species has become abundant, expanding westward and taking advantage of nesting boxes and more woodlands along western streams.*

14421 346th St., Louisville, NE 68037-3001, (402) 234-2217, prsp@ngpc.state.ne.us

The most modern Platte River park is **Eugene T. Mahoney State Park,** which opened southeast of Ashland in 1991 on 706 acres. The park is open year-round with full recreational facilities, including a conference lodge, guest rooms and cabins, RV camping pads, tent camping, restaurant, swimming pool, volleyball court, softball diamond, golf driving range, horseback rides, ice skating rink, summer theater, botanical conservatory and more. There are two small lakes and seven miles of hiking trails through the wooded bluffs. A park permit is required for entry.

• Additional Information: Exit 426 on Interstate 80 between Omaha and Lincoln on southern side of Platte River. Eugene T. Mahoney State Park, 28500 W. Park Hwy., Ashland, NE 68003-3508, (402) 944-2523, etmsp@ngpc.state.ne.us

MICHAEL FORSBERG

*Although found statewide, particularly during fall migration, **Harris's sparrows** are most common in the east. Some overwinter in the southeast and near bird feeders.*

Schramm, Platte River and Mahoney parks are principally deciduous woodlands, similar to those on the bluffs along the Missouri River 20 to 25 miles to the east. Prairie ecologist J.E. Weaver attributed the presence of deciduous woodlands along the lower reaches of the Missouri River's tributaries in part to their deeply cut valleys that decrease winds and evaporation. The steep and dissected bluffs also provided protection from prairie fires. Nearly uninterrupted woodlands historically traced the Platte's course upstream to near Columbus. Farther west, woodlands along the river were sporadic, although there are accounts of enough timber at Grand Island in the 1850s and 1860s to cut for log houses and railroad ties. Red and bur oak, basswood, black walnut, Kentucky coffee-tree, hackberry and sycamore extend up the lower reaches of the Platte River, but the hickories and other oak species found along the Missouri River are gone. Just as Missouri River forests in southeastern Nebraska have a less diverse floral community than deciduous forests in eastern states, the complexity of woodlands along the Platte declines to the west.

The avifauna of the lower Platte River is much like that of the Missouri River, and both are proper elements of the tallgrass prairie region, linear bands of forest tracing the courses of rivers through grassland. During the past 100 years woodlands have spread in breadth and westward along the Platte River, and it has become a travel lane for eastern bird species extending their ranges west. While there are remnants of native grasslands and patches of man-planted grasslands on the bluff tops at Schramm, Platte River and Mahoney parks, the best reason for birders to visit these areas is

to see woodland species. All are good sites for migrating wood warblers in May. Both scarlet and summer tanagers are summer residents and breeders. The lower Platte River woodlands are excellent sites for eastern flycatchers, and for blue-gray gnatcatchers, ruby-crowned kinglets and wood-pewees. Platte River State Park and Schramm Park are perhaps the best places in the state to find the Louisiana waterthrush. Woodland edge species, such as catbirds and eastern bluebirds are well represented. The river adds another

Lower Platte Bird Sampler

Green Heron	White-breasted Nuthatch
Bald Eagle	Carolina Wren
Sharp-shinned Hawk	Ruby-crowned Kinglet
Cooper's Hawk	Blue-gray Gnatcatcher
Broad-winged Hawk	Eastern Bluebird
Red-tailed Hawk	Cedar Waxwing
Wild Turkey	Golden-winged Warbler
Piping Plover	Black-throated Green-
Least Tern	Warbler
Yellow-billed Cuckoo	Yellow-throated Warbler
Ruby-throated	Cerulean Warbler
Hummingbird	Ovenbird
Red-bellied Woodpecker	Louisiana Waterthrush
Hairy Woodpecker	Kentucky Warbler
Eastern Wood-Pewee	Summer Tanager
Eastern Phoebe	Scarlet Tanager
Great Crested Flycatcher	Chipping Sparrow
Yellow-throated Vireo	Indigo Bunting
Black-capped Chickadee	Baltimore Oriole
Tufted Titmouse	House Finch

BUB BLAKE

A female **Baltimore oriole** *gathers horse hair from a thicket for a nest. Baltimore orioles are most common in the east, Bullock's orioles in the west. The two species occasionally hybridize in riparian woodlands in central Nebraska. Until recently both were called northern orioles.*

element to the avifauna. At Schramm park, for example, nesting least terns and piping plovers can often be seen on sandbars. Wading birds, shorebirds and waterfowl are expected. All three areas are excellent sites to watch for migrating hawks riding thermals rising from the bluffs.

• Nearby Birding Destinations: The Plattsmouth Waterfowl Management Area east of Plattsmouth at the mouth the Platte River was acquired by the Nebraska Game and Parks Commission in 1954. In 1980 the name was changed to **Randall W. Schilling Wildlife Management Area,** and today the area encompasses 1,755 acres of Missouri River floodplain. Although the area's riparian woodlands are limited, they provide opportunities to find many migrating and nesting passerines. Public access to two miles of the Missouri River and ½ mile of the Platte River offers opportunities to see waterfowl and waterbirds.

The area was acquired because it attracted snow geese during migration, principally in the fall. Between 1967 and 1996, peak snow goose numbers on Schilling have ranged between 40,000 and 200,000. Since the early-1970s, the period during which snow geese are at the area each fall has declined, perhaps because of changing migration patterns. During the 1960s and 1970s, the snow goose fall migration began in late-September and was prolonged, through October and into November until weather conditions sent the last flocks south. In recent years, mass migrations have been more typical. No build-up of snow geese occurred at Schilling WMA in 1997 or from 1999 through 2002. Few snow geese use the area during spring migration.

Public tours are available in the fall at 4 p.m. on Sundays and Wednesdays when geese are in the area. Group tours can be scheduled other days of the week. Only foot traffic is allowed on the area during spring snow goose migration. Schilling is open to the public daily April 1 through October 15. Camping is not allowed on the area.

• Additional Information: Schilling WMA is located ½ mile east and 1 mile north of downtown Plattsmouth.

Hormel Park, a city park in west Fremont, is a favorite site for migrating warblers and birders. Trails pass through deciduous woodlands, past small ponds and marshes, to the Platte River. Among the species found there in recent years have been migrating cerulean, worm-eating, blackpoll, mourning, Canada and prothonotary warblers.

Wood Duck WMA

The first parcel of the Wood Duck Wildlife Management Area was acquired in 1966, when wood ducks were still a rare sight even in eastern Nebraska. But the area was aptly named. Woodlands and wetlands are intimately intertwined in this Elkhorn River bend.

Deciduous forest borders the prairie river, and abandoned channels are now shadowy oxbow lakes. Willows encircle small spots of marsh created by groundwater seepage in grasslands. Wood Duck WMA has 1½ miles of Elkhorn River frontage and 623 acres of upland grassland, 426 acres of marsh, 67 acres of open water and 264 acres of riparian woodlands. In the mid-1800s, woodlands in Stanton County were probably no more than a fringe of trees and shrubs on the banks and largest islands of the Elkhorn River. Today, willows, indigo bush and cottonwoods line the river's edge, merging into a riparian forest of more long-lived tree species – hackberry, ash, mulberry, silver maple and bur oak.

During migration and nesting seasons, Wood Duck attracts expected deciduous forest species. The Elkhorn River, perhaps more than any other river in the state, still has an abundance of floodplain wetlands, old oxbows abandoned by the river, and these features make this WMA an exceptionally good birding destination. Shallow wetlands in timber attract belted kingfishers and green herons, and cattail marshes in grasslands lure secretive rails and black-crowned night-herons. Puddle and diving ducks pause on their northward migrations and some wood ducks, blue-winged teal, mallards and pied-billed grebes linger to nest. Woodland edge-loving bird species are everywhere at Wood Duck. Spotted sandpipers and great blue herons come to the river's sandbars. Indiangrass and big bluestem grow head-high and attract dickcissels, bobolinks and field sparrows. Eastern kingbirds leave their perches in the tops of lone bur oaks on grassy savannas to snatch flying insects. Few places in northeastern Nebraska match Wood Duck's diversity of habitats and variety of birds.

• Additional Information: Wood Duck WMA is located 1½ miles west of Stanton on Nebraska Highway 24, south 2 miles, west 1½ mile, north 1 mile.
• Nearby Birding Destinations: With 1½ miles of frontage on the Elkhorn River, **Yellowbanks Wildlife Management Area** west of Norfolk offers birders two different woodland types. The high, rugged bluffs on the northern side of the river, for which the area is named, is an upland deciduous woodland dominated by bur oak, and land on the southern side of the river is typical deciduous floodplain forest dominated by cottonwoods. There are grasslands and excellent woodland edge habitat on both sides. To reach Yellowbanks on the northern side of the Elkhorn, from the junction of U.S. 275 and Nebraska Highway 121 (2 miles north of Battle Creek) drive north 1½ miles, west 2¼ miles, north ½ mile, west 1 mile and south ½ mile. To reach Yellowbanks on the southern side of the Elkhorn, from the same junction of highways 275 and 121, drive west 1 mile, north ½ mile, west 2 miles.

Grove Lake WMA

Located in Antelope County, Grove Lake Wildlife Management Area encompasses 2,008 acres in two adjacent tracts and includes a 50-acre impoundment.

The eastern branch of Verdigre Creek passes through the area, supplying a trout-rearing station with abundant cold water. The creek's drainage system also explains the area's rugged and wooded terrain. Verdigre Creek flows into the Niobrara River. Bur oak is the dominant tree species on canyon sides and in ravines. More than 250,000 trees – bur oak, red oak, walnut, green ash and red cedar – shrubs, native grasses and legumes have been planted on the WMA. Hilltops are mostly grasslands. Grove Lake is at the western edge of the tallgrass prairie and far enough north to show the influence of northern prairies. Physiographically, it is on the western margin of a loamy, glaciated region and on the eastern margin of a sandy plain transition to the Sandhills region.

The mix of lake, stream, woodlands and grasslands make Grove Lake an excellent destination for bird watchers, but it has received little attention. Many of the species found on the upper Missouri River and lower Niobrara River should be found at Grove Lake. The lake has an excellent reputation as a fishing lake, attracting human anglers, bald eagles, ospreys and belted kingfishers.

• Additional Information: Grove Lake is located two miles north of Royal. ∎

*A small lake and rugged woodlands at **Grove Lake WMA** attracts bird species similar to those found on the lower Niobrara River.*

Loess Hills and Plains

THE CENTRAL GREAT PLAINS ecoregion is a huge swath of land from central Nebraska southward through Kansas and into Oklahoma. It encompasses central and south-central Nebraska west of the tallgrass prairie region, south of the Sandhills and east of the shortgrass prairie and sandsage prairie in the southwestern counties. With the exception of the Rainwater Basin in south-central Nebraska, the Central Great Plains have well-developed drainage systems – a spider web of intermittent or seasonal trickles feeding creeks that gather to form ever-larger rivers. North of the Platte River, the land is hilly and deeply dissected by thousands of years of erosion. South of the Platte, except along major rivers, the land is gently rolling to flat.

This is mixed-grass prairie country, where the tall grasses of the east and the short grasses of the west merge and blend. It is a transition zone that expands eastward into semihumid grasslands during prolonged drought, and west into semi-arid grasslands during periods of above average precipitation. The mixed-grass prairie region has largely been converted to agriculture, but significant expanses of pastureland are still found in central Nebraska. Before center-pivot irrigation was introduced in the 1970s, there was even

More than other woodpecker species, red-headed woodpeckers prefer woodland edge or trees and groves in open grasslands.

more. After more than 100 years of intensive grazing, many pastures bear scant resemblance to native grasslands. Most botanists consider the Sandhills, also in the Central Great Plains ecoregion, to be mixed-grass prairie but because of its distinctive soils, high water table, and flora and fauna, it will be treated separately.

In 1860, William Gilpin, a writer and speaker on the settlement of the West, compared the topographies of North America and Europe to bowls – North America turned right side up and Europe turned upside down. In North America the continental rims deprive the great interior valleys of atmospheric moisture from the seas. Scant moisture and wildfires limited woodlands on the Great Plains, and to a degree prevented man from making anything of grasslands other than what they are. While the semihumid grasslands of eastern Nebraska were ripe to be plowed and farmed, the more arid western grasslands were best suited for pasture and only grudgingly produced crops until the advent of irrigation. For that reason, more mixed-grass prairie remains than tallgrass prairie.

Much of Nebraska's mixed-grass prairie is found on soils derived from loess (pronounced "luss"), wind-blown silt that settled over much of central North America over hundreds of thousands of years. Silt particles are extremely small but some loess soils in Nebraska are also composed of clay and sand particles. Loess soils are inherently fertile, and only the lack of precipitation precludes a more lush grassland in central Nebraska. Dry hilltops in the Central Great Plains are dominated by blue grama and buffalograss, the most drought resistant of all mixed-grass prairie grasses. Sideoats grama, sand dropseed, June grass and little bluestem are most abundant on hillsides. Tallgrass prairie species – big bluestem, Indiangrass, switchgrass and Canada wild rye dominate the more moist lower slopes and valleys. On an especially good tract of mixed-grass prairie it is possible to see the transition between tallgrass and shortgrass prairie within 300 vertical feet, from mesic, bottomland vegetation to more xeric vegetation on hilltops. More than 230 species of plants have been identified from one loess hills site in Nebraska.

Mixed-grass prairie in the loess hills region of Nebraska once was prairie dog and buffalo country, and the land of the Pawnees. Today, rank woodlands have colonized the canyons and bluffs, and smooth brome and Kentucky bluegrass have spread across pastures and roadsides. In the past three decades red cedar has aggressively invaded pastures – the last remnants of native grasslands in the region. Dryland corn and alfalfa are important agricultural crops, although cattle production remains an integral element to the economy.

While Nebraska's mixed-grass prairie bears scant resemblance to what it was when Stephen Long's party traversed it in 1820, it is more than just cowbird country.

*Before settlement by Euroamericans, the **loess hills** of central Nebraska was mixed-grass prairie broken by ravines and valleys carved by streams and rivers. Fields and pastures dominate the region today and trees are more abundant since the suppression of wildfires.*

The Republican, Platte, Loup and Blue rivers cross the region. There are bur oak draws and backwater sloughs, wooded canyons and bluffs here and there. Sometimes in a pioneer cemetery or along an abandoned rail line, a patch of high-quality native mixed-grass prairie survives. Compared to the bird life of woodlands, mixed-grass prairie avifauna is less diverse and colorful. Like the vegetation, it is a transition between eastern and western grassland species. With the spread of agriculture, the abundance of grassland birds has declined. Today a flock of prairie-chickens, sharp-tailed grouse, nesting upland sandpipers or grassland sparrows, once so common, are rare. The grassland birds that remain are generalists, capable of eking out a living in an impoverished pasture.

Because man controlled prairie fires and planted trees on homesteads and in shelterbelts, woodlands have spread into the central plains. These changes have been a tremendous boon for woodland and edge species not found or uncommon in the region originally – brown thrashers, eastern kingbirds, orioles, blue jays, American goldfinches, bobwhites and many others. In the mid-1930s, *The Nebraska Bird Review* had accounts that both praised the woodland plantings and the birds attracted to them, and that sounded alarm as other species suddenly became more abundant. Common grackles, called bronzed grackles in the early-1900s, became markedly more abundant and were condemned for their habits of raiding the

nests of small birds.

In 1902, Wilson Tout wrote in the *Proceedings of the Nebraska Ornithologists' Union* that he believed Otoe County was about the western limit of the crow in Nebraska. In a 1938 issue of *The Nebraska Bird Review,* Glenn Viehmeyer remarked on the spread of crows as far west and north as the Sandhills during the preceding 25 years. Once it had only been an uncommon migrant, he wrote, "a rare enough bird to cause much excitement when it appeared." Viehmeyer attributed the crow's colonization of the region to tree planting by settlers. In 1958 he again wrote of the increase in crows: "The Eastern Crow followed the settler across the state to feed in his fields and the Magpie moved in from the west to share the loot." By the early-1980s crows were common statewide, and deemed to be noxious pests in south-central Nebraska where they gathered in huge winter roosts. In the winter of 1991, an estimated 500,000 crows roosted at night in the city of Holdrege, and city workers armed with 12-gauge shotguns were stationed on the town's perimeter to discourage the birds' arrival.

The effect of agriculture on native bird life of the Central Great Plains has been incremental and unrelenting, and in the end, enormous. Changes to the land occurred slowly, and were hardly noticed in a lifetime. The loss of wild creatures was small from year to year but incalculable over 150 years. L. Sessions of Norfolk wrote in the 1901 *Proceedings of the Nebraska*

Central Great Plains

BASED ON U.S. GEOLOGICAL SURVEY 2001 MAP

Area Enlarged

Approximately 43 miles

Myrtle Hall WMA

Calamus Reservoir

North Loup River

Middle Loup River

Arcadia Diversion Dam

Lower Loup River WMAs

Wilkinson WMA

Fremont

Columbus

South Loup River

North Loup River

Loup River

A ⊙ Broken Bow

B

Loup City

North Platte

Pressey WMA

Leonard A. Koziol WMA

Grand Island

Crane Meadows

Platte River

Medicine Creek Reservoir

Kearney

Rowe Sanctuary

Fork Big Blue River

Harvard WPA

Red Willow Reservoir

C

Funk WPA

Hastings

Massie WPA

Sacramento WMA

D

The Blue River

Beatrice

McCook

Republican River

Harlan County Reservoir

Cather Prairie

E

NEBRASKA

KANSAS

A **Central Nebraska Loess Plains**
Rolling dissected plains with deep loess soils. Originally mixed-grass prairie. Today a mosaic of rangeland and cropland with irrigation increasing. Red cedars invading pastures.

B **Platte River Valley**
Historically the Platte had braided channels bordered by tallgrass prairie. As upstream irrigation increased, the channel became more narrow, bordered by woodlands and cropland.

C **Rolling Plains and Breaks**
Historically mixed-grass prairie, today a mosaic of cropland and rangeland. Silty soils on loess uplands. A rolling topography cut by the Republican River and smaller streams

D **Rainwater Basin Plains**
Flat to rolling loess plains with poorly developed drainage resulting in many natural wetlands. Former mixed-grass prairie has been converted to row-crop production.

E **Smoky Hills**
A region more extensive in Kansas, where it is a transition between tallgrass prairie and mixed-grass prairie. Loess soils underlain by a sandstone formation. Used for crops and pasture.

Ornithologists' Union about the benefits of tree planting on regional avifauna: "But the birds in their journeying northward stopped to inspect the little grove and soon a partnership was formed with the homesteader, and family after family came to cheer him with their songs, and to aid in successfully combating the hordes of hungry insect pests which came swarming in from all sides."

While welcoming the new birds, Sessions recalled with sadness the loss of those species once so abundant: "I have now in mind one of these ponds, located but a short distance from my home and which covered only about one acre in surface, where in the spring of 1876 I found Blue-winged Teal, Mud Hens, Eared and Pied-billed Grebes, Godwits, Long-billed Curlews, Wilson's Phalaropes, and a long list of sandpipers busily occupied with their homemaking. But herds of cattle have long since destroyed these favorite-nesting places. The same is true of many of our creek valleys

where sheltering thickets of wild plum, willow and other shrubs formerly afforded attractive homes for tree birds. But now well trodden muddy banks, close-cropped herbage and broken thickets afford but little attraction for our songsters."

A change in the common name of *Molothrus ater* succinctly tells the history of the Central Great Plains' avifauna. In the 1800s it was called the buffalo bird; in the 1900s it became the cowbird.

Cather Prairie

Perhaps the largest public-access tract of mixed-grass prairie remaining in Nebraska is just north of the Kansas border and south of Red Cloud in Webster County. In 1974, The Nature Conservancy, acting for the Willa Cather Pioneer Memorial and Educational Foundation and funded by the Woods Charitable Fund, purchased 610 acres of virgin prairie and named it for author Willa Cather, who moved with her family to Webster County when she was nine years old. Cather became one of the state's best-known authors, her novels describing the grasslands she knew as a child in the 1880s and 1890s. "This country was mostly wild pasture and as naked as the back of your hand," she wrote, "I was little and homesick and lonely and my mother was homesick and nobody paid any attention to us. So the country and I had it out together and by the end of the first autumn, that shaggy grass country had gripped me with a passion I have never been able to shake."

When The Nature Conservancy acquired Cather Prairie, parts of the tract had been abused by livestock for years. The grassland is still recovering. Hal Nagel and students from the University of Nebraska-Kearney have identified 250 species of plants at Cather. The landscape is large and undulating, with broad ridge tops and steep valley sides falling away into drainages. Standing in the middle of the prairie it is possible to imagine what all of south-central Nebraska once was. Here and there on the grassland are limestone outcrops and occasional towering hackberries prospering in well-watered ravines. Look for Fendler's aster and Fremont's clematis, plants with southern ranges barely reaching Nebraska. Birders have largely ignored the area, and it deserves more attention because of its southerly position and expanse of grassland.

• Additional Information: Willa Cather Memorial Prairie is located 5 miles south of Red Cloud, west of U.S. Highway 281.

Myrtle Hall WMA

The Myrtle E. Hall Wildlife Management Area straddles the Loup-Custer county line southwest of Taylor. Received by the Nebraska Game and Parks Commission as a bequeath in 2000, the WMA's 1,960 acres cover tableland and breaks that fall off into the North Loup River Valley. There are two tracts three miles apart. The eastern tract's 1,280 acres have more diverse habitat. Its northern and southern ends are rugged, dissected by canyons, ravines and draws filled with woodlands dominated by red cedar but including hackberry, Siberian elm, box elder, green ash and cottonwood. Patches of woody shrubs – wild plum, chokecherry, smooth sumac and snowberry – are common. There are about two miles of mature shelterbelts with ponderosa pines and deciduous trees, and an extensive woodlot of about 160 acres on the northern side of the area.

The western tract of 680 acres is principally grassland. Only about three percent of the WMA is wooded. About a quarter of the area was used as cropland when it was acquired, and wildlife food plots are now grown there. About 1,240 acres of native grassland on both areas have a mix of grasses and forbs. To set back cool-season invasive grasses like smooth brome and Kentucky bluegrass and to control the expansion of red cedars, managers will be using rotational burning.

The North Loup River, only five miles north, marks

ROD NABHOLZ

Indigo buntings expanded their range westward along river valley woodlands and hybridize with the western lazuli bunting.

the transition between Sandhills prairie to the north and Central Loess Plains to the south. Both influence Myrtle Hall's avifauna. Expect to find grassland and edge species with some woodland species. The best of the native grassland provides an excellent sampling of regional wildflowers.

• Additional Information: The eastern tract of Myrtle E. Hall WMA is 8 miles west and 1 mile south of Taylor. The western tract is 11½ miles west and 1 mile south of Taylor. Both areas are accessible by all-weather county roads.

Pressey WMA

The lure of owning land brought schoolteacher H.E. Pressey from England to Custer County in 1904. After buying land on the South Loup River south of Broken Bow for $6 an acre, Pressey and his wife, Kate, built a cabin from cedar logs, and planted crops and a big garden. They raised cattle, sheep, hogs and chickens. She planted flowers and he planted fruit and nut trees and berry bushes. He corresponded with university horticulturists and experimented with new varieties and trees beyond their normal range. Pressey was to Custer County what Jules Sandoz was to Sheridan County, a man with a vision to make his new country a bit more like his old country. After Pressey had a leg amputated, he went to the river, selected a fine hackberry and fashioned his own peg leg.

In 1930, Pressey deeded 80 acres of land to the Game, Forestation and Parks Commission to become a state park. Only months before he died in 1943, he deeded an additional 1,520 acres to be used "for public recreation or for the propagation of wildlife and fish." Included was more than 640 acres of unplowed mixed-grass prairie.

Today, Pressey Wildlife Management Area's 1,692 acres

Willow flycatchers are found statewide in shrubby habitats but they prefer willow thickets during the nesting season.

ROCKY HOFFMANN

are a diverse mix of deciduous floodplain forest (including a few remaining exotic trees and shrubs planted by Pressey), native grassland and former river bottom cropland seeded to native grasses and wildlife food plots. Nebraska Highway 21 and the South Loup River pass through the area. The best of the woodlands are west of the highway. Birders will find extensive grasslands with woodland pockets on the rugged valley wall east of the highway and south of the county road. Watch for nesting wood ducks near the small pond. There are service roads throughout the area.

Pressey WMA offers birders diverse viewing opportunities for central Nebraska woodland species, grassland species and woodland edge species within a small area. The shallow South Loup River attracts wading birds and shorebirds. An active great blue heron rookery is in tall cottonwoods on the southern side of the river near the western end of the area.

• Additional Information: Pressey WMA is 5 miles north of Oconto on Nebraska Highway 21.

Arcadia Diversion Dam WMA

Encompassing 925 acres, Arcadia Diversion Dam Wildlife Management Area is in northeastern Custer County. Situated on both sides of the Middle Loup River, the Arcadia area has bur oak floodplain forest, marshy backwater sloughs, and tree and native grass plantings for wildlife in addition to river access. The

river channel and sandbars are excellent habitat for waterbirds, especially during migrations. Gulls, terns, great blue herons, summertime great egrets, bald eagles and belted kingfishers find fishing opportunities below the diversion dam. Sandbars and shallow water on the riverbed are used by shorebirds. Dead-water sloughs on the western side of the river, such as where Spring Creek enters from the west, are encircled with lush marsh vegetation and used by wood ducks, blue-winged teal, green herons, American bitterns and rails. Woodlands at the river's edge are thick with underbrush, attracting both woodland and edge passerine species, particularly during migration. The 640 acres of wildlife land east of the river is a mix of grasslands and scattered woodlands, weedy areas and wildlife food plots. The WMA has primitive campsites, toilets and wells on both sides of the river. Foot traffic is allowed across the 7,960-foot-long dam that diverts water for Sherman Reservoir.

• Additional Information: To access the east side of Arcadia Diversion Dam WMA from Comstock, drive south four miles. To access the west side from Comstock, drive 1 mile west of the town, crossing the river, and then south about 5 miles on county roads jogging along the river.

• Nearby Birding Destinations: Located 4 miles east and 1 mile north of Loup City, **Sherman Reservoir State Recreation Area and Wildlife Management Area** encompass 6,002 acres, of which 2,845 are the reservoir. The U.S. Bureau of Reclamation completed Sherman Dam in 1962. The reservoir is used principally to store water for irrigation. Camping facilities are available. Look for migrating waterbirds spring and fall, possible rare pelagic species in fall and early winter, and grassland and edge passerine species year-around. Sherman Reservoir is one of three demonstration sites for the Focus on Pheasants program initiated by the Commission and Pheasants Forever in 2002. Under that program, trees and shrubs on public land have

Pressey Bird Sampler

Wood Duck	Black-billed Magpie
Great Blue Heron	Horned Lark
Red-tailed Hawk	White-breasted Nuthatch
Swainson's Hawk	Eastern Bluebird
Northern Harrier	Gray Catbird
Wild Turkey	Brown Thrasher
Spotted Sandpiper	Swainson's Thrush
Yellow-billed Cuckoo	Orange-crowned Warbler
Great Horned Owl	American Redstart
Eastern Screech-Owl	Spotted Towhee
Red-headed Woodpecker	Lark Sparrow
Downy Woodpecker	White-crowned Sparrow
Hairy Woodpecker	Grasshopper Sparrow
Northern Flicker	Vesper Sparrow
Eastern Phoebe	Rose-breasted Grosbeak
Eastern Kingbird	Black-headed Grosbeak
Western Kingbird	Blue Grosbeak
Bell's Vireo	Orchard Oriole
Warbling Vireo	Baltimore Oriole

been removed and the area is being reseeded to grassland. The program should benefit nongame grassland species as well as pheasants.

Leonard A. Koziol WMA

The Leonard A. Koziol Wildlife Management Area, formerly named the Loup Junction WMA, occupies 328 acres of land at the confluence of the North Loup and Middle Loup rivers. It is diverse floodplain habitat with about 100 acres of timber and 100 acres of grassland. About 90 acres of bench land on the western end of the area were formerly used as cropland. They have either been seeded to native grasses or are used as wildlife food plots. The most extensive timberland, lying along the North Loup River and where the rivers merge, is composed principally of cottonwood, red cedar, green ash, box elder, silver maple and mulberry. There are two shelterbelts on the site. Former pastureland is being allowed to regain a diversity of grasses and forbs. A small creek with slough-like aspects flows diagonally across the tract and there is a two-acre, non-flowing slough on the southern edge of the area. The Koziol WMA provides access to about a mile of North Loup River and ½ mile of Middle Loup River.

The area's woodland edge and grassland avifauna is enhanced with species expected on floodplain wetlands and a sandbar-laced river. Watch for post-breeding least terns feeding in shallow backwaters. An access road into the area is closed during the hunting seasons, but it is open most of the year to allow fishing access. Camping is available nearby at North Loup State Recreation Area four miles north of St. Paul.

• Additional Information: To access Koziol WMA from St. Paul, drive north 2½ miles on U.S. 281, then east 2 miles and north ½ mile on county roads.

Lower Loup River WMAs

A complex of wildlife lands in Nance and Platte counties on the lower Loup River provide excellent riparian woodland birdwatching opportunities. The **George Syas Wildlife Management Area** is located on an inside bend of the Loup River. Immediately to the south is a slender, eastern outlier of Sandhills prairie, now largely converted to row crop production. Native Sandhills wildflowers are still often found on the Syas area.

The area's 917 acres are entirely in the river floodplain, offering birders expected riverine habitats and avifauna. An abandoned channel of the Loup River cuts the area diagonally, spawning dead-water sloughs and wet lowlands filled with cordgrass and tallgrass prairie forbs. Much of the WMA is wooded with floodplain species – towering cottonwoods and an understory with eastern red cedar, green ash, hackberry, catalpa, box elder, black walnut; shrub and vine thickets of dogwood, indigo bush, prickly ash, wild plum, wild grape, Virginia creeper and bittersweet.

Many eastern deciduous forest passerines come to Syas WMA during the spring migration and nesting

Eskimo Curlew

During the last half of the 19th century, the number of Eskimo curlews plummeted from hundreds of thousands to the point that a sighting was rare. If any exist today, their numbers are few. Nebraska was in the center of the curlew's northward migration, and they gathered in uncountable numbers on prairies, especially on recently burned prairies, where they gorged themselves with insects and insect eggs before continuing north to breeding grounds in the treeless tundra of northern Canada.

Market hunting played a role in the decline of the species, but destruction of grasslands and the elimination of wildfires ultimately would have led to their near extinction. Eskimo curlews were highly social shorebirds, traveled in enormous flocks and relied on specific habitat sites, leading some ornithologists to believe their numbers were reduced below a socially sustainable level.

During the early-20th century, several Eskimo curlew sightings were from Nebraska. A flock of 70 to 75 was observed in Merrick County in April 1900, and smaller groups were seen in York and Madison counties from 1904 through 1910. Seven were shot from a flock of eight in April 1911 in Merrick County, and a single curlew was shot near Norfolk in April 1915. On April 8, 1926, A.M. Brooking, a reliable amateur ornithologist, reported eight Eskimo curlews east of Hastings in the Rainwater Basin.

Throughout the mid- and late-1900s there were occasional reports of Eskimo curlews from the East Coast, along the species' traditional southward migration route, from the coast of Texas in the spring and from Arctic Canada. On April 16, 1987, a U.S. Fish and Wildlife Service biologist and avid birder reported a single Eskimo curlew feeding with a marbled godwit and greater yellowlegs in a wet meadow along the Platte River near Grand Island. The observation was not documented with a photograph.

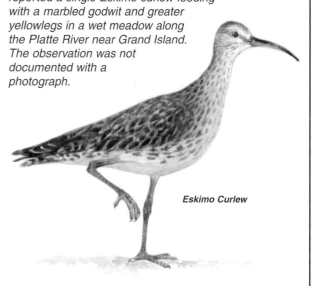

Eskimo Curlew

seasons. There are expanses of native and restored grassland. The southern edge has wildlife food plots and shelterbelts with chokecherry and wild plum thickets. The Loup River is shallow most of the year because water upstream is diverted into the Loup Power District canal constructed during the 1930s. Walking along the river shallows and sandbars is a

Eurasian Collared-Dove

The Eurasian collared-dove was introduced to the Bahamas in the mid-1970s and quickly spread westward after reaching the North American continent. In large part, their rapid and successful colonization of the New World can be attributed to the availability of seed in backyard bird feeders and the availability of urban trees and shrubs providing roosting and nesting sites. Spilled grain at elevators provides a year-round food source in many small towns. It seems likely this European native will become a widespread member of Nebraska's avifauna.

The first Eurasian collared-dove was reported at a feeder in Shelton in Buffalo County in November 1997. Successful nesting was documented in Kearney in April 1998, and they were reported that same year in Nuckolls County. By the spring of 1999, nesting pairs were reported in Pierce County, and in the winter of 1999-2000, they were reported at Ogallala, Dakota City and Elmwood. In the spring of 2000 they moved to the city, appearing in Omaha. By the spring of 2001 they were in the Panhandle, and by the spring of 2003 had been reported in 52 of Nebraska's 93 counties.

With food available year-round, there appears to be no limiting factors to prevent the Eurasian collared-dove from becoming widespread and common in the state. What, if any, effect the species will have on native birds, particularly the mourning dove, is unknown.

BOB GRIER

Eurasian collared-doves were first reported in Nebraska in 1997.

of native grass and weedy areas, and 15 acres of food plots. Watch for sedge wrens, yellowthroats and swamp sparrows in grasslands and emergent vegetation bordering wetlands. Bald eagles use the lower Loup during waterfowl migration in early- and late-winter. The land that was in crop production when it was acquired has been mostly converted into native grassland and tree and shrub plantings.

• Additional Information: Prairie Wolf WMA is 1½ miles south of Genoa in Nance County, west of Nebraska Highway 39.

Loup Lands Wildlife Management Area is owned by the Loup Power District and leased to the Nebraska Game and Parks Commission. Located upstream from Prairie Wolf, Loup Lands is composed of two tracts at the Loup Power District headgates where water is diverted from the river into a canal. The small tract is south of the river immediately west of the headgate, and the large tract is on both sides of the river below the headgates. Most of the area is riparian woodland. There are 65 grassland acres, 30 acres of wetlands and marsh and access to the Loup River. The headgates area is an excellent site to see nesting and feeding least terns in June and July, and shorebirds frequent the sand spoil sites at the head of the canal.

• Additional Information: The northern side of the large tract north of the river is 3 miles southwest of Genoa in Nance County on Nebraska Highway 22. The larger portion of that tract south of the river is 2½ miles south of Genoa on Nebraska Highway 39, then on country roads travel west ½ mile, south ½ mile, west ½ mile, south ½ mile and west 3 miles.

Wilkinson WMA

Another lower Loup site, but one providing a different birding opportunity, is Wilkinson Wildlife Management Area. Soil survey maps from the early-1900s show

pleasant way to access the northern edge of the WMA. Watch for the expected riverine species – great blue and green herons, shorebirds such as spotted sandpipers, summertime least terns, migrating waterfowl and spring-nesting wood ducks. Bell's vireo, a species apparently most abundant in Nebraska on the lower Loup, should be found. Syas WMA is little used beyond the fall hunting seasons.

• Additional Information: To reach Syas WMA from Genoa, travel south 2½ miles on Nebraska Highway 39, then east 1 mile, and north 1 mile.

Prairie Wolf Wildlife Management Area is similar to the Syas area in terrain, flora and avifauna. Sitting astride the Loup River with 1½ miles of frontage, the 926-acre area is composed of about 350 acres of riparian timber, 60 acres of river and marsh wetlands, 500 acres

Lower Loup Bird Sampler

Wood Duck	Red-eyed Vireo
Great Blue Heron	Tree Swallow
Bald Eagle	Northern Rough-winged
Red-tailed Hawk	Swallow
Piping Plover	Bank Swallow
American Woodcock	Black-capped Chickadee
Least Tern	White-breast Nuthatch
Black-billed Cuckoo	Sedge Wren
Yellow-billed Cuckoo	Wood Thrush
Eastern Screech Owl	Gray Catbird
Red-headed Woodpecker	Yellow Warbler
Red-bellied Woodpecker	Common Yellowthroat
Downy Woodpecker	Field Sparrow
Hairy Woodpecker	Grasshopper Sparrow
Northern Flicker	Rose-breasted Grosbeak
Eastern Wood-Pewee	Blue Grosbeak
Willow Flycatcher	Dickcissel
Great-crested Flycatcher	Bobolink
Bell's Vireo	Orchard Oriole
Warbling Vireo	Baltimore Oriole

Least terns nest on sandbars exposed after high spring flows have receded. On the lower Loup River, nesting takes place in June or July most years, and postbreeding birds typically remain through August and into September.

the area as an elliptical pool of water over a mile long surrounded by marsh and wet meadow. Since the late-1880s, landowners have attempted to drain the wetlands for farming. More than 100 years later, defying a deep ditch excavated through the middle, the land is still water-covered most years. A playa wetland complex, Wilkinson is located on an ancient floodplain terrace between the Loup River and Shell Creek. Like wetlands in the Rainwater Basin of south-central Nebraska, these wind-carved wetlands are characteristically small, shallow, clay-lined and located in closed drainage regions. (See the Rainwater Basin chapter, beginning on page 66, for additional information.)

At the urging of Conservation Officer Lyman Wilkinson, the Izaak Walton Wetlands Foundation was established in 1989 to raise money to acquire and protect the area. Later the Todd Valley Wetland Foundation was organized to take up the torch. Two grants from the Nebraska Environmental Trust, along with funds from local and regional partners, made the initial land purchases possible in the mid-1990s. In 1997 the Nebraska Game and Parks Commission accepted ownership and management responsibilities. Today, the 957-acre wetland complex is managed specifically for waterbirds with a system of low-level dikes, nine man-made wetland cells, 17 stop-log drain tubes and four irrigation wells. Wetland cells can be drained or filled with water individually. By manipulating the water level, the vegetation is managed to provide the best habitat. The Wilkinson area has a clay pan bottom that is nearly impervious to seepage.

The shallow wetlands and lush aquatic vegetation surrounded with grassy and weedy dry land is a mecca for migrating waterfowl, primarily geese and puddle ducks. In recent years snow geese have discovered the wetlands and use it during their spring migration. As many as 40,000 snow geese and thousands of other species of geese and ducks have been on the area in one day during spring migration. Shorebirds, wading birds, rails, red-winged blackbirds and yellowthroats

also quickly adopted the wetlands. Grass and weed areas are filled with native sparrows. Bobolinks nest on the area. The spring migration from early-March into April is the time to find the largest number and variety of birds. Nearly 200 acres of cropland on the western end of this three-mile-long area was planted to a high diversity (120 or more species) of native grasses and forbs. Wilkinson is an excellent birding area for grassland and wetland edge passerines, and will become even better in future years.

• Additional Information: Wilkinson WMA is located 5 miles west and 1 mile north of Columbus on U.S. Highway 81, west of the highway and south of the town of Platte Center.

• Nearby Birding Destinations: Part of the Loup Power District canal system, **Lake Babcock** and **Lake North,** three miles north of Columbus, are only five miles east of Wilkinson. Babcock is the older of the two and has marsh on its western end. Look for gulls, ducks, waders and snow geese in March. ■

Wilkinson Bird Sampler

Greater White-fronted Goose	Lesser Yellowlegs
Snow Goose	Hudsonian Godwit
American Wigeon	Pectoral Sandpiper
Northern Shoveler	Wilson's Snipe
Redhead	Bell's Vireo
Pied-billed Grebe	Sedge Wren
Eared Grebe	Marsh Wren
American Bittern	Common Yellowthroat
Great Blue Heron	Clay-colored Sparrow
White-faced Ibis	Field Sparrow
Northern Harrier	Vesper Sparrow
Merlin	Savannah Sparrow
Peregrine Falcon	Swamp Sparrow
Prairie Falcon	Dickcissel
Virginia Rail	Bobolink
Sora	Yellow-headed Blackbird
	Great-tailed Grackle

Rainwater Basin

THE RAINWATER BASIN lies in the flat to gently rolling, mixed-grass loess plains of south-central Nebraska. Like the Sandhills, the Rainwater Basin is geologically young and has not developed a system of streams to drain surface water. Runoff gathers in shallow basins as small lakes, marshes and sheet water in fields. Once there were nearly 4,000 major wetlands totaling nearly 100,000 acres in the 4,200 square-mile, 17-county region. Today fewer than 400 remain.

Most were from one to 40 acres, but the largest covered more than 1,000 acres. Larger wetlands were perennial marshes, except during periods of prolonged drought, and filled with native aquatic vegetation – bulrushes, cattails, pondweeds and smartweeds. Few were more than five feet deep.

The origin of Rainwater Basin wetlands has long been the subject of speculation. Most researchers believe wind scoured shallow depressions when vegetation lost its grip during arid periods and the soil surface was broken by disturbances such as wallowing buffalo. Radiocarbon dating indicates the basins were created near the end of the Ice Age, 20,000 to 25,000 years ago, but might have been enlarged and new ones created as recently as 3,000 years ago. Over thousands of years, minute clay particles accumulated in the bottoms of the basins, effectively sealing them and preventing standing water from seeping away. Today, these impervious clay pans are six to 72 inches thick. In their natural state, the larger basins collected snowmelt and rain runoff from several square miles and, if precipitation was adequate, probably held water through most years. Wetlands of this type are called playa wetlands.

Playa wetland complexes are found elsewhere in Nebraska, although not as extensively as in the Rainwater Basin. Some are located south of the Platte River in Saunders County along an ancient valley of the Platte River called the Todd Valley. Often grouped with the Todd Valley complex for convenience are playas north of the Platte River between Platte and Dodge counties and as far north as Wayne and Thurston counties. There are other playa regions in Custer County, southwestern Nebraska and the southern Panhandle. Statewide, playa wetlands have been degraded or destroyed by agriculture.

Land in the Rainwater Basin was cheap or even free to settlers in the late-1800s. In the early years, farmers

tolerated the marshes and farmed around them. As land became more valuable, farmers looked for ways to drain the wetlands to increase their crop acreage. Landowners formed local drainage districts. Ditches dug by hand or with horse-drawn scrapers drained small wetlands, but large basins defied these efforts. Networks of tile drains were laid beneath the surface of some basins to carry unwanted water away. But, often there was nowhere for the water to drain, so larger basins persisted.

"Drain the bogs, and what can the jacksnipes and the woodcock do for a living?" Sandy Griswold asked in a 1910 *Omaha World-Herald* column. "Reclaim all the wet lands, and ditch away the water of the ponds and small lakes, but after it is done look in vain for dowitcher, yellow leg, willet, turnstone or plover, mallard, teal, spoonbill or widgeon. It is true that the plume gatherers have killed thousands and thousands of herons right here in Nebraska, but the farmers' drains – the sluiceways, irrigating ditches and filled-in swails [swales] – whereby vast areas of watery feeding grounds have been made dry, have killed millions."

After World War II, large earthmoving equipment became available and agriculture intensified in south-central Nebraska. Raising county road grades and deepening roadside ditches drained many wetlands. Drainage ditches on private land carrying water to roadsides accounted for more than half the wetlands destroyed in the Rainwater Basin. Small wetlands were filled with soil from higher ground, and dugouts or reuse pits were excavated to concentrate water in larger basins.

JON FARRAR

White-faced ibis have become more common in recent years in shallow wetlands in the Rainwater Basin and Sandhills. There are only three Nebraska nesting records.

Gone, too, were the grasslands. Most of the remaining pastures in the 1960s were plowed with the advent of center-pivot systems in the 1970s, allowing irrigation of rolling land. During the early-1900s, the Rainwater Basin was the favored hunting grounds for upland sandpipers and American golden-plover. Even then, both species, especially the golden plover, were much diminished in abundance. In 1905, Griswold wrote that when he came to Nebraska in 1886, upland sandpipers "were so plentiful all over the big grazing lands of the state and so easily approached and shot down that there was but little incentive to hunt them." In 1918, the Migratory Bird Treaty Act protected these upland shorebirds from the gun, but

The Rainwater Basin of south-central Nebraska is one of the state's most intensively farmed regions. Before settlement there were nearly 4,000 major wetlands in the region. Today, fewer than 400 remain. The best are protected as public lands.

neither returned to their former abundance in the Rainwater Basin country. Lost, too, were the other grassland species in south-central Nebraska.

Federal wetlands acquisition was first authorized by the Migratory Bird Conservation Act of 1929, with the intent of establishing a national system of publicly financed bird refuges. But few appropriations were made for land purchases, prompting the passage of the Migratory Bird Hunting Stamp Act in 1934, which established a special fund financed by the sale of duck stamps to hunters. For 70 years, funds generated by the Migratory Bird Hunting and Conservation Stamp Program, as it is called today, have been used to acquire wildlife refuges nationwide. Amendments to the act in 1958 authorized the purchase of waterfowl production areas as well as migratory waterfowl refuges, and set the stage for the purchase of wetlands in the Rainwater Basin.

In 1963, the U.S. Fish and Wildlife Service began acquiring waterfowl production areas in the Rainwater Basin on a willing-seller basis. Massie Waterfowl Production Area (WPA) in Clay County was the first area purchased. Today, the American public owns, and the U.S. Fish and Wildlife Service manages, 61 WPAs in the Rainwater Basin, ranging from 38 to 1,989 acres

and totaling 23,821 acres.

The Nebraska Game and Parks Commission acquired its first wetland in the Rainwater Basin in 1940. Only after the Nebraska Legislature passed a bill creating the Nebraska Habitat Program in 1976 were funds available to accelerate land purchases. One priority of the program has been to preserve wetlands in the Rainwater Basin. In dry years, Nebraska Habitat Stamp funds are used to pump water into enough state- and federally owned basins to accommodate migrating waterfowl. Habitat program funds are also available through natural resources districts to landowners who set aside and preserve wetlands. By the mid-1960s, the Commission owned and managed 29 areas in the Rainwater Basin totalling about 6,800 acres, of which about 3,800 acres were wetlands and 2,800 acres were associated uplands.

The northern boundary of the Rainwater Basin region parallels the Big Bend stretch of the central Platte River. During the early weeks of spring migration, waterfowl move freely between the Platte and Rainwater Basin marshes. Some biologists consider the Platte a "release valve" for migrating waterbirds to use when the shallow basins are dry or ice-covered. The Platte River and the Rainwater Basin marshes are

*The number of **snow geese** staging on Rainwater Basin wetlands during spring migration has increased dramatically since the 1970s. Nearly five million snow geese are estimated to pause in these wetlands each spring in recent years.*

complementary and inseparable components to one of the most important wetland complexes on the continent. Waterfowl biologists believe no other midway stopover between wintering grounds and nesting grounds can replace the combination of wetlands and grain fields found in south-central Nebraska.

Commission wetlands biologist Ted LaGrange enumerated the importance of Rainwater Basin wetlands to birds in *Guide to Nebraska's Wetlands and Their Conservation Needs*: "They host seven to 14 million spring-migrating ducks and geese annually, providing the nutrient reserves necessary for migration and reproduction farther to the north. Approximately 90 percent of the mid-continent population of about 750,000 greater white-fronted geese passes through the region during spring migration with as many as 200,000 present at one time. Fifty percent of the mid-continent population of mallards and 30 percent of the continent population of northern pintails use the Basins during spring migration. Recent surveys have identified that a minimum of 200,000 to 300,000 shorebirds represented by over 30 different species migrate through the basins during the spring. In some years the Basins also produce substantial numbers of ducks. About 250 species of birds have been recorded in the Rainwater Basin. The USFWS lists 96 species as having nested on WPAs in the region. Rainwater Basin wetlands are used by the federally endangered whooping crane, piping plover, and the threatened bald eagle. Forty-two percent of confirmed whooping crane observations in Nebraska have been at Rainwater Basin wetlands."

As snow goose breeding grounds expanded westward in the Arctic in recent years, the number of geese pausing in the Rainwater Basin during spring migration has dramatically increased, from about 15,000 in 1974 to 353,000 in 1985, and to nearly to five million today.

The large concentrations of snow geese using the basins during spring migration have probably contributed to die-offs. In a two-week period in March 1975, wildlife workers picked up more than 13,000 ducks and geese that died of avian cholera in the Rainwater Basin, the first major outbreak in the state. Two to three times that many are thought to have died. From 1975 through the 1994 spring migration season, an estimated 200,000 to 237,000 ducks and geese died from avian cholera in the Rainwater Basin. There has not been a major outbreak since 1998, but the bacterium causing avian cholera is believed to be present in some birds using the wetlands every spring. New outbreaks could easily occur in the overcrowded basins if prolonged periods of severe weather holds birds in the area. Even without disease, overcrowding is a concern. A snow goose can consume as much as a pound of corn per day. The millions of snow geese compete with other goose species and ducks for both limited water and for the waste corn in fields.

Early migrants – Canada geese, snow geese, white-fronted geese, mallards, green-winged teal and pintails – begin arriving in mid- to late-February and early-March depending on the retreat of winter. Migrating birds pass through the Rainwater Basin wetlands through May. Some pause briefly, others remain for several weeks. For migrating waterfowl it is not just a stopover of convenience. Ahead of them is an exhausting flight of thousands of miles to their nesting grounds. The fat reserves ducks and geese put on during their Rainwater Basin layover are often the thin margin between successful nesting and failure, and influence the size and vigor of their clutches and broods.

When there were more wetlands that held water later into the summer, and when grasslands surrounded them, large numbers of waterbirds nested in the Rainwater Basin. Studies from the mid-1980s estimated only about 10,000 ducks are raised to flight stage annually in the region, principally on state and federal wetlands. The most common breeding species are blue-winged teal, mallards and gadwall. When the marshes were pools of clear water in a sea of grass, northern harriers, black-crowned night herons, pied-billed and eared grebes, American and least bitterns, black terns and several species of shorebirds also regularly nested in Rainwater Basin marshes. Today, their nests are fewer, but they can be found during wet years when marshes provide adequate habitat. Today, south-central Nebraska wetlands contribute to the North American waterbird populations by sending breeding birds to northern nesting grounds in good physical condition.

A variety of wading birds and shorebirds are found in the Rainwater Basin, especially during spring migration. Before 1900, sandhill cranes were documented nesting in the Sandhills lake country to the north, but there are no early-day nesting records in the Rainwater Basin. Through the 1990s there were occasional reports of sandhill cranes in the region during nesting season. A pair with two juveniles was reported in 1994, and adults with young again were reported in 1995, 1998, 1999 and 2003. Outside of the central Platte River Valley, the Rainwater Basin is the most likely location to observe migrating whooping cranes. Great egrets have become common late-summer visitors to the Rainwater Basin. Also increasingly common are cattle egrets and white-faced ibis.

Second only to the spectacular gatherings of migrating waterfowl is the shorebird migration. Most shorebirds pass through during the last two weeks of April and the first two weeks of May. When water is present in the basins from late-July through September, fall migrants can be found. Joel Jorgensen has intensively studied shorebirds in the Rainwater Basin for the past 10 years. His records are detailed, but for birders new to the region they can be generalized as follows: Relatively common spring migrants are black-bellied plover, American golden-plover, semipalmated plover, greater and lesser yellowlegs, willet, upland sandpiper,

Ross's Goose

Ross's geese, considered rare throughout North America in the early-1900s, have increased in abundance in recent years and are more common during spring migration in Nebraska. About six to seven percent of the "white geese" passing through the state are Ross's. Until recent decades, Ross's geese were principally a Pacific Flyway species and most commonly seen in the Nebraska in the Panhandle during spring migration, and even then rarely. In the early-1950s, it was estimated only 2,000 to 3,000 remained in the wild.

Ross's geese traditionally nested in the central Canadian Arctic. During the past 20 years, the nesting grounds of Ross's geese have shifted southeasterly. Historically, their principal wintering grounds were in the Central Valley of California. Ever increasing numbers winter in Arkansas, Louisiana, New Mexico, Texas and northern Mexico, which, along with more easterly nesting grounds, explain their more common appearance in Nebraska. Ross's geese are often found in the company of snow geese, as the two species share colonies. Ross's geese have increased dramatically in recent years for all the same reasons that snow geese have multiplied.

Size is the first clue to distinguishing the Ross's goose from the white-phase snow goose. A mature Ross's goose weighs less than three pounds and has a wingspan of about 45 inches. A mature snow goose weighs over five pounds with a wingspan of about 53 inches. The Ross's goose has a relatively short neck, giving it a more abbreviated silhouette. Ross's geese are less vocal than snows and their squealing keek-keek call is higher pitched and more rapid. An adult, snow goose is likely to have a stained head and neck. Seen from the ground, the head of a Ross's goose is more rounded and the bill relatively shorter, more stubby and lacking the black "grin patch" between the upper and lower mandibles. Vascular, warty protuberances or caruncles are often visible at the base of the bills of mature males. The protuberances become more pronounced with age and are believed to be a symbol of maturity and status, limiting competition with other males for females during the breeding season.

Ross's goose

Snow goose

JON FARRAR

Least bitterns *are seldom-seen wading birds, which frequent dense stands of marsh vegetation. They nest in loose colonies and have been reported breeding in Rainwater Basin wetlands. They are most conspicuous in late-June when feeding young.*

Hudsonian godwit, dunlin, short-billed and long-billed dowitcher, Wilson's snipe, Wilson's phalarope and semipalmated, least, white-rumped, Baird's, stilt and buff-breasted sandpipers. Less common spring migrants are American avocet, solitary sandpiper, marbled godwit and pectoral sandpiper. Relatively common late-summer migrants are greater and lesser yellowlegs, long-billed dowitcher, Wilson's snipe and solitary, upland, least, semipalmated, pectoral and stilt sandpipers. Less common late-summer migrants are black-bellied plover, American golden-plover, semipalmated plover, American avocet, willet, short-billed dowitcher, Wilson's phalarope and Baird's and buff-breasted sandpipers. Rare migrants are the snowy plover, whimbrel and ruff.

The Rainwater Basin region is an important spring migration stop for buff-breasted sandpipers. Their migration corridor is through mid-continent. The world population of buff-breasted sandpipers is estimated to be only about 15,000. So it is possible that on the right day at the right location, an observer might see a significant percentage of the species. Look for them in mid-May feeding on invertebrates in recently plowed or disked fields, often in the company of American golden-plovers. They use wetlands for drinking and bathing in late afternoon.

There are other species that should be on a birder's watch-list in the Rainwater Basin. Look for the

occasional cinnamon teal during spring migration, especially in the western basins. Peregrine falcons often follow the shorebird migration because they are a preferred prey species, and bald eagles follow the waterfowl migration. There have been several reports of avocets nesting in the region in recent years. In March, do not miss the ever-present courtship flights of pintails. Great-tailed grackles were first reported in Nebraska in the Rainwater Basin in 1976 and they are more common there today than elsewhere in the state.

To locate wildlife management areas and waterfowl production areas in the Rainwater Basin, obtain a current copy of the *Nebraska Hunt Guide and Public Hunting Lands* from any Commission office or at most permit vendors; or a copy of *Visitors Guide to the Federal Waterfowl Production Areas and State Wildlife Management Areas* from the Rainwater Basin Wetland Management District, P.O. Box 1686, Kearney, NE 68848, (308) 236-5015, rainwater@fws.gov. A county map or an atlas showing county roads, or the visitors guide is essential to locating WPAs and WMAs in the Rainwater Basin.

Nowhere in Nebraska are there so many quality, public-access, bird-viewing areas as in the Rainwater Basin, not just for waterbirds but also for upland species. While every wetland is unique, those in the Rainwater Basin are remarkably similar, varying principally in size and depth – the factors that dictate the composition and extent of open water and aquatic vegetation. As needed, water is pumped into some of the larger state and federal wetlands before spring and fall migrations. They are reliable birding destinations, but ignoring small wetlands might mean missing some species. Nebraska birders have devoted more hours observing some wetlands than others in recent years. That is usually a good indication that they find the variety or species they seek there. Some of those wetlands are listed below with notes of specialty species seen in recent years.

Knee-high or hip boots are often needed to approach open water closely enough for a good view. A canoe is an excellent way to observe birds, especially the secretive species that dwell in emergent vegetation. And a word of caution – the silty-clay, gumbo soils of the Rainwater Basin make ungraveled county roads and access roads to some of the basins virtually impassable when wet. In March, many roads are frozen in early morning but a quagmire by noon.

Sacramento WMA

The first tract of land for Sacramento Wildlife Management Area was acquired by the Commission in 1948, making it the oldest public wetland site in the Rainwater Basin. The timing was fortuitous, preceding the 1950s when intensive agriculture led to the destruction of many wetlands in the region. Beginning in the late-1950s, a network of dikes was constructed on the area to impound water for migrating waterfowl.

During the same period, the first of miles of shelterbelts were planted to provide year-round habitat for resident wildlife. Intensively managed for all species of wildlife, the area has extensive native and exotic grasslands, food plots and weedy areas. Irrigation wells are used to fill wetlands when needed before migration.

Better known to locals as the Sacramento Game Farm, the area has a long history of raising game birds for stocking, including chukar partridges, crested tinamous, wood ducks and pheasants. For 27 years, from 1970 through 1997, the Sacramento area was the home of a large captive flock of the giant race of Canada geese. More than 10,000 juvenile birds raised there were used to stock and reestablish the race throughout the state.

Today, Sacramento WMA is composed of four unconnected but closely located tracts totaling 3,023 acres. The largest is the original purchase, where maps and public-use information are available at a headquarters building. On the main area, birders will find a sampling of all habitats except riverine – small, deep-water ponds, expansive smartweed marshes, shelterbelts and woodland groves, native and nonnative grasslands and cropland planted for wildlife food plots. The state's first ruff was recorded at Sacramento in mid-April 1994. Interior roads provide access to much of the area.

• Additional Information: Sacramento WMA is 2¼ miles west of Wilcox in Phelps County. Follow county road signs to the headquarters building and principal access.

Funk WPA

Funk Waterfowl Production Area is one of the largest public wetlands in the western Rainwater Basin, and one of the most popular with birders because it is near the Platte River and sandhill crane viewing during March. During the first half of the 1900s, neighboring farmers and people from nearby towns came to Funk to ice skate, swim, boat and hunt waterfowl. By the 1960s most of the basin was farmed. During the 1970s, seepage from the Tri-County canal system transporting water from the Platte River to south-central Nebraska for irrigation began to raise the water table. Low-lying land in the seepage shadow of the canal became too wet to farm. A plan to ditch and drain the basin in the early-1980s was never pursued because "swampbuster provisions" in the 1985 federal farm bill made landowners who drained wetlands ineligible for many federal farm programs.

In 1985 and 1986, the U.S. Fish and Wildlife Service purchased the heart of the basin and it became a waterfowl production area. In the early-1990s, dikes and water-control structures were installed to better control water levels and provide the shallow-water habitat that produces waterfowl foods. Former farmland surrounding the basin has been reseeded to native warm-season grasses. Today, Funk WPA encompasses 1,989 acres, of which 1,163 are wetlands.

Birders have reported more than 250 species from Funk WPA. The area attracts large numbers of ducks and geese during spring migration, especially during dry years when other basins hold little or no water. Large numbers of greater white-fronted geese rest and

*Shallow wetlands in the Rainwater Basin are critically important rest stops for migrating **whooping cranes**.*

Great-tailed Grackle

In 1900, the northern limits of the great-tailed grackle barely extended north into Texas. By the end of the century it was reported nesting in at least 14 states and occurring in 21 states and three Canadian provinces. The species rapidly expanded northward from Texas during the 1960s in response to habitat created by increased irrigation and urban development.

The great-tailed grackle was separated from the boat-tailed grackle as a distinct species in the late-1950s. The species prefers to nest in scattered trees near standing water, but also does well in tall, emergent wetland vegetation such as cattails. Great-tailed grackles adapted quickly to urban life and are often found foraging in parks, garbage dumps, lawns and golf courses.

Great-tailed grackles were first reported in Nebraska at the Sacramento WMA in Phelps County in 1976, but they were not confirmed to be nesting. In the spring of 1977, they were reported nesting at two sites – southeast of Hastings and west of Omaha. By 1981 they were reported in Platte and Lancaster counties and in 1990, a flock of 150 was reported in Lancaster County. While the Rainwater Basin remained the core of the species's breeding grounds in Nebraska, they expanded across the state during the 1990s, and by the spring of 1998 were documented nesting at Kiowa WMA in Scotts Bluff County.

Today, breeding great-tailed grackles are most common in the Rainwater Basin and the central Platte River Valley, but it is no longer surprising to encounter them in marsh habitat anywhere in the state.

A male great-tailed grackle displays for nearby females.

roost at this WPA.

Because of its reliable water level, size, and popularity with birders, a number of interesting bird reports have come from Funk in recent years. The first curlew sandpiper documented in the state was at Funk. There are records of snowy plovers, white-faced ibis, piping plover, dunlins, ruddy turnstones, black-necked stilts and red phalaropes in addition to expected, yet uncommon shorebirds like the marbled godwit. Black-necked stilts nested at Funk in the summer of 2003. Yellow-crowned night-herons have been seen at Funk and postbreeding great egrets are visitors in late summer. Yellow-headed blackbirds, great-tailed grackles, least bitterns and Virginia rails are documented

breeding species on Funk WPA, and a breeding population of swamp sparrows resides on the wetland.

About 20 species of ducks are reported, including an occasional cinnamon teal. Bald eagles are frequently seen in late-February and March and whooping cranes have been sighted at Funk in both April and October.

• Additional Information: Funk WPA is 1 mile east and 3 miles north of Funk in Phelps County. The area has a wheelchair-accessible viewing blind.

Harvard Marsh WPA

Clay County has more public-access WMAs and WPAs than any other Rainwater Basin county. One of the largest, covering more than two sections of land, is Harvard Marsh Waterfowl Production Area. The area's 1,484 acres are about equally divided between uplands and wetlands. The marsh is at the center of a large basin, which is deep and semipermanent. Small and shallow isolated wetlands and bays to the marsh's south offer excellent shorebird viewing when water levels fall, exposing mudflats. This WPA contains tracts of unplowed, native prairie.

During the peak of migration, Harvard holds hundreds of thousands of ducks and geese – as many as a million geese on a single day. Watch for the diminutive Ross's geese among the snows. When late-migrating puddle ducks arrive in mid-March, look for cinnamon teal among the bluewings. American avocets have been documented nesting at Harvard. In 1999, the first documented nesting of sandhill cranes in Nebraska since the late-1800s was made at Harvard. That year a pair of cranes with one chick was also observed at Kissinger Basin WMA.

Birders also find ibis at Harvard. In the summer of 2001, 25 white-faced ibis nests were confirmed at Kissinger Basin WMA, but the nests were abandoned when water levels dropped. Subsequently, 78 birds, probably from the failed nesting attempt at Kissinger, were reported at Harvard WPA. In the same year, two glossy ibis were seen on Harvard, the second Nebraska record for the species. During the breeding season watch for least and American bitterns, northern harriers, grassland sparrows and common yellowthroats. In winter look for short-eared owls.

• Additional Information: Access to the eastern end of Harvard WPA is 2 miles west and ½ mile north of the town of Harvard. To reach the main parking area from the town of Harvard, drive south 1 mile, west 4 miles, and north 1 mile. There is an information kiosk at this location. Access to the southern side of the marsh is via a trail road. Ungraveled roads should be avoided when muddy.

Massie WPA

Massie Waterfowl Production Area is another large wetland basin in Clay County, and, like Harvard, one of the most reliable for water and bird viewing in the early spring. Massie is one of several WPAs and WMAs in the region where water is usually pumped

*More than 30 shorebird species use Rainwater Basin wetlands during spring and fall migrations. The **stilt sandpiper** is one of them.*

good at Massie as in some other basins. It is an excellent spot to see shoreline, edge and grassland species. Watch for migrating sparrows in brushy areas.

● Additional Information: Massie WPA is 3 miles south of Clay Center, east of Nebraska Highway 14.

● Nearby Birding Destinations: Any Rainwater Basin marsh, large or small, can provide outstanding birdwatching opportunities on the right day. In addition to the wetlands previously described, the following sites, listed by county, are favorites of biologists and birders with experience in the Rainwater Basin.

Hamilton County: **Deep Well WMA,** 238 acres, 1½ miles north, 2 miles east of I-80 Exit 318. **Pintail WMA,** 478 acres, 2½ miles south, 2 miles east of Aurora I-80 exit.

Clay County: **Kissinger Basin WMA,** 490 acres, immediately north of Fairfield. **Hultine WPA,** 1,000 acres, 5 miles west of Sutton, 2 miles north of U.S. Highway 6. **Green Wing WMA,** 80 acres, 5 miles west, and 1½ miles north of Shickley. **White-front WMA,** 280 acres, 2 miles west and 1½ miles north of Clay Center. **Bulrush WMA,** 240 acres, 1 mile east, and 3 miles south of Fairfield.

Fillmore County: **Sandpiper WMA,** 160 acres, 5 miles west, and 1½ miles south of Geneva. **Mallard Haven WPA,** 1,087 acres, 2 miles north of Shickley. **Redhead WPA,** 160 acres, 5 miles west, and ½ mile north of Shickley.

Thayer County: **Father Hupp WMA,** 160 acres, 2 miles west of Bruning.

Seward County: **Straight Water WMA,** 240 acres, 2½ miles north, and 1 mile west of Goehner. ■

from wells in dry years to ensure migration habitat. There are 494 wetland acres and 359 upland acres.

Massie is a large, elliptical basin that once occupied almost two sections of land. Before acquisition as a WPA, the area was cut into four quarters by county roads. There is access from all directions but the eastern and western roads are not developed. A rock road on the south leads to a parking area, information kiosk and an elevated viewing tower, which provides an inspiring view of masses of ducks and geese leaving the area before sunrise to feed in the fields. Typically, geese and puddle ducks return in mid-morning to loaf, and there is a second feeding period at the end of the day. The elevated blind also puts birdwatchers at eye level with pintail courtship flights that are constant over the marsh during March.

Massie has not been as extensively observed as some other Rainwater Basin wetlands. Because it has been heavily colonized with emergent vegetation, Massie lacks large pools and thus is not as attractive to a variety of waterbirds as some other basins are. Disking, burning and haying are being used as management tools to create more open water and reduce late-succession plant species such as cattails. Emergent plants still dominate the marsh by early summer. The best bird viewing opportunity at Massie is during the spring migration. Expect to find all species of geese and puddle ducks. Smartweed shallows in the southwestern corner are usually good for white-fronted geese and pintails. While diving ducks are found on larger Rainwater Basin marshes, they are greatly outnumbered by puddle duck species. Shorebird viewing is probably not as

Rainwater Basin Bird Sampler

Greater White-fronted Goose	Greater Yellowlegs
Snow Goose	Lesser Yellowlegs
Ross's Goose	Willet
Canada Goose	Upland Sandpiper
American Wigeon	Marbled Godwit
Blue-winged Teal	Semipalmated Sandpiper
Northern Shoveler	Least Sandpiper
Northern Pintail	White-rumped Sandpiper
Green-winged Teal	Baird's Sandpiper
Pied-billed Grebe	Pectoral Sandpiper
Least Bittern	Dunlin
Great Egret	Stilt Sandpiper
Cattle Egret	Buff-breasted Sandpiper
Black-crowned Night-Heron	Long-billed Dowitcher
White-faced Ibis	Wilson's Snipe
Bald Eagle	Wilson's Phalarope
Northern Harrier	Short-eared Owl
Peregrine Falcon	Sedge Wren
Sora	Marsh Wren
Whooping Crane	American Pipit
Black-bellied Plover	Song Sparrow
American Golden-Plover	Swamp Sparrow
Semipalmated Plover	Lapland Longspur
	Yellow-headed Blackbird
	Great-tailed Grackle

Central Platte River Valley

IN THE PREFACE TO *CRANE MUSIC*, published in 1991, Nebraska ornithologist Paul Johnsgard wrote of his first view of sandhill cranes on the Platte River in 1962: "On a magical Saturday in March, I drove with a graduate student out to the central Platte Valley west of Grand Island, as much to see the spring waterfowl migration as to see sandhill cranes. At that time the cranes had received very little publicity as a birding spectacle, but I felt that I should investigate them nonetheless. It was perhaps just as well that I wasn't emotionally prepared for the sight of countless cranes punctuating the sky from horizon to horizon, or gracefully wheeling about overhead as if they were caught in some ultraslow-motion whirlwind, their vibrato calls drifting downward like the music of an angelic avian chorus. Not since the days of my boyhood, when I first saw vast migrating spring flocks of snow geese and Canada geese dropping into eastern North Dakota's prairie marshes, was I so completely enthralled, and it was certainly on that particular day of epiphany that I realized that cranes would become as important to my well-being as my beloved waterfowl."

The Platte River is Nebraska's most prominent topographical feature and sandhill cranes now rival the prairie schooner as the Platte's symbol. Born from the merged North Platte and South Platte rivers, which rise from snowmelt in the Rocky Mountains, the Platte River proper drains more than half of the state before emptying into the Missouri River. Writer Washington Irving, a Great Plains traveler in the 1830s, described the Platte as "the most beautiful and useless of rivers," useless in Irving's mind because it was too shallow to float a boat of commerce.

Lieutenant James Henry Carleton, in 1884, described the Platte riverbed near Columbus as "but one wide expanse of quicksand, which is formed in bars, and these are continually changing and driving about." Historical accounts suggest the Platte's many channels, taken as a whole, ranged from three-quarters of a mile to three miles wide, while its valley was as much as 15 miles wide. Once the Platte was the textbook example of a braided river, its channels shifting at will across a broad floodplain. The amount of water the Platte carried from year to year was erratic, characterized by high spring flows and relatively low summer flows. Periodically, stretches of the Platte, above the mouth of the Loup were dry or nearly so during drought years.

Above the Big Bend area, from Overton to Grand Island, the river was essentially treeless. Most sandbars had no vegetation; others had a temporary growth of annual plants or willows thriving until the next ice breakup or high spring flow washed them away. Downstream from Grand Island, the Platte was sparsely wooded where trees were protected from wildfires. Carleton described the Platte near Columbus as "filled with beautiful islands. They are all well wooded, but only here and there is there any timber growing upon the main banks."

A century and a half ago, the Platte River Valley was a westward highway for pioneers. Today, Interstate 80, paralleling the river, is still an important travel corridor. Just as overland trails, railroads and highways faithfully traced the Platte's course, so do Nebraska's population centers. And, some of the state's richest agricultural land is in its valley.

The first recorded diversion of water from the Platte River's main stem was in 1856 near Wood River. Early irrigation efforts were no more than small ditches taking water directly from the river to irrigate floodplain fields. Later, larger canals carried water downstream to crops on benches above the valley floor. By the early-1870s, homesteaders occupied much of the land in the Big Bend area of the Platte. By the 1880s the volume of water approved for summer irrigation diversion in the South Platte River exceeded the total river flows available at times. Most years, valley land close to the river was too wet to farm, and ditches were dug to drain it. To supplement fickle summer rains in

MICHAEL FORSBERG

Canada geese winter on the central Platte River where open water is available. Migrants swell their numbers beginning in late-February and early-March.

*Once the classic textbook example of a braided stream, the **Platte River** had many channels weaving around islands and sandbars, providing roosting sites for waterfowl and wading birds, and nesting and feeding grounds for shorebirds.*

fields farther from the river, canals were dug to carry river water to crops otherwise not suited to central and western Nebraska. The first significant diversion of the main-stem Platte River was the Kearney canal, completed in 1882. As agriculture expanded in the Platte River Valley and its principal tributaries, summer river flows became increasingly unreliable and inadequate. As a solution, the Pathfinder Dam was built in 1909 on the North Platte River southwest of Casper, Wyoming, to capture high flows from mountain snowmelt for release during the summer irrigation season. Since then, seven additional dams

have been built on the North Platte River and the Laramie River, the North Platte's principal Wyoming tributary. Construction of Nebraska's largest irrigation project – Kingsley Dam on the North Platte River north of Ogallala, impounding Lake McConaughy – was completed in 1941. By the 1980s, more than 250 water diversion and storage projects existed on the Platte River system. Deprived of historical flows, the Platte River, especially between North Platte and Overton, is but a shadow of its former self.

Extensive diversion and storage of water has significantly altered the physical character of the

*At least 70 percent of the world's **lesser sandhill crane** population, an estimated 500,000 birds, pauses on the Platte River each spring during the birds' migration northward to nest. It is the largest gathering of any crane species anywhere in the world.*

Platte. At Overton, the lower end of the stretch most depleted by upstream withdrawals, the channel was a mile wide before development. By 1965 the channel width had been reduced to 1,108 feet. In a two-mile segment near Odessa the channel has been reduced 87 percent. On average, nearly 70 percent of the water-carrying channel area has been lost in the Big Bend stretch. In addition to the loss of river channel, most Platte Valley grasslands and wetlands have been converted to agricultural uses. In the Big Bend segment of the Platte, 72 percent of the lowland grasslands and wet meadows adjacent to the river channel have been destroyed. Those that remain are small, dispersed, highly degraded tracts. Approximately 90 percent of the wetland acres once associated with the central Platte have been destroyed.

Since high spring flows were impounded by upstream reservoirs, trees and other woody plants have colonized islands, sandbars and channels. In the 60 years since Kingsley Dam was closed, the process has accelerated. Today, the Platte, from the confluence of the North and South Platte rivers to near Kearney, is a meandering band of forest, not the broad and braided prairie river it once was. This transformation has benefited some wildlife species. Woodland animals, such as white-tailed deer, wild turkey, raccoons and cardinals, have prospered. Cranes, waterfowl, shorebirds, and the full complement of grassland animals have been the losers. Still, what remains of the Platte Valley ecosystem is critically important.

Sixty percent of the bird species reported in Nebraska have been reported along the Platte River system. At least 121 of approximately 200 species of birds reported to breed in the state nest in the Platte Valley. The Platte Valley from Lexington to Shelton is one of nine areas in the United States designated as critical habitat for migrating whooping cranes by the

U.S. Fish and Wildlife Service, and the only one of the nine areas not protected as a federal refuge. As early as 1930 an effort was made to establish a federal refuge on the central Platte, but refuges are not easily carved out of valuable agricultural land. The central Platte River is one of the whooping crane's principal stopover sites on its 2,400-mile migration. Approximately 80 percent of all pre-1980 reports of whooping cranes in Nebraska were along or near the Platte between Lexington and Grand Island. Of 15 crane species in the world, 11 are either threatened or endangered.

At least 70 percent of the world's lesser sandhill crane population pauses during migration in the Platte Valley each spring – the largest gathering of any crane species in the world. All three of the migratory subspecies of sandhill cranes can be seen during spring migration. The most numerous are lesser sandhill cranes. Canadian sandhills account for about 15 percent of the cranes on the Platte and greater sandhill cranes about five percent. Although influenced by weather conditions, the first sandhill cranes usually reach the Platte in mid-February. Crane numbers peak in mid-March and the majestic birds are usually gone by the second week in April. Crane viewing and photography at roosts might be better later in the stopover period because the birds have put on the body fat they need, and they linger later on the river in the morning and return earlier in the evening. Whooping cranes might appear as early as late-March, but their numbers usually peak during the first half of April.

A century ago, the entire lengths of the North Platte and Platte rivers in Nebraska provided roosting and feeding habitat for cranes. During the 20th century, the stretches of river meeting the requirements of both sandhill and whooping cranes – broad, treeless channels with shallow water and vegetation-free sandbars bordering on wetlands and meadows for feeding – have become increasingly shorter and more isolated. In the 1940s and 1950s, before the full effect of storage and diversion of water at Lake McConaughy became evident, sandhill cranes were distributed from Cozad to Grand Island. Today, most sandhill cranes are found between Kearney and Grand Island and between North Platte and Sutherland. In 1980, for example, of an estimated 541,000 sandhill cranes on the Platte, nearly 400,000 were concentrated in that 45-mile stretch where the central Platte most resembles its predevelopment character.

While cranes have stolen the spotlight on the central Platte, it is important to other bird life, too. Bald eagles are common winter residents in the Platte Valley. In recent years, bald eagles have probably benefited from the increasing number of large trees for roost sites, open water found in winter below power generation plants, and extensive miles of shorelines around reservoirs well supplied with fish and waterfowl. Wintering bald eagles peak in abundance on the central Platte from late-February through mid-March.

Before settlement, most of the Platte River system in Nebraska probably provided suitable nesting habitat for least terns and piping plovers. During the past 50 years, however, sandbars free of perennial vegetation have become increasingly rare or absent on the Platte between North Platte and Columbus. Today, in the central Platte River Valley, terns and plovers nest primarily on sand and gravel pits next to the river, and on isolated river sandbars between Overton and Grand Island. Conservation groups now mechanically clear sandbars of vegetation at considerable cost, re-creating on a small scale the habitat that high spring flows once created and maintained. Piping plovers return to the central Platte in mid- to late-April and least terns from mid- to late-May. The U.S. Highway 34 bridge southeast of Grand Island has been a reliable post-breeding site. Look for plovers there in mid-July.

Cranes, terns, plovers and eagles are the Platte's showpiece avian species – the birds attracting attention because they are large, gather in spectacular numbers

Colloquial Bird Names

Language works when everyone agrees to use the same words to mean the same thing. But humans are an imaginative and sometimes perverse lot, applying their own descriptive names to things. Birds are an excellent example. Few of us memorizes the latest American Ornithologists' Union checklist of names for North American birds. And, there are times when colloquial names just make more sense than accepted names.

While DNA evidence is difficult to argue with, marsh hawk still seems like a more accurate description of Circus cyaneus *than does northern harrier, and butcher bird seems an apt name for the loggerhead shrike. Calling the common nighthawk a bullbat requires a bit more thought, linking the ideas of a bird that flies like a bat and a bird that sounds like a bellowing bull during territorial displays.*

No group has hung so many appellations on so few birds as have wildfowl hunters. Their colloquial names usually describe a bird's appearance, behavior or desirability as table fare. In the days when shorebirds were hunted, yellowlegs were often called tell-tales for their alertness and habit of warning less suspecting shorebirds of the approach of danger. American coots were also called blue Peters, a rather obscure reference to the similarity in appearance of the coot's white patch of feathers on the underside of the tail to a blue signal flag with a white square in the center that merchant vessels once raised when setting sail. Shitepoke once was a common colloquial name for any heron or bittern species, but especially for the American bittern – perhaps a reference, fortunately in German, to the bird's value in the kitchen or habit of evacuating before flushing.

Perhaps no species of waterfowl garnered more local names than the ruddy duck, known through the years as butterball, bull-necked teal, booby, greaser, sleepy broadbill, sleepy coot, food duck, stiff-tail, turkey tail, spine-tail, stick-tail diver and bristle-tail. Other waterfowl species have aptly descriptive common names – specklebelly and laughing goose for the greater white-fronted goose, wavie

A drake ruddy duck performs its courtship bubble display for a hen.

JON FARRAR

for the snow goose because of its flight habit, warty-nosed wavie for the little Ross's goose, and sprig-tail or spike-tail for the northern pintail. Spoonbill or spoonie seems an appropriate name for the northern shoveler.

Both wood ducks and blue-winged teal were commonly called summer duck because they nested at lower latitudes than most other duck species. The American wigeon and gadwall were often lumped together as gray ducks in the field and in the meat market because neither species bore strikingly marked plumages. Butterball is a name most often assigned to the bufflehead in times past because they are extraordinarily fat ducks. Sawbill once was a commonly used name for any merganser because of their serrated mandibles. Blackjack was a common name for the ring-necked duck, but also was applied to the lesser scaup by those who could not tell them apart.

Today, just as television has homogenized American culture and language, the American Ornithologists' Union is standardizing the world of bird names, sprinkling a hyphen here and there, creating species, subsequently demoting them to subspecies and then making them species again. Through it all, though, a Bullock's oriole is still a Bullock's oriole in the minds of most, and for some the upland sandpiper will forever be a plover.

MARK DIETZ

Resembling diminutive meadowlarks, **dickcissels** *are common migrants and nesters, preferring disturbed grasslands.*

breast of the distant bluffs, stood like banks of snow upon the yellow of the rolling plain, or like flotillas of foam floated down the broad current of the river. The clanging cackle of the speckled-fronts was as common as the constant twittering of restless blackbirds. But that was in the fabled days of old, when it made little difference where you lingered along those historic shores, geese were to be seen in such quantities as surpasses the credulity of the sportsman of today."

While Griswold would be saddened by the Platte today, few modern birders are disappointed when they see some of the 500,000 sandhill cranes and 10 million ducks and geese still drawn to this prairie river and wetlands to the south. Four federally threatened or endangered species – the bald eagle, whooping crane, piping plover and least tern – can be found on the central Platte at the right times and places, and the chance of sighting a fifth listed species – the Eskimo curlew – remains the hope of birders.

But the central Platte is not just about seeing spectacular birds, it is about the variety of species. For more information on when and where to find other species and a checklist, consult Gary Lingle's *Birding Crane River: Nebraska's Platte*, the most thorough guide to finding birds on the central Platte and the Rainwater Basin. Lingle notes that cranes and waterfowl compose less than 10 percent of the 300-plus species reported in the central Platte River Valley. Over half of those 300 species are Neotropical migrants. Lingle lists 115 breeding species. It is along the central Platte, too, where eastern and western passerine species and subspecies merge and hybridize – rose-breasted and black-headed grosbeaks, indigo and lazuli buntings, yellow-shafted and red-shafted flickers and Baltimore and Bullock's orioles. Lingle's book is filled with detailed information on when and where to find specific species, and it is a valuable traveling companion for any birder, experienced or novice, going to the central Platte.

during migration or are threatened with extinction. But, the central Platte and the wetlands of the Rainwater Basin to its south form an important habitat complex for migrating waterbirds of many species. When the basins are frozen, ducks and geese shift to the Platte's open water. Unlike the Rainwater Basin, where outbreaks of avian cholera since 1975 have killed hundreds of thousands of waterfowl, the Platte has not had serious cholera outbreaks because the infectious bacterium does not flourish in flowing water.

As spectacular as the waterbird migration on the central Platte is today, it pales in comparison to what once was. The best descriptions of that abundance come not from ornithologists but from sportsmen of the period. Sandy Griswold, sporting editor for the *Omaha World-Herald*, frequently recalled his first hunt on the central Platte in 1892. Descriptions from a column published on February 23, 1902, re-created a haunting visual image of his beloved Platte. "Before the prairies on either shore became so numerously dotted with pretentious farm houses it was the favorite early spring resort of countless millions of these royal birds," he wrote of the geese that once gathered on the Platte River near Chapman. "The bars in the broad stream's bed, both up and down, was literally packed with Canadas and Hutchins geese, while the stretching prairie and distant hillsides were dotted with countless others of the white variety. Long after the big gray birds had left the bars, the 'white brant,' as the snow geese were commonly called, were always in view. Like lines of silvery cloud they streamed along the

Rowe Sanctuary

While a national wildlife refuge was never established on the central Platte River as had been proposed in the 1930s and again in the 1970s, private conservation organizations have stepped in to preserve and manage this critical wildlife resource. The Lillian Annette Rowe Sanctuary, commonly called the Rowe Sanctuary, was established in 1974 by the National Audubon Society with a purchase of 782 acres in the Platte River Valley southwest of Gibbon. Rowe Sanctuary is at the heart of sandhill crane concentrations on the central Platte. Additional land acquisitions have increased the sanctuary to 1,248 acres, including 2.5 miles of river channel and wet meadows. Although west of the tallgrass prairie region, a fine example of tallgrass prairie vegetation can be found on the floodplain at Rowe. It is an excellent site for bobolinks and other native grassland species. Also watch for regal fritillary butterflies. Deciduous woodlands bordering the river provide a third type of habitat for birds and birders.

The recently opened Iain Nicolson Audubon Center,

constructed with native red cedar posts and straw bales, offers a commanding view of the Platte River and sandhill cranes during spring migration. Rowe has four observation blinds and three photography blinds overlooking sandhill crane roosts on the river. There is a charge to use the blinds and children under the age of eight are discouraged because tours last two to three hours and the blinds are unheated. Reservations are on a first-come, first-served basis and may be made beginning January 2 of each year. Group sizes are limited to provide a quality experience. Guided bird viewing and educational opportunities for school and other groups are also available. Coinciding with the sandhill crane migration in the third week of March is the annual Rivers and Wildlife Celebration, sponsored by Audubon and held in Kearney. The three-day conference is open to anyone and provides tours to see cranes and other Platte River and Rainwater Basin waterfowl, greater prairie-chicken booming grounds and a prairie dog town. Educational programs and prominent speakers are part of the conference. Participants must register in advance of the conference.

• Additional Information: Rowe Sanctuary, 44450 Elm Island Rd., Gibbon, NE 68840, (308) 468-5282, email rowe@nctc.net, web site www.rowesanctuary.org Information about the Rivers and Wildlife Celebration is available from Audubon Nebraska at 5000 Central Park Drive, Suite 101, Lincoln, NE 68504 (402) 466-1220. www.audubon.org/states/ne

Crane Meadows Nature Center

Crane watchers new to the area might want to start their visit with a stop at the Crane Meadows Nature Center at Exit 305, the Alda exit, on Interstate 80. The center is open year-round. Crane Meadows was established in 1989 as a private, non-profit organization to provide environmental education and outdoor recreation opportunities in the central Platte River Valley. It is funded entirely by donations. The nature center's exhibits and self-guided trails are a good initiation to Platte River and sandhill crane ecology. There is a pedestrian bridge over the Platte River, an elevated observation tower and more than seven miles of hiking trails, including a 250-acre prairie tract. Lingle recommends the area for passerine birding after the cranes have moved north. During spring migration the bird-feeding station at the center attracts Harris's sparrows, eastern towhees, American goldfinches, American tree sparrows, chipping sparrows, clay-colored sparrows and an occasional northern mockingbird. Breeding season species include willow flycatchers, Bell's vireo, bobolinks, upland sandpipers, wild turkeys, field sparrows and black-billed magpies.

The nature center has a gift shop with crane and nature related items. Tours to sandhill crane river roosts are available March 1 through April 10. There is a charge and children under 10 years of age are not allowed in the viewing blinds. Youngsters are allowed on a guided evening tour near a crane roost. Arrangements may be made for large group tours.

A photo blind is also available.

• Additional Information: Crane Meadows Nature Center, 9325 S. Alda Rd., Wood River, NE 68883, (308) 382-1820, Info@cranemeadows.org

Other Viewing Opportunities

The **Platte River Whooping Crane Maintenance Trust** was formed in 1978 as part of a court settlement concerning construction of Grayrocks Dam on a tributary of the North Platte River in Wyoming. To resolve litigation brought by the State of Nebraska and the National Wildlife Federation, the owners of the Grayrock project made a one-time payment of $7.5 million to compensate for negative, ecological effects on the Platte River in Nebraska. Income from that endowment finances the habitat acquisition and protection work of the Trust. Today, the Trust owns and manages about 10,000 acres of Platte Valley habitat. A viewing bunker formerly operated by the Trust is now used by the Crane Meadows Nature Center. Trust

ROCKY HOFFMANN

*A common breeder statewide, the **belted kingfisher** nests in burrows excavated in banks near water with an abundant supply of fish.*

land is open only by permission.

Another destination away from the hustle and bustle of roadways in March is Fort Kearny State Historical Park and the **Fort Kearny State Recreation Area** southwest of Kearney. The hike-bike trail bridge over the Platte River at the recreation area is popular in early morning when cranes are leaving their river roosts or returning at the end of the day. In late-April through May, birders on this trail often see migrating warblers and other passerines. From late-March into May listen for displaying male American woodcocks. The restored fort offers a bit of early Platte Valley history. During the spring crane season, films about

Migration Corridors

Central Nebraska is often described as the constriction of the migration hourglass for lesser sandhill cranes, a justifiable analogy. Sandhill cranes winter in a broad swath from the Gulf of Mexico in southern Texas westward across New Mexico and into Arizona and south into northern Mexico. Their breeding range is more expansive, across Canada, Alaska and into Siberia.

During migration about 80 percent of the world's population of lesser sandhill cranes pauses for a month or more along 150 miles of the Platte River. Sandhill cranes are not the only bird species passing through the neck of the hourglass in Nebraska during migration. The Missouri River was the traditional travel lane for snow geese migrating between their winter and nesting grounds. As wetlands vanished along the Missouri River snow geese shifted westward and now pause each spring in awesome numbers in the Rainwater Basin. The Missouri River corridor is still used by snow geese, especially during the fall migration, when they hop from one wildlife refuge to another.

The migration routes of other waterbirds, particularly shorebirds, are similarly squeezed down on the Great Plains as wetlands are scant from Nebraska's Panhandle west. Twice each year these birds pass through Nebraska, where a ladder of wetlands in the Rainwater Basin, Platte River and Sandhills provide places to rest and feed. Species not so dependent on water, such as bobolinks, a Neotropical migrant, make a beeline between wintering grounds in Brazil and Argentina to familiar nesting grounds in Nebraska and the rest of North America.

Sandhill crane

Snow goose

Bobolink

Lesser sandhill crane wintering range, breeding range and migration routes.

Snow goose wintering range, breeding range and migration routes.

Zone of overlap of lesser sandhill crane and snow goose wintering range, breeding range and migration routes.

cranes and other birds migrating through the Platte Valley are shown at the fort. A state park permit is required.

• Additional Information: Fort Kearny State Historical Park, 1020 V Rd., Kearney, NE 68847-8043. Call (308) 865-5305 or e-mail at ftkrny@ngpc.state.ne.us. For more information go the Commission web site, outdoornebraska.org, click on "wildlife," then "things to do" for a spring migration and crane watcher's guide.

Birders have ample opportunities to see sandhill cranes both on the river and in nearby fields and meadows. Their first step should be to obtain a copy of the current *Central Nebraska Wildlife Guide* from the Commission or central Platte River conservation organizations. Birders can safely park and watch cranes away from the river at three roadside turnouts. Two are on the Platte River Drive west of Doniphan, and the third is west of Rowe. There are two public viewing decks on the river. One is east of Rowe Sanctuary, south of the Gibbon I-80 exit 285, and another is south of Crane Meadows Nature Center, south of the Alda I-80 exit 305.

Sandhill cranes feeding in grain fields can be observed from county roads. The Platte River Road from Doniphan west to the Alda Road on the southern side of the river is a favorite spot. The Shoemaker Island Road on the south side of the river from the Alda Road (I-80, Exit 305) west to the Wood River Road (I-80 Exit 300) is about six miles long and passes through extensive tracts of lowland prairie. Land along this road is privately owned but many species can be observed from the road. Crane watchers who want to avoid crowds, or who are closer to western Nebraska than the central Platte, will find about 160,000 sandhill cranes most years between North Platte and Sutherland. Information and a crane viewing blind are available at the **Buffalo Bill Ranch State Historical Park** in North Platte.

Crane watchers should check out Wings Over the Platte events held in Grand Island during spring migration. Guided tours to see

*The **house finch** was unknown in Nebraska before 1900. Spreading from the west, especially along the Platte River Valley, it arrived in the central Platte Valley in the 1980s. Found in urban areas, it frequents feeders and nests in conifers.*

cranes, prairie-chickens and waterfowl are offered along with seminars, wildlife art competition and a banquet. For information call (800) 658-3178, www.visitgrandisland.com

A chain of small lakes along Interstate 80 in the central Platte region was created by gravel-mining operations and barrow pits for construction of the interstate. Many are wildlife management areas and open the public. **Bassway Strip WMA** between I-80 and the Platte River is 725 acres with 7 miles of river frontage. The area is almost entirely wooded with about 90 acres of lakes and old sandpits. It is located south of Minden I-80 Exit 279 on Nebraska Highway 10, then east at the marked access road. **Martin's Reach WMA** is only 89 acres but has about ½ mile of Platte River frontage and riparian woodlands. It is located ½ mile south and 3 miles west of Wood River I-80 Exit 300. For a complete list of central Platte Valley WMAs, consult the current issue of *Nebraska Hunt Guide and Public Hunting Lands*.

From late-December through February, **Central Nebraska Public Power and Irrigation District** eagle viewing facilities are open to the public at the J-2 Hydroelectric Plant south of Lexington. Bald eagles often gather in impressive numbers to feed on fish they catch in the open water of the canal below the plant. The facility was closed for renovation in the winters of 2002-2003 and 2003-2004, but it is expected to reopen by the winter of 2004-2005. Viewing is through large windows from bleachers within the heated plant. Spotting scopes are available and volunteer guides are present on weekends. The facility is open weekends from 8 a.m. to 4 p.m. Group tours are

available on weekdays by special arrangement. There is no charge for admission. Bald eagles can also usually be found near the inlet at nearby Johnson Lake. The J-2 plant is located 7 miles south of Lexington on U.S. Highway 283 across the Platte River, then follow signs. Another eagle viewing facility is provided at Kingsley Dam north of Ogallala.

• Additional Information: Central Nebraska Public Power and Irrigation District, P.O. Box 740, Holdrege, NE 68949-0740, (308) 995-8601, J-2 phone (308) 324-2811. ■

Central Platte Bird Sampler

Greater White-fronted Goose	Bell's Vireo
Snow Goose	Warbling Vireo
Canada Goose	White-breasted Nuthatch
Northern Pintail	Sedge Wren
Common Merganser	Eastern Bluebird
Bald Eagle	Gray Catbird
Rough-legged Hawk	Common Yellowthroat
Prairie Falcon	Eastern Towhee
Sandhill Crane	American Tree Sparrow
Whooping Crane	Grasshopper Sparrow
Piping Plover	Henslow's Sparrow
Spotted Sandpiper	Song Sparrow
Upland Sandpiper	Indigo Bunting
American Woodcock	Dickcissel
Least Tern	Bobolink
Belted Kingfisher	Orchard Oriole
Eastern Phoebe	Baltimore Oriole
	American Goldfinch

ROCKY HOFFMANN

Southwestern Reservoirs

IN THE DECADES FOLLOWING WORLD WAR II, impounding rivers seemed to be the principal mission of the U.S. Bureau of Reclamation and the U.S. Army Corps of Engineers on the Great Plains. No region of Nebraska gained as many surface acres of water as did the southwestern counties. A single disaster in the heart of the prolonged drought of the 1930s prompted federal funding to build the reservoirs.

In late-May and early-June of 1935, heavy rains in the Republican River watershed unleashed a devastating flood that raged down the valley. Accounts put the number of people drowned between 94 and 135. Some bodies were never recovered. Livestock losses were estimated to be over 20,000 head. The flood destroyed 515 bridges, and 275,000 acres of farmland were temporarily taken out of production. Following World War II, the federal government responded to local political pressure to ensure that the Republican River flood of 1935 was never repeated.

In 1949, Medicine Creek was dammed, creating Medicine Creek Reservoir in Frontier County, followed in 1951 by Enders Reservoir on Frenchman Creek in Chase County and Harlan County Reservoir on the lower Republican River in 1952. Swanson Reservoir on the Republican River in Hitchcock County was completed in 1954. The last impoundment, Red Willow Reservoir on Red Willow Creek in Frontier County, began holding water in 1962.

The Republican River begins as three streams rising from grass-covered sands in northeastern Colorado. It drains a basin that contains more than 26,000 square miles. While both its headwaters and mouth are outside Nebraska, the Republican is mostly a Nebraska river. About 40 percent of its basin and 250 river miles of its channel are within Nebraska's boundaries.

In contrast to its historical legacy, the Republican River has had too little water during the past 10 years. The river is so depleted by irrigation – directly from the river and indirectly from groundwater wells in the valley – that many southwestern reservoirs have shriveled to record-low levels. In 2002, after prolonged legal battles costing the states of Nebraska and Kansas each at least $12 million, an out-of-court agreement was reached to resolve Kansas's contention that Republican River flows out of Nebraska were chronically less than agreed in a 1943 compact. The agreement recognizes that groundwater withdrawals, in addition to irrigation diversions, effect river flows.

Historically, the Republican River was wooded along its course upstream to the mouth of Frenchman Creek. Lieutenant Francis T. Bryan of the U.S. Corps of Topographical Engineers traveled down the Republican in September of 1856 and recommended it as a superior route to the Oregon Trail along the Platte because the Republican had more trees. Since man has largely controlled wildfires, woodlands in the

ERIC FOWLER

Medicine Creek Reservoir in Frontier County was the first of several flood-control and irrigation impoundments constructed in the Republican River watershed from 1949 to 1962. The large bodies of water attract bird species not formerly present in the region.

*Harlan County Reservoir is one of the best sites in the state to find a **great egret** (above) in July and August. Most are postbreeding birds from nesting grounds to the east and south. Snowy egrets are also often present but they are less common.*

ROCKY HOFFMANN

Common loons are casual reservoir visitors during any season when open water is available.

Yellowlegs Comparison

Both greater and lesser yellowlegs are fairly common, statewide migrants in Nebraska. Of the two sandpiper species, the lesser yellowlegs is more abundant. The two species can be difficult to distinguish unless seen near each another, when their size difference is readily apparent. Greater yellowlegs are 12 to 14 inches long, and lesser yellowlegs are about 9 to 10 inches, a size difference of 25 to 30 percent.

Other clues will also help birders make accurate identifications. The best feature to look at is the length and shape of the bill, the greater's being noticeably longer than the head, about 1½ times, usually slightly upturned and often greenish or yellowish at the base. The lesser's bill is shorter – only slightly longer than the length of its head – thinner, straighter and usually brownish or yellow-brown at the base. In breeding plumage, the breast and flanks of the greater yellowlegs is more heavily barred than the lesser yellowlegs.

In movements, the lesser seems more dainty and active when feeding – picking and jabbing at small prey, and often running through shallow water. The call of the greater is a loud teu-teu-teu on a descending scale, the lesser's call is less clear and ringing.

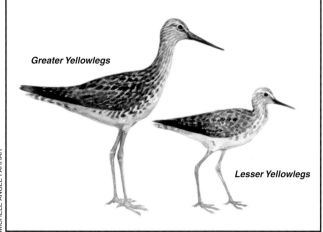

Greater Yellowlegs

Lesser Yellowlegs

MICHELE ANGLE FARRAR

Republican Valley have become even more extensive, and during the 20th century eastern bird species followed the wooded corridor west. Red-bellied woodpeckers, for example, were an unknown species on the lower Republican before 1935. By 1980 they were reported as far west as Dundy County.

The chain of man-made lakes along the Republican and its tributaries provides water recreation in a region that previously had little surface water. The water and woodland habitats created by impoundments in the Republican Valley have been a boon for species not formerly found there, or found in limited numbers. Because these are public areas, they have also been a boon for birdwatchers. Regional birders prefer Harlan County, Red Willow and Medicine Creek reservoirs. Enders Reservoir is described in the sandsage prairie section of this book.

Because the southwestern reservoirs are far from population centers and most birders in the state, their avifauna is not well documented with the exception of Harlan County Reservoir. Because of its southern location in the state, the Republican River Valley offers a mix of bird species – eastern passerines that have expanded westward, southern species near the northern limit of their range, native grassland species, and waterbirds that have come with the reservoirs. Several eastern and western passerine species merge and hybridize along the Republican River.

While birding the southwestern reservoirs, watch for the stick and bark ground nests of the eastern wood rat in woodlands.

Harlan County Reservoir

Uncommon and rare waterbirds have attracted birders to Harlan County Reservoir. Hundreds of bald eagles gather near the dam every winter to feed on waterfowl, principally mallards and Canada geese, and injured fish in the spillway. The number and variety of ducks and geese vary from winter to winter depending on the severity of the weather, but mallards and Canada geese are almost always present. Being the most southern large body of water in the state, Harlan County Reservoir is among of the first to see large numbers of migrating geese and ducks in late-winter, especially when wetlands to the north are still frozen. Harlan County Reservoir is a late-winter staging area for common mergansers, which are often found in open water immediately above the dam. In mid-March 2003 an estimated 200,000 were at Harlan. Red-breasted mergansers and hooded mergansers are often found at the same time.

As on other large reservoirs in the state, reports of uncommon or rare gulls have proliferated at Harlan in recent years. Most sightings have been made during December, but can occur any time from November through March. Herring, slaty-backed, glaucous, California, Thayer's, lesser black-backed and Sabine's gulls have all been reported. Large migrating flocks of Franklin's gulls, which birders expect to find in plowed fields during spring migration, are occasionally reported at Harlan. A flock estimated at 27,000 birds was seen in mid-September 2000, and another flock estimated at 23,000 was noted in mid-September 2001.

Nonbreeding ring-billed gulls are the most common gull species on Harlan and other Nebraska reservoirs in the summer, their numbers increasing in August and September when postbreeding birds drift south. Nonbreeding American white pelicans are common in summer months. Other interesting waterbird sightings at Harlan include the common loon, black-legged kittiwake, parasitic jaeger, little blue heron, white-faced ibis, black-necked stilt, dunlin and osprey.

Harlan County Reservoir can be expected to have post-breeding season great egrets, sometimes numbering in the hundreds, peaking in numbers in July and August. Snowy egrets, a relatively rare species in the state and more common in the east than west, have been reported at Harlan and other southwestern reservoirs, usually during spring migration or late summer. There has been a small double-crested cormorant rookery at the western end of the lake since 1995 and a great blue heron rookery downstream from the dam.

Large numbers of cormorants can often be found at Harlan, especially during migration periods. In recent years, with the lake at record low levels, mudflats have provided extraordinarily good shorebird habitat. Because Harlan is lowered for downstream irrigation during the growing season, the reservoir typically has

BOB GRIER

Ospreys are occasionally seen at southwestern reservoirs, most often during migration but also during summer. The summer birds are probably nonbreeding, immature individuals.

Harlan County Bird Sampler

Wood Duck	Red-headed Woodpecker
Mallard	Red-bellied Woodpecker
Common Goldeneye	Northern Flicker
Common Merganser	Eastern Phoebe
American White Pelican	Say's Phoebe
Double-crested Cormorant	Western Kingbird
Great Blue Heron	Eastern Kingbird
Great Egret	Bell's Vireo
Snowy Egret	Warbling Vireo
Turkey Vulture	Tree Swallow
Bald Eagle	Northern Rough-winged
Northern Harrier	Swallow
Cooper's Hawk	Bank Swallow
Red-tailed Hawk	Cliff Swallow
American Kestrel	Yellow Warbler
Greater Prairie-Chicken	Yellow-rumped Warbler
Wild Turkey	Wilson's Warbler
Semipalmated Plover	Yellow-breasted Chat
American Avocet	Field Sparrow
Lesser Yellowlegs	Vesper Sparrow
Long-billed Curlew	Lark Bunting
Franklin's Gull	Grasshopper Sparrow
Bonaparte's Gull	Rose-breasted Grosbeak
Black Tern	Black-headed Grosbeak
Black-billed Cuckoo	Blue Grosbeak
Yellow-billed Cuckoo	Lazuli Bunting
Barn Owl	Indigo Bunting
Eastern-Screech Owl	Dickcissel
Burrowing Owl	Orchard Oriole
Long-eared Owl	Baltimore Oriole

Conquering Starlings

European starlings probably had their beginning in North America with the release of 80 to 100 birds in Central Park in New York City in 1890 and 1891. The stocking of starlings was sponsored by the American Acclimatization Society in its effort to introduce to America all species mentioned in William Shakespeare's writings. Today, more than 200 million starlings are distributed across the continent, more in eastern states than in western states. By the late-1940s, the starling was present in nearly all of the United States and provinces of Canada. By 1970s it was established in Alaska.

Starlings were first reported in Nebraska, and first reported breeding, in 1932 on a farm near Western in southern Saline County. At least two pair nested, one above a track used for taking hay into the barn. A cat killed one young bird and another was sacrificed for science and became a University of Nebraska State Museum specimen. Myron Swenk in the Nebraska Ornithologists' Union Letter of Information *for that year noted that "they will increase in abundance rapidly, and soon the obnoxious traits of the species will be revealed," adding that the starling "nicely combines all the detestable features of the English sparrow and bronzed grackle, and adds a few of its own for good measure." By 1939 starlings had reached Nebraska's western border along the North Platte and South Platte valleys, and colonized all of eastern Nebraska. By the end of the 1940s, starlings were found statewide.*

The secret to the starling's success is that it prospers in disturbed habitat, urban or agricultural, and by the early-1900s, disturbed habitat was unlimited in the United States. Unfortunately, the starling competes with native cavity-nesting species, especially woodpeckers. Starlings aggressively evict woodpeckers, wood ducks, tree swallows and bluebirds from occupied nest cavities. Starlings are prolific, and 60 percent or more of females attempt and often bring off a second brood per season.

KEN BOUC

European starling.

extensive mudflats, especially on the western end south of Alma, even during periods of normal precipitation. At full pool, the reservoir has about 75 miles of shoreline. Birders should not overlook the extensive habitat west of U.S. Highway 183 or the Prairie Dog Creek arm on the southern side. A county map or sportsman's atlas is helpful in finding access roads. Trail roads are a mix of gravel, sand and clay. Drivers should exercise judgment when traveling these roads when they are wet.

The passerine bird life of Harlan County Reservoir is poorly documented. The lake is surrounded with extensive tracts of deciduous woodlands, brushy edge,

grassland and weedy areas that should attract a wide variety of perching birds. Eastern towhees, eastern wood-pewees, blue-headed vireos, orange-crowned warblers, winter wrens, yellow-breasted chats and scarlet tanagers have been reported there in recent years. Carolina wrens have been found in winter near Methodist Cove. Watch for hybrid species, such as crosses between closely related grosbeaks, orioles, buntings and towhees.

Harlan County Reservoir is the third largest lake in Nebraska, with 13,250 acres of surface water at full pool and 17,750 acres of land. There are two nature trails on the area, including one passing through native prairie. Unlike most reservoirs in Nebraska, recreation lands at Harlan County are administered by U.S. Army Corps of Engineers. There are extensive camping facilities and private concessions. No state park entry permit is required.

• Additional Information: A brochure including a map showing trail roads is available from the Harlan County Project Office, U.S. Army Corps of Engineers, 70788 Corps Road A, Republican City, NE 68971, (308) 799-2105, www.nwk.usace.army.mil/haco/harlan_home.htm

Medicine Creek Reservoir

Although much smaller than Harlan County Reservoir, Medicine Creek Reservoir is in many ways ecologically more interesting. At full conservation pool the lake is 1,850 acres. The Nebraska Game and Parks Commission manages 6,726 acres of land surrounding the lake. About 3,500 acres are grasslands, and about 926 acres are riparian woodlands and seasonal wetlands. There are cropland and wildlife food plantings as well.

Medicine Creek is a narrow, snaky reservoir with arms extending into canyons and up feeder streams. The steep canyon sides, some rising 200 feet above the lake, are separated by flat-topped ridges. The land surrounding the reservoir is wooded with cottonwood, American elm, hackberry, box elder and eastern red cedar, and abundant shrubby areas of wild plum, sumac, chokecherry and western snowberry. Woodlands are intermittent along the upper end of the reservoir, broken by grassland and bluffs. Trail roads are a mix of gravel, sand and clay. Drivers should take care when traveling these roads when they are wet. Maps of the reservoir are available at the park office on the western side of the dam and the wildlife management office on Trail 10. A state park entry permit is required to enter park areas at Medicine Creek but not for wildlife management areas.

Medicine Creek probably does not attract the number or variety of waterbirds, such as gulls and grebes, drawn to the state's larger reservoirs, but during spring migration birders usually find ample numbers of water species. Mallards, Canada geese and other waterfowl overwinter there, attracting attendant bald eagles. Ospreys are occasionally found at Medicine Creek, and pelicans and cormorants are expected. As with most reservoirs, mudflats during low-water and

Large migrating flocks of Franklin's gulls often pause on the southwestern reservoirs in September. Larger ring-billed gulls are frequently found among them. More rare gulls, including herring, California, Thayer's and Sabine's have been reported at Harlan County Reservoir.

migration periods bring good shorebird opportunities. Watch for barn owls nesting in cut banks during the breeding season and gatherings of wood ducks in late summer.

Medicine Creek Reservoir has not produced as many sightings of rare species as Harlan County Reservoir, but it is an area where birders might find 70 or more species during a day. A good place to look for passerines is in the woodlands at the campground. The upper end of the reservoir along Medicine Creek also has stands of deciduous woodlands. While some of the grasslands have been invaded by smooth brome, they offer a variety of grassland birds such as dickcissels, lark sparrows and occasionally lark buntings. Expect to see large numbers of turkey vultures in summer.

- Additional Information: From Cambridge, drive west 2 miles on U.S. Highway 6 and 34, then north 7 miles.
- Nearby Destinations: **Red Willow Reservoir WMA** is 6,016 acres, including a 1,628-acre reservoir at full conservation pool. The Nebraska Game and Parks Commission manages about 4,400 acres of Red Willow. Like Medicine Creek, Red Willow is in erosion-dissected canyon country, but it is less heavily wooded. About 555 acres are woodlands and riparian wetlands, and most of the site is grassland.

At Red Willow's 11-acre prairie dog town look for burrowing owls. Birders will find grasslands and shrubby habitat on the eastern side of the area and between the two arms of the reservoir. The southern side of the reservoir is accessible by trail road and is another good birding area. Trail roads are a mix of gravel, sand and clay. Judgment should be exercised when traveling wet roads. Some of the area requires a state park permit, but these areas are clearly marked. Maps of the area are available . Merlins, northern shrikes, eastern and mountain bluebirds, spotted towhees and pine siskins have been reported there. Location: Red Willow Reservoir is 11 miles north of McCook on U.S. Highway 83. ▪

Medicine Creek Bird Sampler

Greater White-fronted Goose	Eastern Kingbird
Wood Duck	Bell's Vireo
Great Blue Heron	Warbling Vireo
Great Egret	Tree Swallow
Turkey Vulture	Northern Rough-winged Swallow
Bald Eagle	Bank Swallow
Northern Harrier	Cliff Swallow
Cooper's Hawk	Yellow-rumped Warbler
Red-tailed Hawk	Common Yellowthroat
American Kestrel	Yellow-breasted Chat
Greater Prairie-Chicken	American Tree Sparrow
Wild Turkey	Field Sparrow
American Avocet	Lark Sparrow
Lesser Yellowlegs	Lark Bunting
Black-billed Cuckoo	Grasshopper Sparrow
Yellow-billed Cuckoo	Song Sparrow
Barn Owl	Harris's Sparrow
Eastern-Screech Owl	Rose-breasted Grosbeak
Burrowing Owl	Black-headed Grosbeak
Red-headed Woodpecker	Blue Grosbeak
Red-bellied Woodpecker	Lazuli Bunting
Northern Flicker	Indigo Bunting
Eastern Phoebe	Orchard Oriole
Say's Phoebe	Baltimore Oriole
Western Kingbird	

Sandhills

UNLIKE THE LOESS HILLS, which mostly have been converted to agricultural land, Nebraska's Sandhills region remains largely as it was before settlement. The 19,000-square-mile Sandhills region is the largest sand dune area in the Western Hemisphere, and one of the largest grass-stabilized dune regions in the world. The region's shallow, erosion-prone soils discourage widespread conversion to cropland.

During the early-1900s, thousands of farmers came to claim 640 acres of government land under the Kinkaid Act, scratching in small fields on narrow bands of river floodplain and terraces. In time all the farms failed, and grass reclaimed the land, but a hundred years later the full complement of Sandhills vegetation is only beginning to return. In the 1970s, with the encouragement of federal farm programs and tax incentives, investors swept into the more-rolling eastern and southern Sandhills like the Kinkaiders had before them, buying land cheap, bulldozing hilltops and installing center-pivot irrigation systems that could walk across a quarter section of corn. Except in regions of low relief and silty soils, they have not prospered, and again grasses are beginning to reclaim the land. Most of the Sandhills, though, were untouched during the boom in center-pivot irrigation development and native grasslands are still about 90 percent of the region. Ninety-seven percent of the land in the region is privately owned.

Compared to many other North American landforms, the Nebraska Sandhills is a mere child. Only 12,000 years ago, north-central Nebraska was pine-aspen parklands and scattered spruce woodlands. Not until the last continental ice sheet retreated northward was the region shaped into the landscape we know today. Sand and gravel carried eastward across the Great Plains by ancient rivers coursing from the eroding Rocky Mountains and from eroding high plains in northwestern Nebraska and neighboring states are the parent materials of today's Sandhills. During warm and dry climatic intervals 8,000 and 5,000 years ago, prevailing northwesterly winds worked these coarse, yellowish-brown sands into enormous dune ridges, some rising 400 feet above valley floors and running 20 miles long.

The sparse vegetation of Sandhills grasslands make it an optimum habitat for **horned larks.**

During a second episode of prolonged drought from 3,500 to 1,500 years ago, many of the east-west oriented dunes were reshaped. Only 1,500 years ago a sparse covering of plants again spread over the dunes and bound them in place. Since that time, the region's topography has been largely unchanged.

From the early recorded history of the Sandhills, Euroamericans saw the region as one of great desolation, an irreclaimable desert. W.B. Lawson, commissioned by the Burlington Railroad to study the feasibility of building a rail line across the Sandhills, reported in 1883 that the region was "an endless and dreary succession of white-topped, wind-driven hills and ridges of tiresome sand, heaped up and piled and scooped out and re-heaped and piled, with no apparent system or order, over and over again, until apparently the wind itself became bewildered and whirling round and round, scooped out the hill sides and tops into all manner of shaped holes and pits, without regard to shape or position or depth or size." Today, the Sandhills is more often viewed as Nebraska's greatest natural treasure.

In this seemingly inhospitable, semiarid land, precipitation is scant – ranging from an average of 23 inches annually in southeastern counties to less than 17 inches in western counties. And despite vast extremes in temperatures, incessant winds, and thin and relatively infertile soil, an unexpectedly lush grassland dotted with freshwater lakes has evolved.

Underlying the deep dunes of the Sandhills is an immense, subterranean reservoir of water-saturated sand and gravel – the Ogallala Aquifer. From 200 to 900 feet thick, it holds 700 to 800 million acre-feet of water, 350 to 400 times larger than Nebraska's largest reservoir – the 30-mile-long Lake McConaughy. This vast supply of buried, ancient water bubbles to the surface in seeps and springs, feeding Sandhills rivers – the Loups, Dismal, Calamus and Snake – with unfaltering flows. These rivers, and dozens of small streams, pour their waters into larger rivers – the Niobrara, which defines the region's northern edge, and the North Platte and Platte rivers, which border the Sandhills' southern margin. Because the Sandhills is geologically young, its natural drainage systems are poorly developed in some areas – a system of rivers and creeks to carry away surface water has not yet formed. Where groundwater rises above valley floors it creates lakes and marshes. About 1,600 lakes of 10 acres or more are estimated to dot the Sandhills region. Lakes and marshes are especially abundant in the north-central and western areas of the region. There are an estimated 177,000 acres of open water and marsh, and more than 1.1 million acres of wet meadows in the region.

Sandhills lakes are small and shallow. The longest is Dads Lake, at four miles long and about a half-mile wide. The largest natural lake in the Sandhills is Marsh Lake, which covers about 2,300 acres in eastern Cherry County. About 80 percent of these wetlands cover less than 10 acres and only about 10 are more than 10 feet

Cottonwood/Steverson Wildlife Management Area north of Hyannis is typical Sandhills terrain – grass-covered sand dunes with natural lakes in valleys. As recently as 1,500 years ago, the dunes were active and moving in the region.

deep. Most are less than six feet deep, and the average Sandhills lake is two to four feet deep. The smallest wetlands are ephemeral, covering a few acres of subirrigated meadow in the early spring. Some lakes and ponds in the western Sandhills are highly alkaline with open, unvegetated shorelines favored by shorebirds.

Of about 700 plant species recorded in the Sandhills only about 50 are not native – a remarkably small number for such an expansive area. While Sandhills grasslands might appear uniform, specific plant communities have adapted to microhabitats of soil, moisture and topography. Characteristic upland grass species are big, little and sand bluestems, prairie sandreed, Indiangrass, tall dropseed, sand lovegrass, Junegrass, hairy and blue grama, needlegrass, blowout grass and Sandhill muhly. While grasses dominate, the region is also rich in forbs and many showy wildflowers spread across the dunes from late-April through September. In pockets often found on northern-facing slopes or in ravines where snow gathers and moisture is more abundant, woody shrubs such as wild plum, chokecherry, snowberry, poison ivy and sand cherry gather. Trees are few in the Sandhills. Restricted to streamsides and lake shorelines, some willows, cottonwoods, hackberry and ash grow, forming woodland islands attractive to migrating and nesting passerines.

Because of the presence of native grasslands and abundant wetlands, the Sandhills remains an important

nesting ground and stopover for migratory birds. Some species such as sandhill cranes, which nested in the region before 1900, have not returned as breeding birds, while others, such as trumpeter swans and Canada geese, have. Many species of grebes, ducks, wading birds, shorebirds, rails and terns are common breeding species. The region is a stronghold for sharp-tailed grouse and greater prairie-chickens and the full complement of grasslands birds – long-billed curlews, upland sandpipers, grassland sparrows and raptors. From May through June, when migrants and species that linger to nest flood the Sandhills, what once was still is. The American Bird Conservancy, a non-profit organization dedicated to the conservation of wild birds and their habits in the Americas, described the Nebraska Sandhills as the "best grassland bird place in the United States."

Calamus River Headwaters Lakes

The Calamus River rises from a cluster of lakes, marshes and wet meadows in southwestern Brown County, the eastern edge of the complex of wetlands in the north-central Sandhills region. Public-access lakes located within a few miles of each other make the area an outstanding destination for birders.

The American Game Association deeded the 160 acres composing **American Game Marsh Wildlife Management Area** to the Nebraska Game and Parks

Nebraska Sandhills Region

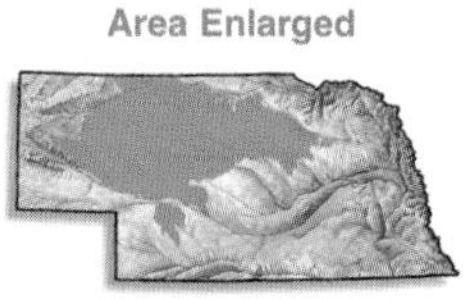

Area Enlarged

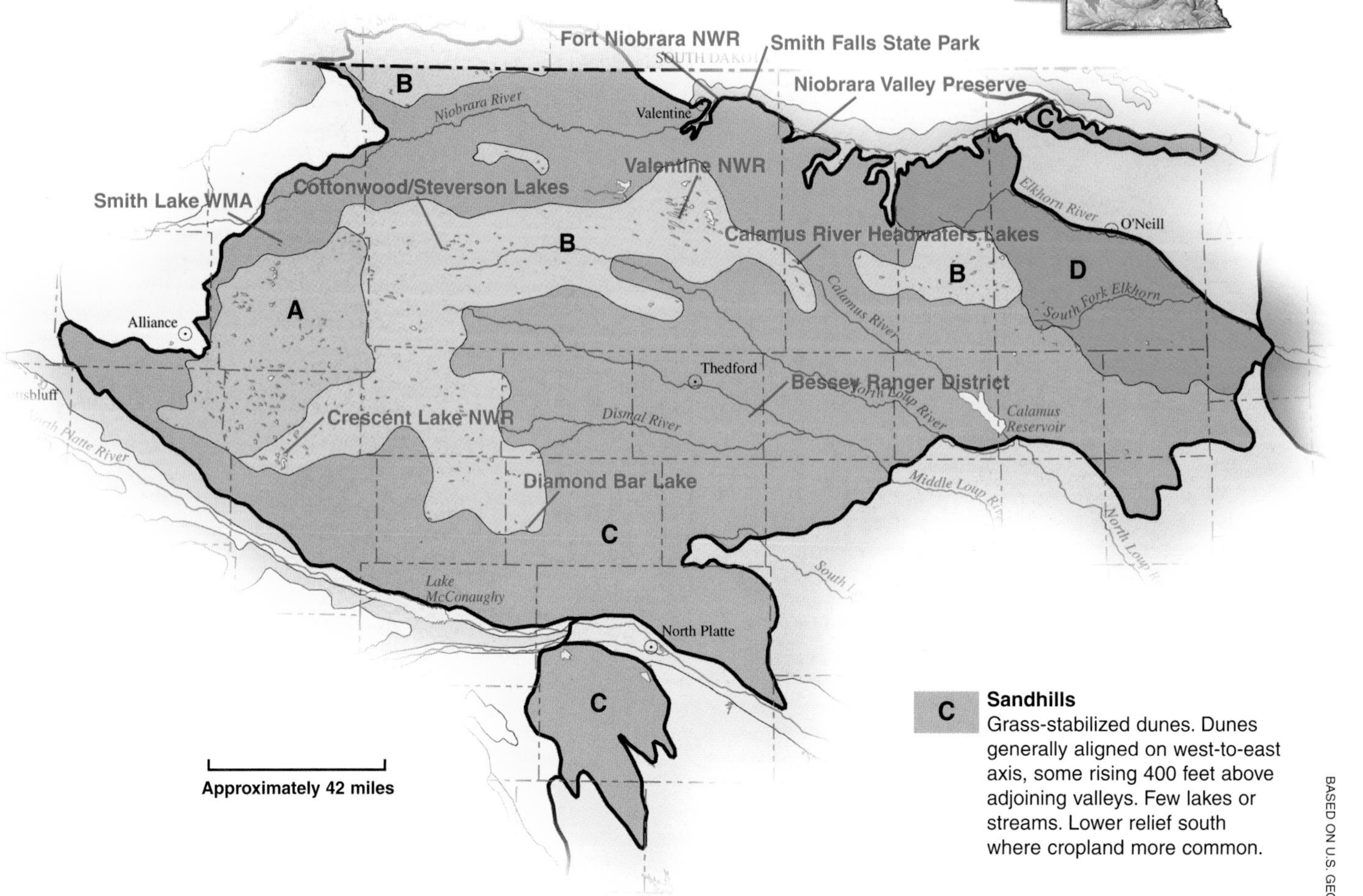

Fort Niobrara NWR
Smith Falls State Park
Niobrara Valley Preserve
Valentine
Niobrara River
Valentine NWR
Cottonwood/Steverson Lakes
Smith Lake WMA
Calamus River Headwaters Lakes
O'Neill
Elkhorn River
South Fork Elkhorn
Alliance
Thedford
Bessey Ranger District
Crescent Lake NWR
Dismal River
Calamus Reservoir
Diamond Bar Lake
North Platte River
North Loup River
Middle Loup R.
Lake McConaughy
North Platte
South L

Approximately 42 miles

A	**Alkaline Lakes Area** Grassy dunes with small lakes and wetlands. Limited groundwater influence and devoid of streams, resulting in high alkalinity and the presence of salt-tolerant vegetation and sparse aquatic vegetation.
B	**Lakes Area** Poorly developed system of streams and outcropping of the water table results in many lakes and other wetlands. Wetlands are only mildly alkaline. Abundant wet meadows.
C	**Sandhills** Grass-stabilized dunes. Dunes generally aligned on west-to-east axis, some rising 400 feet above adjoining valleys. Few lakes or streams. Lower relief south where cropland more common.
D	**Wet Meadow and Marsh Plain** Sandy plains. A transition from dunes to the west and gravelly, loamy regions to the east. Wet meadows, marshes abundant. Has been extensively converted to irrigated agriculture since 1970s.

Commission in 1965. Founded as the American Game Protective and Propagation Association in New York City in 1911 by a group of wealthy sportsmen, and later renamed the American Game Association, the organization evolved into the American Wildlife Institute, the forerunner of today's Wildlife Management Institute. As part of its mission during its early days, the organization acquired, with private funding, areas considered important to wildlife across the country.

All of the marsh and a fringe of land surrounding it are public land. Of the 160 acres, 120 or more during wet years are water. The lake is shallow and, by summer, thick with submergent and emergent aquatic vegetation. Look for puddle ducks, especially during spring migration; wading birds such as great blue herons, black-crowned night-herons and American bitterns; wetland-edge passerines such as yellow-headed and red-winged blackbirds, marsh wrens, yellowthroats and swamp sparrows; sora, Virginia, yellow and black rails; and when water stands on meadows, look for

willets, yellowlegs and other shorebirds feeding.

To reach American Game Marsh WMA from Johnstown, travel east one mile on U.S. Highway 20, then south 19 miles. From Ainsworth, access is south 18½ miles on Nebraska Highway 7, then southwest 12 miles on a county road, then north about 6 miles. This route passes near both Willow Lake BC WMA and Long Lake SRA.

Willow Lake BC WMA is almost entirely water. The BC designates the lake as in Brown County rather than the Willow Lake on the Valentine National Wildlife Refuge, with which it is sometimes confused. Of its 511 acres, about 450 are covered by a Sandhills lake. There is little upland area on public-access land, and most of it is wet meadow. Willow Lake is deeper and less extensively colonized by aquatic vegetation than American Game Marsh, and it is well supplied with game and forage fish, making it a likely destination for fish-eating species such as herons, bitterns, cormorants, pelicans and Forster's terns. Because of its size, depth and water clarity, the lake attracts diving ducks. A primitive campground with picnic tables, pit toilets and a boat ramp are located on the southern side of the lake near the county road. Public land around the lake's perimeter can be accessed by foot.

From Johnstown, drive east 1 mile on U.S. Highway 20, then south 23 miles. From Ainsworth, travel south 18½ miles on Nebraska Highway 7, then southwest 12 miles on a paved county road, then north about 1 mile.

• Nearby Birding Destinations: Located 3½ miles west of American Game Marsh on a trail road, **South Twin WMA** is a 160-acre area with a 60-acre lake. Access is not as convenient as to Willow Lake BC or American Game Marsh. Because of difficult access, nearby Long Lake State Recreation Area, located about 3 miles from American Game Marsh, is not recommended. Located near the eastern edge of central Brown County, **South Pine WMA** is about 20 miles from the Calamus River headwaters lakes and marshes, but it is worth the time for a birder to find. From Long Pine, this WMA is 11½ miles south. The 420-acre area has about 80 acres of open water and 152 acres of marsh – an excellent mix to attract a wide variety of Sandhills waterbirds both during migration and the summer nesting season.

Valentine NWR

Valentine National Wildlife Refuge was established in 1935 in the heart of the northern Sandhills lake country as a breeding ground for migratory birds and other wildlife. Today it encompasses 71,772 acres, of which approximately 13,000 acres are permanent and semipermanent wetlands – lakes, marshes, fens and seasonal sheet water in wet meadows. The largest natural lakes in the Sandhills are on Valentine NWR. Some lakes, such as Dads Lake, are mildly alkaline with scant shoreline vegetation except where freshwater springs enter the lake near the western end. Most of the refuge's lakes are freshwater and fringed with dense stands of phragmites, cattails and bulrushes. Because of the dense shoreline vegetation, shorebirds are not as abundant as at Crescent Lake NWR. During periods of drought and management drawdowns, sandy beaches at Valentine NWR attract a variety of shorebirds in large numbers and can provide exceptional viewing opportunities.

Of the 272 species on the refuge checklist, 100 are wetland-associated species. The checklist includes five species of grebes, common loons, pelicans, cormorants, nine species of wading birds, two species of swans, three species of geese, 21 species of ducks, three species of mergansers, four species of rails, 31 species of shorebirds and 10 species of gulls and terns. Several waterbird species rarely documented as breeders in Nebraska – including least bitterns, cattle egrets and white-faced ibis – have nested on the Valentine NWR. Wetland passerines such as yellow-headed and red-winged blackbirds, common yellowthroats and marsh wrens are abundant. Although considered rare, swamp sparrows are localized nesters in the Sandhills

JON FARRAR

Sharp-tailed grouse are common throughout the Sandhills. Males gather on display grounds in spring to dance and mate.

and probably more abundant than reported on the Valentine NWR. One of the best ways to observe waterbirds is by canoe. An early morning or end-of-the-day excursion during May or June is an exceptional birding experience.

In addition to wetlands, Valentine NWR encompasses enormous expanses of Sandhills prairie. Throughout the refuge isolated tree groves and clumps of woody shrubs attract species not otherwise present on grasslands – black-billed cuckoos, red-headed woodpeckers, eastern and western kingbirds, tree swallows, gray catbirds, loggerhead shrikes, Bell's vireo, yellow-breasted chats and others. Willow and hackberry groves along some of the larger lakes are excellent traps for Neotropical migrants. The full complement of upland Sandhills birds will be found, from long-billed curlews and upland sandpipers to savannah sparrows and chestnut-collared longspurs.

Eastern Sandhills Lake Bird Sampler

Gadwall	Upland Sandpiper
American Wigeon	Long-billed Dowitcher
Blue-winged Teal	Wilson's Snipe
Northern Shoveler	Forster's Tern
Northern Pintail	Black Tern
Redhead	Common Nighthawk
Pied-billed Grebe	Loggerhead Shrike
Eared Grebe	Marsh Wren
Western Grebe	Yellow Warbler
Double-crested Cormorant	Common Yellowthroat
American Bittern	Vesper Sparrow
Great Blue Heron	Lark Sparrow
Black-crowned	Lark Bunting
Night-Heron	Grasshopper Sparrow
Northern Harrier	Swamp Sparrow
Greater Prairie-Chicken	Yellow-headed Blackbird

Blue-winged teal are the most common breeding duck species in the Sandhills, but during some years they are rivaled and surpassed by mallards. Gadwalls are another common breeding species. Puddle ducks require grasslands adjacent to wetlands for nesting.

Sharp-tailed grouse are abundant and greater prairie-chickens are increasingly common in recent years. Except for two natural areas off-limits for research purposes, the entire refuge is open to foot traffic. The Civilian Conservation Corps Nature Trail on the western end of Hackberry Lake provides a sample of wetlands and uplands and leads to an observation deck on an old fire tower.

The Valentine NWR is open year-round during daylight hours. There is no fee to visit the refuge. Blinds for observing sharp-tailed grouse and greater prairie-chicken spring courtship displays are available from early-April until mid-May by reservation. For visitors who are not able to walk to viewing blinds, refuge personal will recommend grouse leks visible from a road. The refuge headquarters is located on the western end of Hackberry Lake. Refuge brochures and bird checklists are available at two kiosks located on U.S. Highway 83. Little Hay Road crosses the western portion of the refuge from U.S. Highway 83 to the refuge headquarters. This nine-mile rock road passes through grasslands, wet meadows and lakes, and offers excellent opportunities to see birds from a vehicle. All but three lakes on the refuge are closed to waterfowl hunting, making Valentine NWR an excellent location for viewing the fall migration.

Camping is not allowed on the refuge. The closest public camping facilities are at Big Alkali WMA 4 miles west of U.S. Highway 83 on State Spur 16B (which also leads to the Valentine NWR headquarters), then south 1½ miles on a trail road. Big Alkali has primitive campsites, RV camping, cabins and a concession. Campsites, water and toilets are available at Ballards Marsh WMA on U.S. Highway 83 north of the refuge. Both areas offer birding opportunities.

• Additional information: To drive to Valentine NWR headquarters from Valentine, travel south 17 miles on U.S. Highway 83, then west 13 miles on State Spur 16B. The Valentine NWR is managed in conjunction with the Fort Niobrara NWR east of Valentine. For information write Fort Niobrara-Valentine National Wildlife Refuge Complex, HC 14 Box 67, Valentine, NE 69201, call (402) 376-3789 (extension 402 for recorded birding information), or (402) 376-1889 for Valentine NWR Headquarters. For internet information see http://valentine.fws.gov

• Nearby Birding Destinations: The lower Snake River was impounded in 1964 behind a dam 108-feet high and 3,222-feet long, creating **Merritt Reservoir.** Constructed by the U.S Bureau of Reclamation, the dam is operated by the Ainsworth Irrigation District to irrigate 34,540 acres. At full pool the reservoir has about 2,900 surface acres and 44 miles of shoreline. The reservoir is drawn down for irrigation in the summer months (leaving extensive sandy beaches) and is refilled with water flowing from the Snake River and Boardman Creek from fall through spring.

Merritt has not been extensively reported by birders

Valentine NWR Bird Sampler

Canada Goose	Greater Prairie-Chicken
Trumpeter Swan	Virginia Rail
Canvasback	Sora
Redhead	Upland Sandpiper
Ruddy Duck	Long-billed Curlew
Pied-billed Grebe	Forester's Tern
Eared Grebe	Black Tern
Western Grebe	Common Nighthawk
Clark's Grebe	Loggerhead Shrike
American White Pelican	Bell's Vireo
Double-crested Cormorant	Marsh Wren
American Bittern	American Pipit
Cattle Egret	Yellow Warbler
Black-crowned	Common Yellowthroat
Night-Heron	Lark Sparrow
Northern Harrier	Grasshopper Sparrow
Swainson's Hawk	Swamp Sparrow
Ferruginous Hawk	Western Meadowlark
Sharp-tailed Grouse	Yellow-headed Blackbird

but it should provide varied opportunities. Tree plantings in the grassland south of the dam, woodlands along the Powderhorn arm to the north, and wooded reservoir edge along the Boardman arm and the southern side should offer opportunities to see woodland and edge species, especially migrant passerines. Upland grassland and weedy bottomland farther west on the southern side are accessible by a trail road. This road is not recommended for cars and under some conditions not recommended for two-wheel-drive pickups. The upper end of the Snake River arm of the reservoir has extensive mudflats in summer and is an excellent but hard-to-reach location to observe fall shorebird migration.

Merritt is a postbreeding staging area for grebes. Look for western, Clark's and eared grebes from late-August into October. In recent years summering common loons and November-December scoters have been reported. As many as 200 trumpeter swans have been reported wintering on the Snake River arm of the reservoir. The Snake River below Merritt Reservoir is one of the most pristine settings for viewing bald eagles, which subsist in the winter months on fish and overwintering mallards. Access to the Snake River below Merritt is limited. The best spot is at Snake Falls. There are public camping facilities, including a private concession and cabins at Merritt Reservoir. A Nebraska park entry permit is required.

Immediately north of Merritt Reservoir is the eastern end of the **Samuel R. McKelvie National Forest.** Most of the Powderhorn arm of the reservoir borders the forest. President Theodore Roosevelt created the Niobrara Forest Preserve in 1902 (see the Nebraska National Forest Bessey Ranger District text that follows for more information). The area was renamed in honor of Samuel R. McKelvie, editor of *The Nebraska Farmer* and governor of Nebraska from 1919 to 1923. McKelvie owned a ranch south of Valentine, had a keen interest in the Sandhills and was influential in regional issues. Areas of hand-planted coniferous trees account for only about 2,200 acres of the 116,079 acres of choppy Sandhills prairie and intervening broad valleys. The area borders the Niobrara River at two points but it is accessible only by trail roads. Unlike the Sandhills to the south, natural lakes and wetlands are absent on the McKelvie Forest with the exception of the Lord Lakes area along the paved road east of the headquarters. Watch for nesting trumpeter swans on those wetlands.

Pine plantations and limited deciduous groves attract passerine migrants and breeders not expected in open grasslands – pine siskins, spotted towhees, eastern and western wood-pewees, several species of thrushes during migration, migrant warblers, white-breasted and red-breasted nuthatches, a variety of woodpeckers, and even an occasional eastern screech-owl. McKelvie's predominant avifauna is grassland species. Sharp-tailed grouse are common, as are grassland sparrows. Colonies of wild plums and chokecherries, often with a few trees in ridge pockets, account for the frequency of species such as black-billed magpies, eastern and western kingbirds, blue grosbeaks

Cattle Egrets

Unlike native North American herons and egrets, the cattle egret is gregarious outside its breeding season, often feeding in flocks. Elsewhere in the world it is known by such common names as the cow crane or cow heron because of its habit of foraging near livestock and herds of wild ungulates. Insects stirred from the soil and vegetation by grazing animals are the cattle egret's principal food. The birds also occasionally perch on the backs of animals to feed on ticks and other ectoparasites.

Cattle egrets are native to southern Europe, Asia and Africa. The species is described as strongly migratory with high dispersal tendencies. Cattle egrets are believed to have crossed the Atlantic Ocean from western Africa to northeastern South America in the late-1800s. They were first reported in South America in 1880. Cattle egrets are still observed at sea today, apparently making the same crossing. The species came to the United States from South America via the West Indies to Florida. They have dispersed in explosive leaps. Cattle egrets were first sighted in Florida in 1941 and reported nesting there in 1953. By 1957 they were established in Texas. Since then they have expanded across the United States, and are still expanding in Canada.

The first report of a cattle egret in Nebraska came in September 1965, when a single bird was seen near cattle in western Adams County. There were two subsequent sightings in the late-1960s, in the eastern Rainwater Basin region. During the early-1970s reports of cattle egrets continued from south-central counties and others came from southeastern counties. In 1984 one was sighted near the Missouri River in Cedar County. The first documented nesting was on the Valentine National Wildlife Refuge in the spring of 1984 when six active nests were found among nests of black-crowned night-herons and double-crested cormorants. Nesting was first observed there in 1981. Since that time cattle egrets have spread statewide, although they remain less common in the Panhandle. Other nesting sites have been infrequently reported. Breeding is probably under-reported because cattle egrets prefer dense, inaccessible stands of emergent vegetation in marshes.

ROCKY HOFFMANN

Cattle egrets were first documented nesting in Nebraska on the Valentine National Wildlife Refuge in 1984.

*Found statewide in wetlands during migration, **American bitterns** are most common in the Sandhills during the nesting season. The bittern's striped neck and breast pattern mimics cattails, and the birds habitually freeze, with their bills up, when threatened.*

and loggerhead shrikes. Common raptors are northern harriers, rough-legged hawks and Swainson's hawks. Golden eagles are occasionally seen, usually in winter.

A paved road from Merritt Reservoir joins Nebraska Spur 16F just north of the McKelvie headquarters. Four-wheel-drive vehicles are recommended on trail roads crossing forest service land. The entire area is open to foot traffic. An attractive campground near the headquarters offers a range of habitats within walking distance – pine plantings, deciduous groves, woody shrub patches and Sandhills prairie.

• Additional Information: McKelvie Forest is located 10 miles south of Nenzel on Nebraska Spur 16F. Samuel R. McKelvie National Forest, HC 74 Box 10, Nenzel, NE 69219-0000, (402) 823-4154, www.fs.fed.us/r2/nebraska

Anderson Bridge Wildlife Management Area, located north of McKelvie, offers a sampling of woodland species along the Niobrara River. This WMA is on the southern side of the river and is accessed via a bridge on its eastern end. The Niobrara River Valley is conspicuously more narrow there than east of Valentine. Though it has only 137 acres, this WMA includes a mile of river frontage. The bottomland is deciduous woodlands, the valley wall is principally ponderosa pine and the valley top is Sandhills prairie. There is a small, marshy, natural lake covered with water lilies in the summer.

To reach Anderson Bridge WMA from Kilgore, travel south 5½ miles, east 2 miles, and then south 5 miles. There is also access to the area from Nebraska Spur 16F south of Nenzel via county roads on the northern side of the river, allowing a loop drive including Merritt Reservoir, McKelvie and Anderson Bridge. Primitive camping is allowed.

Bessey Ranger District

The Bessey Ranger District of the Nebraska National Forest is composed of 90,465 acres of U.S. Forest Service land between the Middle Loup River and Dismal River in Thomas and Blaine counties. The Nebraska National Forest was conceived in experimental pine plantings in Holt County in the 1890s, and born in 1902 when Charles Bessey, a University of Nebraska botanist, with the help of pioneer conservationist Gifford Pinchot and others, convinced President Theodore Roosevelt to establish forest reserves in the Nebraska Sandhills. Of the tree species planted, ponderosa pine, eastern red cedar and jack pine proved the best adapted and endured, although only red cedar has reproduced naturally. A 1965 wildfire sparked by lightning burned about 20,000 acres, including 11,000 acres of forest service land, nearly half of the trees planted. Today there are about 20,000 acres

of trees on the forest reserve, and the remaining land is principally Sandhills prairie with rolling dunes.

As on McKelvie Forest, the addition of extensive tree plantings adds an avifaunal element otherwise lacking on Sandhills grasslands. The densely wooded, deep canyon of the Dismal River above U.S. Highway 83 south of Thedford probably has long been a resort for both eastern and western woodland passerines not found elsewhere in the region. That stretch of the

Nesting burrowing owls are most frequently found in prairie dog towns, but they also nest in abandoned burrows of larger mammals such as badgers.

Dismal and the forest reserve was a favorite birding destination for University of Nebraska ornithologists in the early-1900s. In 1906, Frank Chapman, author of the *Bird-Life* field guides in the late-1890s and early-1900s, came to Halsey to gather material for a prairie-chicken exhibit at the American Museum of Natural History. University of Nebraska entomologist and ornithologist John T. Zimmer prepared a bird list for the area, published in the 1913 *Proceedings of the Nebraska Ornithologists' Union*, numbering 142 species. Today the species list is well over 200 and apparently growing, in part because more birders are observing the area, and in part because new species are arriving. Ruth Green, who has banded birds at the forest for the past 25 years, has noted an ever-increasing variety of species as eastern and western species expand their ranges.

The species of grassland birds at Bessey are like those at McKelvie, including those drawn to patches of chokecherry and wild plum in the grasslands. Along the Middle Loup River, though, deciduous woodlands with dense underbrush are well developed, especially near the tree nursery, headquarters complex and camping area, and offer excellent opportunities for viewing spring and fall passerine migrants not expected in the Sandhills. Deciduous woodland birds of both eastern and western distributions are there, although not in the numbers found on the Platte or Niobrara rivers. During migration watch for eastern and spotted towhees, black-headed and rose-breasted grosbeaks, lazuli and indigo buntings and for four color phases of dark-eyed juncos – gray-headed, slate-colored,

Shorebird Migration

For 30 years Richard Rosche observed birds across Nebraska and neighboring states, and he specialized in shorebirds in the Panhandle and western Sandhills. The summary of when to find shorebirds that follows is condensed from his article in NEBRASKAland *Magazine's Birds of Nebraska published in 1985.*

Well over half of the 80 shorebird species in North America have been reported in Nebraska, and 13 species nest in the state. Spring migration begins in March with the arrival of killdeer and by the end of the month long-billed curlews are arriving along with the vanguard of greater yellowlegs and Baird's sandpipers, which are species pushing winter to reach their nesting grounds in the far north. The peak of shorebird migration through Nebraska is from mid-April through May, and some shorebirds will still move through during the second week of June. Species wintering in the United States and Central America are the first to arrive – the piping plover, marbled godwit and willet. Long-distance migrants wintering in South America – the American golden-plover, Hudsonian godwit, and pectoral, Baird's,

JON FARRAR

Willets are common spring migrants in central and western Nebraska, but they breed in the state only near shallow lakes in the western Sandhills.

upland and buff-breasted sandpipers – pass through Nebraska later in the spring migration period.

Shorebird migration south begins almost before spring migration has ended. Some years it is impossible to tell in late-June and early-July if an individual lesser yellowlegs is migrating south or north. Least and solitary sandpipers, and lesser yellowlegs, are the first to move south and can be found in Nebraska in early-July. Long-billed dowitchers and stilts, Baird's and pectoral sandpipers follow them. The southward migration is more prolonged than spring migration and so shorebirds are abundant in Nebraska from late-July into early-September and often later if the weather is mild. The maximum number of species occurs in most parts of Nebraska in early-September, the highest number of individuals in August.

While most species of shorebirds passing through Nebraska in spring also pass south in late summer, some have different autumn migration routes. Most American golden-plovers and buff-breasted sandpipers pass off the Atlantic Coast. Greater yellowlegs are more numerous in Nebraska in spring than fall, lesser yellowlegs more common during autumn migration.

Oregon and pink-sided. Green has mist netted red-shafted, yellow-shafted and intermediate orange-shafted northern flickers.

A population of red-breasted nuthatches nest regularly at the forest. During migration look for clay-colored, Harris's, white-crowned, white-throated, field and chipping sparrows near the headquarters building and along the Middle Loup. Look for vesper sparrows in the nursery during migration. Green has also banded lark buntings, and lark, savannah, song and Lincoln's sparrows there. Least flycatchers are common, and both Acadian and Hammond's flycatchers have been banded there during migration. Northern mockingbirds are regular nesters in the deciduous woodlands at the campground on the Dismal River.

Among the uncommon or rare species Green has banded or observed at the forest are the Cape May warbler, great crested flycatcher, brown creeper, winter wren, Swainson's and wood thrush, MacGillivray's warbler, summer tanager and evening grosbeak. Both golden-crowned and ruby-crowned kinglets can be observed on a regular basis. The best warbler grounds are in riparian woodlands along the Middle Loup River. Watch for prairie falcons in the fall. Common poorwills are present in the summer and fall.

Longtime U.S. Forest Service employee and accomplished amateur naturalist Carl Smith estimated there were more than 100 breeding species in 1947. He noted that cardinals were rare before 1934 and that starlings appeared in the mid-1940s. Green has observed that starlings, common grackles and house sparrows are uncommon at the forest. Both Cooper's hawks and long-eared owls are documented breeders.

The Bessey Ranger District does not have natural marshes and lakes. There are several prairie dog towns where burrowing owls can often be found. These disturbed sites are also a favorite for foraging grassland passerines. Great blue heron rookeries in hackberry groves in the grasslands were documented between the Middle Loup and Dismal rivers as early as the 1890s. One persisted at least into the 1970s before it was abandoned. There are still rookeries on the area. Ask for locations at the headquarters. Public-viewing blinds for both greater prairie-chicken and sharp-tailed grouse leks are provided. Cock displays begin in March most years. They peak in mid-April when hens come to mate, and continue with less vigor well into June.

Paved or graveled loop roads pass through the area and there are four-wheel-drive trail roads, one providing access to the Whitetail campground on the Dismal River. The Gaston Road on the western half of the forest leads to U.S. Highway 2 east of Thedford. About a third of the area is closed to vehicle traffic from September 1 through November 30. The main campground near the headquarters has both RV and tent camping sites. There is a picnic ground, swimming pool and other recreational facilities. Check in at the headquarters for an area map, bird checklist and to ask questions.

• Additional Information: Bessey Ranger District

American white pelicans are common on large Sandhills lakes during the summer months. They have laid eggs on Valentine National Wildlife Refuge but there are no records of successful nesting in Nebraska.

headquarters is located 1½ miles west of Halsey in Thomas County on Nebraska Highway 2, south ½ mile on Nebraska Spur 86B. USDA Forest Service, Bessey Ranger District, P.O. Box 39, Halsey, NE 69142-0039, (308) 533-2257, www.fs.fed.us/r2/nebraska

Diamond Bar Lake

Lakes and marshes are clustered in the north-central and western Sandhills, and are uncommon in the central counties where drainage systems are better developed and valleys are typically dry. Lakes are occasional, though not abundant, in the southern Sandhills. Diamond Bar Lake in southwestern McPherson County is one of the southern-most lakes in the Sandhills. It has about 120 surface acres and is essentially the headwaters of Birdwood Creek, which flows south to the Platte River. Diamond Bar Lake is on private land but the owner, Gifford Leu, allows fishing and birdwatching as long as the privilege is not abused.

Diamond Bar has a long history as both a fishing and a birding lake. An intriguing bit of birding history at Diamond Bar comes from the Nebraska Ornithologists' Union's *Letter of Information* in 1930. In that issue it was noted that A.M. Brooking and C.A. Black traveled to Diamond Bar in search of birds in late-March 1930, staying at a fishing resort operated by Roy Coon. They reported the expected Sandhills duck species, numerous Baird's sandpipers, and that an area farmer had seen a swan on the lake earlier in the month. Also in that letter, Black reported "the large flock" of whooping cranes "that usually goes through between Grand Island and North Platte this spring passed over Diamond Bar Lake." Black's source for the information was

Bessey Bird Sampler

Great Blue Heron	Tennessee Warbler
Turkey Vulture	Yellow Warbler
Northern Harrier	Black-throated Blue
Sharp-shinned Hawk	Warbler
Cooper's Hawk	Yellow-rumped Warbler
Swainson's Hawk	Black-and-white Warbler
Rough-legged Hawk	American Redstart
Sharp-tailed Grouse	Ovenbird
Greater Prairie-Chicken	Common Yellowthroat
Wild Turkey	Yellow-breasted Chat
Eastern Screech-Owl	Spotted Towhee
Burrowing Owl	Eastern Towhee
Short-eared Owl	American Tree Sparrow
Common Nighthawk	Chipping Sparrow
Common Poorwill	Vesper Sparrow
Belted Kingfisher	Lark Sparrow
Downy Woodpecker	Lark Bunting
Hairy Woodpecker	Savannah Sparrow
Northern Flicker	Grasshopper Sparrow
Western Wood-Pewee	Harris's Sparrow
Eastern Wood-Pewee	Lapland Longspur
Eastern Phoebe	Rose-breasted Grosbeak
Loggerhead Shrike	Black-headed Grosbeak
Bell's Vireo	Blue Grosbeak
Yellow-throated Vireo	Lazuli Bunting
Warbling Vireo	Indigo Bunting
Red-eyed Vireo	Dickcissel
Black-billed Magpie	Orchard Oriole
Horned Lark	Baltimore Oriole
Red-breasted Nuthatch	House Finch
White-breasted Nuthatch	Red Crossbill
Townsend's Solitaire	Pine Siskin
Gray Catbird	Evening Grosbeak

Eared grebes nest on shallow marshes or on marshy areas of larger lakes. They are colonial nesters and dozens to hundreds of nests may be found at one site. Nests are mats of soggy vegetation attached to emergent plants such as bulrush.

communication from Coon. Black wrote, "Mr. Coon is well acquainted with the Whooping Crane, and viewed them with his binoculars as they flew over, so there is no mistake about the identification." Later in the same *Letter of Information* Black clarified, after additional communication with Coon, the birds had been seen April 2 and there were exactly 59 birds in the flock. Coon reported to Black "he would not have noticed them had he not heard their loud whooping calls" and that he "laid on his back and watched them through his binoculars until they were out of sight." In recent times, whooping cranes have not migrated in such large groups, and 59 would have represented a large percentage of the whooping cranes known at that time.

Birders should not expect flocks of whooping cranes at Diamond Bar Lake today, but they should find a sample of Sandhills waterbirds. The lake is mostly open water fringed with emergent vegetation, with extensive stands of cattails on the southern end. Water quality is good, supporting extensive submergent plants and invertebrates, making it an attractive feeding lake. In addition to expected duck species, there are double-crested cormorants, American white pelicans, Canada geese and often a pair of trumpeter swans. During open winters swans might be seen even in January and February. Marsh-edge species such as rails, shorebirds, yellow-headed and red-winged blackbirds, marsh wrens, pied-billed grebes, coots and waders should be encountered. White-faced ibis, long-billed dowitchers, western sandpipers and white-rumped sandpipers have been reported from Diamond Bar Lake.

Because the lake and land surrounding it is privately owned, birders must not violate the conditions under which access is allowed. A county road passes along the eastern side of the lake. Access is at the swinging gate near the southeastern corner of the lake where signs are posted with fishing regulations. If the gate is open, leave it open; if closed, close it after passing

through. Cattle are sometimes present in the meadow. Birders may park at the gate and walk in or drive closer to the lake on a trail road. Do not leave the trail road. The trail road is not always passable to vehicles with low carriages. If in doubt, walk in. If grasslands are dry, do not park where a vehicle's catalytic converter might start a fire. Land away from the lake is not open to access. Using a canoe or small boat is an excellent way to view waterbirds. Hunting is not allowed on the ranch so fall viewing of waterbirds should be good.

• Additional Information: Diamond Bar Lake is 18 miles west of Tryon on Nebraska Highway 92, then south 3 miles.

Crescent Lake NWR

If there were only one reason for a birder to visit Crescent Lake National Wildlife Refuge it would be shorebirds, but birding opportunities on this 45,849-acre western Sandhills refuge are many. The refuge was created March 16, 1931, with an initial purchase of 36,920 acres, acquired primarily from one large ranch. Additional acres were added between 1932 and 1937. There are 21 wetland complexes – shallow lakes, marshes, seasonal wetlands and wet meadows – on the refuge totaling 8,251 acres and composing about 18 percent of the refuge land.

Crescent Lake NWR is on the southern edge of the closed basin region of northwestern Garden, southern Sheridan and northeastern Morrill counties where wetlands are highly to moderately alkaline. Wetlands on the refuge are only slightly to moderately alkaline – not alkaline enough to preclude shoreline vegetation but often alkaline enough to prevent dense stands of emergent vegetation. That, in part, explains shorebirds' affinity for western Sandhills wetlands. Even though the waters are alkaline, they are rife with invertebrate life, brine shrimp and brine fly larvae in particular, and are rich feeding grounds for shorebirds. About

413 acres of alkaline wetlands have been identified on the refuge. More alkaline wetlands and excellent front-seat shorebird viewing opportunities are found on the road between the refuge and Lakeside on Nebraska Highway 2.

More than 32 species of shorebirds have been reported on the refuge. Especially common during spring migration are American avocets, lesser yellowlegs, long-billed dowitchers, Wilson's phalaropes and Baird's, white-rumped, semi-palmated, least and stilt sandpipers. Watch, too, for red-necked phalaropes. The variety of shorebirds during southward migration is more limited, but pectoral sandpipers are common. Breeding shorebirds include black-necked stilts, American avocets, willets, upland sandpipers, long-billed curlews, Wilson's snipe and Wilson's phalaropes. The eastern half of Border Lake is on the refuge. With 150 acres of alkaline waters, it is an excellent shorebird lake. Biologists have estimated as many as 4,000 American avocets on Border Lake at one time. Shorebird migration begins in late-April and continues through May.

Thirty-two species of waterfowl are reported from Crescent Lake – 22 species of ducks, two species of swans, five species of geese and three species of mergansers. Trumpeter swans and Canada geese breed there. Twelve species of ducks are breeders, with blue-winged teal and mallards the most common. Ruddy ducks are the most common diving duck that nests there, followed by redheads and limited numbers of canvasbacks.

Crescent Lake wetlands are excellent spots to see wading birds and water-birds other than waterfowl. Western, eared and pied-billed grebes are breeders. Double-crested cormorants have long nested on the refuge and about 60 nests can be seen each year on Goose Lake. On Crane Lake there is a great-blue heron rookery, which in recent years has held from 43 to 127 nests. Black-crowned night-herons, American bitterns and Virginia rails and soras are breeding species. Seven species of gulls and terns are reported. Black terns and Forster's terns are breeding birds and common.

Upland plants and grassland birds on Crescent Lake are similar to those found on Valentine NWR and throughout the Sandhills region. The greater

Black-necked stilts *were first reported nesting in Nebraska in 1985 at Crescent Lake National Wildlife Refuge.*

JON FARRAR

prairie-chicken was relatively common in the western Sandhills during the early-1900s when settlers with small land holdings attempted to grow grain crops, but prairie-chickens steadily declined in abundance when large-scale ranching again predominated. Reintroduction projects in the 1970s and 1980s were unsuccessful. Sharp-tailed grouse, the native prairie grouse to the region, remain plentiful although their numbers have been in decline across their range in recent years. Long-billed curlews and upland sandpipers are common breeding species.

There are about 80 acres of trees on the refuge, most of which were planted by the Civilian Conservation Corps in the 1930s. Many of those trees have died or are dying and the refuge is returning to what it naturally was, a grassland with cottonwoods and willows on the shorelines of some wetlands. Twenty-six raptor species are reported from the refuge, of which 10 are breeders – bald eagle, northern harrier, Swainson's hawk, red-tailed hawk, American kestrel, barn owl, eastern screech-owl, great horned owl, burrowing owl and short-eared owl. Ferruginous hawks likely nest on the refuge but have not been confirmed. Look for barn owls using nest boxes on windmills. The limited woodlands are also excellent migrant passerine traps. Cottonwood and willow groves near the headquarters produce some unexpected species in May. If driving to Crescent Lake from Oshkosh, watch for a rare glimpse of MacGillivray's warblers in sagebrush country along the way, especially near Blue Creek. Prairie falcons and least terns are casual visitors during migration. Species whose populations are of concern nationwide and found on Crescent Lake include ferruginous hawks, black terns and log-gerhead shrikes. A pair of bald eagles has nested on the refuge since 1994.

Camping is not allowed on Crescent Lake NWR. The closest accommodations are in Oshkosh, 28 miles south, or in Alliance, which is 26 miles of mostly single-lane road north to U.S. Highway 2, then west 23 miles. The refuge is open during daylight hours. Information about a self-guided Auto Tour Route is available at the refuge. A photo blind for observing sharp-tailed grouse on their display grounds is available by reservation in April. Most sand trails require a four-wheel-drive vehicle.

• Additional Information: Crescent Lake NWR is administered as part of the Crescent Lake/North Platte National Wildlife Refuge Complex, 115 Railway Street, Suite C109, Scottsbluff, NE 69361-3190, (308) 635-7851, e-mail crescentlake@fws.gov, web site http://crescent-lake.fws.gov/ or Crescent Lake National Wildlife Refuge, 10630 Road 181, Ellsworth, NE 69340-6801, (308) 762-4893.

Smith Lake WMA

Located on the northwestern edge of the Sandhills region, Smith Lake Wildlife Management Area includes 640 acres, of which about 200 acres are lake and 20 acres marsh. The natural lake was enlarged with a water-control structure in 1949, two years after the first 320 acres were acquired for wildlife management. Before that time the wetland was a shallow, bulrush marsh of about 40 acres.

Smith Lake and other small lakes and marshes to the south are essentially the headwaters of Pine Creek, which flows northward to the Niobrara River. The WMA includes 1¼ miles of Pine Creek. Smith Lake WMA attracts the expected mix of Sandhills, upland and wetland bird species. Cottonwoods, willows, ponderosa pine and eastern red cedar near the lake, and the area's proximity to the Pine Ridge, account for unexpected raptor and passerine species, especially during migration.

Stephen Jones, author of *The Last Prairie – A Sandhills Journal*, has observed birds on Smith Lake since 1989 and has documented 145 species, of which 49 are confirmed nesting species, 18 probable breeders and 36 possible breeders. Former Nebraska birder Richard Rosche reported marbled godwits nesting in the Smith Lake area in 1990, and in June 2003 Jones observed adult marbled godwits engaged in distraction displays near Smith Lake, suggesting young were present. Marbled godwits are regular breeders at Lacreek NWR

Common nighthawks frequently sleep on fence posts during the day. They are active at dawn and dusk.

Crescent Lake Bird Sampler

Trumpeter Swan	Upland Sandpiper
Cinnamon Teal	Long-billed Curlew
Pied-billed Grebe	Marbled Godwit
Eared Grebe	Wilson's Snipe
Western Grebe	Wilson's Phalarope
Clark's Grebe	Red-necked Phalarope
Double-crested Cormorant	Forster's Tern
American Bittern	Black Tern
Great Blue Heron	Barn Owl
Black-crowned	Short-eared Owl
Night-Heron	Common Nighthawk
White-faced Ibis	Loggerhead Shrike
Bald Eagle	Marsh Wren
Northern Harrier	Yellow-rumped Warbler
Swainson's Hawk	Vesper Sparrow
Sharp-tailed Grouse	Lark Sparrow
Virginia Rail	Lark Bunting
Sora	Grasshopper Sparrow
American Coot	Black-headed Grosbeak
Black-necked Stilt	Blue Grosbeak
American Avocet	Bobolink
Willet	Yellow-headed Blackbird

in South Dakota, 70 miles northeast of Smith Lake. The only confirmed observation of the species breeding in Nebraska was in 1990 in Dawes County. Among the breeding species that Jones has positively documented are the wood duck, ruddy duck, northern harrier, Cooper's hawk, Swainson's hawk, red-tailed hawk, American kestrel, long-billed curlew, eastern screech-owl, long-eared owl, eastern wood-pewee, tree swallow, white-breasted nuthatch, warbling vireo, yellow warbler, lark sparrow, swamp sparrow, Brewer's blackbird, orchard oriole, Baltimore oriole, Bullock's oriole and bobolink.

During the 30 years Rosche observed the avifauna of the western Sandhills, he noted over 200 species between Lakeside and Smith Lake. Among the local rarities he listed were the red-throated loon, greater scaup, surf scoter, northern parula, summer tanager, rose-breasted grosbeak, "gray-headed" dark-eyed juncos, and Townsend's, black-throated green- and palm warblers.

Look for nesting field sparrows in evergreen plantings at Smith Lake, least flycatchers in cottonwoods and willow flycatchers in willow groves. Winter species that Rosche observed included the long-eared owl, red-breasted nuthatch, Townsend's solitaire, pinyon jay and pygmy nuthatch. Ferruginous hawks are probably more common in the western Sandhills than anywhere else in Nebraska. Rosche suggested birders watch for rare MacGillivray's warblers and green-tailed towhees in willow thickets along Nebraska Highway 250 between Lakeside and Smith Lake. During migration Smith Lake is a good place to see diving ducks, especially redheads.

• Additional Information: The lake has an excellent fish population and offers primitive camping with pit toilets. The shady campground is an oasis in the western Sandhills. Smith Lake WMA is located immediately

Trumpeter swans from Lacreek National Wildlife Refuge north of Merriman began pioneering into the Sandhills in the 1960s. While not abundant, they now nest on wetlands throughout much of the region and winter on some Sandhills streams.

west of Nebraska Highway 250, 23 miles south of Rushville and 25 miles north of Lakeside.

Cottonwood/Steverson Lakes

Located in southwestern Cherry County, Cottonwood/Steverson Wildlife Management Area is a long way from anywhere, but worth the drive. Hidden deep in the Sandhills, three lakes on the 2,919-acre WMA attract nearly every species of bird expected in the region. Bring your walking shoes and a sack lunch to see it all, or tie a canoe to the top of your car.

Steverson Lake, the largest at nearly 500 surface acres, and Cottonwood Lake, with about 230 surface acres, were acquired by the Nebraska Game and Parks Commission in 1997. Home Valley Lake, which has about 200 surface acres, was added the following year. Cottonwood Lake has a maximum depth of 20 feet, making it the deepest lake in the Sandhills. The lake's depth is the result of draining other lakes into it and a dam at the outlet. A narrow channel through which boats can pass connects Cottonwood and Steverson lakes. Expect to share the lakes with an angler or two. There are no trails or interior roads. Whether traveling by boat or on foot, access to the area is from a gravel road on the southern side of Steverson Lake.

Except for riverine habitat, birders will find all Sandhills habitats expected in the region – upland Sandhills prairie in choppy hills, lush wet meadow grasslands, a fringe of shoreline emergent vegetation and freshwater lake. There is a fen on the western end of Steverson Lake. Fens are similar to bogs in that they have organic soils (peat and muck), however, fens are fed by groundwater, not surface water, and they are less acidic than bogs. Because of the cold groundwater seepage, dead vegetation is slow to decay and accumulates in thick, peat and muck beds. This unusual microenvironment is home to rare plants such as cottongrass, buckbean, swamp lousewort, rush aster, marsh marigold and western red lily – species that vanished from the rest of Nebraska at the end of the Ice Age 10,000 years ago. Watch for swamp sparrows during the breeding season.

• Additional Information: To reach Cottonwood/Steverson WMA from Hyannis, drive north 30 miles on Nebraska Highway 61, then east 1½ miles. ■

Smith Lake Bird Sampler

Wood Duck	Western Wood-Pewee
Redhead	Great Crested Flycatcher
Common Loon	Warbling Vireo
Western Grebe	Tree Swallow
American White Pelican	Marsh Wren
Double-crested Cormorant	Mountain Bluebird
American Bittern	Yellow Warbler
Osprey	Yellow-rumped Warbler
Northern Harrier	Common Yellowthroat
Cooper's Hawk	Vesper Sparrow
Virginia Rail	Lark Sparrow
Sora	Lark Bunting
Willet	Grasshopper Sparrow
Long-billed Curlew	Swamp Sparrow
Forster's Tern	Black-headed Grosbeak
Black Tern	Bobolink
Eastern Screech-Owl	Yellow-headed Blackbird
Long-eared Owl	Orchard Oriole
Common Nighthawk	Bullock's Oriole
Red-headed Woodpecker	Baltimore Oriole

NEBRASKA SANDHILLS REGION
Central Niobrara River

IF NEBRASKA IS THE BIOLOGICAL CROSSROADS of North America, the precise intersection is the central Niobrara River Valley. Five distinct biotas merge here – Rocky Mountain pine forest, eastern deciduous forest, northern boreal woodlands, Sandhills prairie and northern mixed-grass prairie. In the floodplain, there are also tallgrass-like prairies, adding a sixth floristic element.

Eastern deciduous woodlands are at their northwestern-most limit along the moist Niobrara floodplain and shaded southern canyon wall, while western ponderosa pine forests probe eastward along the dry and rocky northern canyon rim. Paper birch, aspen, mosses and lichens, which were common during the Pleistocene epoch that ended 10,000 years ago, are still found in the cool, moist microenvironments in spring-branch canyons on the southern side of the Niobrara. Ponderosa pine, bur oak, eastern red cedar and a mix of other deciduous trees compose the woodlands found in dry canyons on both sides of the river. The central Niobrara River Valley is the distribution limit for about 160 plant species.

As expected, these diverse floral communities have diverse avifaunal communities. In his book, *The Nature of Nebraska*, ornithologist Paul Johnsgard (citing work done by Mark Brogie and Mike Mossman in 1982, and subsequently by James Ducey), noted 268 species of birds have been reported from the central Niobrara, of which about 125 species breed there. For variety of species, the central Niobrara rivals Nebraska's other birding hotspots – the Missouri River Valley, Lake McConaughy and the Pine Ridge. In the Niobrara Valley east of Valentine, eastern species pioneer westward – northern bobwhite, red-bellied woodpecker, great crested flycatcher, eastern bluebird and gray catbird. Similarly, western species are extending their range eastward – common poorwill, Cassin's kingbird and red-breasted nuthatch.

Even more interesting than the mingling of eastern and western species is the hybridization of closely related species, such as the indigo and lazuli buntings, scarlet and western tanagers, Baltimore and Bullock's orioles, rose-breasted and black-headed grosbeaks, eastern and spotted towhees, and eastern and western wood-pewees. Hybrids between all these species have been found along the Niobrara, as are intermediate

individuals of the "yellow-shafted" eastern race and the "red-shafted" western race of the northern flicker. Charles Sibley, Lester Short and others who studied passerine hybrids on the Great Plains in the late-1950s and early-1960s speculated that glaciers separated ancestral populations of these species during the Pleistocene. When the glaciers retreated, grasslands developed on the northern Great Plains under warmer and drier conditions. For woodland bird species, hundreds of miles of grasslands were as great a barrier as had been glaciers. Separated for thousands of years, the eastern and western forms evolved recognizably different plumages and songs, but they remain closely enough related to hybridize. These eastern and western bird populations merged in recent times after prairie wildfires were controlled and river valleys became more heavily wooded.

Before hybridization studies in the mid-20th century, the avifauna of the Niobrara River was little studied. University of Nebraska zoologist Myron Swenk and others floated the river in a chronically leaky boat from north of Long Pine downstream to the mouth of the Niobrara in the summer of 1902. Their mission was principally entomological in nature, but all were accomplished ornithologists and they noted the river's bird life, including nesting piping plovers and probable nesting least terns. They noted that western black-headed grosbeaks were not immediately replaced by the eastern rose-breasted grosbeak, suggesting those species did not overlap in the central Niobrara Valley at that time. Conversely, Baltimore and Bullock's orioles were found coexisting on the same stretch of river.

William Youngworth and Fred Dille collected and made notes of birds in the central Niobrara River Valley in 1933 and 1947. Following Lester Short's hybridization work on the central Niobrara in 1964, the river was largely ignored by ornithologists until Brogie and Mossman studied it in 1982, two years after The Nature Conservancy had purchased 52,000 acres of land in the heart of the river's transition from east to west.

Three public-access areas to the river are located in the ecologically unique 30 miles downstream from Valentine – the Niobrara Valley Preserve, Smith Falls State Park and Fort Niobrara National Wildlife Refuge.

ROD NABHOLZ

Scarlet tanagers are most common in deciduous forests along the Missouri River. They have expanded their range westward along the Niobrara River.

*The **Niobrara River Valley's** northern rim is dry, rocky and cloaked in ponderosa pines. The floodplain and southern valley wall is colonized by deciduous woodlands with pines on the rim. Five distinct plant communities merge in the central Niobrara Valley.*

Niobrara Valley Preserve

The Nature Conservancy's purchase of land on the Niobrara River came at a critical and contentious time. In 1954, the U.S. Congress, as part of the Pick-Sloan Missouri River Basin Program, authorized a dam on the middle Niobrara, and reauthorized it in 1972 to provide irrigation water for 77,000 acres of farmland in the O'Neill, Atkinson and Springview areas. The Norden dam project would have flooded 19 miles of the river and 30,000 acres of land behind a proposed 180-foot-high earthen dam on the river between Norden and Johnstown. Through the 1970s and into the 1980s, heated debate raged and lawsuits and restraining orders proliferated over the issue. The dam proposal was not laid to rest until 1991, when a stretch of 76 miles of the Niobrara River downstream from Valentine was designated the Niobrara National Scenic River.

The Nature Conservancy's Niobrara Valley Preserve borders about 25 straight-line miles of Niobrara River and now encompasses about 55,000 acres. Most of the conservancy land is on the southern side of the river but easements in recent years have added buffer lands with development restrictions on the northern side. Examples of all biota associations that merge on the central Niobrara River are found within the Niobrara Valley Preserve. The Nature Conservancy uses bison and cattle grazing to manage its grasslands and controlled burns to manage its woodlands. It mechanically removes invasive red cedars on the preserve. While protection of critically important biological resources is the principal mission of the Conservancy, research and education are also priorities. The preserve has been designated a Globally Important Bird Area by the American Bird Conservancy, a nonprofit organization dedicated to the conservation of wild birds and their habitats in the Americas. The preserve's avifauna is better studied than any other area on the central Niobrara.

Brogie and Mossman's research on the Niobrara Valley Preserve and adjacent private land reported 186 bird species, of which 75 were documented breeders and another 30 species were probable breeders. That suggests that well over half of the known breeding species in Nebraska nest on the Niobrara Valley Preserve. The preserve's bird checklist today cites 230 species. Most of the breeding species and probable breeding species found 30 miles downstream from Valentine have eastern affinities. These species include the wood duck, green heron, sharp-shinned hawk,

ROCKY HOFFMANN

*A western species, the **black-headed grosbeak** pioneered eastward along the Niobrara and hybridized with the rose-breasted grosbeak.*

and two similar but slightly shorter trails on the southern side of the river. The longer southern loop, about two miles, passes through spring-branch canyons, eastern deciduous woodlands, into Sandhills prairie used as bison pasture and back along riverbottom woodlands, tallgrass prairie and floodplain marsh. Trail guides and bird checklists are available at the visitor center.

The Niobrara Valley Preserve is open year-round, Monday through Friday, 8 a.m. to 4 p.m., except holidays. No admission is charged, but donations are welcome to support educational and visitor services. Bison and wildflower tours are available by appointment. Vehicle access is limited to public roadways. Camping is not allowed on the preserve but canoeing campgrounds are plentiful upstream on the northern side of the river, and at

Cooper's hawk, American woodcock, black-billed cuckoo, eastern screech-owl, whip-poor-will, red-bellied woodpecker, hairy woodpecker, eastern wood-pewee, great crested flycatcher, eastern phoebe, red-eyed vireo, white-breasted nuthatch, blue-gray gnatcatcher, wood thrush, black-and-white warbler, American redstart, ovenbird, scarlet tanager, northern cardinal, rose-breasted grosbeak, indigo bunting, orchard oriole and Baltimore oriole.

Examples of species with a more-western distribution are the common poorwill, red-shafted races of the northern flicker, western wood-pewee, Say's phoebe, black-billed magpie, violet-green swallow, red-breasted nuthatch, Townsend's solitaire, western tanager, spotted towhee, black-headed grosbeak, lazuli bunting and Bullock's oriole. Several species with breeding ranges to the north are near their southern limits along the central Niobrara Valley. They include the Wilson's snipe, least flycatcher, tree swallow, brown creeper, clay-colored sparrow, chipping sparrow and swamp sparrow. Species with a southern affinity include the turkey vulture, northern mockingbird and Bell's vireo.

Grassland species found along the central Niobrara include the golden eagle, ferruginous hawk, prairie falcon, upland sandpiper, burrowing owl, loggerhead shrike, lark bunting, dickcissel, clay-colored sparrow and grasshopper sparrow. Threatened or endangered species reported on the preserve include whooping cranes, bald eagles, peregrine falcons, piping plovers and least terns.

Self-guided hiking trails on the preserve pass through varied terrain and plant communities, and hence offer opportunities to see varied bird species. The five biotas merging on the central Niobrara can be sampled on the trails. Trails on the northern side of the river begin on the floodplain in dry deciduous woodlands, pass through "go-back prairie," wind to the canyon rim through mixed-grass prairie and ponderosa forest, along the rocky rim, and back to near the river. There is a 1-mile loop trail and a 3-mile loop,

Niobrara Preserve Bird Sampler

American White Pelican	Red-eyed Vireo
Double-crested Cormorant	Black-billed Magpie
Great Blue Heron	Horned Lark
Green Heron	Tree Swallow
Turkey Vulture	Cliff Swallow
Osprey	Red-breasted Nuthatch
Bald Eagle	White-breasted Nuthatch
Sharp-shinned Hawk	Golden-crowned Kinglet
Cooper's Hawk	Ruby-crowned Kinglet
Red-tailed Hawk	Blue-gray Gnatcatcher
Golden Eagle	Eastern Bluebird
Peregrine Falcon	Townsend's Solitaire
Sharp-tailed Grouse	Gray Catbird
Greater Prairie-Chicken	Northern Mockingbird
Wild Turkey	Orange-crowned Warbler
Virginia Rail	Yellow Warbler
Piping Plover	Yellow-rumped Warbler
Spotted Sandpiper	Black-and-white Warbler
Upland Sandpiper	American Redstart
Wilson's Snipe	Ovenbird
American Woodcock	Common Yellowthroat
Least Tern	Yellow-breasted Chat
Black-billed Cuckoo	Scarlet Tanager
Yellow-billed Cuckoo	Spotted Towhee
Eastern Screech-Owl	Chipping Sparrow
Burrowing Owl	Clay-colored Sparrow
Long-eared Owl	Field Sparrow
Common Nighthawk	Vesper Sparrow
Common Poorwill	Lark Sparrow
Whip-poor-will	Lark Bunting
Belted Kingfisher	Song Sparrow
Red-headed Woodpecker	Swamp Sparrow
Red-bellied Woodpecker	Rose-breasted Grosbeak
Northern Flicker	Black-headed Grosbeak
Eastern Wood-Pewee	Blue Grosbeak
Willow Flycatcher	Lazuli Bunting
Least Flycatcher	Indigo Bunting
Eastern Phoebe	Dickcissel
Great Crested Flycatcher	Bobolink
Loggerhead Shrike	Orchard Oriole
Bell's Vireo	Bullock's Oriole
Yellow-throated Vireo	Baltimore Oriole
Warbling Vireo	Pine Siskin

nearby state wildlife and park areas. While the Niobrara River immediately above Norden Bridge is not canoed as often as the upstream reaches, visitors who float it in a canoe will find that is an excellent way to observe birds, especially early and late in the day. Canoeists should exit the river above Norden Bridge because of a dangerous chute. The Niobrara is wider and more shallow below Norden Bridge.

• Additional Information: From U.S. Highway 20 at Johnstown, the Niobrara Valley Preserve is north 16 miles on a county road.

From Norden the preserve is 8 miles south of Nebraska Highway 12. At the Y in the road in the valley, turn east along the northern side of the river to the Norden Bridge. The headquarters and visitors center are on the southern side of the river at the Norden Bridge. Niobrara Valley Preserve, Rt. 1 Box 348, Johnstown, NE 69214, (402) 722-4440, tvodehnal@tnc.org, web site www.nature.org

Smith Falls State Park

Located on the Niobrara River 15 miles east of Valentine, Smith Falls State Park was established in 1992. The 260-acre park includes Smith Falls, where a spring-fed stream cascades 70 feet over a rock ledge, creating Nebraska's tallest waterfall. A campground is located on the northern side of the river. A bridge over the Niobrara provides access to the falls to visitors, including those in wheelchairs.

A mile-long hiking trail on the southern side of the river passes through a spring-branch canyon, eastern deciduous forest and Sandhills prairie. Many bird species found at the Niobrara Valley Preserve will also be found at Smith Falls. The park is an excellent home-base for birders to use as they explore the Niobrara Valley by car, canoe or foot.

There are 23 camping sites but no RV pads. Reservations may be made a year in advance. Picnic

*Formerly considered a distinct species, the myrtle race of **yellow-rumped warbler** is found statewide and it is a common migrant in the Niobrara River Valley. The Audubon's yellow-rumped warbler, the more-western race, breeds in the Pine Ridge and is less common.*

HC 13 Box 25, Valentine, NE 69201-9103, (402) 376-1306, smithfalls@ngpc.state.ne.us

Fort Niobrara NWR

A case can be made that Nebraska's first government-owned bird refuge was on the central Niobrara River. Located east of Valentine, Fort Niobrara was built in 1879 to keep the Sioux on their land in the nearby Dakota Territory. The fort was abandoned by the War Department in 1906, although it served as a remount depot until 1911. By 1912, most of the post buildings had been dismantled and on October 13, 1913, all but about 15,000 acres of the 55-section reservation was opened to settlement.

Marianne Beel, in *A Sandhill Century, Book I, The Land, A History of Cherry County*, published in 1986, recounted the transformation of the former army post into a national wildlife refuge. In 1907, the desirability of establishing a bird refuge on the area was called to the attention of William Dutcher, then president of the National Association of Audubon Societies. G.L. Carter, Chief Deputy Game Warden of Nebraska, was also interested in the project. Because the area remained the property of the War Department, their cause did not advance until in 1908, when Dutcher wrote to President Theodore Roosevelt, who signed an executive order two months later prohibiting all shooting and trapping on the reservation. In 1912 an executive order established the Niobrara Bird and Big Game Reservation.

The preservation of vanishing large game animals overshadowed protecting birds from the reserve's very beginning. In January 1913, Fred M. Dille, Inspector for the U.S. Biological Survey, delivered six bison, 17 elk and two white-tailed deer, the beginning of the reservation's wildlife stock. In subsequent years the reservation grew in size and number of animals. Dille was manager from 1913 until he retired in 1930. He was a member of the Nebraska Ornithologists' Union, an avid collector and dealer in bird specimens, egg sets and out-of-print ornithological books. In 1940 the area was renamed the Fort Niobrara National Wildlife Refuge.

Today, Fort Niobrara NWR encompasses about 19,000 acres on both sides of the Niobrara River, including about 14,400 acres of prairie, 4,356 acres of woodland and 375 acres of wetlands. Nine miles of the Niobrara River pass through the refuge. A self-guided wildlife drive offers opportunities to see grassland birds as well as bison, elk and prairie dogs. Look for burrowing owls in the prairie dog town. Check small, spring-fed impoundments for waterbirds. A hiking trail winds through a deciduous woodlands on the southern side of the river at the Bur Oak picnic grounds and another trail leads to Fort Falls at the mouth of a spring-branch canyon. The Niobrara Wilderness Area on the northern side of the river offers hiking for adventurous birdwatchers through ponderosa

*A migrant and breeder statewide, the **eastern kingbird** is more common along the Niobrara Valley than the western kingbird species.*

BUB BLAKE

tables, restrooms, a concession and pay showers are on the northern side of the river. The park is open from May to mid-November. Because the park is located within the Niobrara National Scenic River, which designates this stretch of river as an ecologically important corridor, development is limited.

• Additional Information: Smith Falls State Park,

Fort Niobrara Bird Sampler

Turkey Vulture	White-breasted Nuthatch
Bald Eagle	Mountain Bluebird
Sharp-shinned Hawk	Black-and-white Warbler
Rough-legged Hawk	American Redstart
Golden Eagle	Ovenbird
Sharp-tailed Grouse	Common Yellowthroat
Greater Prairie-Chicken	Yellow-breasted Chat
Solitary Sandpiper	Scarlet Tanager
Spotted Sandpiper	Western Tanager
Upland Sandpiper	Spotted Towhee
Burrowing Owl	Eastern Towhee
Common Nighthawk	Chipping Sparrow
Belted Kingfisher	Field Sparrow
Western Wood-Pewee	Savannah Sparrow
Eastern Wood-Pewee	Grasshopper Sparrow
Say's Phoebe	Rose-breasted Grosbeak
Great crested Flycatcher	Black-headed Grosbeak
Bell's Vireo	Blue Grosbeak
Red-eyed Vireo	Orchard Oriole
Horned Lark	Bullock's Oriole
Cliff Swallow	Baltimore Oriole

forest and mixed-grass prairie. The refuge bird checklist includes 230 species.

• Additional Information: Fort Niobrara NWR is 5 miles east of Valentine on Nebraska Highway 12. Stop at the visitor center for a refuge brochure, map and bird checklist. The refuge is open year-round from sunrise to sunset. Fort Niobrara National Wildlife Refuge, HC 14 Box 67, Valentine, NE 69201, 402-376-3789, FortNiobrara@fws.gov, web site fortniobrara.fws.gov/

• Nearby Birding Destinations: There are several wildlife management areas and a state recreation area located on streams flowing into the Niobrara River between Valentine and Nebraska Highway 7 north of Bassett. While none of these areas have the diversity of bird species found within the Niobrara Valley Preserve, the variety is similar. All are in rugged, mostly wooded, rocky canyons. Bring a water bottle and wear quality hiking shoes. There are no formal hiking trails, but service roads serve that function. All WMAs are open to primitive camping.

The only wildlife management area north of the river is **Thomas Creek WMA.** Almost a mile of Thomas Creek passes through the western side of the 1,154-acre area, with canyons spreading from it like veins of a leaf. The area is almost entirely wooded – deciduous woodlands in the bottoms, pine forest on the canyon walls and grasslands beyond the canyon rims. To reach Thomas Creek WMA from Springview, drive south 2 miles on U.S. Highway 183, then east 2 miles and south 1 mile on county roads.

Keller Park State Recreation Area serves as an

The clay-colored sparrow is one of several species at the southern edge of its breeding range in the Niobrara River Valley.

excellent headquarters for birding the central Niobrara Valley. The 196-acre area has 10 acres of water in five fishing ponds, RV camping pads, a dump station, water, vault toilets and picnic areas. A state park entry permit is required. The 640-acre **Keller School Land WMA** is adjacent to the park. Bone Creek passes through both areas. To reach Keller Park, travel 3 miles west of Long Pine on U.S. Highway 20, then north 9 miles on U.S. Highway 183.

Pine Glen WMA is only two miles east of Keller SRA, as the crow flies, and a bit farther via county roads. Both Bone Creek and Long Pine Creek pass through the 960-acre area. Native grasslands with shrubs are on the western side of the area. Most of the area is steep canyon country with ponderosa pine, bur oak and eastern red cedar woodlands. Service roads on the southwestern and eastern sides provide access to the area. To reach Pine Glen from Bassett, drive west 7 miles on U.S. Highway 20, then north 9 miles on county roads. If going to Pine Glen from Keller Park, it is shorter to drive north 3 miles on U.S. 183, then east 3½ miles, then south 2½ miles on county roads.

Plum Creek flows through a deep canyon on the northern end of **Bobcat WMA.** Most of the 893 acres in this area are heavily wooded with ponderosa pine and eastern red cedar. The southern end of the area is Sandhills prairie. From Ainsworth, drive north 10 miles on the Meadville Road, then west 1 mile and north 1½ miles. If driving to Bobcat WMA from Meadville in the Niobrara Valley, travel south 4 miles, then west 1 mile and north 1½ miles.

Plum Creek WMA is a relatively new wildlife management area and it has easy access close to a major highway. Two miles of Plum Creek, a coldwater trout stream, passes through the western side of the 1,320-acre area. Plum Creek canyon is wooded, predominantly with eastern red cedar, bur oak and other deciduous species near the stream. The eastern half of the area is Sandhills prairie. From Johnstown, drive west 1½ miles on U.S. Highway 20, then south 1½ miles on a county road. ∎

Turkey vultures are common summer residents in the Niobrara River Valley, nesting on rock ledges and other sites.

North Platte River Valley

CHARLES W. MCCONAUGHY HAD A DREAM. McConaughy moved from Illinois to Holdrege, Nebraska, in 1892 to start a grain business. In 1913 he organized Phelps County farmers to form the Tri-County Supplementary Water Association. McConaughy's idea was to construct a canal system to carry water from the North Platte River during the spring and fall to soak the soil of farmers' fields.

McConaughy died in 1941, but he lived to see his dream realized. Construction of Kingsley Dam on the North Platte River north of Ogallala began in 1936, and the first water was diverted into irrigation canals in 1938. George P. Kingsley, a Minden banker, joined McConaughy in the long battle to gain funding for the project. Drought and Depression during the 1930s finally created the political will for the massive Public Works Administration project. The Tri-County Project, officially completed in 1943 at a cost of $43.5 million, is owned and operated by the Central Nebraska Public Power and Irrigation District (CNPPID).

Lake McConaughy is the largest body of water in Nebraska – 22 miles long and three miles wide near the dam, it covers 35,700 acres and has 105 miles of shoreline at full pool. The impoundment of the North Platte River, coupled with existing irrigation withdrawals, had profound, downstream ecological consequences. It also created a destination for birds and birders unlike any other in the state. Ornithologist Paul Johnsgard, in *The Nature of Nebraska*, said the McConaughy complex "has the largest bird list of any location in the state, including more than 340 species, with 104 known breeders, 17 additional possible breeders, and 184 transients."

Double-crested cormorants hinted at the change that Lake McConaughy and other later reservoirs would bring to the avifauna of Nebraska. Before Lake McConaughy was completed, there were only a handful of reports of small nesting colonies of cormorants in the state. One was associated with flooded trees above a diversion dam east of North Platte and part of the Tri-County irrigation project. In 1945, game warden Loron Bunney reported a rookery with about 40 nests in dead cottonwoods nine miles west of Kingsley Dam. In 1946, he wrote there were "probably 60 nests." When the lake level rose that rookery was abandoned and two new ones were established, the largest holding more than 100 nests in 1947. In subsequent years, the

number of rookeries grew at McConaughy and the number of nesting pairs increased. But when the dead trees over water tumbled, cormorant-nesting habitat vanished, probably by the mid-1950s. Cormorants were only the vanguard of a host of big waterbirds to discover Lake McConaughy in subsequent years.

Richard Rosche exhaustively chronicled Panhandle bird life from 1968 through 1998. His records and publications are the sharpest snapshot of the region's avifauna in that period. In 1994 he published *Birds of the Lake McConaughy Area and North Platte River Valley, Nebraska*. While more recent, rare sightings and records are not included, Rosche's book remains an excellent bird guide to the McConaughy complex. He described the North Platte River Valley from Oshkosh eastward to Keystone, located below Lake McConaughy, as "one of the most outstanding birding areas in the Great Plains" because of its assortment of habitats. He wrote that an experienced birder could expect to observe from 120 to 130 species most weekends from the last week of April through the first three weeks of May. Christmas counts of more than 100 species are now common. Rosche reported 36 species of shorebirds and 24 species of warblers at the McConaughy complex.

The North Platte Valley provides varied bird habitats in addition to its riverine and reservoir components. Sandhills prairie and sandsage prairie border the valley westward nearly to Scottsbluff. To the south is shortgrass prairie. Deciduous woodlands, dominated by large cottonwoods, trace the river's course, and ponderosa pine woodlands are found on the southern valley rim in the midsection. There are rock outcrops on the valley walls, alkaline wetlands on the valley floor in Scotts Bluff and Morrill counties, and lush subirrigated meadows along much of the river. In 1926 the North Platte River in Garden County was designated a waterfowl refuge. It attracts and holds Canada geese, mallards and other waterfowl from fall migration into spring migration. The North Platte River Valley offers ample public land for birders to sample the region's avifauna.

ROCKY HOFFMANN

*Loon species rare to Nebraska, such as this **yellow-billed loon**, have become regular visitors to Lake McConaughy.*

McConaughy and Ogallala Lakes

Sand and gravel to construct Kingsley Dam was taken from the floodplain immediately below the dam, creating Lake Ogallala, a boot-shaped body of water composed of two basins. The eastern basin, called

The spillway below Kingsley Dam at **Lake Ogallala** *is a favorite resort of bald eagles and birdwatchers in winter. The viewing cabin allows birders to look in comfort for other rare species, especially sea ducks, mergansers, gulls and loons seldom seen in Nebraska.*

Western High Plains

Approximately 30 miles

Oglala National Grassland

A

B

B

Chadron

Gilbert-Baker WMA

White River

Nebraska National Forest

C

D

Fort Robinson
State Park

Agate Fossil Beds
National Monument

E

WYOMING

Kiowa WMA

Alliance

Scotts Bluff
National Monument

F

North Platte NWR

Scottsbluff

Cedar Canyon WMA

North Platte River

G

Wildcat Hills SRA

G

Buffalo Creek WMA

G

Clear Creek WMA

Oliver Reservoir

Lake McConaughy and Lake Ogallala

Lake
McConaughy

E

Sidney

H

I

Enders Reservoir

I

H

Rock Creek Lake

A **Semiarid Pierre Shale Plains**
Rolling hills and mixed-grass
prairie with some sagebrush.
Scant rainfall, 15-17 inches per
year, a short growing season
and hot summers have restricted
agricultural development.

B **White River Badlands**
Eroded and water-dissected
grasslands immediately north
of the Pine Ridge escarpment.
Mixed-grass prairie with
sagebrush and other shrubs.
Used principally as rangeland.

C **Pine Ridge Escarpment**
Sandstone and siltstone
bluffs and escarpments with
ponderosa pine woodlands and
mixed-grass prairie. Rugged
terrain precludes agriculture,
used principally as rangeland.

D **Sandy and Silty Tablelands**
Tablelands with moderate relief
and arid climate are used
principally as rangeland. Mixed-
grass prairie with outliers of
Sandhills prairie. Canyons with
rock outcrops along streams.

E **Flat to Rolling Cropland**
Level to rolling plains, few
streams, mostly intermittent.
Loess soils. Mixed-grass prairie
extensively converted to dryland
and irrigated agriculture – wheat,
corn and sugar beets.

G **Scotts Bluff and
Wildcat Hills**
Bluffs, escarpments, steep
valley slopes. Mixed-grass
prairie with ponderosa pine
and juniper woodlands on
ridges and slopes. Used
principally as rangeland.

F **North and South Platte Valley
and Terraces**
Flat alluvial valley, bluffs,
uplands. Tallgrass prairie,
mixed-grass prairie, sandsage
prairie and riparian woodlands.
Cropland and rangeland.

H **Moderate Relief Rangeland**
Plains with moderate slope,
intermittent streams and
perennial streams impoverished
by irrigation. Mostly mixed-grass
prairie north, shortgrass prairie
south. Mostly rangeland.

I **Rolling Sand Plains**
Sandsage prairie. Undulating
plains with scattered sand dunes
and poorly developed natural
drainage. Sandy soils. Former
rangeland largely converted to
irrigated cropland.

*Gull species formerly not found in Nebraska, such as **laughing gulls**, are reported with increasing frequency at reservoirs such as Lake McConaughy.*

Lake Keystone or Keystone Pool, is the shallower basin. Lake Ogallala has 640 acres of water maintained by controlled releases and seepage from Lake McConaughy. From November into March, Lake Ogallala is a waterbird watcher's paradise.

Even when the main lake and most of Lake Ogallala are sealed in ice, open water in the spillway attracts an incredible variety of waterbirds. Visitors may look at the spillway from a CNPPID building through large windows. Bald eagles gather to feed on sick and injured ducks and on fish flushed to the surface. In recent years there have been counts of as many as 368 bald eagles near Kingsley Dam in one day. Most years the maximum number of eagles occurs in January and February. The number varies dramatically from day to day depending on weather conditions, which can create or eliminate feeding opportunities. By mid-March, most of the bald eagles have dispersed. For current eagle information call the Kingsley Dam office at (308) 284-2332.

A concentration of bald eagles is a popular sight for even the most casual birdwatcher, but it is the gatherings of waterbirds not often seen in inland areas that attract advanced birders. Reports of gull species other than ring-billed, Franklin's and herring were scant before the 1990s. The rarer species might have been there, but were not observed and reported. Gull species observed in the Kingsley Dam area in recent years include laughing, little, Bonaparte's, mew, California, Thayer's, Iceland, lesser black-backed, glaucous, glaucous-winged, great black-backed and Sabine's. Most of these species are transients during spring and fall migration periods and can be widely dispersed around the reservoir. Look for them on shorelines, and on sandbars above the reservoir before freeze-up. The best chance to observe rare gulls is in late fall and winter, when they concentrate in the spillway at Lake Ogallala or in open pools above the dam. Rosche recommended looking for rare gulls among herring gulls when they are at their maximum numbers, just before freeze-up or at ice-out in the spring. The state's first black-legged kittiwake specimen was found dead at Lake Ogallala in May 1990 with fish bones lodged in

***Mississippi kites** have been nesting in Ogallala since the early-1990s.*

its esophagus.

Caspian tern reports at Lake McConaughy increased markedly during the 1990s. Look for them from spring through summer. An Arctic tern was reported in May 2003. The only previous sighting for that species was from Lake Minatare in September 2000. Watch for the rare visit of a parasitic or long-tailed jaeger from mid-September into winter. All four North American loon species have been reported at Lake McConaughy. Common loons might be seen any month of the year. Pacific, red-throated and yellow-billed loons are rarer. They might appear during spring or fall migration, but are most likely from October into November.

Lake McConaughy, especially its western end near Clear Creek WMA, is an important staging area for western grebes from August through October. The state record count for the species – an estimated 44,000 birds – occurred at Lake McConaughy in late-September 2000. (See the Clear Creek WMA section below for more information on western grebes.) Horned grebes are occasionally seen at Lake McConaughy, most often near Lake Ogallala, and sometimes in unexpectedly large numbers during spring and fall migration. Look for red-necked grebes from fall into winter. Large numbers of common mergansers can usually be found at Lake McConaughy as soon as there is open water in late winter and again just before freeze-up. Some overwinter in open water in Lake Ogallala. Counts of 40,000 have been made in December. Look for red-breasted mergansers at the same time.

As many as 22 species of waterfowl have been reported at McConaughy in January. Species of special interest are the greater scaup, Barrow's goldeneye, long-tailed duck, and surf, white-winged and black scoters. The first accepted state record for tufted duck was made on Lake Ogallala in December 1999. Trumpeter swans have wintered on open water at Lake McConaughy and Lake Ogallala in recent years. Tundra swans are occasionally seen during spring migration and rarely in winter. About 150,000

*The first state record for **snowy plovers** breeding successfully was on the beach at Lake McConaughy in July 2000. Pairs have successfully nested in subsequent years.*

BUB BLAKE

The kites are regular visitors in the state, observed principally in September, but Ogallala is the only known nesting site. Osprey is another species to watch for at Lake Ogallala, especially during migrations, but also during the summer months. While there are no modern nesting records for osprey in Nebraska, they have been seen in late-June and early-July, early for fall migrants of the species. Some are probably prebreeding-age birds.

While waterbirds are the showstoppers at Lake McConaughy, birders will find many habitats and species year-round. Lake Ogallala SRA has a diverse mix of habitats – riparian woodland, shrub land, grassland, marsh, sand beach, river, ponds and lakes – where many bird species come during the warm months. Bird surveys in the late-1980s and early-1990s found 56 terrestrial and 19 aquatic species, including hybrids of closely related species. More than 30 wood warblers are listed for the Lake McConaughy area. Look for nesting Say's phoebes and rock wrens in rock outcrops, especially on the southern side of Lake McConaughy and along the North Platte River above the reservoir. A rare sighting would be of a Cassin's sparrow in sage grasslands on the northern side of the lake. The eastern end of Lake McConaughy and the woodlands and rock outcrops below the dam have produced reports of white-winged doves, cave swallows, Clark's nutcrackers, northern mockingbirds, white-eyed and Bell's vireos, scissor-tailed flycatchers, winter and Carolina wrens and blue grosbeaks. Cliff swallows are abundant in the McConaughy area. Look for nesting colonies under bridges over the North and South Platte rivers and on concrete structures on

to 170,000 sandhill cranes roost on the North Platte River downstream from Kingsley Dam near North River WMA, four miles north of Hershey.

With record-low water levels in recent years, Lake McConaughy has been an outstanding shorebird destination. Even when the lake is at normal levels, it is an excellent shorebird site. Extensive mudflats exposed on the upper reaches of the reservoir during summer drawdowns attract southward-migrating shorebirds. As many as 3,000 to 4,000 Baird's sandpipers have been reported in August and early-September. Of six documented breeding records for snowy plovers in the state, five are from Lake McConaughy since 2001. Watch for the rare appearance of red knots and buff-breasted sandpipers during southern migration, too. Black-necked stilts were documented as breeding on Lake McConaughy's western end in the spring of 2000. Another shorebird species of interest is the red-necked phalarope. The best chance of finding sanderlings is on northern shore beaches in May. The second state record for the white ibis was made on Lake Ogallala in May 2000.

Piping plovers have been known to nest on the sandy beaches of Lake McConaughy since at least 1978. Several pairs of least terns have nested there in recent years. Both least terns and piping plovers are listed at the state and federal level. The numbers of piping plovers are greatest when the lake is at less than full pool, exposing broad, sandy beaches. CNPPID marks and fences off nesting sites, and traffic is prohibited in specific areas where the two species nest. Nesting birds should be viewed from a distance. The nesting season at Lake McConaughy is from early-May through mid-August. Check at the CNPPID office located in the visitors center for additional information.

Mississippi kites have nested in a residential area of the city of Ogallala since the early-1990s – the first nesting records for Nebraska and the northernmost nesting record for the species. Two nests were confirmed in 1994 and nesting pairs were still present in 2003.

Lake McConaughy Bird Sampler

Trumpeter Swan	Piping Plover
Canvasback	American Avocet
Redhead	Whimbrel
Ring-necked Duck	Baird's Sandpiper
Greater Scaup	Franklin's Gull
Lesser Scaup	Bonaparte's Gull
Long-tailed Duck	Ring-billed Gull
Bufflehead	California Gull
Common Goldeneye	Herring Gull
Barrow's Goldeneye	Thayer's Gull
Ruddy Duck	Glaucous Gull
Common Merganser	Sabine's Gull
Common Loon	Caspian Tern
Horned Grebe	Common Tern
Red-necked Grebe	Forster's Tern
Western Grebe	Least Tern
Clark's Grebe	Northern Saw-whet Owl
American White Pelican	Western Wood-Pewee
Osprey	Willow Flycatcher
Mississippi Kite	Marsh Wren
Bald Eagle	Townsend's Solitaire

Kingsley Dam. Marsh wrens, rails, Townsend's solitaires, and swamp sparrows can often be found in winter.

• Additional Information: Lake McConaughy SRA covers 5,492 acres of land on 12 areas and Lake Ogallala SRA adds another 339 land acres. There are 324 RV pad sites, 268 with electrical hookups, and unlimited non-pad camping sites. There are modern restrooms, coin-operated showers, dump stations, water, vault toilets, picnic tables, shelters and private concessions. CNPPID and the Ogallala/Keith County Chamber of Commerce distribute an attractive bird checklist citing 313 species, of which 103 are breeding species. It is available at the Lake McConaughy

Visitors Center and Water Interpretive Center south of the dam. The center is a good first stop for visitors new to the area. Also ask for the eagle-viewing and piping plover and least tern brochures. Kingsley Dam is located 8 miles north of Ogallala on Nebraska 61. U.S. Highway 26 parallels the southern side of Lake McConaughy and Nebraska Highway 92 travels the northern shore. Lake McConaughy SRA, 1475 Hwy. 61N, Ogallala, NE 69153-5929, 308-284-8800, lakemac@ngpc.state.ne.us

• Nearby Birding Destinations: Sutherland Reservoir, a water storage component of the Nebraska Public Power District's system, is another good site to find

Bald Eagles

Before settlement in Nebraska, bald eagles apparently nested regularly in appropriate habitat – tall trees in old-growth forest relatively close to water for fish foraging opportunities. Those habitat requirements probably restricted nesting bald eagles mostly to the Missouri River Valley, although there is a nesting record from 1845 near Ash Hollow in Garden County. It is likely that bald eagles also nested along the central and lower Niobrara River. By 1900, bald eagles were considered extirpated from the state. The species declined not just in Nebraska but across its range.

The bald eagle was not protected in the United States until 1940, and not until 1952 in Alaska, the last stronghold for the species. From 1917 to 1949 there was a 50-cent bounty on bald eagles in Alaska, and the bounty was increased to $2 in 1949. Between 1917 and 1952, more than 128,000 bounties were paid. In the lower 48 states, both bald and golden eagles were often shot or poisoned when they were perceived as competitors for fish or as killers of livestock. The factor that pushed the bald eagle to the brink of extinction, more than any other, was the introduction of potent pesticides in the 1940s, especially DDT. Like other end-of-the-food-chain species, pesticide residues accumulated in the tissues of bald eagles and caused failed nesting attempts because of thin eggshells. The use of DDT was banned in 1972, but its residues remained in aquatic systems. The southern subspecies of bald eagles received protection in the lower 48 states under the Bald Eagle Protection Act in 1940. The entire North American population received federal protection under the federal Endangered Species Act in 1978. That year the species was listed as endangered in Nebraska under the Nebraska Nongame and Endangered Species Conservation Act. Legislative protection and elimination of harmful pesticides, has allowed the species to increase in abundance.

Populations have increased dramatically across the bald eagle's range since the 1980s. Eagle habitat for all seasons, and especially for breeding, has improved in Nebraska during the past 100 years. Large trees for nesting are now found where once they did not exist, and reservoirs have created a reliable food source.

The first attempted nesting in Nebraska in recent times was along the Missouri River in Cedar County in 1973, when a pair constructed a nest and were observed copulating. Eggs were never documented. Bald eagle pairs constructed nests on the North Platte River in Garden County in 1987, along the Platte River in Lincoln County

in 1989 and another pair nested in 1991 in Garden County, but in none of those cases were eggs documented. The first documented laying of eggs and successful hatching of bald eagles in Nebraska since the late-1800s came in 1991 on the lower Platte River in western Douglas County, but the one chick did not survive to fledge. The following year the first documented successful nesting of bald eagles in Nebraska occurred in Sherman County when two young were fledged. And, in 1993 six young were fledged from two nests, one in Scotts Bluff County and the other in Sherman County.

Since 1991 there have been many nesting attempts and successful nesting records for the state. Nests have been found as far west as Scotts Bluff County and in 45 of Nebraska's 93 counties. Through the 2002 nesting season a total of 203 eagles have fledged from 121 known nesting attempts over the past 12 years.

Not only are bald eagles becoming more regular and widespread nesters in Nebraska, they are increasingly common winter visitors, especially where there are concentrations of waterfowl at reservoirs. The number of bald eagles in Nebraska is highly variable, depending on weather conditions, available open water and abundance of wintering waterfowl. Nebraska Game and Parks Commission winter bald eagle surveys showed an average of 651 birds during the 1980s, 930 during the 1990s and 1,282 during the period of 2000 to 2003. The species status was upgraded from endangered to threatened by the U.S. Fish and Wildlife Service in 1995.

Bald eagles became more common winter visitors with the construction of reservoirs. In recent years they have returned as a breeding species.

Clark's and Western Grebes

Until 1985, the Clark's grebe was considered a color morph of the western grebe. Both species are waterbirds of the western United States. Their ranges overlap extensively, the western's range extending farther north and east than the Clark's. In Nebraska and elsewhere, the western is significantly more abundant.

In most regards the two species appear to be identical, including a characteristic rushing display when mated pairs rise to the surface of the water and run parallel with necks arched. There is a difference, however, in the "advertising call" used during courtship as well as differences in bill color and facial patterns. A study in the early-1960s demonstrated that each species showed a preference for mating with those of its own kind. DNA studies during the 1980s demonstrated as much difference between western and Clark's grebes as between other closely related species. So, where there had been one species, there became two.

The discerning birder will detect a color difference in the bills of the species, the western's being yellowish to dull olive and the Clark's a brighter yellow. The give-away is on the head. If the black crown ends above the eye, it is a Clark's grebe. If the crown extends below the eye, it is a western grebe. The advertising calls heard during early phases of courtship are also different, the western's is a harsh, two-note, cree creet, and the Clark's call is a single note. Where both species are present during early courtship and pair formation, males respond to the calls of females of their species.

During the nesting season, both species select relative large freshwater marshes, or the marshy ends of freshwater lakes, with abundant supplies of fish. Central and western Sandhills lakes and marshes are used by both species during the breeding season. Only a handful of Clark's grebe nesting sites have be documented in Nebraska's western Sandhills and on the marshy upper end of Lake McConaughy.

Clark's grebe

Western grebe

rare gulls, including Bonaparte's, lesser black-backed, great black-backed, Ross's, glaucous, laughing, California and Thayer's. As many as 85,000 Franklin's gulls have been seen at Sutherland during fall migration. The best time to see a rare gull is late-November through early-January. Other uncommon species reported at Sutherland in recent years include the common loon, long-tailed duck, red-necked grebe, Clark's grebe and Neotropic cormorant. Look, too, for large concentrations of common goldeneyes and common mergansers. In recent years double-crested cormorants established a breeding colony on the reservoir. Summer drawdowns leave mudflats and islands that are attractive to southward-migrating shorebirds. Whatever time of year, bring a spotting scope.

Clear Creek WMA

Clear Creek Wildlife Management Area at the upper end of Lake McConaughy slices across braided North Platte River channels and includes land on both sides of the river. With 6,195 acres, it encompasses a variety of habitats on the floodplain and nearly flat stream terraces – river channel, riparian woods and brush, wetlands and wet meadows. The land is owned by CNPPID but has been managed by the Nebraska Game and Parks Commission since 1960. The WMA is divided into three units – the 3,144-acre eastern block is a public hunting area, 600 acres above that is a controlled public shooting area for waterfowl, and farther upstream is a 2,451-acre waterfowl refuge. As many as 9,000 Canada geese and 19,000 mallards have wintered on the refuge in recent years, and a rich mix of waterfowl species can be expected. Water-control structures recently installed on meadows have increased waterfowl use of the area. Both trumpeter and tundra swans use the WMA in fall and winter. Look for cinnamon teal during spring migration and Eurasian wigeons in flocks of American wigeons.

While Clear Creek is managed principally for waterfowl, nonhunted wildlife share equally in the diverse habitats protected and managed there. During spring migration, 12,000 to 14,000 sandhill cranes stage on and near the area, and whooping cranes have rested there during both spring and fall migration. In 1991, 24 sandhill cranes wintered on Clear Creek. American white pelicans are almost always on the area during the summer months. Bald eagles are common when waterfowl gather from fall through spring, and peregrine falcons winter in the area. Both sharp-tailed grouse and greater prairie-chickens use the area in fall and winter. Western grebes, which were first reported breeding at the McConaughy complex in 1993, have had a nesting colony on Clear Creek in recent years when a proper mix of emergent vegetation and water levels are present. Clear Creek is one of a handful of known Clark's grebe nesting sites in Nebraska.

Summer reservoir drawdowns and drought often leave expanses of mudflats that attract shorebirds in great variety and numbers, especially during their

Western grebes are most common as nesters on large lakes and marshes in the central and western Sandhills. Since the early-1990s, western and Clark's grebes have nested on the Clear Creek Wildlife Management Area.

southward migration. Rosche considered Clear Creek WMA the most reliable place to see black-bellied plovers in the region. They are found on wet, plowed fields during spring migration from mid-May to mid-June, and on mudflats from late-August into October during fall migration. He recommended the road south of the headquarters traversing wet meadows and mudflats. Other shorebird species to look for at Clear Creek are the willet, long-billed curlew, marbled godwit, and semipalmated, western, least, white-rumped, Baird's, pectoral, stilt and buff-breasted sandpipers. Ruddy turnstones are rare, but look for them in mid-May on mudflats. Peregrine falcons are most common when shorebirds are abundant during migration. Upland sandpipers are breeders. Virginia and king rails have been reported wintering.

Postbreeding great egrets and snowy egrets are expected, although usually not in the numbers found at reservoirs in southern Nebraska. Eleven waders have been reported in the Lake McConaughy complex, of which only the great blue heron and cattle egret are documented breeding species. Cattle egrets were discovered nesting on the western end of the lake in 1994. Three previous breeding records for the species are all from the Sandhills. Wilson's snipe and least bitterns probably nest on the area. Yellow-headed blackbirds are a common breeding species. The first state record for the rare reddish egret, of which only about 2,000 nesting pairs are believed to exist in the United States, was made on the western end of Lake

McConaughy in late-September 2000. White-faced ibis are regularly seen in spring. River otter sightings have been frequent at Clear Creek since 13 males and nine females were released in 1987 and 1988.

A sampling of woodland passerines, including similar eastern and western species such as the indigo and lazuli buntings and eastern and western wood-pewees, can be found on Clear Creek. Look for Bell's vireo, willow flycatcher, common yellowthroat and swamp sparrows in floodplain brush and willows. Breeding bobolinks and dickcissels are in the meadows and alfalfa fields.

Rosche rated the road south of the North Platte River and Clear Creek WMA as "one of the most important birding roads in the region." Four-wheel-drive vehicles are recommended for portions of that road. Rosche recommended that birders watch for barn owl and great horned owl nests at the base of the cliff that is the northern end of Ash Hollow State Historical Park. Poorwills also are found there in summer. Where the road passes by juniper woodlands watch for the northern parula and magnolia warblers in migration, and red-breasted nuthatches, golden-crowned kinglets and Townsend's solitaires in winter. Marshes north of the road have a large population of swamp sparrows in summer and wintering marsh wrens and rails. Listen for willow flycatchers in willows just beyond the gate to Clear Creek refuge.

• Additional Information: To reach Clear Creek WMA from Lewellen, travel southeast 5 miles on

*A secretive and seldom-seen marsh bird, the **king rail** has been reported in all seasons at Clear Creek Wildlife Management Area.*

BUB BLAKE

Nebraska Highway 92, then at the sign, south 1 mile on an access road. To access the southern side of Clear Creek, turn east on the gravel road off U.S. Highway 26 about ½ mile south of the North Platte River bridge opposite Ash Hollow Cemetery. Roads on Clear Creek are closed during the winter months.

• Nearby Birding Destinations: Located on U.S. Highway 26 south of the North Platte River above Lake McConaughy is **Ash Hollow State Historical Park.** Archaeological excavations indicate early man used the site 6,000 years ago and it remains an outstanding retreat, especially for birders. Windlass Hill, where travelers on the Oregon Trail lowered their wagons into the North Platte Valley, is on the area. There are more than 1,000 acres of grasslands and rock outcrops on the rugged valley wall and canyons for birds and birders. There is a 1-mile hiking trail from the visitor center to a spring in the canyon bottom and a trail west of the highway up Windlass Hill. Ornithologist John Kirk Townsend collected the lark bunting at Ash Hollow in 1834, but he did not scientifically describe it so it is not the type specimen. Additional Information: Ash Hollow SHP, P.O. Box 70, Lewellen, NE 69147-0070, (308) 778-5651, ashhollow@ngpc.state.ne.us

Scotts Bluff National Monument

A prominent natural landmark and favorite campsite for emigrants moving west on the Oregon and California trails, and the nearby Mormon Trail, from the 1840s through the 1860s, Scotts Bluff, Mitchell Pass and adjoining grasslands were set aside as a national monument in 1919. The proclamation President Woodrow Wilson signed creating the national monument stated it was the "highest known point within the State of Nebraska." The monument is 4,649 feet above sea level, rising nearly 800 feet above the North Platte River immediately to the north. The highest known point in Nebraska, however, is a rather nondescript tract of real estate in southwestern Kimball County at 5,424 feet above sea level.

Scotts Bluff National Monument encompasses nearly 3,000 acres, the remnant of an ancient and higher plain formed by material carried by rivers and winds from the uplifted Rocky Mountains about 60 million years ago. Fossils of saber-toothed cats, giant turtles and pigs, rhinoceroses and camels have been found in the eroding bluff. The bluff is named for Hiram Scott, an injured trapper who, according to legend, was abandoned there to die in 1828. A complete history of the site is available at www.nps.gov/scbl/

Ponderosa pine and Rocky Mountain juniper have colonized parts of the summit and sheltered slopes. As would be expected, the area is rocky, with openings of native prairie and shrubland. Scotts Bluff is an excellent site to see western Nebraska wildflowers, especially cushion-plants adapted to semiarid, rocky environments.

Golden eagles and prairie falcons have nested on bluffs and buttes in the area and are a likely sighting, as are other High Plains raptors. Scotts Bluff is one of the most convenient locations to see white-throated swifts. Watch, too, for chimney swifts. There have been reports and records of unexpected species in the Scotts Bluff area in recent years, including a brambling in mid-April 1999, curved-billed thrasher in the winter of 2002-2003, and band-tailed pigeon in May 2000.

Personal vehicles may be driven to the bluff summit. There is a 1.6-mile hiking trail between the summit and the visitor center at the base of the bluff. During the summer season, park rangers shuttle hikers who want to hike only one way. The entrance fee is $5 per vehicle for seven days access. The monument is open from 8 a.m. to 7 p.m. Memorial Day through Labor Day, and 8 a.m. to 5 p.m. the rest of the year. It is closed Thanksgiving, December 25 and January 1. Hours of operation are subject to change. The visitor center features watercolors by William Henry Jackson, a pioneer artist and photographer, as well as paleontological and historical exhibits. Programs and guided nature walks are offered during the summer months. Additional Information: Scotts Bluff National

Scotts Bluff Bird Sampler

Turkey Vulture	Rock Wren
Swainson's Hawk	Townsend's Solitaire
Red-tailed Hawk	Sage Thrasher
Ferruginous Hawk	Yellow-rumped Warbler
Rough-legged Hawk	Yellow-breasted Chat
Golden Eagle	Western Tanager
Prairie Falcon	Green-tailed Towhee
Black-billed Cuckoo	Spotted Towhee
Yellow-billed Cuckoo	Chipping Sparrow
Burrowing Owl	Clay-colored Sparrow
Common Poorwill	Brewer's Sparrow
White-throated Swift	Lark Sparrow
Say's Phoebe	Lark Bunting
Pinyon Jay	Black-headed Grosbeak
Black-billed Magpie	Blue Grosbeak
Horned Lark	Lazuli Bunting
Violet-green Swallow	Bullock's Oriole
Northern Rough-winged	Baltimore Oriole
Swallow	Gray-crowned Rosy Finch
Red-breasted Nuthatch	Red Crossbill

Monument is located 3 miles west of Gering on Nebraska Highway 92. Scotts Bluff National Monument, P.O. Box 27, 190276 Highway 92 West, Gering, NE 69341-0027, (308) 436-4340, SCBL Webmaster@nps.gov

• Nearby Birding Destinations: **Facus Springs WMA** is a North Platte Valley alkaline wetland worth a birder's attention. Acquired in 1996, this 422-acre area is one of the largest alkaline wetlands in the North Platte Valley. Saline ponds and meadows, and freshwater marsh contribute to a diverse avifauna.

Expect many of the same species as found at Kiowa WMA (see below), including nesting cinnamon teal, American avocets and Wilson's phalaropes. The largest population of nesting Savannah sparrows documented in the state is at Facus Springs on the western side of Redington Road, which is the western boundary of the WMA.

There is a large pond on private land west of Facus that can be viewed from Redington Road. Location: Facus Springs WMA is 9 miles west of Bridgeport on U.S. Highway 26 and Nebraska Highway 92. The highway passes diagonally through the northern half of the area. There is a parking lot on the northern side of the highway.

South of Facus Springs on Redington Road is Redington Gap through the rocky southern North Platte Valley wall. Watch for burrowing owls in a prairie dog town on the west side of Redington Road a few miles south of Facus Springs. Redington Gap is worth a stop, especially to see wildflowers in May and June. Watch for Cassin's kingbirds, Brewer's blackbirds and pinyon jays.

While on highways 92 and 26, other Oregon Trail rock monoliths, such as Chimney Rock, Courthouse Rock and Jail Rock, offer opportunities to see golden eagles, prairie falcons, Say's phoebes, rock wrens and white-throated swifts. Yellow-breasted chats nest at Chimney Rock and sage thrashers are occasionally found there in autumn.

There are several excellent birding destinations nearby in the Wildcat Hills. Turn to page 140 for for additional information about birdwatching in the Wildcat Hills Escarpment.

North Platte NWR

The North Platte National Wildlife Refuge was established by executive order in 1916 as a "preserve and breeding ground for native birds," especially for autumn and winter concentrations of mallards and Canada geese. The 2,722-acre refuge is superimposed over four Bureau of Reclamation irrigation reservoirs constructed between 1910 and 1917. Three of those reservoirs – the 430-acre Lake Minatare, 780-acre Winters Creek and 1,377-acre Lake Alice – are part of the refuge. A smaller impoundment, Little Lake Alice

BUB BLAKE

*Most common as migrants, **hooded mergansers** often linger into the summer. More common in eastern Nebraska, they frequent reservoirs in the west during spring and fall migration.*

reservoir, was removed from the refuge in 1961. Since 1963, most of the shoreline and the sport fishery of Lake Minatare have been managed by the Nebraska Game and Parks Commission as a state recreation area.

The refuge includes about 1,439 acres of grassland, mostly native prairie. Since 1985, grazing has been reduced and prescribed burning has been used to restore the grasslands to their natural state. Prospects for viewing native grassland birds improve each year. There are about 315 acres of trees on the area, principally cottonwood and green ash surrounding the lakes. The Bureau of Reclamation still manages the

Clear Creek Wildlife Management Area is one of the most reliable sites in the region to view **black-bellied plovers**.

MICHAEL FORSBERG

North Platte NWR Bird Sampler

Ross's Goose	Least Sandpiper
Canada Goose	Baird's Sandpiper
Wood Duck	Long-billed Dowitcher
Mallard	Wilson's Phalarope
Cinnamon Teal	Red-necked Phalarope
Northern Shoveler	Bonaparte's Gull
Northern Pintail	Ring-billed Gull
Lesser Scaup	California Gull
Common Goldeneye	Herring Gull
Barrow's Goldeneye	Forster's Tern
Common Merganser	Eastern Screech-Owl
Red-breasted Merganser	Common Poorwill
Ruddy Duck	Belted Kingfisher
Common Loon	Red-headed Woodpecker
Eared Grebe	Western Kingbird
Western Grebe	Cassin's Kingbird
American White Pelican	Warbling Vireo
Double-crested Cormorant	Black-billed Magpie
Great Blue Heron	Horned Lark
Black-crowned Night-Heron	Cliff Swallow
Osprey	Marsh Wren
Bald Eagle	Mountain Bluebird
Northern Harrier	Townsend's Solitaire
Ferruginous Hawk	Yellow-rumped Warbler
Merlin	Common Yellowthroat
Peregrine Falcon	Western Tanager
Prairie Falcon	Spotted Towhee
Virginia Rail	Lark Sparrow
Black-bellied Plover	White-crowned Sparrow
Lesser Yellowlegs	Dark-eyed Junco
Long-billed Curlew	Lapland Longspur
Marbled Godwit	Black-headed Grosbeak
Sanderling	Blue Grosbeak
Western Sandpiper	Yellow-headed Blackbird
	Pine Siskin

system for water storage and draws down the lakes to meet summer irrigation demands. Because of seasonal fluctuations in their water levels, Lake Minatare and Lake Alice have little shoreline emergent vegetation. Winters Creek Lake was a natural wetland converted into a storage reservoir and it has an established aquatic plant community.

The refuge bird lists includes 228 species of which 58 are probable or confirmed breeders. Waterbirds are the principal attraction. The refuge list includes six species of grebes, eight species of wading birds, trumpeter swans, four species of geese, 20 species of ducks, three species of mergansers, 18 species of raptors, 28 species of shorebirds and 12 species of gulls and terns. Canada geese, wood ducks, blue-winged teal and mallards nest on the refuge in small numbers. Lake Minatare is listed as "globally significant" by the American Bird Conservancy as a waterfowl wintering area. Lake Minatare is closed in fall and winter as a waterfowl sanctuary. A pair of bald eagles has nested in the great blue heron rookery at Lake Alice every year since 1993, and 27 young eagles have fledged through 2003. The nesting area is closed to the public.

Richard Rosche recommended Winters Creek Lake as the best birding site on the refuge because of its marshy habitat. The lake can be seen from a refuge road on the southwestern side, and from a parallel county road when access to the refuge is closed. Watch for cinnamon teal in spring.

• Additional Information: At the refuge's five primary entry points there are kiosks with refuge information and maps. A stop at one of these sites is essential for finding your way around on the refuge. Sunrise to sunset public access to Winters Creek Lake, Lake Minatare and Lake Alice is allowed from January 15 through October 14. Because the area is designated a waterfowl sanctuary, the refuge and Lake Minatare SRA are closed to the public from October 15 through January 14. Some grasslands sites are closed to the public to provide an undisturbed wildlife sanctuary. Modern camping facilities are available at Lake Minatare SRA. North Platte National Wildlife Refuge, 115 Railway St., Suite C109, Scottsbluff, NE 69361-3190, (308) 636-7851, e-mail crescentlake@fws.gov, web site http://crescentlake.fws.gov/

Kiowa WMA

The first tract of land for Kiowa Wildlife Management Area south of Morrill was acquired in 1993 by the Nebraska Game and Parks Commission with the financial support of other conservation organizations and a bequest from Clive Ostenberg, a Panhandle sportsman. Kiowa is perhaps the best public-access alkaline wetland in the Panhandle. North Platte River Valley alkaline wetlands exist where drainage is poorly developed and rainfall is inadequate to leach naturally occurring salts from the soil. Salts in shallow, standing water precipitate out in the heat of summer, and over centuries they accumulate until wetlands and soils are highly alkaline and saline-adapted plants – inland saltgrass, alkali sacaton, spearscale, sea blite, alkali plantain and others – colonize the areas.

As on alkaline wetlands in the western Sandhills, the open shorelines and abundant hatches of several aquatic invertebrates, especially brine flies and brine shrimp, make these wetlands attractive shorebird feeding grounds. Richard Rosche regularly observed North Platte Valley alkaline wetlands for three decades and recorded about 70 bird species, with shorebirds, wading birds and waterfowl dominating his list. Snow geese and Ross's geese use Kiowa in the spring and as many as 10,000 Canada geese and 30,000 mallards winter there. Between 1984 and 1994, the Commission released 5,000 Canada goose goslings in the North Platte Valley to re-establish a breeding population. Several pairs of Canada geese now nest on Kiowa. About 20 species of waterfowl have been reported at Kiowa. It is probably the best place in the state to find cinnamon teal, principally in the spring and summer. Eared grebes and ruddy ducks often pause on Kiowa during spring migration. A birder's shorebird checklist could easily reach 20 species. Look for nesting American avocets, black-necked stilts, Wilson's phalaropes and Wilson's snipe. Marbled godwits are expected during spring migration, although their stay is usually brief, and red-necked phalaropes and white-faced ibis have been reported. Other shorebirds include lesser yellowlegs, western, least, white-rumped, Baird's and stilt sandpipers. Red-winged and yellow-headed blackbirds are breeders. Kiowa is the western-most documented nesting site for great-tailed grackles in the state. American pipits have been reported.

Kiowa WMA encompasses 540 acres of which 326 are closed as a refuge from October 1 to the end of the dark goose hunting season. On the eastern end of the WMA a low-level dike created a large pool, and there are extensive, seasonal wetlands to the west. A small prairie dog town is immediately east of the pool. Freshwater springs feed the main pool on the southern side and there are extensive stands of emergent vegetation. It is possible to walk the entire area without waterproof boots but knee-high boots are suggested.

• Additional Information: Primary access is 2½ miles south of Morrill. There is a parking lot and a wheelchair-accessible observation deck.

• Nearby Birding Destinations: Since 1990 a 135-acre

diversion project on the North Platte River south of Henry has been managed as part of the North Platte NWR. **Stateline Island** is formed by the North Platte River on the north and Centennial Creek on the south. It is heavily forested with cottonwood and green ash. Prescribed burning has been used since 1994 to setback understory woody plants and to invigorate native grassland. This site is open during daylight hours year-round. Location: 1 mile south of Henry. ■

BUB BLAKE

Marbled godwits are fleeting migrants. The best locations to find them are Clear Creek and Kiowa wildlife management areas and the North Platte National Wildlife Refuge.

Kiowa Bird Sampler

Snow Goose	Ferruginous Hawk
Ross's Goose	Virginia Rail
Canada Goose	Sora
Gadwall	American Coot
American Wigeon	Lesser Yellowlegs
Mallard	Willet
Cinnamon Teal	Marbled Godwit
Northern Shoveler	Western Sandpiper
Green-winged Teal	Least Sandpiper
Pied-billed Grebe	Baird's Sandpiper
Double-crested Cormorant	White-rumped Sandpiper
Great Blue Heron	Long-billed Dowitcher
Great Egret	Wilson's Snipe
Black-crowned Night-	Wilson's Phalarope
Heron	Red-necked Phalarope
Bald Eagle	Burrowing Owls
Northern Harrier	Black-billed Magpie
Red-tailed Hawk	Great-tailed Grackle

Shortgrass Prairie

COMPARED TO MOST OTHER REGIONS of the state, little was written of Nebraska's shortgrass prairie before settlement in the late-1870s and 1880s. Early explorers and naturalists brushed against the semiarid grasslands when they traveled along the North and South Platte rivers, but they found little reason to venture into the seemingly endless expanse. Even promoters of the state's agricultural prospects steered clear of the rocky soils littered with cacti and grasses only halfway to the knees. And, there was the "Indian question" in the northern Panhandle that was not resolved until the 1880s. In June 1886, the Fremont, Elkhorn and Missouri Valley Railroad reached the present site of Harrison in Sioux County, providing a shipping point for cattle, and the northern prairie in Nebraska's Panhandle became the domain of large cattle ranches.

Except for areas in Sioux and Dawes counties north of the Pine Ridge escarpment, the Panhandle grasslands are considered a blending of shortgrass and mixed-grass prairie. Mid-20th century University of Nebraska prairie ecologist J.E. Weaver dismissed shortgrass prairie as nothing more than mixed-grass prairie that had been subjected to "severe drought, overgrazing, burial by dust, and damage by grasshoppers." Because Weaver was the foremost authority of grasslands of the Great Plains of his time, his opinion should be questioned cautiously. But periodic drought, overgrazing, burial by dust and damage by insect hordes is almost a description of North American grasslands, especially the shortgrass plains. Prairie fire should be added to the list of seemingly apocalyptic forces that keep forests at bay and define grasslands.

Other ecologists have defined shortgrass prairie as grasslands where all available soil moisture is depleted by the end of the growing season. The towering Rocky Mountains strip Pacific weather fronts of much of their moisture before it reaches the soils on the western Great Plains. In the western Panhandle, average annual precipitation is 14 to 17 inches, much it falling in May and June.

The eastern edge of the shortgrass prairie region is vaguely defined – a shifting line influenced by long-term fluctuations in precipitation. Shortgrass prairie extends westward to the foothills of the Rocky Mountains. Through its extent, from Texas to northern Montana, the region is sparsely populated. Drought-resistant blue grama and buffalograss are the characteristic plant species, and there are few woody plants. Forb species are fewer in shortgrass prairies than in more mesic grasslands to the east, but they are often showy, blanketing pastures with colorful blossoms when rainfall is abundant. In the shortgrass prairie, where plants live on a thin line between surviving and vanishing, unpalatable forbs, such as native cacti, and toxic species, such as locoweeds and death camas, have evolved to discourage grazing.

More shortgrass prairie exists today than of any other North American grassland type, largely because precipitation is scant for farming and groundwater is too deep and expensive to extract for irrigation in many areas. Other areas of shortgrass prairie have remained in grass because of rocky soils. But, large areas of shortgrass prairie in the central and southern Nebraska Panhandle have been converted to crop production, principally wheat. With the recent introduction of center-pivot irrigation, corn is now more widely planted. Sugar beets are a common crop in some areas of the Panhandle. Throughout the region, however, cattle production remains an important use of the land and shortgrass prairie persists at least in name, if not in original plant composition.

Except where shortgrass prairie is broken by streams sparsely fringed with cottonwoods, and near rocky outcrops, the bird life of this region is meager. Fewer bird species exist in shortgrass prairie than in more complex plant communities to the east. Bird species native to shortgrass prairie are the most rapidly declining bird populations on the continent, largely because of extensive conversion of prairie to dryland cultivation and overgrazing. Still, about 40 percent of the shortgrass region is considered intact. While declines in Neotropical migrant bird species have received considerable attention in recent years, the seriousness of declining grassland species is only beginning to be recognized and studied.

JON FARRAR

Rock wrens nest in rock ledges and outcrops from Lake McConaughy west and are most common in the Panhandle. They nest in May and June.

Characteristic shortgrass prairie birds are the ferruginous hawk, mountain plover, long-billed curlew, burrowing owl, McCown's longspur, horned lark, western meadowlark, lark bunting, and lark, vesper and grasshopper sparrows. Add a cottonwood and both eastern and western kingbirds will be present; add a rubble of rock eroding out of the plains and rock wrens or Say's phoebes are sure to be found; add short woody plants like sage and Brewer's sparrows, sage thrashers and green-tailed towhees are possible. High

*The **Oglala National Grassland** is a landscape of big skies, mixed-grass prairie, sagebrush, and soft rock and clay bluffs. It is the largest expanse of public-access grassland in the Panhandle. Roads crisscross the area, providing birders excellent access.*

buttes and escarpments provide perches and nesting sites for golden eagles, ferruginous hawks and prairie falcons.

Oglala National Grassland

Most botanists and ecologists consider the grassland north of the Pine Ridge in extreme northwestern Nebraska to be mixed-grass prairie. It is included here for convenience and because the avifauna is similar to that found on shortgrass plains to the south. Grasslands north of the Pine Ridge are a blend of mesic eastern plant species and xeric western plant species. They also include a blend of cool-season species from the north, such as wheatgrasses and green needlegrass, and warm-season species from the south, such as buffalograss, blue grama and little bluestem. Near the Wyoming border big and dwarf sagebrush, rabbit brush and greasewood add vertical elements, attracting bird species not found elsewhere in the region.

The topography is perhaps the most interesting in Nebraska – rolling grasslands scarred by eroded drainages carrying water only after rare cloudbursts, soft rock and hard clay bluffs, and bizarre and seemingly inhospitable badlands. To the south is the dark rim of the Pine Ridge, and on crisp autumn days the Black Hills can be seen on the northern horizon.

It is a place, like the Sandhills, where little imagination is required to conjure an image of what the land was like 200 years ago.

The Oglala National Grassland was acquired by the federal government, tract by tract, from failing homesteaders during the drought and Depression of the 1930s. Until 1954 these lands were administered by the Soil Conservation Service, which rehabilitated the effects of overgrazing and dryland farming during the 1930s drought. Today, the 94,400-acre area is managed by the Pine Ridge Ranger District of the Nebraska National Forest, U.S. Forest Service in Chadron. Roads crisscrossing the Oglala grassland are little used and birding can be done safely along them. A county map or a map sold by the forest service is useful in navigating the area. Private lands border public-access lands throughout the Oglala National Grassland. Landowner permission is required to enter private property. Major roads are graveled but many others are not, and traveling these dirt roads when they are wet is not advised.

Singing perches are at a premium because few fences parallel the roads. More than in most regions of the state, birders will want to seek birds wherever there is a break in the uniform grassland. Rock outcrops, isolated tree groves or bands of trees along drainages, and tracts with sagebrush attract migrating and nesting

Ferruginous Hawks nest in grasslands on rock outcrops and buttes, and occasionally in isolated trees, but they also nest on the ground. They are most common in the Panhandle and western Sandhills.

birds. Also watch for birds where there is water – pools standing after a rain and near small impoundments on the Oglala National Grassland.

Expect to see long-billed curlews and upland sandpipers along the roads during the breeding season. Black-billed magpies are permanent residents. Sage thrashers are rare summer residents and suspected breeders in sagebrush, especially near Montrose, Orella and Sugarloaf Butte. MacGillivray's warblers are rare spring and autumn transients, and they are suspected but not confirmed breeders. Look for them in dense brush, often near water. Snowy owls and snow buntings are possible in winter.

In the extreme northwestern corner of Sioux County, it might be possible to find greater sage-grouse. The species occurs only a short distance west in Wyoming and north in South Dakota and it was apparently also found in extreme northwestern Nebraska in the early-1900s. Greater sage-grouse have been sporadically reported in sagebrush country as recently as 1960, 1975 and 1987. Watch for pronghorns, and in the early morning and evening, for a glimpse of the diminutive swift fox. There are black-tailed prairie dog towns on the Oglala Grassland, and prairie rattlesnakes, but few people are fortunate enough to ever see one.

• Additional Information: The Oglala National Grassland is a large area spanning northern Sioux County and extending into Dawes County. Access to the western portion is via a paved road north of Harrison that passes through Gilbert-Baker WMA, another important birding stop. To access the eastern areas of the grassland, from the junction of combined

Nebraska Highway 2 and 71 and U.S. Highway 20 at the northeastern edge of Crawford, drive north a little more than 4 miles on the combined route of Nebraska Highway 2 and 71. Turn west at the sign directing visitors to Toadstool Geologic Park, drive west 2 miles, then turn northwest and follow the road paralleling the rail line past Toadstool Park. U.S. Forest Service roads to the west are marked, providing access through the grassland, and they connect to roads north of Harrison. For additional information contact the Pine Ridge Ranger Station. See information on page 138 under Nebraska National Forest.

Ogalala Grassland Bird Sampler

Northern Harrier	Loggerhead Shrike
Swainson's Hawk	Black-billed Magpie
Ferruginous Hawk	Horned Lark
Rough-legged Hawk	Cliff Swallow
Golden Eagle	Rock Wren
Merlin	Sage Thrasher
Prairie Falcon	MacGillivray's Warbler
Sharp-tailed Grouse	Brewer's Sparrow
Upland Sandpiper	Lark Sparrow
Long-billed Curlew	Lark Bunting
Burrowing Owl	McCown's Longspur
Common Nighthawk	Lapland Longspur
Western Wood-Pewee	Chestnut-collared
Say's Phoebe	Longspur
Western Kingbird	Gray-crowned Rosy-Finch
Northern Shrike	Common Redpoll

• Nearby Birding Destinations: While bizarre badlands topography is the principal attraction of **Toadstool Geologic Park,** it is worth walking the trails there for birds. Say's phoebes and rock wrens are expected. Watch for golden eagles and prairie falcons overhead. Flocks of gray-crowned rosy-finches have been found roosting in rocky areas from October into April. A birder should not expect to find black-throated sparrows anywhere in Nebraska, but one of the two documented records for the species in the state was made at Toadstool. Rabbitbrush west and south of the parking area attracts migrant passerines. There is a campground, picnic shelters, water and restrooms on the area and a mile-long hiking trail. Hikers should be aware of the presence of prairie rattlesnakes. There is a daily vehicle charge.

Agate Fossil Beds

Although Agate Fossil Beds National Monument is only 3,000 acres, it is a worthy stop for birders driving between the North Platte Valley and the Pine Ridge. The Niobrara River passes through the area, only 65 miles downstream from its headwaters. There it is a narrow, deep and fast-running stream quite unlike the Niobrara River most people know. About three-fourths of the area is pristine shortgrass prairie with rocky buttes and outcrops, the remainder is wet meadows associated with the Niobrara River. Agate is best known for the 20-million-year-old Miocene Epoch fossilized mammal bones excavated from rocky knobs on the valley wall in the early-1900s. Many of those fossils can be seen at the University of Nebraska State Museum in Lincoln, and in prestigious eastern museums, such as the Carnegie Museum, the American Museum in New York, and at Yale University.

MICHAEL FORSBERG

McCown's longspurs are common breeders in Panhandle shortgrass prairie.

During the Miocene, the land at Agate Fossil Beds was a grass savanna comparable to today's Serengeti Plains in Africa. Bones of animals of that time – giant pig-like Dinohyus, three-foot-tall camels, rhinoceros, huge horse-like animals with claws, and carnivorous beardogs – are still emerging from the eroding high plain as the Niobrara River carves through geologic history. Fossils are displayed at the visitor center along with an outstanding display of Lakota and Northern Cheyenne artifacts collected by James H. Cook.

Agate has not been extensively observed by birders. The area checklist includes 140 species. A variety of grassland sparrows can be found. McCown's and chestnut-collared longspurs are breeders. Birders

Mountain Plover

The mountain plover, like the upland sandpiper and long-billed curlew, is a shorebird that seldom is found near water. Mountain plovers breed in arid shortgrass plains from northern Montana to southern New Mexico. Market hunting in the late-1800s and destruction of grasslands have led to a dramatic decline in the plover's abundance. Their numbers are estimated to have been reduced by as much as 50 to 89 percent. The current mountain plover population is estimated to be between 8,000 and 11,000 individuals. The species' strongholds are small areas of native prairie in Montana and Colorado. Most mountain plovers winter in the San Joaquin Valley in California, where suitable habitat has also dramatically declined.

Historically, mountain plovers were breeders over most of the Nebraska Panhandle. In recent years they are known principally from Kimball County, a county almost entirely in private ownership and intensively farmed. They have also been documented breeding in Cheyenne County, and adults have been observed in Cherry, Banner, Antelope, Box Butte, Dawes and Sioux counties. The species was classified as threatened in Nebraska in 1976. The mountain plover was proposed for listing as a federally threatened species by the U.S. Fish and Wildlife Service in 1999. In September 2003 USFWS withdrew the listing proposal based on new information suggesting threats to the species were not as significant as previously believed, and because there were conservation and monitoring programs in place.

The species prefers expansive arid flats with very short grass and a high proportion of bare ground. Grazing by bison and prairie dogs once created optimum nesting habitat. Cattle can perform a similar function today. The plover shows a strong preference for heavily grazed pastures and prairie dog towns. The loss of prairie dog towns has probably contributed to a decline in mountain plover nesting habitat. They have been found nesting in fallow wheat fields in Kimball County. Mountain plovers are often described as a "disturbance-evolved species," requiring grasslands with short cover. This should not suggest that abuse of the land is desirable, rather that in a natural environment the habitat requirements of all grassland bird species are present.

Under the Shortgrass Prairie Partnership, the Nebraska Game and Parks Commission and the Rocky Mountain Bird Observatory are surveying and monitoring mountain plovers in western Nebraska and working with landowners to improved nesting habitat.

BOB GRIER

Mountain plovers are rare breeders in the southern Panhandle.

Oliver Reservoir is an anomaly in the shortgrass prairie region – a man-made body of water with deciduous trees and shrubs attracting unexpected passerine species in a semiarid land. Unexpected warblers and flycatchers have been recorded.

should use binoculars to scan the sky and rock outcrops for golden eagles, prairie falcons, and rough-legged and ferruginous hawks. Golden eagles and ferruginous hawks nest on rock ledges along this portion of the Niobrara River. Short-eared owls might be seen over meadows bordering the river. Say's phoebes and rock wrens are common at rock outcrops and cottonwood groves attract migrating passerines. Cushion-type wildflowers adapted to the region's semiarid climate and harsh environment are found in bloom on rock outcrops in May and June. There are

Agate Birding Sampler

Great Blue Heron	Loggerhead Shrike
Northern Harrier	Horned Lark
Swainson's Hawk	Rock Wren
Red-tailed Hawk	Yellow Warbler
Ferruginous Hawk	Common Yellowthroat
Rough-legged Hawk	Yellow-breasted Chat
Prairie Falcon	Lark Sparrow
Sharp-tailed Grouse	Lark Bunting
Upland Sandpiper	Grasshopper Sparrow
Long-billed Curlew	McCown's Longspur
Burrowing Owl	Chestnut-collared
Common Nighthawk	Longspur
Northern Flicker	Red-winged Blackbird
Western Wood-Pewee	Western Meadowlark
Say's Phoebe	Brewer's Blackbird
Western Kingbird	Orchard Oriole
Eastern Kingbird	Bullock's Oriole

prairie rattlesnakes at Agate.

• Additional Information: Agate Fossil Beds is located 3 miles east of Nebraska Highway 29 at a point 22 miles south of Harrison and 34 miles north of Mitchell. A county road east of Agate, parallels the Niobrara River and ends at combined Nebraska Highway 2 and 71 about 18 miles south of Crawford. The area is open daily, the visitor center is open except on Thanksgiving, Christmas and New Year's days. Hours are 8 a.m. to 5 p.m. Labor Day to Memorial Day and 8 a.m. to 6 p.m. Memorial Day to Labor Day. Guided tours and informational talks are available in the summer months. There are covered picnic areas but no camping facilities. There is an entrance fee. Agate Fossil Beds National Monument, 301 River Road, Harrison, NE 69346-2734, (308) 668-2211, lil_morava@nps.gov, www.nps.gov/agfo

• Nearby Birding Destinations: For birders who want to get off the beaten path, and be invigorated by big skies and endless landscapes, the county road paralleling the Wyoming-Nebraska state line between Henry in the North Platte River Valley and Harrison is a great drive. From Henry take Nebraska S-79A north. There is an easterly jog from Henry before the road turns north. The road is paved for the first 8 miles, then graveled. The first 9 miles pass through farmland but there are wooded drainages that attract passerines. Beyond that point is shortgrass prairie rangeland. About 17 miles north of Henry the road passes through a gap in a rocky ridge. There is a prairie dog town south of the ridge on the western side of the road. Burrowing owls can usually be found there. Stop at the rock ridge to look for wildflowers and raptors, especially golden eagles that nest on the sides of the buttes. In winter watch for gray-crowned rosy-finches coming to roost in mid- to late-afternoon. Just north of the ridge, the western-most extent of Sandhills dunes can be seen in the distance to the east. Eventually the road turns to the east and jogs to Nebraska Highway 29 about 6 miles south of Harrison. Land on both sides of the road is privately owned. The road has little traffic and is wide, so birding can be done from a vehicle.

Oliver Reservoir SRA

The Kimball Irrigation District organized in 1909. Two years later a dam on Lodgepole Creek east of Bushnell was constructed with steam tractors, horses and hand labor, and the impoundment began to provide water for irrigation to one of the state's driest counties. Water flowed from the reservoir to irrigate crops until 1974, when the dam was declared a hazard by the Nebraska Department of Water Resources.

In 1976 the dam was breached and the lake was drained. Through the efforts of many people, and adoption of the reservoir by the South Platte Natural Resources District, the dam was improved to meet the new standards. The new reservoir's primary uses became recreation and flood control. In 1984 the Nebraska Game and Parks Commission began managing the area's recreation and it was designated the Oliver Reservoir State Recreation Area.

The area includes 270 acres of lake and 917 acres of uplands. Surrounded by grasslands, fringed with willows and cottonwoods, and its shallows filled with aquatic vegetation, Oliver Reservoir is an oasis in a semiarid land. The highest point in Nebraska, 5,424 feet above sea level, is only a few miles southwest of the reservoir.

Oliver Reservoir SRA has been described as a "migrant trap par excellence." Mist netting and observations by Steve Dinsmore in 1999 and 2000 confirmed suspicions and provided surprises about the avifauna of Oliver Reservoir and the Panhandle. In 2000 he spent four days catching birds in a mist net between August 26 and September 20. His net and sightings produced 26 species. Wilson's warblers were the most abundant. Three dusky flycatchers were captured and Hammond's flycatchers were observed, suggesting those species might be common fall migrants in the Panhandle. Also captured were Cassin's vireo, the Rocky Mountain subspecies of hermit thrush, western and eastern wood-pewees, ruby-crowned kinglet, clay-colored sparrow, black-headed grosbeak, northern waterthrush, common yellowthroat, and Townsend's, MacGillivray's and orange-crowned warblers. On other occasions Dinsmore confirmed gray, least and cordilleran flycatchers, and black-throated gray, black-throated blue and Virginia's warblers.

Other species reported from Oliver in recent years are the green-tailed towhee, willow flycatcher, Cassin's kingbird, plumbeus vireo, veery and western tanager.

Cliff swallows are more common breeders in western Nebraska than in the east, nesting in large colonies on rock outcrops and bridges.

Wilson's snipe have been reported nesting in the marshes at the western end of the lake, and dense thickets at Oliver are the only known regular breeding site for song sparrows in the Panhandle. Unexpected waterbirds reported there are the Clark's grebe and white-winged scoter. Post-nesting juvenile Mississippi kites have been reported at Oliver.

Recreational facilities are on the northern side of the lake. The southern and western sides are maintained as natural areas. Facilities include 75 camping pads and 100 nonpad sites, neither with electrical hookups. There are vault toilets, picnic tables, shelters, and grills all under a towering canopy of cottonwoods. Fishing is excellent at Oliver and there are two boat ramps. A state park entry permit is required.

• Additional Information: Oliver Reservoir State Recreation Area is 8 miles west of Kimball on U.S. Highway 30. ■

Oliver Bird Sampler

Canada Goose	Ruby-crowned Kinglet
Ruddy Duck	Swainson's Thrush
Pied-billed Grebe	Hermit Thrush
Eared Grebe	Northern Mockingbird
Western Grebe	Sage Thrasher
American White Pelican	Orange-crowned Warbler
Great Blue Heron	Virginia's Warbler
White-faced Ibis	Yellow-rumped Warbler
Cooper's Hawk	Townsend's Warbler
Golden Eagle	Northern Waterthrush
American Kestrel	MacGillivray's Warbler
Willet	Common Yellowthroat
Broad-tailed Hummingbird	Wilson's Warbler
Rufous Hummingbird	Western Tanager
Belted Kingfisher	Green-tailed Towhee
Western Wood-Pewee	Clay-colored Sparrow
Eastern Wood-Pewee	Song Sparrow
Willow Flycatcher	White-crowned Sparrow
Hammond's Flycatcher	McCown's Longspur
Dusky Flycatcher	Chestnut-collared
Cassin's Kingbird	Longspur
Northern Shrike	Black-headed Grosbeak
Plumbeus Vireo	Yellow-headed Blackbird
Cassin's Vireo	Bullock's Oriole

Sandsage Prairie

MOST GEOGRAPHERS AND BOTANISTS consider the sandy soil grasslands in parts of Dundy, Chase, Perkins and Hayes counties of southwestern Nebraska an extension of the Sandhills region. The origin of the sands and the time and means of deposition in both regions are similar. Radiocarbon datings from a blowout in Dundy County suggest dune sand was deposited in three periods, between 8,800 and 10,000 years ago, again between 8,000 and 3,000 years ago, and finally during the last 1,000 years. Dune relief in southwestern Nebraska is gentler than in the central Sandhills, but some ridges are 10 miles long, rise 50 to 150 feet above adjacent valleys and are pitted by blowouts. As in the eastern and southern Sandhills, sandsage prairie soils are very silty.

What makes southwestern Nebraska's sandsage prairie distinct from north-central Nebraska's Sandhills prairie are the plants dominating and defining each – a reflection of geographic position, climate and soils. Just as the plant composition of the Sandhills falls within the influence of the northern Great Plains, the sandsage prairie's plant composition is somewhat influenced by species with ranges to the south and southwest. The most diagnostic plant species of sandsage prairie is the sand sagebrush (*Artemisia filifolia*), a compact, woody shrub seldom more than three feet tall. Sand sagebrush is also found on sandy soils in the Nebraska Panhandle on the southwestern margins of the Sandhills in Keith, Garden, Morrill and Box Butte counties. That band is often considered a transition zone between Sandhills prairie and sandsage prairie.

"We found suddenly that the nature of the country had entirely changed," wrote Brevet Captain John C. Fremont of the U.S. Topographical Engineers in late-June 1843 upon entering the sandsage country of what is now Dundy County. "Bare sand hills everywhere surrounded us in the undulating ground along which we were moving; and the plants peculiar to a sandy soil made their appearance in abundance. With the exception of one or two distant and detached groves, no timber of any kind was to be seen; and the features of the country assumed a desert character, with which the broad [Republican] river, struggling for existence among the quicksands along the treeless banks, was strikingly in keeping. We traveled now for several days through a broken and dry sandy region, about 4,000 feet above the sea, where there were no running streams; and some anxiety was constantly felt on account of the uncertainty of water, which was only to be found in small lakes that occurred occasionally among the hills. The discovery of these always brought pleasure to the camp, as around them were generally green flats, which afforded abundant pasturage for our animals; and here were usually collected herds of buffalo, which now were scattered over all the country in countless numbers."

By 1876, the buffalo herds south of the Platte River were gone, and cattlemen were bringing stock to graze the Republican River Valley grasslands. From 1880 through 1886, Texas cattle were trailed north to Ogallala through Dundy County west of Benkelman, 150,000 in 1886 alone – the last year of the big trail drives. For a few years, Benkelman's saloons were filled with cowboys and drovers, and the town was called "the wickedest city between McCook and Denver." Ranches were soon established, running their herds on government-owned open range.

*Once common in sandsage prairie, **greater prairie-chickens** have been much diminished in abundance by the conversion of grassland to cropland.*

JON FARRAR

As in the Sandhills to the north, ranchers established headquarters along the region's streams and in watered valleys. Without water, the dry uplands were useless to farmers, and so, for a while, ranchers grazed far more land than they held by title. The cattle empires were short-lived. By the mid-1880s, settlers had flooded the region to claim 160 acres of land under the 1862 Homestead Act. By 1887, the only unclaimed tracts remaining in Dundy County were sandy hills in the northwestern corner of the county.

In the blink of an eye, longhorns had taken the place of buffalo, and just as quickly milk cows, hogs and chickens replaced the longhorns. Prairie was turned under, and crops were planted. Some farmers endured under great hardship. From the beginning, it was evident that for farming to consistently succeed, rainfall would have to be supplemented with irrigation. The oldest water appropriation rights on the Republican River were assigned to the Phelan Ditch, which began taking water from Rock Creek near Parks in 1882. Water, however, was never far below the surface. Over most of Nebraska's sandsage prairie country, a 20-foot well

*Most **sandsage prairie,** especially tracts of low relief, have been converted to cropland under center-pivot irrigation. Even those grasslands that remain have been altered in plant composition by many years of herbicide application to eliminate sand sagebrush.*

would supply all the water required for domestic use.

During the first half of the 20th century, agriculture in southwestern Nebraska settled into an uneasy compromise with the land and the climate. By 1900, ditch irrigation was flourishing along streams where gravity would carry water in canals to downstream valley land. Farming became more important than ranching in the southwestern counties, but the grassy dunes continued to be used for livestock grazing. Irrigation was so extensive in southwestern Nebraska that, as early as 1936, some streams were dry during the growing season. In response to the shrinking supply of surface water for irrigation, pump irrigation from wells steadily increased during the 1940s and 1950s.

In the early-1960s, most Sandhills land in the sandsage counties was still in native prairie pasture. Land with heavier soils grew wheat, and the more sandy soils with low relief were mostly planted to corn. Center-pivot irrigation technology profoundly altered farming practices, the economy and natural resources in southwestern Nebraska.

Sprinkler systems came into use after World War II, but they were primitive affairs. The earliest were no more than sections of pipe with nozzles on risers that had to be disassembled and moved by hand. The first self-propelled center-pivot system in Dundy County was installed in 1965. For the first time, technology provided a means to farm large tracts of land on

rolling terrain. Unlike gravity-flow systems, land with a center pivot does not need to be level, and water is distributed evenly over an entire field. Add to that formula the low cost of rangeland, abundant groundwater and generous tax incentives for developers and investors, and plowing the sandy hill country was just too good a proposition to pass up. Irrigated acres in Dundy County jumped from 14,700 to 114,000 between 1960 and 1990.

In August 1977, in response to a steadily falling water table, the state's first groundwater control area was established in Perkins, Chase and Dundy counties. But for the sandsage prairie and its wildlife, it was too late. Springs once feeding Frenchman Creek no longer flowed. In 1952, Frenchman Creek was a perennial stream about a mile below the Colorado-Nebraska border. By 1973, because of irrigation withdrawals from groundwater feeding the creek, the stream did not flow until eight or 10 miles downstream from the state border. Enders Reservoir on Frenchman Creek southeast of Imperial has not held a full pool of water since 1968. Most artesian wells no longer flow, and the upper reaches of many small streams in Chase and Dundy counties are now dry, and the flows in their lower reaches are much diminished.

Drained of its once abundant water that surfaced as ponds and fed streams, and with most of the native grassland acres plowed and growing corn under center-pivot irrigation systems, Nebraska's sandsage

*Before Euroamerican settlement, shallow wetlands were abundant in sandsage prairie, attracting shorebirds such as **long-billed dowitchers** (above) during migration. Today, shorebirds are most commonly found in the region on the mudflats of Enders Reservoir.*

prairie, like tallgrass prairie in the east, has nearly disappeared. There are still tracts of grassland where the rugged terrain defied pivot irrigation, but for decades the land has been sprayed with herbicides to kill the sand sagebrush, a process that killed most of the native forbs. Finding even a small tract of native sandsage prairie is nearly impossible. The best examples persist in narrow strips of grass between county roads and fences, or on bluffs above the region's streams.

Falling water tables spelled the end for wetland and subirrigated meadow avifauna in the sandsage prairie, a mix not unlike what is still found in the Sandhills today. Simplification of the grassland community made it unsuitable for many bird species, and fragmentation of suitable habitat contributed to the disappearance of others. Today, for the most part, only generalist grassland bird species remain – horned larks, lark buntings, western meadowlarks, grasshopper sparrows and lark sparrows.

University of Nebraska ornithologists Myron Swenk and John Zimmer, noting that the bird life of Dundy, Chase and Perkins counties was poorly studied, compiled a list of 53 species that they observed during several trips between 1901 and 1911. They noted that the Arickaree River, which enters Nebraska in southern Dundy County and courses northeasterly only three miles before merging with the Republican River, was typically depleted of water by irrigation, but its course was marked by gatherings of willows and clumps

of trees, which attracted birds. They noted that upland sandpipers were "the most plentiful of all the species present," an observation perhaps more accurately stated as "the most conspicuous." Burrowing owls were "perched like so many statues on the fence posts and sleepily turning their heads to watch the passing buggy and its occupants."

And there were short-eared owls, yellow-headed blackbirds and the expected grassland passerines.

Swenk and Zimmer did not note Cassin's sparrows, a species typically associated with sandsage grasslands. The Chihuahuan raven, another species of southwestern states, has periodically been reported in southwestern Nebraska, perhaps even nesting, but the records are poorly documented. In

***Yellow-headed blackbirds** nest on Rock Creek Lake in Dundy County.*

recent years more birders have been searching Nebraska's southwestern counties for species with ranges to the southwest. Southern, southwestern and western species, such as the ash-throated flycatcher, bushtit, canyon towhee, Scott's oriole, sage sparrow, black-throated sparrow, and Brewer's sparrow conceivably might find their way into Nebraska's sandsage prairie, but they are yet to be reported.

It is likely that three species of prairie grouse have inhabited Nebraska's sandsage prairie. The traditional distribution of greater prairie-chickens and sharp-tailed grouse is poorly documented, but it is likely that the native grouse of sandsage prairie was the sharp-tailed grouse. Greater prairie-chickens probably followed homesteaders westward from their traditional range in the tallgrass prairie. During the first decade of the 20th century, prairie-chickens were still plentiful enough in the sandsage country that they were hunted for the market and in the 1920s haying crews were still regularly fed young prairie-chickens. Even more of a mystery is if lesser prairie-chickens were once found in Nebraska's sandsage prairie. Hunters seldom made a distinction between sharptails and prairie-chickens, and so distinctions between greater and lesser prairie-chickens are even less likely.

Today, the range of lesser prairie-chickens stops south of Nebraska, where they are associated with arid, sandy soil grasslands with sagebrush. The northern-most extent of lesser prairie-chickens in recent times is in the sandsage prairie of southwestern Kansas and southeastern Colorado although they are reported expanding their range northward in western Kansas. Some range maps show the presettlement distribution of lesser prairie-chickens extending nearly to Nebraska's southwestern border. In 1901, University of Nebraska ornithologist Lawrence Bruner wrote that the lesser prairie-chicken "was formerly much more plentiful than at present." Bruner's colleague, Robert Wolcott, writing in 1909,

Northern flicker and egg

The Color of Bird Eggs

Bird eggs are marvelous objects but their function is strictly utilitarian. To produce the next generation, eggs must survive in a world of egg eaters until the young hatch. The first bird eggs were probably white, like the eggs of the reptiles from which birds evolved. Many species of birds still lay white eggs, but there is considerable variation in color and pattern from species to species.

Ground-nesting birds typically lay brown or tan eggs marked with darker blotches, specks or streaks to camouflage them at the nest site. Blotched eggs are created when the egg is stationary in the oviduct at the time pigment is secreted; swirled patterns are created when the egg is moving.

White eggs are common in bird species that nest in holes – owls, woodpeckers and kingfishers. There was no evolutionary advantage for these species to have colored eggs. Ducks, geese and grebes lay white eggs but their clutches are covered with vegetation when an adult is not incubating. Species that begin incubation when the first egg is laid and seldom leave the eggs uncovered – great blue herons, northern harriers, doves and hummingbirds – also have white or solid-colored eggs.

There are variations in egg shapes, too. Eggs of ground-nesting species, particularly shorebirds, have pointed ends so they roll in a circle and not out of the shallow nest. Shorebirds typically lay clutches of three or four eggs arranged with the pointed ends together, a compact circle easily covered by the adult. Cavity-nesting species typically have more rounded eggs, and eggs of species nesting in open-cupped nests are between those extremes.

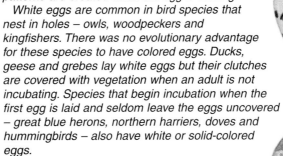

Black tern nest and egg

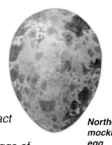

Wood thrush egg

Baltimore oriole egg

Northern mockingbird egg

Enders Reservoir *was completed on the Frenchman River in Chase County in 1951. Grasslands, including sandsage prairie, mudflats and deciduous woodlands attract a wide variety of birds during migration and breeding seasons.*

noted that lesser prairie-chickens had not been seen in the state since the early-1870s. There are records of lesser prairie-chickens from southwestern Nebraska, the most recent from the 1920s, when three specimens were collected in Red Willow County just to the east of Nebraska's sandsage prairie. Recent researchers, however, consider these specimens questionable, or suggest they represent only temporary movements of lesser prairie-chickens north of their normal range.

Enders Reservoir

Although not located in rolling sand dunes, and hence not a textbook example of sandsage prairie, Enders Reservoir is one of the largest tracts of public land with that floral community in southwestern

Nebraska. Enders Dam impounded Frenchman Creek in Chase County in 1951 as an irrigation reservoir. At full conservation pool the reservoir is 1,707 surface acres with 26 miles of shoreline. Since the late-1960s, the reservoir has not been at full pool because of extensive irrigation development in the watershed. Constructed by the U.S. Bureau of Reclamation, Enders Reservoir is surrounded by about 3,900 acres of wildlife lands, which are managed by the Nebraska Game and Parks Commission. There are about 650 acres of woodlands and 2,097 acres of shortgrass, mixed-grass and sagebrush prairie, including a 135-acre black-tailed prairie dog town. Because the area encompasses the Frenchman Creek Valley, much of the land is rocky bluffs cut by drainages. It is especially rugged on the southern side of the reservoir. The best expanse of sandsage prairie is on the northern side of the upper end of the reservoir. Frenchman Creek flows through extensive deciduous woodlands above the reservoir and birders should walk through the area when looking for migrating and breeding passerines. The creek is shallow and is a good travel lane for birders who do not mind getting wet or wearing knee-high boots. Extensive mudflats on the upper end during irrigation drawdown periods or drought create shorebird habitat.

Perhaps the most interesting piece of topography is along the trail road on the southern side of the reservoir. The road passes through a variety of plant and bird communities. Look for rock wrens at rocky outcrops. Turkey vultures are regular traveling companions. Ravines are wooded and uplands are shrubby, and have both mixed-grass and sandsage prairies. The grasslands are rife with native wildflowers.

Enders Reservoir Bird Sampler

Wood Duck	Eastern Phoebe
Western Grebe	Red-eyed Vireo
American White Pelican	Black-billed Magpie
Double-crested Cormorant	Loggerhead Shrike
Green Heron	Bell's Vireo
Ferruginous Hawk	White-breasted Nuthatch
Wild Turkey	Northern Mockingbird
American Avocet	Yellow Warbler
White-rumped Sandpiper	Yellow-breasted Chat
Forster's Tern	Spotted Towhee
Yellow-billed Cuckoo	Cassin's Sparrow
Burrowing Owl	Lark Sparrow
Common Poorwill	Yellow-headed Blackbird
Belted Kingfisher	Orchard Oriole

In September look for patches of buffalo-gourd in grasslands along the trail and ornate box turtles on the road. Prairie rattlesnakes are found on the southern side of the reservoir so walkers should be alert, though not alarmed. High-clearance vehicles are recommended, and at times four-wheel-drive vehicles are required.

Enders, like other southwestern reservoirs, should provide gull-viewing opportunities during migration and in late and early winter, but it has not been well observed. Clark's grebes, red-necked grebes and common loons have been reported. A 1,650-acre portion of the upper half of the reservoir is designated as a waterfowl refuge and is closed to vehicle traffic from October 1 through February 28. Foot traffic is allowed and large numbers of ducks and geese, and some bald eagles, can be found there from fall migration to well into the winter months. Golden eagles are occasionally seen and have been reported nesting in the region. Expect to sample the full complement of shorebirds, including American avocets and white-faced ibis, on mudflats during migration periods. Virginia rails have been reported in marshes on the upper end of the reservoir during the breeding season.

• Additional Information: Land around Enders Reservoir is designated as both a state recreation area and wildlife management area. There are eight RV camping pads with electrical service and 160 nonpad camping sites, modern restrooms, coin-operated showers and a dump station. Tent camping is allowed elsewhere around the lake. Enders Reservoir is 5 miles east and 4½ miles south of Imperial in Chase County on U.S. Highway 6.

Rock Creek Lake SRA

Rock Creek Lake State Recreation Area includes a 50-acre lake and 54 acres of surrounding land. In the summer of 1933, about 200 World War I veterans – Nebraskans enrolled in the Depression-era's Veterans Conservation Corps – arrived to construct a dam on Rock Creek and create a lake for fishing and recreation in a region lacking surface water. The lake was opened for fishing in 1935. Since that time the lake has filled with silt and undesirable rough fish supplanted desirable game fish. In 2002, Rock Creek Lake was drained and sediment was removed. The lake has refilled and has been stocked with game fish. Nearby Rock Creek Fish Hatchery has been located on the stream's headwaters since 1924. The hatchery raises coldwater species, such as rainbow and brown trout, as well as warmwater game fish and pan fish.

Like other southwestern birding destinations, Rock Creek Lake is far from population centers and its bird life has been poorly documented. The lake and fish hatchery are wooded, watered oases in a semiarid land and should be a magnet for birds. Pine trees and deciduous woodlands surround most of the lake and fill with migrant passerines during spring and fall. The upper end of the lake is an extensive marsh and accessible by a trail road. Grassland and shrub thickets, including remnants of sandsage prairie, are on the

southern end of the lake.

• Additional Information: Campsites, picnic areas and water are available at Rock Creek SRA. To travel to Rock Creek SRA from the small town of Parks on Highway 34, drive north 2 miles, then west ¾ mile, and northwest 1 mile. ■

Rock Creek Bird Sampler

Blue-winged Teal	Western Kingbird
Ruddy Duck	Warbling Vireo
Eared Grebe	Marsh Wren
Western Grebe	Townsend's Solitaire
Cooper's Hawk	Northern Mockingbird
Swainson's Hawk	Cedar Waxwing
Rough-legged Hawk	Yellow Warbler
Virginia Rail	Northern Waterthrush
Spotted Sandpiper	Yellow-breasted Chat
Upland Sandpiper	Cassin's Sparrow
Eastern Screech-Owl	Lark Sparrow
Burrowing Owl	Lark Bunting
Common Nighthawk	Black-headed Grosbeak
Belted Kingfisher	Yellow-headed Blackbird
Red-headed Woodpecker	Bullock's Oriole
Western Wood-Pewee	Baltimore Oriole

JON FARRAR

Upland sandpipers *have declined in abundance as grassland meadows were plowed and converted into cornfields.*

WESTERN HIGH PLAINS
Panhandle Escarpments

SOME 65 TO 130 MILLION YEARS AGO the center of the North American continent was under a great inland sea. Then the Rocky Mountains began to rise. Streams flowing eastward from the mountains deposited gravel, sand and silt on what is now the Great Plains. Those deposits were reworked by the wind and eventually consolidated into beds of fine sandstones, coarse siltstones and conglomerates of coarse sand and gravel. These beds, nearly 2,000 feet thick in places, filled the once-vast inland sea, building a tableland with higher elevations to the west. The rise of the Rockies was also a time of great volcanic activity in the western United States, and thick beds of ash were laid down over parts of what has become the Nebraska Panhandle. During the past 35 million years, sediments from the west continued to be deposited, and all the while that new land was eroded and carried farther east.

Today, these ancient deposits, known to geologists as the Arikaree and the White River groups, are exposed where the North Platte River and the White River have carved deeply into them at places like Scotts Bluff National Monument and the badlands of northern Sioux County. As streams cut deeper valleys, the Wildcat Hills and Pine Ridge became isolated islands of the tableland that once was continuous across the Panhandle. Today one can stand atop Scotts Bluff or on a butte at Fort Robinson and be near the surface of the ancient tableland, gazing across deep valleys carved through the ancient outwash of the Rocky Mountains.

The Pine Ridge separates two great continental regions – the High Plains extending southward almost to Mexico, and the Missouri River Plateau stretching northward into Canada. The Pine Ridge covers some 2,700 square miles and rises more than 5,000 feet above sea level, declining in elevation from west to east. Annual precipitation in the Pine Ridge is only about 18 inches, and the growing season is short, averaging about 110 days, nearly 50 days shorter than along the Missouri River in eastern Nebraska. The combination of low rainfall, a short growing season, relatively

In Nebraska, **pygmy nuthatches** are documented as breeding only in the Pine Ridge and Wildcat Hills.

infertile soils and rugged topography has kept the Pine Ridge region in native grasslands and woodlands little altered from their natural condition.

The Wildcat Hills escarpment rises above the North Platte River to the north and Pumpkin Creek Valley to the south. The escarpment is about 70 miles long and 10 miles wide in the west, narrowing and falling in elevation to the east. The highest buttes and ridges exceed 4,600 feet and the canyons are often deep and large. In places, passes cut the escarpment where roads go today. Courthouse and Jail rocks are at the eastern end of the escarpment. Except on the escarpment's northern side, the Wildcat Hills has less relief than the Pine Ridge. It is a drier environment, less dissected by small streams and has less extensive canyon-bottom deciduous woodlands. In the Wildcat Hills ponderosa pines are shorter and more spreading than those in the Pine Ridge. Nearly pure stands of mountain mahogany, a western shrub, are found in some areas of the Wildcat Hills.

Ponderosa pine dominates the rolling-to-steep rocky slopes in the Pine Ridge. Junipers are more conspicuous in Wildcat Hills woodlands. In the Rocky Mountains, ponderosa pine occurs on drier, fire-prone, lower slopes and typically grows in open stands, minimizing competition for moisture. In the Pine Ridge, where dense forest prevails on north- and east-facing slopes, the understory is composed of shrubs, grasses and forbs of northern and mountain affinities. In more open, sunny, south-facing locations, stands of mixed-grass prairie grow in the pine understory, providing forage for cattle and some elk.

Historically, when wildfires periodically swept through the Panhandle escarpments, pine woodlands were open, park-like savannas with small gatherings or individual trees where fire did not reach. Today, with wildfires largely controlled, ponderosa pines grow where they never grew before settlement, in thick stands often composed of stunted trees. Today, about 200,000 acres of ponderosa pines are spread across the Pine Ridge alone. During the last 20 years of the 19th century, most of the Pine Ridge forest was

RICHARD HOLMES

*Buttes in the **Pine Ridge** escarpment are remnants of a once higher tableland that eroded away over millions of years. The area is arid, cloaked in ponderosa pines and its avifauna is much like that of the Black Hills in South Dakota or eastern slopes of the Rocky Mountains.*

cut to build growing communities, to provide ties for expanding railroads, and to construct barns and forts to hold the Lakota at bay. Most of today's pines are second growth, creating a 100-year-old forest, but on steep ridges a few 200-year-old patriarchs remain.

Logging returned to the Pine Ridge on a limited scale during the past 20 years to allow thicker, more luxuriant grass for livestock forage and to limit wildfires. On some public lands, controlled fires now remove tinder that could fuel large, out-of-control wildfires. Three large wildfires in the Pine Ridge between 1973 and 1989 burned about 54,000 acres of pine forest. Early in the 20th century the Lewis's woodpecker had been reported in the Pine Ridge, but it essentially had vanished by the middle of the 1900s after wildfires were largely controlled. The Lewis's woodpecker, which is at the eastern edge of its range in Nebraska, most often nests in burned pine trees, but has also been found nesting in dead cottonwood snags in riparian areas. A few years after the Dead Horse fire in and near Chadron State Park in 1973, as many as 25 Lewis's woodpeckers returned, and they have come back to other areas after large fires.

Green ash, box elder, cottonwood and the bleached skeletons of American elm stand along rivers and streams. Twenty-seven species of deciduous trees, 44 species of shrubs and five species of vines are associated with ponderosa pine forest in the

Panhandle. The Pine Ridge is at or near the most southern or eastern range of dwarf and creeping juniper, mountain birch, quaking aspen, mountain mahogany, Oregon grape, blue larkspur, silvery lupine, harebell, mariposa lily, sego lily, stonecrop and a host of other shrubs, forbs and northern or montane shrubs, forbs, grasses and sedges. The edge between pine forest and deciduous woodlands is rich with bird life and warrants birders' attention.

In climate, vegetation and avifauna, the Pine Ridge is more like the Rocky Mountains than other parts of Nebraska. The region shares many avifaunal features with the Black Hills in western South Dakota.– the white-winged race of the dark-eyed junco, nesting Swainson's thrushes and nesting flycatchers with western ranges.

Ornithologist Paul Johnsgard estimated about 128 species breed in Sioux County, more than in any other region of the state except the deciduous woodlands along the Missouri River and the lower Niobrara Valley. Because the Pine Ridge has changed little from its natural state, there are more native bird species in the Pine Ridge than in the Missouri Valley. Western species have pioneered eastward from the Pine Ridge along the Niobrara Valley and from the Wildcat Hills along the North Platte Valley. And, as those river valleys grew more wooded with deciduous trees during the past 100 years, eastern birds have

*During migration, **mountain bluebirds** might be encountered as far east as central Nebraska, but during nesting season they are found only in the Panhandle, especially in the Pine Ridge and Wildcat Hills. In summer they prefer pine woodlands at the upper ends of canyons.*

come to the coniferous forests of the Panhandle. As in the Niobrara and Platte valleys, hybrids of Bullock's and Baltimore orioles, black-headed and red-breasted grosbeaks, lazuli and indigo buntings, western and eastern wood-pewees, and yellow-shafted and red-shafted morphs of the northern flicker are found in the Pine Ridge.

But, birders come to the Pine Ridge to see its characteristic western species – the common poorwill, Lewis's woodpecker, pinyon jay, pygmy nuthatch, mountain bluebird, red crossbill, plumbeous vireo and western tanager. Look for migrating rufus and broad-tailed hummingbirds from mid-July through early-September. Watch for nesting rock wrens and Say's phoebes in rock outcrops. Juncos are abundant in the Pine Ridge in winter and it is possible to see several races at one time, including the Oregon, the pink-sided, the slate-colored and the white-winged. House finches, once only winter visitors, have exploded in numbers since the early-1980s. Richard Rosche, who observed birds in the Pine Ridge for 30 years, noted some western species, such as the Cassin's finch, gray jay and Clark's nutcracker, periodically appeared in irruptions. The abundance of red crossbills in the Pine Ridge is contingent on the ponderosa pine seed crop. When production is poor, crossbills leave for better feeding grounds. Nesting is also dependent on the pine seed crop, being most common when seeds are abundant, and nesting can occur almost any time of the year except the dead of winter.

The Wildcat Hills avifauna is like the Pine Ridge in most regards, but the two areas have distinct differences, too. More species and more breeding species are found in the Pine Ridge because it has more diverse habitats. But, some species, particularly those with southwesterly distributions adapted to drier habitats, such as Cassin's kingbirds, sage thrashers and green-tailed towhees, are more frequently found in the Wildcat Hills than the Pine Ridge. Breeding by red-breasted nuthatches was first noted in the Wildcat Hills in the mid-1980s, and pygmy nuthatches have recently been found nesting there. And as in the Pine Ridge, the Wildcat Hills is a zone of overlap for orioles, wood-pewees, grosbeaks and others. Wayne Mollhoff, coordinator of *The Nebraska Breeding Bird Atlas* who studied Wildcat Hills breeding birds, said eastern, western and Cassin's kingbirds sometimes nest within 100 yards of each other.

Public land has always been abundant in the Pine Ridge and birders have observed it intensively since the early-1900s.

Gilbert-Baker WMA

No area in the Pine Ridge has been studied by birders more extensively or for a longer period than Monroe Canyon in northern Sioux County. During the 1900s, University of Nebraska zoologists returned to the area again and again, camping for weeks at a time, to study avifauna. Today, Monroe Canyon, on the northern side of the Pine Ridge escarpment, is part of the Gilbert-Baker Wildlife Management Area.

Because it is the western-most tract of public land in the Pine Ridge, Gilbert-Baker is a reliable location to find western passerine species, including rare breeders such as the Townsend's solitaire and rare visitors such as

JON FARRAR

the Clark's nutcracker. Pinyon jays, assumed to be occasional breeders in the Panhandle escarpments since the early-1900s, were first documented nesting in Nebraska at Gilbert-Baker in the spring of 1999. Nesting Swainson's thrushes are as likely at Gilbert-Baker as anywhere in the state. Even through Lewis's woodpeckers prefer burned areas for nesting, they have been seen at Gilbert-Baker. Watch, too, for white-throated swifts nesting in crevices of rock faces, and for rock wrens and Say's phoebes near buttes and rock outcrops.

Violet-green swallows, common poorwills, cordilleran flycatchers, plumbeous vireos and western tanagers are also found at the WMA. Spring migrants include green-tailed towhees, MacGillivray's warblers and Townsend's warblers. The red-naped sapsucker breeds in the Black Hills in western South Dakota and has occasionally been seen as a migrant in Monroe and Sowbelly canyons. Merlins, golden eagles and prairie falcons nest in buttes in the area.

On the steep northern face of t the Pine Ridge escarpment cut by Monroe and East Monroe creeks, Gilbert-Baker is a rugged tract of land. Canyon bottoms are filled with deciduous woods, and canyon sides are cloaked with ponderosa pine. Look for moutain birch and mountain maple, two tree species found in Nebraska at only a few Pine Ridge sites. Least chipmunks might also be seen. There are tracts of mixed-grass prairie, rock outcrops and buttes on the area, which encompasses 2,537 acres. The best birding opportunities are in rugged terrain. While the area has no trails, it is entirely open to foot traffic. A two-acre trout pond is located in the northeastern part of the area and two parking areas are along Monroe Canyon Road. Primitive camping is allowed and there are pit toilets and water.

- Additional Information: Gilbert-Baker WMA is 4½ miles north of Harrison on Monroe Canyon Road.
- Nearby Birding Destinations: East of Gilbert-Baker WMA, **Sowbelly Creek** flows from the

Woodpecker Adaptations

Woodpeckers are wonderfully designed for their way of life. Most species have two opposing toes rather than one to better grip vertical surfaces. Tail feathers are stiff, providing a brace against trees while they hammer away. Woodpeckers have strong beaks with a chisel-shaped tip rather than a delicately pointed tip. Woodpecker's skulls are thick and relatively spongy, with cartilage at the base of the mandible to cushion the impact of blows. The mandibles are attached to the skull by powerful muscles, distributing the force of impact, and the skull tightly encloses the brain to prevent concussions. A pileated woodpecker can strike wood at a remarkable rate of 20 times per second and up to 12,000 times a day. A millisecond before each strike thick, nictitating membranes cover the eyes, protecting them from flying debris and keeping the eyes from popping out of their sockets.

Lewis's woodpecker

Perhaps the most fascinating woodpecker feature is the tongue. The hard tip is barbed for impaling larger insects and coated with sticky saliva for gathering small insects. The tongue is remarkably extensible. A red-bellied woodpecker's tongue can extend three times the length of its bill. The woodpecker has cleverly solved the problem of storing its long tongue when it is not being used. The tongue forks in the throat, passes below the jaw and wraps behind and over the skull where the forks rejoin and attach in the right nostril. Yellow-bellied sapsuckers, also woodpeckers, are an exception. They feed on sap oozing from quarter-inch holes they drill in living trees rather than insects. Their tongues are relatively short and bristly to lap up sap.

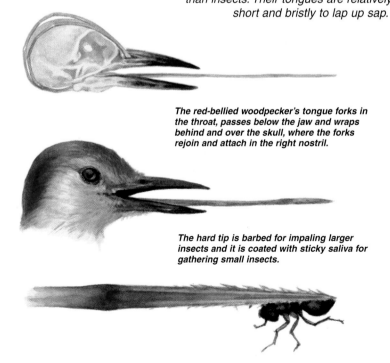

The red-bellied woodpecker's tongue forks in the throat, passes below the jaw and wraps behind and over the skull, where the forks rejoin and attach in the right nostril.

The hard tip is barbed for impaling larger insects and it is coated with sticky saliva for gathering small insects.

Pinyon jays are found in the Pine Ridge but probably are more abundant in the Wildcat Hills. They are breeding birds in both areas.

RICHARD HOLMES

canyons, birders should use caution when birding along it. Coffee Park at the base of the escarpment is a good place to park and observe birds in deciduous woodlands near the creek. Birders walking along Sowbelly Canyon Road at some times of the year should have opportunities to see or hear many of the Pine Ridge specialty species. Watch for Cassin's kingbirds, plumbeous vireos, pygmy nuthatches and cordilleran flycatchers. The state's single record for a sage sparrow came from Sowbelly Canyon. Clark's nutcrackers have been reported breeding there. Other expected species are the golden eagle, common poorwill, white-throated swift, violet-green swallow, rock wren, western tanager, eastern phoebe, great crested flycatcher, yellow-rumped warbler, the white-winged form of the dark-eyed junco and Bullock's oriole. Birders are likely to see pygmy nuthatches on the upper reaches of Sowbelly Canyon. Most of the regional specialty species found in Sowbelly Canyon can also be found at Gilbert-Baker WMA.

To access Sowbelly Canyon Road from Harrison, travel north on Nebraska Highway 29 one mile, then turn east. To loop to Gilbert-Baker WMA from Sowbelly Canyon Road, travel north until connecting with Pants Butte Road. Drive north 5½ miles, then turn west for 6½ miles on Prairie Dog Road, then south 3½ miles on Monroe Canyon Road to Gilbert-Baker.

Pine Ridge escarpment and is a favorite spot of birders. The graveled road that parallels Sowbelly Creek passes through privately owned land. Because the road is narrow and falls away into deep, rocky

Fort Robinson State Park

Fort Robinson was established as a post-Civil War Indian agency in 1874. In 1919 it became a remount depot, and subsequently the U.S. Army's largest training and breeding center for horses and mules. During the 1930s the U.S. Olympic Equestrian Team trained at the fort. In the 1940s the fort housed the War Dog Reception and Training Corps and was a prisoner-of-war camp. In 1948 the fort was declared surplus and transferred to the U.S. Department of Agriculture, which used it as a beef research station. In 1955, the fort was transferred to the Nebraska Game and Parks Commission and became a state park.

Many of Fort Robinson's original buildings have been renovated and others have been reconstructed. The fort offers a worthy glimpse of the old American West and is an excellent home base while birding in the Pine Ridge.

The White River and Soldier Creek pass through Fort Robinson State Park and are lined with deciduous woodlands, attracting passerine species. The park is laced with hiking trails that take birders through several habitats, including dramatic, towering buttes. Bighorn sheep have been reintroduced to the park and are

---

Bone Structure

Few other groups of animals rival birds in specialized skeletal adaptations, from the evolution of the large keel-like breastbone, which anchors the wing muscles, to modifications of the forelimbs for flight. Some bones common to higher vertebrates are eliminated or fused in birds.

While a bird's skeleton must be light to allow flight, it must also be strong and elastic. To accomplish this, the long bones of limbs are often hollow and the outer shell is supported by a complex, internal network of struts that makes the construction of an airplane's wings seem like child's work.

Hollow bones are more flexible and stronger than solid bones of the same weight. In diving birds, such as cormorants and loons whose weight is not of great importance and for whom buoyancy is a disadvantage, bones are solid. Those birds are plodding fliers, laboring under heavy wing loads and expending more energy in flight than lighter birds.

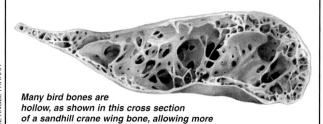

MICHELE ANGLE FARRAR

Many bird bones are hollow, as shown in this cross section of a sandhill crane wing bone, allowing more flexibility and strength than solid bones of the same weight.

Say's phoebes prefer arid habitats, particularly in grasslands where they hawk for insects. They nest in crevices in rock outcrops, in abandoned or little-used buildings and under bridges. Migrants occur east of their Panhandle breeding range.

likely to be seen in the rocks, as are nesting golden eagles, prairie falcons and merlins. The first documented nesting of prairie falcons in the state was made on Saddle-back Butte (called Saddle Rock today) at Fort Robinson in May 1901 by University of Nebraska ornithologist M.A. Carriker. Abandoned golden eagle nests on buttes are sometimes adopted by great horned owls, and red-tailed and ferruginous hawks. The Smiley Canyon Scenic Drive passes through a bison pasture and into pine-covered buttes, offering birdwatching from a vehicle.

● Additional Information: Fort Robinson State Park is located 3 miles west of Crawford on U.S. Highway 20. Many park facilities are available, including RV and primitive camping, lodging in historic buildings, a restaurant and an array of family activities in the summer months. Fort Robinson State Park, 3200 U.S. Hwy. 20, P.O. Box 392, Crawford, NE 69339-0392, (308) 665-2900, ftrobsp@ngpc.state.ne.us

● Nearby Birding Destinations: The 2,460-acre **Peterson Wildlife Management Area** abuts Fort Robinson. Soldier Creek northwest of Fort Robinson is lined with deciduous woodlands attracting passerine species. Hiking trails from the parking area at the end of Soldier Creek Road access **Soldier Creek Wilderness,** which has 7,794 acres with 15 miles of developed trails and is administered by the U.S. Forest Service. Soldier Creek trailhead facilities located just outside the wilderness area include primitive campsites, vault toilets and water. Soldier Creek Wilderness was added to the National Wilderness Preservation System in 1986. Nebraska's largest recorded forest fire burned about 48,000 acres, including areas in Fort Robinson, Peterson WMA and Soldier Creek Wilderness in 1989. Soldier Creek Wilderness is being allowed to recover

Western tanagers are common breeders in the Pine Ridge, and have extended their range eastward along the Niobrara River.

BOB GRIER

Golden eagles are Panhandle residents, nesting on buttes and cliffs in the Pine Ridge and Wildcat Hills. The bird shown above is a juvenile with white tail feathers and wing patches.

vehicle access and there are more than 80 miles of recreational trails.

East Ash and West Ash creeks are popular birding sites on the forest service lands. Roads paralleling the creeks pass through the Pine Ridge and take drivers through upland pine forest and bottomland deciduous woodlands. Most of the western passerine species of the Pine Ridge are found there. Wayne Mollhoff found eight pygmy nuthatch nests with eggs in 1997 near West Ash Creek. Before that find, the only reports of breeding pygmy nuthatches in the state were by Richard Rosche in Sowbelly and Monroe canyons where he observed adults feeding young in nesting cavities.

Since 1999, Mollhoff has made detailed observations of Lewis's woodpeckers nesting in the 1985 McIntosh burn west of West Ash Creek Canyon. Mollhoff also documented white-throated swifts nesting in crevices in soft rock faces over West Ash Creek. The state's first accepted record for nesting Swainson's thrush was made by Rosche on West Ash in 1973. Clark's nutcrackers have been reported there in recent years.

• Additional Information: A county map, sportsman's atlas or a Pine Ridge map is essential for birders who want to fully explore U.S. Forest Service lands in the Pine Ridge. Excellent maps can be obtained at the U.S. Forest Service office in Chadron. Also ask for a Pine Ridge hiking trail brochure and the "Birds of the Nebraska Pine Ridge" checklist covering the Oglala National Grassland as well. The checklist includes 235 bird species. Drivers should exercise judgment before leaving paved or graveled roads in the Pine Ridge when they are wet or snow-covered. There are two forest service campgrounds – Red Cloud Campground, located a mile south of Chadron State Park on U.S. Highway 385, and the Roberts Tract Campground. To drive to the Roberts campground from Chadron, travel west 8 miles on U.S. Highway 20, then south 7½ miles, and then east 1½ miles. A $5 per night camping fee is charged from Memorial Day weekend through Labor Day weekend. Nebraska National Forest – Pine Ridge Ranger Station, 1240 West 16th, Chadron, NE 69337, (308) 432-4475, nnf_info @fs.fed.us, www.fs.fed.us/r2/nebraska

• Nearby Birding Destinations: As Fort Robinson serves as a home base for birders in the western Pine Ridge, **Chadron State Park** provides birding opportunities to the east, and is close to forest service land and several large wildlife management areas. Located 9 miles south of the town of Chadron on U.S. Highway 385, the state park was established in 1921 when the Nebraska Legislature created the State Park Board within the Department of Public

naturally. Expect fewer pines and a more open landscape. Lewis's woodpeckers have been reported from the burned tracts. For more information contact the Pine Ridge Ranger District at locations provided with U.S. Forest Service lands section later in this chapter.

In topography, vegetation and avifauna, **Ponderosa WMA** is much like Fort Robinson. The 3,660-acre area includes rocky buttes and pine forest on higher elevations, deciduous woodlands along drainages and mixed-grass prairie on more level tracts. A two-mile stretch of Squaw Creek flows through the area. The eastern side of the area was burned in the McIntosh fire in 1985 and in the 2000 Sawlog Fire. Lewis's woodpeckers have been reported nesting in standing, charred pines and Clark's nutcrackers are also occasionally seen. There are several parking lots in the area and service roads serve as hiking trails. The Rim of the World Trail at parking area 5 offers panoramic views. From Crawford, drive south 3 miles on U.S. Highway 20, then east 4 miles.

Nebraska National Forest

South of U.S. Highway 20 between Crawford and Chadron is a patchwork of U.S. Forest Service land designated as the Pine Ridge National Recreation Area and Nebraska National Forest, Pine Ridge Unit, which totals 41,500 acres. The forest service land traces the Pine Ridge escarpment and is deeply cut by streams coursing northward to the White River. Ponderosa pine forest dominates the uplands and is broken by tracts of mixed-grass prairie at higher elevations. Deciduous woodlands of cottonwood, hackberry, box elder, green ash and woody shrubs trace the stream courses. Dominant grasses are western wheatgrass, little bluestem, big bluestem, prairie sandreed, needle-and-thread and blue grama. County roads provide

Works and set aside a section of school land in the Pine Ridge for a park. Ponderosa pine woodlands occupy most of the park along with some deciduous draws and mixed-grass prairie. This 972-acre state park is a likely location to find poorwills, western tanagers, pinyon jays and violet-green swallows. Watch for pygmy nuthatches near dead pine snags, which they often use as nest sites. The park offers 22 housekeeping cabins, RV and tent camping, hiking trails and other amenities. Chadron State Park, 15951 Hwy. 385, Chadron, NE 69337-7353, (308) 432-6167, chadronsp@ngpc.state.ne.us

Two large wildlife management areas in the eastern Pine Ridge deserve the attention of birders. **Metcalf WMA,** a 3,076-acre area crossed by Little Beaver Creek, has deep canyons and high ridges interspersed with mixed-grass prairie. Ponderosa pines dominate the uplands and deciduous woodlands follow the creek's course. Metcalf is the eastern-most canyon on the Pine Ridge with public access. Species typical of the Pine Ridge – the white-throated swift, pinyon jay and Clark's nutcracker – have been found there. Elk use the area seasonally. To reach Metcalf WMA from Hay Springs, drive north 2 miles on Beaver Creek Road,

BOB GRIER

Red crossbills are Pine Ridge residents. Their numbers vary with the pine seed crop, and time of nesting is often tied to it as well.

JON FARRAR

Blue-gray gnatcatchers are most common as breeders in the lower Missouri Valley, but in recent years they have become regular breeders in the Wildcat Hills as western populations in Colorado have expanded northward.

then east ½ mile and north 9½ miles. There are parking areas on the WMA's southern and eastern sides. The area has no vehicle trails but hiking trails lead from the parking areas.

Bordeaux Creek WMA is located 3 miles east of Chadron on U.S. Highway 20, then south on Bordeaux Road. Nearly three miles of Big Bordeaux Creek passes through the 1,857-acre area. Ponderosa pine forest covers the uplands and deciduous woodlands trace the creek's course. Bordeaux Creek is one of the most likely places to catch a glimpse of free-ranging elk that returned to the Pine Ridge in recent years.

Wildcat Hills Escarpment

Until recent years there was little public land in the Wildcat Hills. Consequently, its bird life was not as extensively observed as that in the Pine Ridge. Since new wildlife management areas have been established, the Wildcat Hills escarpment has revealed unexpected avifauna as well as confirming what was long expected. Unfortunately, university zoologists did not frequent the Wildcat Hills in the early-1900s as they did the Pine Ridge, so changes in the escarpment's avifauna are not known.

Wayne Mollhoff has searched the Wildcat Hills to document breeding birds in recent years. "Early workers in the Nebraska Panhandle commented on some western and southwestern species barely reaching the area, such as the house finch, and others that might be expected in the future, such as Cassin's kingbirds," he said. "Their comments have proven prophetic, even conservative." Mollhoff attributed the arrival of species from the south and southwest to climatic warming trends in the past half-century.

Pine Ridge Bird Sampler	
Turkey Vulture	White-breasted Nuthatch
Cooper's Hawk	Pygmy Nuthatch
Red-tailed Hawk	Brown Creeper
Golden Eagle	Rock Wren
Merlin	Mountain Bluebird
Prairie Falcon	Townsend's Solitaire
Sharp-tailed Grouse	Swainson's Thrush
Wild Turkey	Yellow-rumped Warbler
Barn Owl	Blackpoll Warbler
Northern Saw-whet Owl	Black-and-white Warbler
Common Poorwill	American Redstart
White-throated Swift	Ovenbird
Broad-tailed Hummingbird	MacGillivray's Warbler
Rufous Hummingbird	Yellow-breasted Chat
Lewis's Woodpecker	Western Tanager
Northern Flicker	Spotted Towhee
Western Wood-Pewee	Brewer's Sparrow
Cordilleran Flycatcher	Lark Sparrow
Say's Phoebe	Grasshopper Sparrow
Great Crested Flycatcher	Dark-eyed Junco
Western Kingbird	Black-headed Grosbeak
Cassin's Kingbird	Blue Grosbeak
Plumbeous Vireo	Lazuli Bunting
Pinyon Jay	Brewer's Blackbird
Clark's Nutcracker	Orchard Oriole
Black-billed Magpie	Bullock's Oriole
Violet-green Swallow	Red Crossbill
Red-breasted Nuthatch	Pine Siskin

Reports of Cassin's kingbirds in the Wildcat Hills became more common in the early-1960s, and apparently red crossbills began to move into the region at about the same time. Red-breasted nuthatches were found nesting in the Wildcat Hills in the mid-1980s, and pygmy nuthatches were seen nesting in the late-1990s. Today, blue-gray gnatcatchers are regular breeders. Pinyon jays were assumed to be occasional breeders in the Panhandle in the early-1900s. Young begging for food were observed during *The Nebraska Breeding Bird Atlas* project, but young in the nest were not observed until 1999 in the Pine Ridge. Mollhoff believes pinyon jays are more common as breeders, and more easily found, in the Wildcat Hills than elsewhere in the Panhandle. Violet-green swallows, common poorwills and white-throated swifts have all been reported in recent years from the escarpment. As more birders work the Panhandle escarpments, their reports suggest that sharp-shinned hawks might be rare but regular breeders.

Mollhoff said that sage thrashers are found in the Wildcat Hills but not regularly, and that sightings of green-tailed towhees have become more frequent during the fall and winter. He said he expects to find Virginia's warblers, which breed in adjacent states, nesting in tracts of mountain mahogany in the Wildcat Hills. He has found Cassin's kingbirds to be more common at some locations than western or eastern kingbirds. The best time to look for Cassin's kingbirds is September, when most of the western and eastern kingbirds have already moved south. Mollhoff

Rare migrants and uncommon but regular breeders,
Cordilleran flycatchers *nest in the Pine Ridge in late-June.*

RICHARD HOLMES

Ponderosa pine woodlands are a preferred habitat of **Steller's jays.** *They are uncommon winter visitors in the Panhandle, and are most frequently reported at feeders in November and December. The North Platte River Valley near Scottsbluff is the area of most reports.*

Cedar Canyon Wildlife Management Area is on the rugged northern face of the Wildcat Hills. Eroded sandstone bluffs drop abruptly into grasslands. Birders should not be surprised to see bighorn sheep released on the area in 2001 and now numbering about 40.

suggested that birders watch for Richardson's merlins, a western subspecies. Cassin's vireos are rare during migration, and Steller's jays and mountain chickadees are rare winter visitors. Townsend's solitaires are common in winter where juniper berries are plentiful.

Wildcat Hills SRA

For birders new to the area, the best first stop is the Wildcat Hills State Recreation Area Nature Center. The Nebraska Game and Parks Commission acquired its first tract of land in the Wildcat Hills in 1929. During the 1930s Depression years, the Civilian Conservation Corps and Works Progress Administration constructed most of the area's buildings, using native stone quarried nearby and pine logs cut on the area. The Wildcat Hills SRA's 935 acres offer views of the North Platte River Valley and Scotts Bluff National Monument to the northwest. One of the oldest trees documented in Nebraska is a ponderosa pine on the area dating to 1618.

With the cooperation and financial support of local organizations, the Commission opened the Wildcat Hills Nature Center in 1995. Situated on a hilltop, the center gives visitors a commanding view of rugged Wildcat Hills topography. Large, tinted windows permit close-up views of birds coming to feeders and wildlife plantings near the building. Designed as an educational facility, museum and interpretive center, the building houses state-of-the-art exhibits and

interactive computer displays with an emphasis on the region's bird life, especially Neotropical migrants. There is also a 240-acre wildlife management area on the eastern edge of the complex.

Wildcat Hills SRA is designed for day-use. While it has no camping facilities, the area has stone picnic shelters, water and vault toilets. More than three miles of nature trails wind through the canyons and rocky bluffs. A short trail near the nature center is accessible to hikers of all ages and abilities; other trails have rather steep grades. A state park entry permit is required for visits longer than 20 minutes.

• Additional Information: Wildcat Hills SRA is located 10 miles south of Gering on Nebraska Highway 71. Wildcat Hills SRA and Nature Center, 210615 Hwy. 71, P.O. Box 65, Gering, NE 69341-0065, (308) 436-3777, wildcat@ngpc.state.ne.us

Buffalo Creek WMA

The initial land for Buffalo Creek Wildlife Management Area along the northern side of the Wildcat Hills escarpment was purchased in 1985. The acquisition of adjoining tracts enlarged the WMA to 4,262 acres, and it is about five miles long. Western and southern portions of the area have the greatest topographic relief. Birders will find rugged ridges and canyons cloaked in pine and juniper with mixed-grass prairies on tracts with lower relief. Intermittent drainages originating in the buttes merge on the grassland, and near the center of the area there is a seven-acre pond, which adds yet another habitat element. The area also has nine natural springs. Because of limited precipitation, the woodlands are open, often with parkland meadows surrounded by trees. Isolated rock outcrops with pines and other woody plants in the grassland are excellent sites to look for birds and western wildflowers.

Buffalo Creek is an outstanding birding area for those who are willing to walk. Vehicle access is limited to two designated parking areas, but foot traffic is allowed throughout. Primitive camping is allowed but open fires are prohibited.

• Additional Information: To drive to Buffalo Creek WMA from Melbeta, travel south 4 miles, then west 2½ miles. Wildcat Hills SRA is only two miles west, but no road directly connects the two tracts.

Cedar Canyon WMA

With 2,200 acres, Cedar Canyon Wildlife Management Area is not as large as Buffalo Creek WMA, but if vertical acres were factored in it would be a close race. Cedar Canyon occupies the rugged northern face of the Wildcat Hills escarpment. The area's northern boundary is defined by a meandering ribbon of eroded sandstone buttes abruptly falling 500 feet or more to bottomland. The plateau atop the buttes on the northern boundary is accessible along breaks carved by thousands of years of erosion. The trek to the top is arduous, but the panoramic view is worth the effort. A high ridge also defines the area's southern boundary. Between those bands of buttes is an intermittent drainage through an eroded landscape. Several springs emerge from the buttes and trickle over cast-off sandstone rubble. Higher elevations are cloaked in sparse stands of ponderosa pine and Rocky Mountain juniper. Gatherings of cottonwoods trace the drainage and north-facing slopes have stands of mountain mahogany. Mixed-grass prairie covers the majority of the gentle side slopes. Bighorn sheep were released on the area in 2001 and now number about 40 animals. Visitors are likely to see them on northern buttes. Cedar Canyon should be an excellent site for viewing raptors, especially during migration periods.

Cedar Canyon WMA was acquired in 1998 with the cooperation of local supporters and funds from the Nebraska Environmental Trust Fund and from the sale of Habitat Stamps to hunters and trappers. Vehicle access is limited to a designated parking area on the eastern end. There is a service road that extends almost to the western edge of the WMA along a drainage and another road provides access to the south. There are no formal hiking trails, but foot traffic is allowed throughout the area. Primitive camping is allowed but open fires are prohibited.

• Additional Information: To reach Cedar Canyon WMA from Gering, drive south 2 miles on Nebraska Highway 71, then 4 miles west on Carter Canyon Road, and then 2 miles south on a gravel county road. ∎

Wildcat Hills Bird Sampler

Turkey Vulture	Pygmy Nuthatch
Swainson's Hawk	Rock Wren
Red-tailed Hawk	Ruby-crowned Kinglet
Ferruginous Hawk	Blue-gray Gnatcatcher
Golden Eagle	Eastern Bluebird
Prairie Falcon	Mountain Bluebird
Wild Turkey	Townsend's Solitaire
Barn Owl	Swainson's Thrush
Burrowing Owl	Sage Thrasher
Common Nighthawk	Virginia's Warbler
Common Poorwill	Yellow-rumped Warbler
White-throated Swift	MacGillivray's Warbler
Broad-tailed Hummingbird	Yellow-breasted Chat
Rufous Hummingbird	Western Tanager
Western Wood-Pewee	Green-tailed Towhee
Cordilleran Flycatcher	Spotted Towhee
Say's Phoebe	Lark Sparrow
Cassin's Kingbird	Lark Bunting
Western Kingbird	White-crowned Sparrow
Loggerhead Shrike	Dark-eyed Junco
Cassin's Vireo	McCown's Longspur
Warbling Vireo	Black-headed Grosbeak
Steller's Jay	Blue Grosbeak
Pinyon Jay	Lazuli Bunting
Clark's Nutcracker	Brewer's Blackbird
Black-billed Magpie	Orchard Oriole
Horned Lark	Bullock's Oriole
Violet-green Swallow	Cassin's Finch
Bank Swallow	House Finch
Cliff Swallow	Red Crossbill
Mountain Chickadee	Pine Siskin
Red-breasted Nuthatch	American Goldfinch

RICHARD HOLMES

Green-tailed towhees and other species with ranges to the southwest are more common in the Wildcat Hills than the Pine Ridge.

HOW TO FIND BIRDS

ABOUT 70 MILLION PEOPLE in the United States – about one in four – consider themselves birdwatchers. They are a diverse lot – from casual birdwatchers who peer at cranes from their car windows one weekend a year or who watch birds at a backyard feeder to birders who drive across the state or fly across the country at the drop of a feather to add some vagrant species to their life list. Those who search for birds regularly become very good at finding them. They seem to have a sixth sense about where and when to look. While luck always plays a role in finding birds, it is experience and technique that guides expert birders to their quarry. Equally important is the amount of time spent searching. Birds are not found by sitting on a sofa reading the Sunday newspaper.

Time and Place

Perhaps the greatest difference between those who find birds they seek and those who do not is knowing when and were to look. Such knowledge comes with experience, but there are shortcuts for birders who are

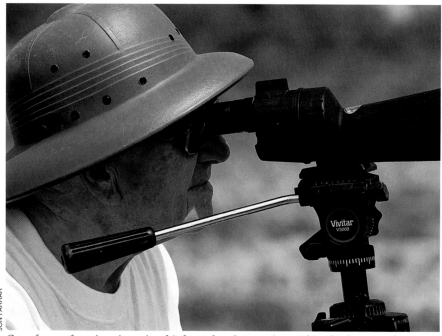

*One of every four Americans is **a birdwatcher**. Interest in watching birds ranges from casual to intense, from those who walk nature center trails once or twice a year to those who drive through the night to glimpse a rare species.*

JON FARRAR

beginners or who are in unfamiliar locations. Such information can be found in a general sense in most field guides, but more precise information is available in regional books that give the range and migration peak for each species. Weather can delay or advance when a species passes, arrives and departs, but on average, birding when a species's migration is at or near its peak enhances the chances of finding it. These

books typically provide information about what region of a state a species is most likely to be found in, its preferred habitat and often precise locations. The best book for such information about Nebraska birds is *Birds of Nebraska* by Roger S. Sharpe, W. Ross Silcock and Joel G. Jorgensen.

A good source of information about Nebraska's breeding species is *The Nebraska Breeding Bird Atlas, 1984-1989,* by Wayne J. Mollhoff. Based on real observations, species accounts in *The Breeding Bird Atlas* have detailed descriptions of where each species is found during its breeding season and of the habitat it nests in. To optimize your chances of locating a particular species, learn everything there is to know about its life history and habitat requirements.

There is, of course, an alternative to seeking a certain species. It is simply going to a place that birds frequent and being delighted with whatever you find.

A birder can never have too many maps. County maps and bound atlas maps of Nebraska are valuable aids in locating wildlife management areas tucked away in a maze of county roads. In an area like the Rainwater Basin, where public bird areas are abundant, a county map allows birders to plan routes from one area to another, and to the closest small town with a cafe. Birders with a sense of adventure look at county or atlas maps and discover out-of-the-way roads through good birding areas. Roads passing through drainages, woodlands or wetlands are usually good birding routes. Some atlas maps are plotted over a base topographic map suggesting the type of terrain and land cover likely to be encountered. While exploring new places far from home adds an element of adventure to birding, do not overlook nearby places that may be birding hotspots. Many city parks are wooded and have either ponds or streams that attract migrating passerines. Cemeteries with coniferous trees are also good spots.

Beginning birders should seek the recommendations of more experienced birders. As a rule, birders generously share information. If there is a birding club near you, join it and learn from others. If not, make arrangements to accompany such groups on any of their regular field trips or counts.

The Nebraska Bird Review is filled with field reports of where other birders have found certain species and when. There are on-line discussion sites, bird chat

*Poised to flee, a **warbling vireo** might offer a birder no more than a second to make an identification. To avoid alarming birds and to get longer views, birders should remain quiet, move slowly and wear clothing that does not stand out in the natural environment.*

*Urban birds, such as the female **cardinal** (above), are accustomed to being near humans. Attracted to feeders and water, they often allow a close approach but are best observed at close range through a window. Even then, sudden movements or noise will cause them to leave.*

rooms and rare-bird alerts specific to Nebraska. (See Additional Sources, page 150). When visiting a wildlife refuge or sanctuary, talk with a local biologist or naturalist. He or she can often narrow your search for specific species to the best sites.

Clothing

It is not necessary to dress like a commando to be a successful birder, but dressing in a way that alarms birds should be avoided. The best circumstances to view birds occur when birds are relaxed, unaware or at least accepting of the presence of the birder. Longer views allow birders to distinguish field marks and make positive identifications, and increase the chances a birder will see interesting behavior. Birds obviously see colors, otherwise bright nuptial plumages would not exist, and they will detect an upright creature wearing bright colors. Earth- and plant-colored clothing that blends with a bird's environment is less likely to cause alarm. Birders should avoid white clothing. A flash of white is one of the most common visual alarms in the natural world. Consider the message transmitted

by the bobbing, white patch of a white-tailed deer's tail, or the marginal tail feathers of a flushing junco. Camouflaged clothing provides the ultimate in concealment, which is especially important if a birder's object is more than simply seeing and documenting a species. Quiet clothing is twice important. Stiff clothing is noisy, alerting birds to the presence of danger, and it muffles birds' vocalizations, which are clues to their identity and location.

Limit Movement

Nearly as important as blending with the bird's environment is limiting sounds and movements that cause alarm. Many birders find these skills difficult to master. As a species, humans seem to be constantly talking and moving, especially when in groups. While birding is often a social endeavor, talking is best reserved for after the observation is complete or at the end of the day.

Most birders actively stalk their quarry – a tactic that usually increases the number of species they see. It is best to move slowly and stop often. Skilled birders do not just look for birds, they look for parts of birds – a patch of glowing red on a red-winged blackbird deep in cattails, or a tree sparrow's beady black eye in a tangle of chokecherry bush. Motion, a sudden flit of brown in woodlands, is often the only hint of a bird's presence. Watch for it. The elaborate vocalizations of birds are evidence of their keen sense of hearing. Moving quietly increases the number of species birders see. Following trails, whether man-made or a deer trail, minimizes alarming noises made by crushing dry leaves or snapping twigs.

If you flush a bird unexpectedly, especially a passerine species, remain motionless and settle into a comfortable position. The bird might have an attraction to that location, perhaps a nest or a source of food or water, and will return. To approach a bird more closely, move a few steps, then pause, allowing it to become comfortable with your presence. Approaching a bird obliquely is less alarming than moving directly toward it. If a bird is distressed by your presence, it is likely the bird has a nest or young nearby. Back away and observe from a distance. No observation is worth jeopardizing a pair of birds the one chance a year they have to produce young.

Sitting still in good bird habitat and allowing birds to reveal themselves and resume their normal activity can be a rewarding experience. While the glimpse of a rare Sabine's gull or cordilleran flycatcher is an exciting observation in Nebraska, watching a pair of American coots at their nest for a morning reveals far more about the life of birds. Clothing appropriate for the situation is important if a birder is to remain comfortable and nearly motionless for long periods of time. A swath of camouflaged netting makes a lightweight and portable blind from which to observe birds at close range.

As a rule, with conspicuous exceptions, birds are most active in the early morning hours and at the end of the day. After a night on the roost, birds are eager to spread their wings and search for food. And at the end of the day, most want to feed again before night falls. Males are conspicuous early and late as they claim and defend territories during the breeding season. During

Niches

So far as is known, no two bird species have the same ecological requirements. Ecologists call this the "competitive exclusion principle." Subtle differences separate the ecological niches of one species from another. Nature wonderfully fashioned a species for every conceivable way and place of making a living in varied habitats of all ecosystems. Seemingly uniform environments are filled with variety for birds. While a horned lark seeks a disturbed grassland, a Henslow's sparrow looks for lush, wet grassland. In between those extremes, there are other species. In a woodland, the preferred environment of each species could be mapped horizontally as towering forest trees yield to smaller trees better adapted to the Great Plains' harsh environment, and those trees give way to shrubs that venture into grassland. Bird species also sort vertically in woodlands.

Scarlet tanagers prefer mature deciduous woodlands, especially oaks, and for feeding and nesting they favor the upper forest canopy. During the breeding season they are almost exclusively insectivorous, capturing insects and spiders from leaves and branches and "hawking" from a perch to capture flying insects. Most migrant warblers occupy similar niches, but they have evolved to become specialists, minimizing competition. Red-bellied woodpeckers are also adapted to mature hardwood forests, but they occupy the mid-story for nesting, extracting insects and insect larvae from tree trunks and large limbs. Eastern towhees feed both on the forest floor and at the shrub level, and may nest either on the ground or in shrubs only a few feet above it. Add to these three species dozens of other passerines found in woodlands, and vertical and horizontal sorting becomes incredibly complex, each species having evolved to exploit a rather narrowly defined set of environmental circumstances. Knowing where a species is most likely to be found is an important aid to the birder.

Bird species in a forest sort vertically to avoid competition for food and nest sites. Each species has its own niche.

the heat of summer, most nesting birds need to be on the nest in midday to shade eggs or young. Even grassland species adapted to Great Plains summers seek shade in woody thickets or the shadow of bunchgrass. Fortunately, periods early and late in the day are also the most pleasant times to be afield, especially in the summer, when the light is soft and winds are usually light. The best birders do not sleep in, but like the birds they seek, they may nap in midday.

Isolated trees and water on grasslands attract a variety of bird species, especially during migration periods. During the breeding season isolated trees are almost sure to have one or more bird nests, whether a Swainson's hawk or Baltimore oriole.

JON FARRAR

*Give a bird a perch, even a **Wilson's snipe,** and it is sure to use it to advertise its territory, watch for danger or preen.*

Hunt the Edge

Passerines, the perching birds, are the largest order of birds. That alone suggests that a birder wanting to find a large number of species should look where there are perches. Forty-eight percent of Nebraska's breeding bird species are associated with woodlands. Nebraska was a prairie state and much of it yet today remains sparsely wooded. That does not mean there are no birds where there are no trees.

But even grassland passerines – species so well adapted to treeless plains the courtship songs of some are issued while in flight – appreciate a perch. For a grasshopper sparrow, a perch may be no more than a milkweed stalk. Others, such as sedge wrens, do quite nicely perching on nothing more than several grass stems clutched in their feet. Small grassland birds do not need trees, but where a fence runs through a grassland they will perch, sing, preen and peruse for danger from fence posts and barbed wire. To attract birds, edge habitat does not need to be the textbook example of towering forests stair-stepping down to shorter pioneer trees, then shrubs, then grassland. A patch of scrubby willows or wild indigo along a Sandhills stream draws migrating and nesting birds like a magnet.

If there is a rule to finding the maximum number of birds in an area, it is to not neglect any landforms or vegetation deviating from what is most abundant. In a woodland, look for grassy openings. And conversely, any break in uniform grasslands is sure to attract birds – fences, shrubby plants like sage, rock outcrops, a gathering of trees and water. The best of all is a cluster of cottonwoods or willows around a small pool of water. Sit quietly near one of these migrant traps in May, and you will be rewarded with a variety of perching birds. Water – whether open water in a spillway below a reservoir in the depth of winter or a temporary pool of rainwater in a Panhandle grassland – attracts birds and is seldom a disappointing stop for birders.

While many bird species are associated with woodlands, dense, mature woodlands are relatively impoverished in both species and individuals. Find a break in a dense woodland, where a giant oak or cottonwood has fallen or where a small wetland allows sunlight to penetrate, and there will be more birds of different species than in deep woods. Grassy openings and the outer margins of woodlands support a greater and more varied avifauna than deep woods. Where ponderosa pine woodlands merge with deciduous woodlands along drainages in the Pine Ridge is an incredibly rich zone for bird life. However, some species, such as ovenbirds, seem to shy away from sunlight. To find them a birder must search the forest.

Finding and watching birds should never be anything but a delightful experience. We are a competitive species, prone to count and name every creature, and to compare our accomplishments with others. But when the joy of birding becomes something other than the joy of viewing the Earth's most wondrous creations we have lost our way. ∎

JON FARRAR

*For grassland and edge species, such as the **American** **goldfinch**, a common mullen flower stalk is a desirable perch.*

Code of Ethics

Everyone who enjoys birds and birding must always respect wildlife, its environment, and the rights of others. In any conflict of interest between birds and birders, the welfare of the birds and their environment comes first.

Promote the welfare of birds and their environment. To avoid stressing birds or exposing them to danger, exercise restraint and caution during observation, photography, sound recording, or filming. Limit the use of recordings and other methods of attracting birds, and never use such methods in heavily birded areas or for attracting any species that is threatened, endangered, or is of special concern or rare in your local area. Keep well back from nests and nesting colonies, roosts, display areas, and important feeding sites. In such sensitive areas, if there is a need for extended observation, photography, filming, or recording,
try to use a blind or hide, and take advantage of natural cover. Use artificial light sparingly for filming or photography, especially for close-ups. Before advertising the presence of a rare bird, evaluate the potential for disturbance to the bird, its surroundings, and other people in the area, and proceed only if access can be controlled, disturbance minimized, and permission has been obtained from private landowners. The sites of rare nesting birds should be divulged only to the proper conservation authorities. Stay on roads, trails, and paths where they exist; otherwise keep habitat disturbance to a minimum.

Respect the law and the rights of others. Do not enter private property without the owner's explicit permission. Follow all laws, rules, and regulations governing use of roads and public areas. Practice common courtesy in contacts with
other people.

While group birding, each individual has responsibilities as a group member. Respect the interests, rights, and skills of fellow birders, as well as people participating in other legitimate outdoor activities. Freely share your knowledge and experience. Be especially helpful to beginning birders. If you witness unethical birding behavior, assess the situation, and intervene if you think it prudent. When interceding, inform the person(s) of the inappropriate action, and attempt, within reason, to have it stopped. If the behavior continues, document it, and notify appropriate individuals or organizations. Be an exemplary ethical role model for the group. Teach through word and example. Keep groups to a size that limits its effect on the environment, and does not interfere with others using the same area.

Condensed from the American Birding Association's Principles of Birding Ethics.

Additional Sources

Books About Nebraska Birds

Ducey, James E. 2000. *Birds of the Untamed West – The History of Birdlife in Nebraska, 1750 to 1875.* Making History [Press]: Omaha, NE. 299 pages, 33 maps and illustrations. Paper. The role of birds in Nebraska Native American daily life, myth and religion, and accounts of birds in Nebraska during the period of exploration. $25.

Johnsgard, Paul A. 2003. *Great Wildlife of the Great Plains.* University Press of Kansas. 328 pages, 68 line drawings, 5 maps. Cloth. Written sketches of 121 Great Plains species, including birds, their ecology, behavior and life histories. Organized by biotic communities. $29.95.

——. 2003. *The Birds of Nebraska.* Privately published. 139 pages, range maps. Paper cover, spiral binding. A good choice for birders wanting a portable condensation of similar information found in *Birds of Nebraska* by Sharpe, et al. Includes accounts of all Nebraska species – frequency, abundance, distribution, breeding/migration status, migration peaks, habitats and additional information. Available from author, School of Biological Sciences, University of Nebraska-Lincoln, Lincoln, NE 68588, $12 includes postage.

——. 2001. *Prairie Birds – Fragile Splendor in the Great Plains.* University Press of Kansas. 352 pages 47 drawings, 14 maps. Highly readable accounts of 33 characteristic grasslands birds. Filled with natural history and behavior information and Great Plains ecology. Includes list of prairie preserves. $29.95.

——. 2001. *The Nature of Nebraska.* University of Nebraska Press. 402 pages, 10 maps, 56 illustrations. Cloth. The natural history of Nebraska organized by nine ecosystems, including historical geology, biology, botany and ecology. Includes a guide to public and private wildlife viewing areas. $29.95

Lingle, Gary R. 1994. *Birding Crane River: Nebraska's Platte.* Harrier Publishing, Grand Island. 121 pages, maps, art, charts. Paper cover, spiral binding. Where and how to find birds in the central Platte River Valley. Description of area, birding areas by counties, specialty species, checklist. $11.95.

Mollhoff, Wayne J. 2002. *The Nebraska Breeding Bird Atlas, 1984-1989.* Nebraska Game and Parks Commission. 233 pages. Paper cover. Maps, charts. Information derived from a six-year study of breeding birds in Nebraska. Species accounts of 191 species breeding in the state including historical references. $29

Rosche, Richard. 1994. *Birds of the Lake McConaughy Area and the North Platte River Valley, Nebraska.* Published by the author. 119 pages, line art. Paper, spiral-bound. While not designed as a bird-finding guide, it serves that purpose quite well. Organized taxonomically by species. $10 + $3 postage for Priority Mail, $1.50 for Media Mail. Richard Rosche, 110 Maple Road, East Aurora, NY 14052-1729

Sharpe, Roger S., W. Ross Silcock and Joel G. Jorgensen. 2001. *Birds of Nebraska.* University of Nebraska Press. 510 pages, maps, color photographs. Cloth. Species accounts including historical reports, distribution, abundance, time of migration, breeding records. A book to consult for specific information on all bird species reported in the state. $69.95.

Identification Guides

Birds of North America: A Guide to Field Identification. St. Martin's Press, 2003. Written by Chandler S. Robbins et al. 360 pages. Hardcover list price $19.95, paper cover list price $15.95. The most recent edition of the long-popular Golden Guide book. Compact and lightweight. Organized taxonomically with range maps on same page as species accounts and illustrations. Bird illustration adequate but not as good as some field guides. Covers both eastern and western species.

National Geographic Field Guide to the Birds of North America. National Geographic Society, 4th edition, 2002. 480 pages. Paper cover list price $21.95. Larger than most field guides (5 by 8 inches). New edition conforms to current taxonomy. All North American species are included with species descriptions and identification marks, measurements and notes on vocalizations. Small, updated range maps appear with species accounts. The 800 illustrations by 21 different artists clearly show identification features. Typically three to five species per two-page spread. Age, sex and seasonal differences are illustrated, as are birds in flight.

Peterson Eastern and Western Field Guides. Peterson's guides have long been a bane to birders in midcontinent because the 100th meridian – located in the middle of Nebraska – divides the editions. Peterson's illustrations are classics, using small arrows to point out identifying features. Small enough to carry in the field (7¼ by 4½ inches). Detailed range maps. *A Field Guide to the Birds of Eastern and Central North America.* Houghton Mifflin Co., 5th edition, 450 pages. Paper cover list price $22, hardcover list price $30. Species accounts includes description, voice, habitat and range. 1,800 illustrations. *A Field Guide to Western Birds: A Completely New Guide to Field Marks of All Species Found in North America West of the 100th Meridian and North of Mexico.* Houghton Mifflin Co., Reissue of 1998 edition, 432 pages. Paper cover list price $18, hardcover list price $27. Includes 700 species in 160 color plates.

Sibley Guide to Birds. Alfred A. Knopf, 2000. Written and illustrated by David Allen Sibley. Durable soft cover, 544 pages, list price $35. An oversized field guide (9¾ by 6½ inches) weighing 2½ pounds with 6,600 illustrations including 810 species. Includes species of contiguous 48 states and Canada. Each bird is shown in several positions, an average of eight pictures per species, illustrating plumage changes by age, sex and season. Usually two species per page. Most birds also shown in flight. Range maps on same page as species account. Contains less life history and habitat information than some other guides. The original Sibley guide was criticized as too large for field use. More compact eastern and western editions are now available at a list price of $19.95 each.

The above field guides are widely used by birders. Recently several additional field guides have been published. They are not yet widely used, but might meet the needs and interests of some birders.

Smithsonian Handbooks, DK Publishing, 2001. Written by Fred J. Alsop III. Three volumes. *Birds of North America* includes 930 species, 1,024 pages, cloth cover list price $60. *Birds of North America: Eastern Region* includes 706 species, 752 pages, soft cover list price $25. *Birds of North America: Western Region* includes 706 species, 752 pages, soft cover list price $25. Photo-encyclopedic design. Includes more life history information than most field guides. Concise, user-friendly text. All three volumes are too large and heavy to be considered field guides but suitable for use in a vehicle or as home reference.

Stokes Field Guide to Birds: Eastern Region and *Stokes Field Guide to Birds: Western Region.* Little, Brown & Co., 1996. Written by Donald and Lillian Stokes. 496 and 560 pages respectively, list price of both $17.95. Small enough to be considered field guides. Good starter field guides. One species per page is illustrated with one to several color photos usually showing plumage differences in age, sex and season. More life history information than most field guides.

Birds of North America (Kaufman Focus Guides). Houghton Mifflin Co., 2001. Written by Kenn Kaufman et al. 384 pages. Flexicover list price $22. A compact, lightweight field guide illustrated with 2,000 photos digitally edited to emphasize identifying characteristics and eliminate confusing backgrounds and lighting.

Birds of Nebraska. Adventure Publications, Inc., 2003. Written by Stan Tekiela. 304 pages, paper cover, list price $12.95. Compact (4 by 6 inches). 117 common species, illustrated with photographs. Brief description of species. Will leave users wondering about identities of more than 300 other species found in the state.

Maps

Nebraska Sportsman's Atlas, Sportsman's Atlas Company, P.O. Box 132, Lytton, IA 50561, 1997. Spiral-bound, 79 pages, 16 by 11 inches, $21.95. Available at many book and sporting goods stores as well as on the Internet. A full set of county road maps reproduced from those issued by the Nebraska Department of Roads. Shows county roads, rural residences, state and federal wildlife management areas and refuges with brief descriptions of each. Also includes accommodations and site index. Laminated cover. Useful for navigating the state's back country.

Nebraska Atlas and Gazetteer, Delorme Publishing Company, P.O. Box 298, Freeport, ME 04032, 2000. Staple-bound, 80 pages, 16 by 11 inches, $19.95. Available at many book and sporting goods stores as well as on the Internet. County lines, highways, county roads and towns superimposed over 1:200,000 scale topographic maps. Includes GPS grids and tick marks, placename index, information on attractions, scenic drives, historic sites, wildlife management areas, refuges and recreational information.

Nebraska Birding and Conservation Organizations
- Audubon Society of Omaha – Omaha-based Audubon chapter. 11809 Old Maple Road, Omaha, NE 68164, (402) 445-4138, www.audubon-omaha.org
- Big Bend Audubon Society – Kearney-based Audubon chapter. PO Box 1575, Kearney, NE 68848-1575.
- Bluebirds Across Nebraska – www.bbne.org
- Lueshen's Birders – Jan Uttecht, P.O. Box 823, Stanton, NE 68779, (402) 439-2114. Norfolk-based birding club.
- Audubon Nebraska - 5000 Central Park Drive Suite 101, Lincoln, NE 68504, (402) 466-1220, www.audubon.org/states/ne
- Nebraska Ornithologists' Union – Quarterly publishes *The Nebraska Bird Review,* the state's best source for information on birds and birding. Web site includes current Nebraska checklist, rare bird alerts, link to NEBirds chatroom, information on birding areas and more. http://rip.physics.unk.edu/NOU/
- The Nature Conservancy-Nebraska – www.nature.org/wherewework/northamerica/states/nebraska
- Wachiska Audubon Society – Lincoln-based Audubon chapter for southeastern Nebraska. 4547 Calvert Street, Suite 10, Lincoln, NE 68506-5643, (402) 486-4846, www.wachiskaaudubon.org
- Wildcat Audubon Society – Scottsbluff/Gering-based Audubon chapter for the Panhandle. www.audubon.org/states/ne/wildcat.html

Internet Birding and Conservation Sites
- American Bird Center: www.americanbirdcenter.com/abc-nebraska.html
- American Birding Association: www.americanbirding.org
- American Breeding Bird Survey: www.mp2-pwrc.usgs.gov/bbs
- American Ornithologists' Union: www.aou.org
- BIRDNET: www.nmnh.si.edu/BIRDNET/index.html
- Birding.com: www.birding.com/
- Cornell Laboratory of Ornithology: www.birds.cornell.edu/
- U.S. Fish and Wildlife Service: www.fws.gov
- Nebraska Game and Parks Commission: outdoornebraska.org
- NGPC Spring Migration Guide: outdoornebraska.org/wildlife/guides/migration/migration.asp
- NGPC Nongame Program: outdoornebraska.org/wildlife/programs/nongame/nongame.asp
- NGPC Interactive Bird Guide: outdoornebraska.org/wildlife/guides/birds/findbirds.asp
- Northern Prairie Wildlife Research Center: www.npwrc.usgs.gov

Checklist of Nebraska Birds

Checklist information largely adapted from Birds of Nebraska *by Roger S. Sharpe, W. Ross Silcock and Joel G. Jorgensen. Other sources used were* The Nebraska Breeding Bird Atlas *by Wayne Molhoff and records of the Nebraska Ornithologists' Union.*

COMMON-SCIENTIFIC NAME	BREEDER	MIGRANT	HABITAT	ADDITIONAL INFORMATION
FAMILY ANATIDAE **ducks, geese and swans**				
Black-bellied Whistling-Duck *Dendrocygna autumnalis*		A	Lakes, marshes, streams.	Two state records, both in Rainwater Basin.
Bean Goose *Anser fabalis*		A	Lakes, marshes, streams.	Two state records, DeSoto NWR and Funk WMA.
Greater White-fronted Goose *Anser albifrons*		C	Marshes, lakes, large rivers with sandbars, cropland.	Rainwater Basin, Platte River, spring. Less common in fall.
Emperor Goose *Chen canagica*		A	Lakes, marshes, streams.	One state record, Harvard WMA, Rainwater Basin. May mix with Canada geese.
Snow Goose *Chen caerulescens*		C	Lakes, marshes, large rivers, cropland.	Most abundant in spring migration, Missouri River, Rainwater Basin. Hypothetical breeder.
Ross's Goose *Chen rossii*		C	Lakes, marshes, large rivers, cropland.	Migrate with snow geese. Missouri River, Rainwater Basin. Panhandle during spring. migration.
Canada Goose *Branta canadensis*	C	C	Lakes, marshes, large rivers, cropland.	Statewide. Common breeders since 1970s.
Brant *Branta bernicla*		R	Lakes, marshes, streams.	Usually found with Canada Geese. Spring and fall migration. Statewide.
Trumpeter Swan *Cygnus buccinator*	L/UC	L/UC	Large marshes, streams.	Resident, breeder in Sandhills, winters on western streams.
Tundra Swan *Cygnus columbianus*		R	Shallow lakes, marhses, flooded fields.	Rare winter visitor. Usually in small flocks. Statewide reports. March and November.
Wood Duck *Aix sponsa*	C	C	Wetlands near woods, marshes.	More common as breeder and migrant in east.
Gadwall *Anas strepera*	C	C	Lakes, marshes.	Common breeder in Sandhills.
Eurasian Wigeon *Anas penelope*		R	Ponds, lakes.	Most often seen with American wigeon in Rainwater Basin. More likely spring.
American Wigeon *Anas americana*	UC	C	Lakes, ponds, marshes.	Uncommon regular breeder in north-central and northwest.
American Black Duck *Anas rubripes*		R	Lakes, marshes.	Usually with mallards. Rare visitor year-round. More likely east.
Mallard *Anas platyrhynchos*	C	C	Lakes, marshes, streams.	Overwinters. One of state's two most common breeding ducks.
Mottled Duck *Anas fulvigula*		A	Lakes.	One state record, Howard County. Hybridizes with mallards.
Blue-winged Teal *Anas discors*	C	C	Marshes, ponds, sloughs, shallow water.	Late spring migrant, early fall migrant. One of state's two most common breeding ducks.
Cinnamon Teal *Anas cyanoptera*	UC	UC	Marshes, ponds, shallow water.	Most common west. Kiowa and Facus Springs WMAs, Crescent Lake NWR.
Northern Shoveler *Anas clypeata*	C	C	Ponds, lakes, marshes, shallow water.	Locally common breeder in Sandhills. Late spring migrant, early fall migrant.
Northern Pintail *Anas acuta*	UC	C	Lakes, marshes, shallow water.	Large numbers in March in Rainwater Basin. Uncommon regular breeder in Sandhills.
Garganey *Anas querquedula*		A	Lakes, marshes.	Two records. Migrate with blue-winged teal.
Green-winged Teal *Anas crecca*	UC	C	Lakes, marshes, streams.	Rare, regular breeder in Sandhills. Frequently overwinters.

Key   **A** – Accidental – Reported but cannot be expected to occur again.
R – Rare – Fewer than 50 reports exist.
UC – Uncommon – Some present every year in expected habitats.

C – Common – Expected to be found in the proper habitat at appropriate times.
L – Local in occurrence.

COMMON-SCIENTIFIC NAME	BREEDER	MIGRANT	HABITAT	ADDITIONAL INFORMATION
Canvasback *Aythya valisineria*	UC	C	Lakes, large rivers, marshes.	Regular breeder in small numbers, principally western Sandhills.
Redhead *Aythya americana*	C	C	Lakes, marshes.	One of two most common breeding, diving ducks in Sandhills.
Ring-necked Duck *Aythya collaris*		C	Lakes, marshes.	Reported as breeder in Sandhills pre-1920.
Tufted Duck *Aythya fuligula*		A	Lakes.	One record, Lake Ogallala.
Greater Scaup *Aythya marila*		UC	Lakes and rivers.	More common spring than fall, regular winter visitor. Lake McConaughy best site.
Lesser Scaup *Aythya affinis*	R	C	Lakes, large marshes, streams.	Small breeding population extreme western Sandhills.
King Eider *Somateria spectabilis*		A	Lakes.	One record, DeSoto NWR November 1985.
Common Eider *Somateria mollissima*		A	Lakes, streams.	One record, early winter, 1967, Lincoln County.
Harlequin Duck *Histrionicus histrionicus*		A	Lakes, rocky shores.	Three state records. May associate with buffleheads.
Surf Scoter *Melanitta perspicillata*		R	Lakes, large rivers.	Most likely at Gavins Point Dam, Lake McConaughy with diving ducks.
White-winged Scoter *Melanitta fusca*		R	Lakes, large rivers.	Missouri River, Lake McConaughy and other large reservoirs in fall.
Black Scoter *Melanitta nigra*		R	Lakes, large rivers.	Most likely during fall migration.
Long-tailed Duck *Clangula hyemalis*		R	Lakes, large rivers.	Regularly seen at Lake Ogallala in winter. Scattered reports elsewhere.
Bufflehead *Bucephala albeola*	A	C	Lakes, large marshes.	Single breeding record in Brown County in 2000.
Common Goldeneye *Bucephala clangula*		C	Lakes, large rivers.	Regular winter visitor in open water below dams.
Barrow's Goldeneye *Bucephala islandica*		R	Lakes, large rivers.	Most reports December to February, Lake Ogallala.
Hooded Merganser *Lophodytes cucullatus*		UC	Lakes, streams.	Hypothetical breeder in Missouri Valley. One state breeding record.
Common Merganser *Mergus merganser*	R	C	Lakes, large rivers.	Three breeding reports. Large numbers late fall at Harlan County Reservoir and winter at Sutherland Reservoir and Lake McConaughy.
Red-breasted Merganser *Mergus serrator*		UC	Lakes, large rivers.	Uncommon migrant, especially in west. In winter look at Lake Ogallala, Gavins Point Dam.
Ruddy Duck *Oxyura jamaicensis*	L/C	C	Large lakes and marshes.	One of two most common breeding, diving ducks in Sandhills. Occasional breeder in wet years in Rainwater Basin.
PHASIANIDAE **partridges, turkeys**				
Gray Partridge *Perdix perdix*	R		Cropland, pasture, grassy and weedy edge.	Resident. Primarily in north, especially northeast. Subject to population cycles.
Ring-necked Pheasant *Phasianus colchicus*	C		Weedy grasslands, cropland.	Resident. First introduced 1890s, expanded in abundance and statewide in 1920s.
Ruffed Grouse *Bonasa umbellus*			Deciduous woodlands.	Native to Missouri Valley, extirpated by 1900.
Greater Sage-Grouse *Centrocercus urophasianus*		R	Sagebrush grassland.	Never abundant, restricted to extreme northwest, possibly extirpated.
Sharp-tailed Grouse *Tympanuchus phasianellus*	C		Shortgrass and mixed-grass prairie.	Resident. Most abundant in Sandhills, less abundant in Panhandle.
Greater Prairie-Chicken *Tympanuchus cupido*	L/C		Native grasslands, especially near scattered cropland.	Resident. Most common in southern and eastern Sandhills, remnant populations elsewhere.
Lesser Prairie-Chicken *Tympanuchus pallidicinctus*			Sandsage prairie.	Possibly native to southwestern counties. Extirpated.
Wild Turkey *Meleagris gallopavo*	C		Floodplain and pine forests, shelterbelts, other woodlands.	Extirpated from eastern counties before 1900, reintroduced 1960s in Pine Ridge. Now found statewide.

COMMON-SCIENTIFIC NAME	BREEDER	MIGRANT	HABITAT	ADDITIONAL INFORMATION
ODONTOPHORIDAE quail				
Northern Bobwhite *Colinus virginianus*	C		Where grasslands, cropland, brush and woodlands merge.	Resident. Most common south of Platte River and eastern third of state.
FAMILY GAVIDAE loons				
Red-throated Loon *Gavia stellata*		R	Lakes.	Reported October-November at Lake McConaughy, Branched Oak Lake.
Pacific Loon *Gavia pacifica*		R	Lakes.	Winter visitor. Most in fall at Lake McConaughy and eastern reservoirs.
Common Loon *Gavia immer*		UC	Lakes.	Most reports from April-May and November-December. Occasionally found in summer months.
Yellow-billed Loon *Gavia adamsii*		A	Lakes.	Three state records. October-November. Lake McConaughy.
FAMILY PODICIPEDIDAE grebes				
Pied-billed Grebe *Podilymbus podiceps*	C	C	Marshes, lakes, ponds with with emergent vegetation.	Common breeder in Sandhills, less common statewide.
Horned Grebe *Podiceps auritus*		UC	Lakes during migration, marshes in breeding season.	Hypothetical breeder in Sandhills. Flocks of 100 or more during migration. Lake McConaughy, North Platte NWR.
Red-necked Grebe *Podiceps grisegena*		R	Lakes.	Most commonly reported late-October.
Eared Grebe *Podiceps nigricollis*	L/C	C	Lakes, marshes during breeding season.	Locally common breeder Sandhills. Postbreeding on reservoirs, large lakes.
Western Grebe *Aechmophorus occidentalis*	L/C	C	Lakes, marshes during breeding season.	Breeder in central, western Sandhills. Post-breeding on reservoirs, large lakes.
Clark's Grebe *Aechmophorus clarkii*	R	UC	Lakes, marshes during breeding season.	Rare breeder western Sandhills, Clear Creek WMA. Probably underreported. Found with western grebes.
PELECANIDAE pelicans				
American White Pelican *Pelecanus erythrorhynchos*		C	Lakes, large marshes, rivers.	Common migrant, nonbreeding birds present in summer. Breeds in southern South Dakota.
Brown Pelican *Pelecanus occidentalis*		R	Lakes, large rivers.	Five accepted state records, most reports along Missouri River.
PHALACROCORACIDAE cormorants				
Neotropic Cormorant *Phalacrocorax brasilianus*		R	Lakes.	Seven state records. Travel with double-crested cormorants.
Double-crested Cormorant *Phalacrocorax auritus*	L/C	C	Lakes, large marshes, rivers.	Increased in abundance and as breeders with reservoir construction since 1940s.
ANHINGIDAE darters				
Anhinga *Anhinga anhinga*		A	Rivers, oxbows.	Three state records, spring and fall, Missouri River Valley.
ARDEIDAE herons, bitterns				
American Bittern *Botaurus lentiginosus*	UC	UC	Wetlands with heavy emergent vegetation.	Locally common breeder in Sandhills.
Least Bittern *Ixobrychus exilis*	R	UC	Wetlands with heavy emergent vegetation.	Probably a more common breeder in east, particularly Rainwater Basin wet years.
Great Blue Heron *Ardea herodias*	C	C	Lakes, marshes, streams.	Colonial breeder in tall trees.

Key
A – Accidental – Reported but cannot be expected to occur again.
R – Rare – Fewer than 50 reports exist.
UC – Uncommon – Some present every year in expected habitats.

C – Common – Expected to be found in the proper habitat at appropriate times.
L – Local in occurrence.

COMMON-SCIENTIFIC NAME	BREEDER	MIGRANT	HABITAT	ADDITIONAL INFORMATION
Great Egret *Ardea alba*	A	UC	Lakes, marshes, streams.	One state nesting record, Sarpy County. Most common as postbreeders late summer. Harlan County Reservoir in August.
Snowy Egret *Egretta thula*		UC	Marshes, streams.	Hypothetical breeder. Most reports from Rainwater Basin, migration and summer. More common in east.
Little Blue Heron *Egretta caerulea*		R	Marshes, lakes, streams.	Most reports in south and east, Rainwater Basin, spring and summer.
Tricolored Heron *Egretta tricolor*		R	Marshes, lakes.	Five state records. Spring and summer, Rainwater Basin.
Reddish Egret *Egretta rufescens*		A	Marshes, lakes.	One state record, Lake McConaughy, August-September 2000.
Cattle Egret *Bubulcus ibis*	R	UC	Flooded grasslands, shallow marshes.	Often seen near livestock. Five breeding records, first in 1984 at Valentine NWR. Probably underreported as breeder.
Green Heron *Butorides virescens*	L/C	UC	Wooded streams and lakes.	Most common in east.
Black-crowned Night-Heron *Nycticorax nycticorax*	L/C	C	Marshes with dense emergent vegetation.	Locally common breeder in Sandhills marshes.
Yellow-crowned Night-Heron *Nyctanassa violacea*	A	R	Wooded wetlands.	One nesting state record, Fontenelle Forest. Might be an irregular breeder in southeast.
THRESKIORNITHIDAE **ibises, spoonbills**				
White Ibis *Eudocimus albus*		A	Shallow wetlands.	Four state records. Most likely in Rainwater Basin.
Glossy Ibis *Plegadis falcinellus*		A	Shallow marshes.	Three documented state records.
White-faced Ibis *Plegadis chihi*	R	L/C	Shallow wetlands, flooded fields, wet meadows.	Six state nesting records, Rainwater Basin and Sandhills.
Roseate Spoonbill *Platalea ajaja*		R	Marshes, lakes.	Mostly likely in south-central and southeast. Four documented state records. Associate with little blue herons and snowy egrets.
CICONIIDAE **storks**				
Wood Stork *Mycteria americana*		A		One documented state record, Fontenelle Forest.
CATHARTIDAE **vultures**				
Black Vulture *Coragyps atratus*		A		One accepted state record.
Turkey Vulture *Cathartes aura*	L/C	C	Forest edge and open country.	Most often nests in river valleys providing nest sites. Communal roosts late summer.
ACCIPITRIDAE **ospreys, kites, hawks, eagles**				
Osprey *Pandion haliaetus*		UC	Rivers, lakes with abundant fish for foraging.	Hypothetical breeder. Summer birds probably non-breeders.
Swallow-tailed Kite *Elanoides forficatus*			Wooded streams.	Extirpated since early-1900s.
White-tailed Kite *Elanus leucurus*		R	Grasslands.	Rare summer visitor south and west. Three state records.
Mississippi Kite *Ictinia mississippiensis*	R	R	Scrub and open woodlands near water, urban.	Ogallala only known breeding site.
Bald Eagle *Haliaeetus leucocephalus*	UC	C	Larger tree-lined rivers and lakes.	Found over most of state. Increasing as breeder. Winters at reservoirs and along large rivers.
Northern Harrier *Circus cyaneus*	L/UC	C	Grasslands and marshes.	Highest breeding numbers in Sandhills. Remain in Nebraska during open winters in appropriate habitat.
Sharp-shinned Hawk *Accipiter striatus*	R	UC	Open woodlands, forest.	Most summer reports in southeast and central Niobrara River Valley. Few breeding records.

COMMON-SCIENTIFIC NAME	BREEDER	MIGRANT	HABITAT	ADDITIONAL INFORMATION
ACCIPITRIDAE **ospreys, kites, hawks, eagles** *(continued)*				
Cooper's Hawk *Accipiter cooperi*	UC	UC	Woodlands, woodland edge.	Most common in southeast. Increasingly common as breeder.
Northern Goshawk *Accipiter gentilis*		R	Forests, woodlands.	Rare migrant and winter visitor statewide, rare in summer in northwest.
Harris's Hawk *Parabuteo unicinctus*		A		Two state records. Fall and winter visitor.
Red-shouldered Hawk *Buteo lineatus*	LR	LR	Riverbottom woodlands.	Fontenelle Forest only known breeding site.
Broad-winged Hawk *Buteo platypterus*	LR	UC	Mature, deciduous forest, migrants in open country.	Rare in west. Few breeding records, all in Missouri Valley.
Swainson's Hawk *Buteo swainsoni*	C	C	Open country in migration. Prefers grasslands with scattered trees when breeding.	Migrates statewide, most common as breeder in western Nebraska.
Red-tailed Hawk *Buteo jamaicensis*	C	C	Open country with scattered trees, forest edge.	Nests statewide. Might overwinter in large numbers.
Ferruginous Hawk *Buteo regalis*	UC	UC	Shortgrass prairie with rock outcrops or scattered trees.	Most common western Sandhills and Panhandle. Prefers rock outcrops for nesting.
Rough-legged Hawk *Buteo lagopus*		LC	Grasslands.	Winters statewide.
Golden Eagle *Aquila chrysaetos*	UC	UC	Grasslands with rock buttes or outcrops.	Most breeders in Panhandle, winters statewide. Pine Ridge, North Platte Valley.
FALCONIDAE **falcons**				
American Kestrel *Falco sparverius*	L/C	C	Grasslands with scattered trees.	Males commonly overwinter.
Merlin *Falco columbarius*	R	UC	Pine forest edge.	Breeding principally in Pine Ridge, winters statewide.
Gyrfalcon *Falco rusticolus*		R	Open prairies, plains.	A few reports most winters. Prey on grouse, Sandhills.
Peregrine Falcon *Falco peregrinus*	R	UC	Urban, wetlands.	Only known breeding sites restocked birds in Omaha and Lincoln. Frequents wetlands with shorebirds during migration.
Prairie Falcon *Falco mexicanus*	UC	UC	Grasslands.	More common in west year-round. Nests in cliffs near grasslands.
RALLIDAE **rails, gallinules, coots**				
Yellow Rail *Coturnicops noveboracensis*		R	Marshes with grass or sedge borders.	Most reports in eastern counties.
Black Rail *Laterallus jamaicensis*		R	Marshes, wet meadows.	Hypothetical breeder. Possible statewide migrant.
Clapper Rail *Rallus longirostris*		A		One winter record, Logan County.
King Rail *Rallus elegans*	R	R	Marshes with abundant shoreline emergent vegetation.	Summer visitor statewide, rare breeder in east. Reported at Jack Sinn WMA.
Virginia Rail *Rallus limicola*	L/C	L/C	Marshes with abundant shoreline emergent vegetation.	Regular breeder in north and west. Winter in North Platte Valley.
Sora *Porzana carolina*	L/C	C	Marshes with abundant shoreline emergent vegetation.	May breed statewide, most common Sandhills.
Purple Gallinule *Porphyrio martinica*		A	Wooded wetlands.	One record, Adams County.
Common Moorhen *Gallinula chloropus*	R	R	Ponds and marshes with abundant emergent vegetation.	Occur in wet cycles, principally in southeast and eastern Rainwater Basin. Nests in dense cattail marshes.
American Coot *Fulica americana*	C	C	Open wetlands with abundant shoreline emergent vegetation.	Common breeder in Sandhills marshes.

Key   **A** – Accidental – Reported but cannot be expected to occur again.   **C** – Common – Expected to be found in the proper habitat at appropriate times.
R – Rare – Fewer than 50 reports exist.
UC – Uncommon – Some present every year in expected habitats.   **L** – Local in occurrence.

COMMON-SCIENTIFIC NAME	BREEDER	MIGRANT	HABITAT	ADDITIONAL INFORMATION
GRUIDAE **cranes**				
Sandhill Crane *Grus canadensis*	R	C	Large, open, shallow rivers, marshes, wet meadows.	Spring staging, less common in fall. Recent breeding records in Rainwater Basin area.
Common Crane *Grus grus*		R	Large, open, shallow rivers.	Five state records, all with sandhill cranes on Platte River.
Whooping Crane *Grus americana*		R	Large, open, shallow rivers, marshes, lakes.	Stops over during spring and fall migrations in central Nebraska.
CHARADRIIDAE **plovers**				
Black-bellied Plover *Pluvialis squatarola*		UC	Wetlands, mudflats, fields.	Most reports from Rainwater Basin and Lake McConaughy in late-May.
American Golden-Plover *Pluvialis dominica*		UC	Open fields, short grasslands, shorelines.	More common in spring migration than fall, eastern counties.
Snowy Plover *Charadrius alexandrinus*	R	R	Sandy beaches of lakes and rivers.	Recent breeding at Lake McConaughy, Missouri River.
Semipalmated Plover *Charadrius semipalmatus*		C	Mudflats, wetlands, shorelines.	More common in east and spring.
Piping Plover *Charadrius melodus*	L/C	UC	Sandbars, sandy beaches of large streams and lakes.	Nests on sandy beaches and sandbars, Lake McConaughy, lower Platte and Niobrara rivers.
Killdeer *Charadrius vociferus*	C	C	Wetlands, open grasslands, exposed ground.	Nests statewide in variety of habitats. Flocks July-October.
Mountain Plover *Charadrius montanus*	R	R	Shortgrass prairie, barren cropland.	Nests in Kimball, Cheyenne, Banner counties.
RECURVIROSTRIDAE **stilts, avocets**				
Black-necked Stilt *Himantopus mexicanus*	R	UC	Alkaline ponds and marshes.	Localized breeding western Sandhills. Scattered breeding reports elsewhere.
American Avocet *Recurvirostra americana*	C	C	Alkaline ponds and marshes.	Nests near alkaline ponds and lake margins, principally in western Sandhills.
SCOLOPACIDAE **sandpipers, phalaropes**				
Greater Yellowlegs *Tringa melanoleuca*		C	Ponds, marshes, creeks, mudflats, flooded meadows.	Early spring migrant. More numerous in spring than fall.
Lesser Yellowlegs *Tringa flavipes*		C	Ponds, marshes, creeks, mudflats, flooded meadows.	More common than greater yellowlegs. More common in fall.
Solitary Sandpiper *Tringa solitaria*		UC	Shorelines.	Prefers shallow wetlands, marshes and wooded streams.
Willet *Catoptrophorus semipalmatus*	C	C	Low prairie near shallow wetlands, wet meadows.	More common in west. Breed primarily in western Sandhills.
Spotted Sandpiper *Actitis macularia*	UC	UC	Sparsely vegetated shorelines, streams, lakes.	Breeds statewide in small numbers. Does not mix with other shorebirds.
Upland Sandpiper *Bartramia longicauda*	L/C	L/C	Native prairies.	Found in variety of grasslands, including restored grasslands. Most common as breeder in Sandhills.
Eskimo Curlew *Numenius borealis*			Native prairies.	Extirpated, possibly extinct. Last accepted Nebraska record in 1926.
Whimbrel *Numenius phaeopus*		R	Flooded grasslands, sandbars, shorelines.	Rare migrants statewide, most reports in central and west, most in mid-May.
Long-billed Curlew *Numenius americanus*	UC	UC	Sandhills uplands, shortgrass and mixed-grass prairies.	Usually near water, most common central and western Sandhills, Panhandle.
Hudsonian Godwit *Limosa haemastica*		UC	Marshy ponds, wet grasslands, flooded fields.	Spring migrant only. Rare in west.
Marbled Godwit *Limosa fedoa*	R	UC	Mudflats, wet fields, sandbars, lake shorelines.	Spring and fall migrant more common in west. One state breeding record.
Ruddy Turnstone *Arenaria interpres*		R	Marsh, lake and river mudflats and sandbars.	Less common in west and fall. Most likely in mid-May. Lake McConaughy, Rainwater Basin, Platte River.
Red Knot *Calidris canutus*		R	Variety of wetland habitats.	Statewide migrant, a third of reports from Lancaster County. Best time August to early September.

COMMON-SCIENTIFIC NAME	BREEDER	MIGRANT	HABITAT	ADDITIONAL INFORMATION
SCOLOPACIDAE **sandpipers, phalaropes** **(continued)**				
Sanderling *Calidris alba*		C	Sandy beaches, mudflats on large lakes.	Most sightings at Lake McConaughy. More common in fall, late-July and August.
Semipalmated Sandpiper *Calidris pusilla*		C	Mudflats, sandbars, flooded fields, shorelines.	More common east. Rainwater Basins in May.
Western Sandpiper *Calidris mauri*		UC	Mudflats, open shorelines.	Statewide, more common in fall, peak late-August.
Least Sandpiper *Calidris minutilla*		C	Mudflats, shallow ponds, marsh edge, flooded meadow.	Common spring-fall migrant statewide, peak early-May and August.
White-rumped Sandpiper *Calidris fuscicollis*		C	Ponds, flooded pasture, shorelines.	Spring migrant only, statewide. Peak counts in late May.
Baird's Sandpiper *Calidris bairdii*		C	Ponds, flooded pasture, shorelines.	Early spring migrants, peak in April, statewide.
Pectoral Sandpiper *Calidris melanotos*		C	Mudflats, sandbars, flooded fields, shorelines.	More common east, peak late-April to mid-May, August.
Sharp-tailed Sandpiper *Calidris acuminata*		A	Mudflats, sandbars, flooded fields, shorelines.	Three state records.
Dunlin *Calidris alpina*		UC	Muddy shorelines, mudflats.	More common in east in spring, statewide fall. Flooded fields mid-May.
Curlew Sandpiper *Calidris ferruginea*		A	Freshwater pools.	One state record, Funk WPA, July 1997.
Stilt Sandpiper *Calidris himantopus*		C	Shallow water in wetlands.	Common spring and fall statewide. Peak mid-May, late-August to mid-September.
Buff-breasted Sandpiper *Tryngites subruficollis*		UC	Wetlands and flooded fields.	Most common spring in eastern Rainwater Basin. Forages in freshly worked fields.
Ruff *Philomachus pugnax*		R	Shorelines, mudflats.	Six state records, most Rainwater Basin. More common in east and central.
Short-billed Dowitcher *Limnodromus griseus*		UC	Shallow water in wetlands, flooded grasslands.	Less common than long-billed dowitcher. More common in east.
Long-billed Dowitcher *Limnodromus scolopaceus*		C	Shallow water in wetlands, flooded grasslands.	Common spring and fall. Best area Rainwater Basin, late-April to early-May, August and September.
Wilson's Snipe *Gallinago dilicata*	UC	C	Marshes, sloughs, wetlands with organic soils.	Breeds in northern and western Nebraska, rare in winter.
American Woodcock *Scolopax minor*	UC	UC	Wet forests and woodlands usually along streams.	More common in east, expanding west. Begin displaying in mid-March.
Wilson's Phalarope *Phalaropus tricolor*	UC	C	Shallow water in wetlands, especially alkaline waters.	Most common as migrants and breeders in Sandhills and Panhandle.
Red-necked Phalarope *Phalaropus lobatus*		UC	Open-water marshes, shallow lakes.	More common west, peak in late-May.
Red Phalarope *Phalaropus fulicarius*		R	Shorelines, mudflats.	Rare fall migrant in central and west.
LARIDAE **jaegers, gulls, terns**				
Pomarine Jaeger *Stercorarius pomarinus*		R	Lakes.	Eleven fall state records, most at Lake McConaughy.
Parasitic Jaeger *Stercorarius parasiticus*		R	Lakes.	Five fall state records, most at Lake McConaughy and eastern reservoirs.
Long-tailed Jaeger *Stercorarius longicaudus*		R	Lakes.	Four fall state records, most at Lake McConaughy and eastern reservoirs, September and October.
Laughing Gull *Larus atricilla*		R	Lakes.	Ten state records, most at reservoirs, but also elsewhere. Summer.
Franklin's Gull *Larus pipixcan*	A	C	Lakes, marshes, disked or plowed fields.	Statewide migrant. Two breeding records, both in Garden County in 1960s.
Little Gull *Larus minutus*		R	Lakes.	Eleven state records, most at western reservoirs, September and October.

Key

A – Accidental – Reported but cannot be expected to occur again.
R – Rare – Fewer than 50 reports exist.
UC – Uncommon – Some present every year in expected habitats.

C – Common – Expected to be found in the proper habitat at appropriate times.
L – Local in occurrence.

COMMON-SCIENTIFIC NAME	BREEDER	MIGRANT	HABITAT	ADDITIONAL INFORMATION
Black-headed Gull *Larus ridibundus*		A	Lakes.	One record state in August, Sheridan County.
Bonaparte's Gull *Larus philadelphia*		UC	Rivers, marshes, large lakes.	Increasingly common on reservoirs statewide in spring and fall.
Mew Gull *Larus canus*		R	Lakes.	Eighteen records, most in spring at Lake McConaughy.
Ring-billed Gull *Larus delawarensis*		C	Lakes, reservoirs, rivers, marshes.	Most common summer gull, nonbreeders.
California Gull *Larus californicus*		L/UC	Lakes, reservoirs, rivers, marshes.	Most records from Lake McConaughy, late summer and fall.
Herring Gull *Larus argentatus*		C	Lakes, reservoirs, rivers, marshes.	Increasing as reservoirs mature. Might be found any month.
Thayer's Gull *Larus thayeri*		UC	Lakes.	Small numbers each year, sightings increasing. Lake McConaughy, winter.
Iceland Gull *Larus glaucoides*		R	Lakes.	Eighteen state records, statewide but most reports mid-winter at Lake McConaughy.
Lesser Black-backed Gull *Larus fuscus*		R	Lakes.	Small numbers most years. Most reports Lake McConaughy, Branched Oak Lake.
Glaucous-winged Gull *Larus glaucescens*		A	Lakes.	Two records, both at Lake McConaughy, April and December.
Glaucous Gull *Larus hyperboreus*		UC	Lakes.	Present statewide as migrant and winter visitor.
Great Black-backed Gull *Larus marinus*		R	Lakes.	Eight state records. Reported throughout the year, mostly at Lake McConaughy.
Sabine's Gull *Xema sabini*		R	Lakes.	Very rare in spring. Most reports at western reservoirs, September-October.
Black-legged Kittiwake *Rissa tridactyla*		R	Lakes.	Most records at Gavin's Point Dam in November.
Ross's Gull *Rhodostethia rosea*		A	Lakes.	One state record, Sutherland Reservoir, December 1992.
Caspian Tern *Sterna caspia*		UC	Large rivers, deep marshes, lakes.	More frequent in east, May and September.
Common Tern *Sterna hirundo*		UC	Lakes, rivers, marshes.	Similar to Forster's tern. More common on lakes and reservoirs, not as common on marshes as Forster's terns.
Arctic Tern *Sterna paradisaea*		A	Lakes.	One documented record, Lake Minatare, September 2000.
Forster's Tern *Sterna forsteri*	L/C	C	Lakes and rivers during migration, marshes breeding.	Locally common breeder on large Sandhills lakes and marshes.
Least Tern *Sterna antillarum*	UC	UC	Rivers, lakes.	Nests on sandbars of Platte, Niobrara, Loup, Missouri rivers, and at sandpits.
Black Tern *Chlidonias niger*	L/C	C	Migrants in variety of aquatic habitats, marshes breeding.	Nests on Sandhills lakes and marshes.
ALCIDAE **murrelets**				
Ancient Murrelet *Synthliboramphus antiquus*		A		One state record, specimen from Missouri River, Burt County, 1929.
COLUMBIDAE **pigeons, doves**				
Rock Pigeon *Columba livia*	L/C	L/C	Human habitations, bluffs and buttes in western Nebraska.	Feral pigeons may occasionally nest on rock ledges in Panhandle.
Band-tailed Pigeon *Patagioenas fasciata*		A	Woodlands.	Two state records, Scotts Bluff County.
Eurasian Collared-Dove *Streptopelia decaocto*	UC		Principally rural towns.	First reported breeding in state in1998, now probably present in all counties and expected to increase in abundance.
White-winged Dove *Zenaida asiatica*		R	Variable.	All records since 1988, expanding range northward. Look for them in Panhandle and southwest in summer.
Mourning Dove *Zenaida macroura*	C	C	Grasslands, woodland edge, croplands.	Some winter in southeast and Platte Valley.

COMMON-SCIENTIFIC NAME	BREEDER	MIGRANT	HABITAT	ADDITIONAL INFORMATION
COLUMBIDAE **pigeons, doves** *(continued)*				
Passenger Pigeon *Ectopistes migratorius*				Extinct.
Inca Dove *Columbina inca*		R	Open areas, woodland edge.	Four state records, most likely late fall. Expanding northward.
Common Ground-Dove *Columbina passerina*		R	Open areas, woodland edge.	Two state records, most likely fall.
PSITTACIDEA **parakeets**				
Carolina Parakeet *Conuropsis carolinensis*				Extinct.
CUCULIDAE **cuckoos, anis**				
Black-billed Cuckoo *Coccyzus erythropthalmus*	UC	UC	Wooded habitats with understory of shrubs, vines.	Less common than yellow-billed, most common in northeast.
Yellow-billed Cuckoo *Coccyzus americanus*	L/C	L/C	Moderately dense thickets, second growth woodlands.	Less common in west.
Groove-billed Ani *Crotophaga sulcirostris*		A	Woodland edge, thickets, open areas.	Three state records, all from September-November.
TYTONIDAE **barn owls**				
Barn Owl *Tyto alba*	LC	LC	Grasslands with nesting sites.	Most numerous in southwest, nests in holes in banks, cliffs and in farm structures.
STRIGIDAE **typical owls**				
Eastern Screech-Owl *Megascops asio*	L/C		Woodlands, woodland edge, urban woods.	Nonmigratory, statewide resident. Gray morph more common than red and brown morphs.
Great Horned Owl *Bubo virginianus*	C		Forests, woodlands, also in unwooded habitats.	Resident statewide, most abundant in riparian woodlands. A few winter visitors from north.
Snowy Owl *Bubo scandiacus*		UC	Open fields, plains.	A few reported each winter when food is limited in north.
Northern Hawk Owl *Surnia ulula*		A		One state record, 1912, Sheridan County.
Burrowing Owl *Athene cunicularia*	L/C	L/C	Grasslands, prairie dog towns.	Most common western two-thirds of state, declined as prairie dogs eradicated.
Barred Owl *Strix varia*	L/C		Dense riverbottoms, deciduous woodlands.	Resident, most common in southeast, and along Missouri River Valley.
Great Gray Owl *Strix nebulosa*		A		One state record, Dixon County, January 1978.
Long-eared Owl *Asio otus*	R	UC	River bottoms, parks, orchards, woodlots.	Scattered breeding locations, winter roosts in conifers, more rare in west.
Short-eared Owl *Asio flammeus*	UC	UC	Grasslands, often near marshes.	Nomadic and gregarious in winter. Most common in Sandhills and Rainwater Basin in early winter.
Boreal Owl *Aegolius funereus*		A		One state record, Clay County, 1916.
Northern Saw-whet Owl *Aegolius acadicus*		UC	Dense coniferous and deciduous forests.	Winter visitor, principally in eastern Nebraska. Possible Pine Ridge breeder. Former Missouri Valley breeder.
CAPRIMULGIDAE **goatsuckers**				
Common Nighthawk *Chordeiles minor*	C	C	Grasslands and other open areas, also urban.	Nest in grasslands and on graveled roofs Large flocks in fall migration.

Key

A – Accidental – Reported but cannot be expected to occur again.
R – Rare – Fewer than 50 reports exist.
UC – Uncommon – Some present every year in expected habitats.

C – Common – Expected to be found in the proper habitat at appropriate times.
L – Local in occurrence.

COMMON-SCIENTIFIC NAME	BREEDER	MIGRANT	HABITAT	ADDITIONAL INFORMATION
Common Poorwill *Phalaenoptilus nuttallii*	C	C	Rocky habitats with scrubby vegetation.	Most common in west, migrants possible statewide, range expanding eastward. May nest in Niobrara Valley.
Chuck-will's-widow *Caprimulgus carolinensis*	UC	UC	Oak-hickory, woodland edge.	Most common east. Indian Cave SP a good location.
Whip-poor-will *Caprimulgus vociferus*	C	C	Oak-hickory forest.	Prefers woodland with intact understory. Most common Missouri Valley.
APODIDAE **swifts**				
Chimney Swift *Chaetura pelagica*	C	C	Open habitats, most common in towns and cities.	Few in Panhandle but increasing. Roosts and nests in man-made structures, formerly in mature woodlands.
White-throated Swift *Aeronautes saxatalis*	L/C	L/C	Cliffs, buttes, canyons with vertical rock faces.	Panhandle only, principally Pine Ridge and Wildcat Hills.
TROCHILIDAE **hummingbirds**				
Ruby-throated Hummingbird *Archilochus colubris*	UC	L/C	Woodlands, towns.	Uncommon breeder, principally Missouri and lower Platte valleys.
Costa's Hummingbird *Calypte costae*		A		One state record, Dawson County.
Calliope Hummingbird *Stellula calliope*		R	Woodland edge, towns.	Ten state records, mostly in Panhandle in fall.
Broad-tailed Hummingbird *Selasphorus platycercus*		UC	Woodland edge, towns.	Most reports from Panhandle in August at feeders and in flower gardens.
Rufous Hummingbird *Selasphorus rufus*		UC	Plains, foothills, gardens.	Most reports from Panhandle in August at feeders and in flower gardens.
ALCEDINIDAE **kingfishers**				
Belted Kingfisher *Ceryle alcyon*	L/C	L/C	Streams, lakes, ponds with abundant fish.	Nests in vertical dirt banks near water.
PICIDAE **woodpeckers**				
Lewis's Woodpecker *Melanerpes lewis*	L/UC	L/UC	Forest edge, principally pine, with standing dead trees.	As a breeder restricted to Pine Ridge. Rare late-May and August-September migrant principally in Pine Ridge and Wildcat Hills.
Red-headed Woodpecker *Melanerpes erythrocephalus*	C	C	Open forest, isolated trees and groves.	More common in east. Declining in numbers nationwide.
Acorn Woodpecker *Melanerpes formicivorus*		A		One record, Holt County, 1996.
Red-bellied Woodpecker *Melanerpes carolinus*	C		Woodland edge, open woodlands, forests.	Permanent resident east. Expanding west in riparian woodlands.
Williamson's Sapsucker *Sphyrapicus thyroideus*		A	Woodland edge.	Three records, all central and east. Expected more common in Panhandle pine woodlands.
Yellow-bellied Sapsucker *Sphyrapicus varius*		UC	Various woodlands, especially poplars and aspens.	Most reports in southeast, Missouri Valley. Most conspicuous in winter and southeast.
Red-naped Sapsucker *Sphyrapicus nuchalis*		R	Coniferous woodlands, woodland edge.	Six records, most Pine Ridge. Breeder in Black Hillls, South Dakota. September and April most likely times for sightings.
Downy Woodpecker *Picoides pubescens*	C		Varied woodland habitats.	Nonmigratory resident statewide, more common east.
Hairy Woodpecker *Picoides villosus*	C		Mature forests, woodlands.	Nonmigratory resident statewide, more common east.
American Three-toed Woodpecker *Picoides dorsalis*		A	Burned pine woodlands.	Two records, both Panhandle. Most likely in Pine Ridge, winter. Look for them in burned areas.
Northern Flicker *Colaptes auratus*	C	C	Riparian woodland, woodland edge.	Permanent resident statewide, red-shafted form east, yellow-shafted west, hybrids.
Pileated Woodpecker *Dryocopus pileatus*	R		Mature eastern deciduous forest.	Recent breeding at Fontenelle Forest and Indian Cave SP. Could be found anywhere in lower Missouri Valley.

COMMON-SCIENTIFIC NAME	BREEDER	MIGRANT	HABITAT	ADDITIONAL INFORMATION
TYRANNIDAE **tyrant flycatchers**				
Olive-sided Flycatcher *Contopus cooperi*		UC	Woodlands, trees with dead upper branches.	Most numerous in Missouri Valley during migration, rare west.
Western Wood-Pewee *Contopus sordidulus*	L/C	L/C	Open pine and riparian woodlands and forests.	Most common western Nebraska, breeder in Pine Ridge and Wildcat Hills. Might hybridize with eastern wood-pewee.
Eastern Wood-Pewee *Contopus virens*	L/C	L/C	Deciduous woodlands and forests.	Most common in Missouri, lower Platte and Elkhorn valleys. Found westward along Platte and Niobrara rivers.
Yellow-bellied Flycatcher *Empidonax flaviventris*		UC	Second growth woodlands.	Most likely in Missouri Valley, late-May and August-September.
Acadian Flycatcher *Empidonax virescens*	R	UC	Shady riparian woodlands.	Hypothetical fall migrant. Best location Indian Cave SP in early-June.
Alder Flycatcher *Empidonax alnorum*		UC	Shrubby woodland edge.	Most likely east during spring migration, especially late-May in Missouri Valley.
Willow Flycatcher *Empidonax traillii*	L/C	L/C	Shrubs near water.	Nests in willow thickets, larger eastern river valleys.
Least Flycatcher *Empidonax minimus*	R	L/C	Floodplain forest, scattered woodlands.	Breeds along Niobrara River, mid-May migrants in Missouri Valley.
Hammond's Flycatcher *Empidonax hammondii*		R	Woodland edge, riparian.	Most likely in west. Willow thickets. Oliver Reservoir best site.
Gray Flycatcher *Empidonax wrightii*		R	Arid habitats.	Look in arid habitats, late May, southern Panhandle.
Dusky Flycatcher *Empidonax oberholseri*		R	Woodland edge.	Western Nebraska. Oliver Reservoir best site.
Cordilleran Flycatcher *Empidonax occidentalis*	UC	R	Shaded canyons, riparian, deciduous shrubs.	Pine Ridge, Wildcat Hills. Best sites Sowbelly Canyon and Gilbert-Baker WMA.
Eastern Phoebe *Sayornis phoebe*	L/C	L/C	Woodlands near water.	Nests on manmade structures, bridges, outbuildings.
Say's Phoebe *Sayornis saya*	L/C	L/C	Open dry habitats, grasslands.	Western Nebraska. Nests on manmade structures and ledges of rock outcrops.
Vermilion Flycatcher *Pyrocephalus rubinus*		R	Riparian areas.	Four reports, one documented. Most likely southwest.
Ash-throated Flycatcher *Myiarchus cinerascens*		A		One state record, Dawes County, 1987.
Great Crested Flycatcher *Myiarchus crinitus*	C	C	Mature deciduous woodlands.	Common spring-fall migrant in east, uncommon in west. Best sites Fontenelle Forest and Indian Cave SP in May-June.
Cassin's Kingbird *Tyrannus vociferans*	UC	UC	Grassland, pine woodland edge.	Best sites Wildcat Hills and Pine Ridge.
Western Kingbird *Tyrannus verticalis*	C	C	Open areas with trees.	Statewide breeder, more common in west. Breeds in drier habitats than eastern kingbird.
Eastern Kingbird *Tyrannus tyrannus*	C	C	Open areas with trees.	Statewide breeder, more common in east.
Scissor-tailed Flycatcher *Tyrannus forficatus*	R	R	Grassland with scattered trees.	Most common in southeast. Nine state breeding records. Best sites are southeastern WMAs.
LANIIDAE **shrikes**				
Loggerhead Shrike *Lanius ludovicianus*	L/C	L/C	Open habitat with scattered shrubs, small trees.	Absent in winter. More common in north and west where habitat is more abundant.
Northern Shrike *Lanius excubitor*		UC	Grasslands with scattered trees, shrubs.	Winter visitor, more common in west, western Sandhills and Panhandle.
VIREONIDAE **vireos**				
White-eyed Vireo *Vireo griseus*		R	Bottomland understory, thickets near streams.	Prefers dense undergrowth adjacent to woodlands, often near water. Best sites Fontenelle Forest, Indian Cave State Park.

Key   **A** – Accidental – Reported but cannot be expected to occur again.
R – Rare – Fewer than 50 reports exist.
UC – Uncommon – Some present every year in expected habitats.

C – Common – Expected to be found in the proper habitat at appropriate times.
L – Local in occurrence.

COMMON-SCIENTIFIC NAME	BREEDER	MIGRANT	HABITAT	ADDITIONAL INFORMATION
Bell's Vireo *Vireo bellii*	L/C	L/C	Grasslands with shubs and thickets near water.	More common in east, especially in Loup River Valley.
Black-capped Vireo *Vireo atricapilla*		A		One state record. Sarpy County, May 1921.
Yellow-throated Vireo *Vireo flavifrons*	UC	UC	Mature, moist deciduous forests.	Spring and fall migrant. Best locations Missouri, lower Platte and Niobrara valleys.
Plumbeous Vireo *Vireo plumbeus*	UC	UC	Pine woodlands.	One of three species formerly called "solitary vireo." Oliver Reservoir, Wildcat Hills, Gilbert-Baker WMA.
Cassin's Vireo *Vireo cassinii*		UC	Woodland, woodland edge.	Western Nebraska. One of three species formerly called "solitary vireo." Oliver Reservoir, possibly Wildcat Hills.
Blue-headed Vireo *Vireo solitarius*		L/C	Woodland, woodland edge.	Principally in eastern Nebraska. One of three species formerly called "solitary vireo."
Warbling Vireo *Vireo gilvus*	C	C	Riparian woodlands.	Statewide migrant in variety of woodland types. Most often breeds in cottonwoods.
Philadelphia Vireo *Vireo philadelphicus*		UC	Open woodlands, streamside and lakeside thickets.	Most common east half of the state, principally Missouri Valley.
Red-eyed Vireo *Vireo olivaceus*	C	C	Deciduous forests with large trees.	Most numerous in Missouri Valley. Extending range west along river systems.
CORVIDAE **crows, jays, ravens**				
Gray Jay *Perisoreus canadensis*		R	Coniferous, mixed forests.	Reported in towns in winter. Two documented state records, northwest.
Steller's Jay *Cyanocitta stelleri*		UC	Principally coniferous forests.	Most reports from winter feeders in Panhandle.
Blue Jay *Cyanocitta cristata*	C	C	Woodlands, woodland edge.	Less abundant in west than east.
Pinyon Jay *Gymnorhinus cyanocephalus*	L/UC	UC	Pine woodlands.	First documented breeding in Pine Ridge in 1999. Probably more common as breeders in Wildcat Hills.
Clark's Nutcracker *Nucifraga columbiana*	A	UC	Pine woodlands.	One state breeding record. Reported eastward during irruptions years. Best sites Gilbert-Baker, Sowbelly Canyon in fall and winter.
Black-billed Magpie *Pica hudsonia*	C		Grasslands with scattered trees or shrubs.	More abundant west, but breeding documented statewide.
American Crow *Corvus brachyrhynchos*	C	C	Wide variety of habitats.	More abundant in east during breeding season. Common urban dwellers.
Chihuahuan Raven *Corvus cryptoleucus*	R	R	Arid grasslands with trees.	Most likely south-central, southwest. No records since 1979.
Common Raven *Corvus corax*		A	Open woodlands, grasslands.	Apparently statewide before disappearance of bison. Two documented state records since 1900.
ALAUDIDAE **larks**				
Horned Lark *Eremophila alpestris*	C	C	Sparse grasslands, barren cropland.	Regular migrant, breeder, winter visitor statewide. Sandhills optimum habitat.
HIRUNDINIDAE **swallows**				
Purple Martin *Progne subis*	L/C	L/C	Martin houses, usually near water.	More common in east, rare in Panhandle. Occasionally nesting on cliffs, old woodpecker holes.
Tree Swallow *Tachycineta bicolor*	C	C	Grasslands with trees near water.	Common in east, becoming rare in west. Commonly nests in bluebird houses as well as natural tree cavities.
Violet-green Swallow *Tachycineta thalassina*	LC	LC	Open pine woodlands.	Principally in Pine Ridge, Wildcat Hills. Migrants farther east in fall.
Northern Rough-winged Swallow *Stelgidopteryx serripennis*	C	C	Wooded streams with vertical banks.	Common migrant, breeder statewide. Nests in dirt or sand banks, roadcuts. Generally not colonial.
Bank Swallow *Riparia riparia*	L/C	C	Vertical banks near water.	Typically nest in banks of soft substrate near lakes and streams. Often in large colonies.

COMMON-SCIENTIFIC NAME	BREEDER	MIGRANT	HABITAT	ADDITIONAL INFORMATION
HIRUNDINIDAE **swallows (continued)**				
Cliff Swallow *Petrochelidon pyrrhonota*	C	C	Open country. Nests on rock outcrops, bridges near water.	Abundant migrant, breeder statewide. Nest in large colonies where mud is available.
Cave Swallow *Petrochelidon fulva*		R		Four state records, all in Keith County. Sometimes seen with cliff swallows.
Barn Swallow *Hirundo rustica*	C	C	Open habitats with buildings, cliffs, bridges.	Common breeder and migrant statewide.
PARIDAE **chickadees, titmice**				
Black-capped Chickadee *Poecile atricapillus*	C	C	Mature woodlands, forest, woodland edge.	Common resident statewide. Breeding least common in southwest and southern Panhandle. Common at winter feeders.
Mountain Chickadee *Poecile gambeli*		R	Woodland edge.	Winter visitor, principally North Platte Valley.
Tufted Titmouse *Baeolophus bicolor*	C		Oak-hickory woodlands and forests.	Resident southeast. Breeding in counties bordering Missouri River north to Washington County.
SITTIDAE **nuthatches**				
Red-breasted Nuthatch *Sitta canadensis*	UC	UC	Pine forests and woodlands.	Regular breeding in Wildcat Hills, Pine Ridge and more recently in Thomas County.
White-breasted Nuthatch *Sitta carolinensis*	C	UC	Mature deciduous woodlands and woodland edge.	Common resident north and east. Not migratory. Eastern and western races.
Pygmy Nuthatch *Sitta pygmaea*	UC		Pine forests and woodlands.	First confirmed nesting in Pine Ridge in 1957, Wildcat Hills in 1996. Fall flocks of 50+ birds.
CERTHIIDAE **creepers**				
Brown Creeper *Certhia americana*	R	UC	Mature deciduous forests and woodlands.	Documented nesting in Fontenelle Forest and Pine Ridge. Possible nesting on central Niobrara.
TROGLODYTIDAE **wrens**				
Rock Wren *Salpinctes obsoletus*	L/C	L/C	Arid grasslands with rock outcrops, badlands.	Common migrant, breeder west. Usually nests in rock cavities but sometimes nests in dirt banks and trees.
Canyon Wren *Catherpes mexicanus*		A	Cliffs, steep rocky canyons.	Rare migrant, winter visitor northwest and north. Two documented records in Sioux and Knox counties.
Carolina Wren *Thryothorus ludovicianus*	L/C		River-bottom forests, woodland edge.	Non-migratory residents in southeastern Nebraska. Numbers decline in cold winters.
Bewick's Wren *Thryomanes bewickii*		R	Open woodlands, brushy areas, farmsteads, towns.	Present but rare all seasons in east and central. Few records since 1960s.
House Wren *Troglodytes aedon*	C	C	Forests, woodlands, woodland edge, urban.	Common migrant, breeder statewide. Most numerous in Missouri Valley woodlands.
Winter Wren *Troglodytes troglodytes*		UC	Riparian woodlands, ravine thickets along streams.	As a spring and fall migrant and winter visitor more common in east, and rare in west.
Sedge Wren *Cistothorus platensis*	R	C	Wet grass-sedge meadows, lowland grasslands.	Sporadic breeder in July and August. Few breeding records since 1960.
Marsh Wren *Cistothorus palustris*	C	C	Emergent vegetation of freshwater marshes, streams.	Common Sandhills nester. Seldom nest south of Platte River.
CINCLIDAE **dippers**				
American Dipper *Cinclus mexicanus*		R	Rapidly flowing streams in wooded areas.	Rare, fall through spring visitor. Three documented state records. Niobrara and White rivers are likely habitats.

Key

A – Accidental – Reported but cannot be expected to occur again.
R – Rare – Fewer than 50 reports exist.
UC – Uncommon – Some present every year in expected habitats.

C – Common – Expected to be found in the proper habitat at appropriate times.
L – Local in occurrence.

COMMON-SCIENTIFIC NAME	BREEDER	MIGRANT	HABITAT	ADDITIONAL INFORMATION
REGULIDAE **kinglets**				
Golden-crowned Kinglet *Regulus satrapa*		L/C	Forests, woodlands, woodland edge.	Common spring and fall migrant statewide. More common winter visitor in southeast. Prefers conifers.
Ruby-crowned Kinglet *Regulus calendula*		C	Forests, woodlands, woodland edge.	More common migrant in east than west, and winter visitor southeast.
SYLVIIDAE **gnatcatchers**				
Blue-gray Gnatcatcher *Polioptila caerulea*	L/C	L/C	Lowland deciduous forest woodlands, upland shrubby sites.	Until recently a breeder principally in Missouri Valley in southeast and as migrant in eastern third of the state. Breeding population now established in Wildcat Hills.
TURDIDAE **thrushes**				
Eastern Bluebird *Sialia sialis*	C	C	Grasslands with scattered trees, woodland edge.	Until recent years a breeder in eastern third of the state. Range has expanded westward, largely because of presence of nesting boxes.
Mountain Bluebird *Sialia currucoides*	L/C	L/C	Migrants in open country, breeders in open woodlands.	Common migrant in west, central. Breeder in northwest, Pine Ridge, Wildcat Hills.
Townsend's Solitaire *Myadestes townsendi*	R	C	Pine and juniper forests.	Winter visitor in western Nebraska in junipers. Rare breeder Pine Ridge.
Veery *Catharus fuscescens*		R	Forests close to running water.	Migrant statewide, most common Missouri Valley. Best sites Fontenelle Forest, Indian Cave State Park in mid-May.
Gray-cheeked Thrush *Catharus minimus*		UC	Heavy shrubbery, deciduous woodlands.	Most common in east, especially Missouri Valley. Best sites shady areas near streams at Fontenelle Forest, Indian Cave SP.
Swainson's Thrush *Catharus ustulatus*	A	C	Floodplain forest, parks, shelterbelts.	Seeks shady riparian woodlands. Statewide migrant. One state breeding record, Dawes County, August 1973.
Hermit Thrush *Catharus guttatus*		UC	Deciduous woodlands, viney tangles, shrubbery.	Seeks dense, shaded woodlands. More common in east. Eastern and western races. Late-April, early-May best times.
Wood Thrush *Hylocichla mustelina*	L/C	L/C	Mature deciduous forests.	More common in east. Most common as breeder in Missouri and central Niobrara valleys.
American Robin *Turdus migratorius*	C	C	Forests, woodland edge, urban.	Erratic regular winter visitor where juniper berries and other wild fruit available, often riparian woodlands.
Varied Thrush *Ixoreus naevius*		R	Coniferous forest, open woodlands.	32 records, statewide. Attracted to feeders. Prefer coniferous woodlands. Most reports from towns and cities.
MIMIDAE **mockingbirds, thrashers**				
Gray Catbird *Dumetella carolinensis*	C	C	Brushy habitats. thickets, woodland edge.	Common migrant, breeder in east. Uncommon in west.
Northern Mockingbird *Mimus polyglottos*	UC	UC	Grasslands with scattered trees and shrubs.	Migrant and breeder statewide, more common in southeast. Best sites southeastern WMAs.
Sage Thrasher *Oreoscoptes montanus*		R	Sage-dominated grasslands, open prairies.	Rare spring and fall migrant, summer visitor. Hypothetical breeder in sagebrush grasslands of northwestern Sioux County.
Brown Thrasher *Toxostoma rufum*	C	C	Open woodlands, shrubby, brushy habitats.	Common spring and fall migrant, breeder statewide.
Curve-billed Thrasher *Toxostoma curvirostre*		A	Woodland edge.	Five records, North Platte west. Most likely in late fall, winter in southwest or southern Panhandle.
STURNIDAE **starlings**				
European Starling *Sturnus vulgaris*	C	C	Human habitation, urban and rural.	Resident statewide, becoming uncommon in northwest. First state record in 1930.

COMMON-SCIENTIFIC NAME	BREEDER	MIGRANT	HABITAT	ADDITIONAL INFORMATION
MOTACILLIDAE **pipits**				
American Pipit *Anthus rubescens*		C	Bare shorelines of wetlands, moist grasslands.	Statewide spring-fall migrants where sparse vegetation. In fall found on reservoir margins. More common in northwest in fall.
Sprague's Pipit *Anthus spragueii*		R	Dense vegetation of plains, prairies.	Spring and fall migrant most common central. Best sites are short pastures central in early-October.
BOMBYCILLIDAE **waxwings**				
Bohemian Waxwing *Bombycilla garrulus*		UC	Fruit-bearing trees.	Erratic winter visitor principally in northwest. Periodic irruptions eastward. Feed on Russian olive, juniper, hackberry fruit.
Cedar Waxwing *Bombycilla cedrorum*	UC	UC	Fruit trees in urban areas.	Common migrant, winter visitor statewide. Breeder east and west. Most conspicuous in October-November and February-March.
PTILOGONATIDAE **silky-flycatchers**				
Phainopepla *Phainopepla nitens*		A		One state record, Alliance, January 1983.
PARULIDAE **wood warblers**				
Blue-winged Warbler *Vermivora pinus*		R	Woodland edge, thickets, pastures.	Rare spring-fall migrant east, even less common west. Apparently a breeder in Missouri Valley before 1900.
Golden-winged Warbler *Vermivora chrysoptera*		R	Second-growth woodlands, thickets.	More common migrant east. Best time first two weeks of May in Missouri Valley.
Tennessee Warbler *Vermivora peregrina*		C	Deciduous woodlands.	Statewide migrant most common in east.
Orange-crowned Warbler *Vermivora celata*		C	Deciduous woodland, brush.	Spring-fall migrant statewide. Late-April, early-May best time.
Nashville Warbler *Vermivora ruficapilla*		UC	Second-growth woodlands, brushy undercover.	Common spring-fall migrant in east, rare in west. Mid-May, Fontenelle Forest, Indian Cave SP.
Virginia's Warbler *Vermivora virginiae*		R	Woodland edge, brush.	Rare spring migrant in west. Eight records, all Panhandle. Oliver Reservoir, Wildcat Hills.
Northern Parula *Parula americana*	UC	UC	Swampy woods, parks, orchards.	Spring migrant, breeder east, rare west. Most breeding reports from Missouri Valley.
Yellow Warbler *Dendroica petechia*	C	C	Woodland edge, brush.	Common spring and fall migrant, breeder statewide. Prefer willow thickets in summer.
Chestnut-sided Warbler *Dendroica pensylvanica*		UC	Thickets, woodland edge.	Spring-fall migrant in east, rare in west. Hypothetical breeder.
Magnolia Warbler *Dendroica magnolia*		UC	Thickets, woodland edge, both deciduous, coniferous.	Spring-fall migrant in east, rarer in west. Mid-May, Missouri Valley. Found in more dense woodlands than most warblers.
Cape May Warbler *Dendroica tigrina*		R	Forests, parks, gardens.	Rare spring and fall migrant east. Most reports from Missouri Valley. Prefers to forage for insects in oaks, conifers.
Black-throated Blue Warbler *Dendroica caerulescens*		R	Low shrubby areas, parks, woodlands, gardens.	Rare spring-fall migrant statewide, more common in fall from September to mid-October. Forages low.
Yellow-rumped Warbler *Dendroica coronata*	UC	C	Variety of wooded habitats, thickets.	Perhaps the most common migrant warbler, statewide. Audubon's subspecies breeds in Pine Ridge, Gilbert-Baker, Sowbelly Canyon.
Black-throated Gray Warbler *Dendroica nigrescens*		A	Pine, juniper woodlands, riparian habitats.	One documented state record, Oliver Reservoir, 1986.
Black-throated Green-Warbler *Dendroica virens*		UC	Variety of woodlands, often second growth, riparian.	More common in east, rare in west. Best site Missouri Valley early-May and September. Forages at medium heights.

Key ✎   **A** – Accidental – Reported but cannot be expected to occur again.
     R – Rare – Fewer than 50 reports exist.
     UC – Uncommon – Some present every year in expected habitats.   **C** – Common – Expected to be found in the proper habitat at appropriate times.
     L – Local in occurrence.

COMMON-SCIENTIFIC NAME	BREEDER	MIGRANT	HABITAT	ADDITIONAL INFORMATION
Townsend's Warbler *Dendroica townsendi*		R	Woodlands.	Migrants in oak, juniper, pine, riparian woodlands. Rare migrant in west, principally in Panhandle in fall.
Hermit Warbler *Dendroica occidentalis*		A		One poorly documented report.
Blackburnian Warbler *Dendroica fusca*		UC	Deciduous woodland.	More common in east, rare in west. Mid-May, Missouri Valley. Forages high in trees.
Yellow-throated Warbler *Dendroica dominica*	R	R	Wet deciduous woodlands.	Most often in sycamores, forages near top. Best site is Fontenelle Forest.
Pine Warbler *Dendroica pinus*		R	Pine woodlands.	Also in deciduous woodlands, especially fall. As migrant, mostly in east in fall. About 20 state records.
Prairie Warbler *Dendroica discolor*		R	Brushy fields, red cedars.	Rare spring migrant statewide. Six state records. Best habitat is fields with scattered cedars, edge of oak-hickory woodlands.
Palm Warbler *Dendroica palmarum*		UC	Brushy fields, open woods, woodland edge.	More common in spring and east than in fall and west. Best time early to mid-May in Missouri Valley.
Bay-breasted Warbler *Dendroica castanea*		UC	Variety of coniferous and deciduous woodlands.	Found in deciduous, coniferous and mixed woodlands. More common in east and in fall. Indian Cave SP, Fontenelle Forest.
Blackpoll Warbler *Dendroica striata*		L/C	Tall deciduous trees in streamside woodlands.	More common in east and spring. Best sites are Fontenelle Forest and Indian Cave State Park in mid-May.
Cerulean Warbler *Dendroica cerulea*	R	R	Mature deciduous woodlands.	Rare migrant in east, even less common in central and west. Rare breeder east. Fontennelle Forest a good site.
Black-and-white Warbler *Mniotilta varia*	LC	LC	Riparian deciduous woodlands.	Migrant statewide, more common in east. Breeder north in deciduous or coniferous woodlands on lower Niobrara Valley. Early- and mid-May in Missouri Valley.
American Redstart *Setophaga ruticilla*	C	C	Deciduous riparian woodlands.	Common spring-fall migrant in east, less common in west. Breeder in northwest, north, east.
Prothonotary Warbler *Protonotaria citrea*	UC	UC	Wetlands in deciduous woodlands.	More common in east and spring. Uncommon regular breeder. Best site is Great Marsh at Fontenelle Forest.
Worm-eating Warbler *Helmitheros vermivorus*		R	Riparian or hillside woodlands with shrubby understory.	Rare spring migrant statewide, rare fall migrant in east. Prefers deep ravines near water. Most reports in Missouri Valley.
Swainson's Warbler *Limnothlypis swainsonii*		A	Brushy thickets near water.	One questionable state record.
Ovenbird *Seiurus aurocapilla*	L/C	L/C	Pine, deciduous woodlands.	Spring and fall migrant statewide. Breeder in north and east. Most common as breeder in Missouri and Niobrara valleys.
Northern Waterthrush *Seiurus noveboracensis*		L/C	Riparian woodlands, edge.	Common spring and fall migrant in east, rare in west. Best sites Missouri Valley in mid-May are brush areas near standing water.
Louisiana Waterthrush *Seiurus motacilla*	UC	UC	Deciduous woodlands near streams.	Uncommon migrant and breeder principally in east. Best sites Missouri Valley, Fontenelle Forest, Indian Cave State Park.
Kentucky Warbler *Oporornis formosus*	UC	UC	Dense upland woodlands with heavy understory.	Regular spring-fall migrant in east, rare or absent west. Rare breeder in east. Best sites Indian Cave SP, Fontenelle Forest and Hummel Park in Omaha.
Connecticut Warbler *Oporornis agilis*		R	Low deciduous woodlands with brushy tangles.	About 35 state records, all eastern Nebraska. Forages on ground. Best site Missouri Valley, mid-May.
Mourning Warbler *Oporornis philadelphia*		L/C	Thickets, woodland edge along streams.	Common spring and fall migrants in east, becoming rare in west. Best location Neale Woods in mid-May.
MacGillivray's Warbler *Oporornis tolmiei*		LC	Brushy thickets near water.	Regular spring and fall migrant in west, becoming increasing rare in east. Best sites are riparian thickets in Pine Ridge and Oliver Reservoir.

COMMON-SCIENTIFIC NAME	BREEDER	MIGRANT	HABITAT	ADDITIONAL INFORMATION
PARULIDAE **wood warblers** *(continued)*				
Common Yellowthroat *Geothlypis trichas*	C	C	Wetland edge.	Common spring-fall migrant and breeder statewide. Abundance declines from east to west.
Hooded Warbler *Wilsonia citrina*		R	Moist, mature forests with heavy understory, urban.	Rare spring migrant statewide, more common in east. About 50 records. Best sites Indian Cave SP, Schramm Park.
Wilson's Warbler *Wilsonia pusilla*		C	Woodland edge, brush, often near streams.	Spring-fall migrant statewide, less common west. Preference for willow thickets. Best time mid-May east, early September west.
Canada Warbler *Wilsonia canadensis*		UC	Deciduous woodlands.	Prefer brushy riparian woodlands. Spring and fall migrant more common in east. Best time mid-May in Missouri Valley.
Yellow-breasted Chat *Icteria virens*	C	C	Streamside thickets, edge.	Spring and fall migrant and breeder, less common east. Populations have disappeared from southeast.
THRAUPIDAE **tanagers**				
Hepatic Tanager *Piranga flava*		A	Pine woodlands.	One state record, January 1999 at West Point. Closest populations in Colorado and Wyoming.
Summer Tanager *Piranga rubra*	L/C	L/C	Mature deciduous woodlands.	Rare migrant east, uncommon but regular breeder east. Best sites Indian Cave State Park and Schramm Park.
Scarlet Tanager *Piranga olivacea*	L/C	L/C	Mature deciduous woodlands.	Uncommon spring-fall migrant in east, less common in west. Regular breeder east, central Niobrara Valley.
Western Tanager *Piranga ludoviciana*	L/C	L/C	Coniferous woodlands.	Regular spring and fall migrant in west, less common to east. In a variety of woodlands during migration.
EMBERIZIDAE **towhees, new world sparrows, longspurs**				
Green-tailed Towhee *Pipilo chlorurus*		R	Arid environments, thickets, shrubs, sage.	Rare spring and fall migrant in Panhandle. Occasionally reported farther east. Best sites Scotts Bluff National Monument, Wildcat Hills, Oliver Reservoir.
Spotted Towhee *Pipilo maculatus*	C	C	Riparian woodland edge, thickets.	Breeder in western two-thirds of the state. Leaves the Panhandle in winter.
Eastern Towhee *Pipilo erythrophthalmus*	C	C	Brushy fields, thickets, edge, woodland edge, urban.	Common breeder in southeast, less common south and southwest. Absent in winter. Eastern towhee and spotted towhee had been lumped as rufous-sided towhee until recently.
Cassin's Sparrow *Aimophila cassinii*	UC	UC	Sage grasslands.	Erratic, regular breeder, migrant in west and southwest. Best sites Enders Reservoir, Rock Creek Lake, Dundy County.
American Tree Sparrow *Spizella arborea*		C	Woodland edge, brush.	Spring and fall migrant, and winter visitor statewide.
Chipping Sparrow *Spizella passerina*	C	C	Woodland edge, orchards, urban.	Breeding birds prefer coniferous woods, migrants might be in deciduous woods. Common spring and fall migrant, breeds statewide, less common southwest.
Clay-colored Sparrow *Spizella pallida*		L/C	Thickets, weed patches in grasslands with shrubs.	Common spring and fall migrant statewide, hypothetical breeder in northern counties.
Brewer's Sparrow *Spizella breweri*	L/C	L/C	Scrubland, shortgrass plains with sagebrush.	Spring and fall migrant west, breeder in western Panhandle. Best sites include Ogalala Grassland and near Wyoming border.

Key   **A** – Accidental – Reported but cannot be expected to occur again.
R – Rare – Fewer than 50 reports exist.
UC – Uncommon – Some present every year in expected habitats.

C – Common – Expected to be found in the proper habitat at appropriate times.
L – Local in occurrence.

COMMON-SCIENTIFIC NAME	BREEDER	MIGRANT	HABITAT	ADDITIONAL INFORMATION
Field Sparrow *Spizella pusilla*	C	C	Open grasslands with scattered shrubs.	Common spring and fall migrant and breeder in east, rare in west.
Vesper Sparrow *Pooecetes gramineus*	C	C	Grassland edge or mix of shrubs and trees.	Spring and fall migrant statewide, breeder in north and northwest. Most common in Sandhills.
Lark Sparrow *Chondestes grammacus*	C	C	Grassland, grassland edge with scattered trees, shrubs.	Common spring and fall migrant, breeds statewide with largest numbers in north and west.
Black-throated Sparrow *Amphispiza bilineata*		R		Rare spring migrant in east and west, rare winter visitor in east. Five state reports, three documented.
Sage Sparrow *Amphispiza belli*		A	Sagebrush grasslands.	One state record, Sioux County, August 1989.
Lark Bunting *Calamospiza melanocorys*	C	C	Shortgrass and mixed-grass prairie with shrubs and weedy areas.	Shortgrass and mixed-grass prairie. Abundant spring and fall migrant in west, less common in east, common breeder in west. Large flocks in late summer.
Savannah Sparrow *Passerculus sandwichensis*	L/UC	C	Migrants in low wet grasslands.	Spring and fall migrant statewide. Local breeder in west. Best known breeding site is Facus Springs WMA.
Grasshopper Sparrow *Ammodramus savannarum*	C	C	Grasslands.	Statewide migrant in spring and fall. More common breeder west.
Baird's Sparrow *Ammodramus bairdii*		R	Grasslands.	Rare spring and fall migrant in west and central. Most likely in shortgrass prairie or western Sandhills in early-May or mid-September. Few records.
Henslow's Sparrow *Ammodramus henslowii*	R	R	Moist, weedy pastures and fields.	Spring-fall migrant east and central. Best site is Burchard Lake in Pawnee County, also Spring Creek Prairie.
Le Conte's Sparrow *Ammodramus leconteii*		UC	Wet meadows, marsh edge.	Spring and fall migrant in east, less common in west. Best sites are low grasslands in Missouri Valley, early-October. Also Jack Sinn WMA.
Nelson's Sharp-tailed Sparrow *Ammodramus nelsoni*		R	Wet edges, marshes, sloughs.	Spring and fall migrant east, more common fall. Best sites are Jack Sinn WMA and eastern Rainwater Basin marshes.
Fox Sparrow *Passerella iliaca*		UC	Woodland edge, brushy areas.	Spring and fall migrant in east, becoming rare in west. Best locations in Missouri Valley in early-April and late-October.
Song Sparrow *Melospiza melodia*	L/C	C	Weedy areas, thickets, streamside, woodland edge.	Spring and fall migrant in east, uncommon in west. Breeder north and east. Best sites are Rainwater Basin wetlands.
Lincoln's Sparrow *Melospiza lincolnii*		L/C	Thickets, weedy areas.	Spring and fall migrant in east, uncommon in west. Usually close to water. Best sites in Missouri Valley in early-October.
Swamp Sparrow *Melospiza georgiana*	L/C	C	Wetlands with emergent vegetation.	Spring and fall migrant in east, becoming less common in west. Breeds in brushy cattail marshes. Most breeding records Sandhills and Loup Valley.
White-throated Sparrow *Zonotrichia albicollis*		C	Woodland edge, thickets, weedy fields, winter feeders.	Spring and fall migrant in east, less common in west. Some winter in southeast.
Harris's Sparrow *Zonotrichia querula*		C	Woodland edge, brush.	Spring and fall migrant in east, less common in west. Winter visitor southeast. Missouri Valley an important migration corridor.
White-crowned Sparrow *Zonotrichia leucophrys*		C	Woodland edge, brush.	Spring and fall migrant statewide, uncommon winter visitor statewide.
Golden-crowned Sparrow *Zonotrichia atricapilla*		R	Woodland edge, brush.	Rare spring and fall migrant in west and central. Three documented state records. Often migrate with white-crowned sparrows.
Dark-eyed Junco *Junco hyemalis*	UC	C	Woodland edge, brush.	Common spring and fall migrants and winter visitors statewide. "White-winged" subspecies breeds in Pine Ridge.
McCown's Longspur *Calcarius mccownii*	UC	UC	Shortgrass prairie.	Spring and fall migrant in west, regular breeder in western Panhandle. Often mixed with Lapland longspurs.

COMMON-SCIENTIFIC NAME	BREEDER	MIGRANT	HABITAT	ADDITIONAL INFORMATION
EMBERIZIDAE **towhees, new world sparrows,** **longspurs** *(continued)*				
Lapland Longspur *Calcarius lapponicus*		C	Short grasslands or cultivated fields.	Common spring and fall migrant winter visitor statewide. Look for them with horned larks on winter roadsides.
Smith's Longspur *Calcarius pictus*		R	Open areas	Usually on short grasslands or cultivated fields. Spring migrant in southeast, fall migrant statewide. More common in fall.
Chestnut-collared Longspur *Calcarius ornatus*	L/C	L/C	Plains, pastures with short grass.	Spring and fall migrant in west becoming less common in east. Common breeder in west, less common in north-central.
Snow Bunting *Plectrophenax nivalis*		UC	Open areas, short vegetation, roadsides, fields, beaches.	Spring and fall migrant, winter visitor statewide.
CARDINALIDAE **cardinals, grosbeaks,** **new world buntings**				
Northern Cardinal *Cardinalis cardinalis*	C		Woodlands, woodland edge, urban.	Nonmigratory. More common in east. Has spread west in riparian woodlands. Now almost statewide.
Rose-breasted Grosbeak *Pheucticus ludovicianus*	C	C	Deciduous woodlands.	Spring and fall migrant and breeder in east, less common west. Prefers woodland with well-developed understory.
Black-headed Grosbeak *Pheucticus melanocephalus*	LC	LC	Open woodlands with well-developed understories.	Spring and fall migrant and breeder in west and central, less common in east. Hybridizes with rose-breasted in central.
Blue Grosbeak *Passerina caerulea*	L/C	L/C	Weedy pastures, old fields, edge, thickets, hedgerows.	Spring and fall migrant and breeder statewide. Most common in grasslands with brush or riparian edge.
Lazuli Bunting *Passerina amoena*	L/C	L/C	Open, shrubby forest, second-growth woodlands.	Spring and fall migrant and breeder in west, rare migrant east.
Indigo Bunting *Passerina cyanea*	C	C	Open, shrubby forest, second-growth woodlands.	Spring and fall migrant and breeder in east, less common in west. Hybridizes with Lazuli in central Nebraska, particularly along Niobrara and Platte rivers.
Painted Bunting *Passerina ciris*		R	Brushy riparian habitat.	Nine state records. Mostly likely to be found in central or western Platte Valley in May.
Dickcissel *Spiza americana*	C	C	Grasslands, croplands with shrubs.	Spring and fall migrant and breeder in east, less common west.
ICTERIDAE **meadowlarks, blackbirds, orioles**				
Bobolink *Dolichonyx oryzivorus*	L/C	L/C	Meadows, pastures.	Spring-fall migrant statewide. Nests in wet meadows in river valleys.
Red-winged Blackbird *Agelaius phoeniceus*	C	C	Migrants often in fields, breeders in wetlands.	Spring-fall migrant and breeder statewide. Large flocks conspicuous from late July into October.
Eastern Meadowlark *Sturnella magna*	C	C	Tall and mixed-grass prairie, meadows.	Common spring-fall migrant and breeder east, less common west.
Western Meadowlark *Sturnella neglecta*	C	C	Prairies, hayfields, weedy cropland borders, meadows.	Spring-fall migrant and breeder statewide, rare northwest.
Yellow-headed Blackbird *Xanthocephalus xanthocephalus*	C	C	Breeds in marsh, lake edge, heavy emergent vegetation.	Spring-fall migrant statewide, more common west. Most common as breeder in Sandhills.
Rusty Blackbird *Euphagus carolinus*		UC	Woodlands near water.	Spring-fall migrant east, less common west. Winter visitor east.
Brewer's Blackbird *Euphagus cyanocephalus*	L/C	C	Migrants in pastures, barnyards, grainfields.	Breeds in short grasslands with brush or scattered trees. Spring-fall migrant and breeder west. Best sites are Ogalala grasslands, Wildcat Hills.
Common Grackle *Quiscalus quiscula*	C	C	Woodland edge, farmsteads, urban, shelterbelts.	Spring-fall migrant and breeder statewide. Gather in large flocks in fall.

Key   **A** – Accidental – Reported but cannot be expected to occur again.   **C** – Common – Expected to be found in the proper habitat at
R – Rare – Fewer than 50 reports exist.   appropriate times.
UC – Uncommon – Some present every year in expected habitats.   **L** – Local in occurrence.

COMMON-SCIENTIFIC NAME	BREEDER	MIGRANT	HABITAT	ADDITIONAL INFORMATION
Great-tailed Grackle *Quiscalus mexicanus*	C	C	Cattail marshes, open ground, croplands near water, urban.	Most common as breeders in Rainwater Basin and central Platte Valley. First reported in state in 1976.
Brown-headed Cowbird *Molothrus ater*	C	C	Grasslands with scattered trees, fields, pastures.	Common spring-fall migrant and breeder statewide.
Orchard Oriole *Icterus spurius*	C	C	Open woodlands, woodland edge.	Spring-fall migrant and breeder statewide. Expanded westward in 20th century.
Bullock's Oriole *Icterus bullockii*	L/C	L/C	Coniferous woodlands.	Spring-fall migrant and breeder west. Hybridizes with Baltimore oriole.
Baltimore Oriole *Icterus galbula*	L/C	L/C	Wooded river bottoms, shelterbelts, urban.	Spring-fall migrant and breeder east and central, rare west. Until recently lumped with Bullock's as northern oriole.
Scott's Oriole *Icterus parisorum*		A	Woodland edge.	One record, Hall County, June 1975.
FRINGILLIDAE **finches**				
Brambling *Fringilla montifringilla*		A		One record, Scotts Bluff County, April 1999.
Gray-crowned Rosy-Finch *Leucosticte tephrocotis*		UC	Rock outcrops in open grasslands.	Erratic winter visitor in western Panhandle at feeders and roosting in rock outcrops in grasslands. Most likely late-October and early-November. Roost in late afternoon.
Black Rosy-Finch *Leucosticte atrata*		A	Rock outcrops in open grasslands.	One record, Sioux County, November 2000. Found with gray-crowned rosy-finch.
Pine Grosbeak *Pinicola enucleator*		R	Conifers, fruit trees.	Rare winter visitor statewide. Few recent reports, most during irruption years. Look in winter in central Niobrara Valley.
Purple Finch *Carpodacus purpureus*		UC	Woodlands, woodland edge, feeders.	Spring-fall migrant and winter visitor east, rare west. Usually seen at feeders.
Cassin's Finch *Carpodacus cassinii*	A	R	Coniferous woodlands, feeders.	Rare visitor, principally northwest but also North Platte Valley.
House Finch *Carpodacus mexicanus*	C	C	Open woods, river thickets, scrubby vegetation, urban.	Common resident statewide. First recorded west, but spread statewide from introduced eastern U.S. population, becoming common by 1990s.
Red Crossbill *Loxia curvirostra*	UC	C	Coniferous woodlands, and forest, sunflower and ragweed patches.	Spring-fall migrant and breeder northwest, rare elsewhere. Probable breeding in Wildcat Hills since 1960s.
White-winged Crossbill *Loxia leucoptera*		R	Coniferous forests.	Uncommon winter visitor statewide. Often with red crossbill. Cemeteries with spruce and hemlock trees.
Common Redpoll *Carduelis flammea*		UC	Coniferous and deciduous woodlands, fields, feeders.	Most common in northwest and north in winter, but reported statewide. An erratic winter visitor.
Hoary Redpoll *Carduelis hornemanni*		A	Woodland edge, feeders.	Rare winter visitors statewide. Usually with common redpolls.
Pine Siskin *Carduelis pinus*	C	L/C	Wooded, treeless areas where weed seed available, feeders.	Breed in pine woodlands in Pine Ridge. Spring-fall migrant and winter visitor statewide in a variety of woodland habitats. Common at feeders.
Lesser Goldfinch *Carduelis psaltria*		R	Woodland edge, brush.	Seven records, summer visitor northwest. Look in flocks of American goldfinches, Panhandle, June and July.
American Goldfinch *Carduelis tristis*	C	C	Thickets, weedy grasslands, feeders.	Spring-fall migrant and breeder statewide. Frequent feeders in winter and spring. Nest June into September.
Evening Grosbeak *Coccothraustes vespertinus*		R	Coniferous woodlands, feeders.	Erratic winter visitor and hypothetical breeder northwest. Most common in the Panhandle during irruption years.
PASSERIDAE **old world sparrows**				
House Sparrow *Passer domesticus*	C	C	Areas of human habitation.	Introduced, permanent resident statewide.

APPENDIX
Index

Northwestern Glaciated Plains, 32
Northwestern Great Plains, 32, 33 (map)
Nutcracker, Clark's, 112, 134, 135, 136, 138, 139, 140, 143
Nuthatch
  Pygmy, 100, 132 (photo), 134, 136, 138, 139, 140, 143
  Red-breasted, 44, 93, 96, 97, 100, 102, 104, 115, 116, 134, 140, 143
  White-breasted, 22, 40, 43, 45, 51, 53, 55, 62, 64, 81, 93, 97, 100, 104, 106, 130, 140
Nuttall, Thomas, 111

Oglala National Grassland, 110 (map), 121 (photo), 122, 138
Ogallala Aquifer, 88
Ogallala, Lake, 108, 109 (photo) 110 (map), 111, 112, 113
Oliver Reservoir SRA, 110 (map), 124 (photo), 125
Omaha Audubon Society, 23, 25, 29, 41
Omaha (Indian), 8, 9, 40
Omaha Nature Study Club, 23, 25
Omernik, James M., 32
Oregon Trail, 82, 116, 117
Oriole
  Baltimore, 44, 49, 51, 53, 55, 56 (photo), 62, 64, 78, 81, 85, 87, 97, 100, 101, 102, 104, 106, 116, 131, 134, 148
  Bullock's, 56, 77, 78, 100, 101, 102, 104, 106, 116, 124, 125, 131, 134, 136, 140, 143
  Orchard, 43, 44, 49, 51, 53, 62, 64, 81, 85, 87, 97, 100, 101, 104, 106, 124, 130, 140, 143
Osprey, 43, 45, 85 (photo), 101, 104, 112, 118
Ostenberg, Clive, 118
Otoe (Indian), 10, 11
Otoe County, 11, 59
Ovenbird, 40, 43, 44, 55, 97, 104, 106, 140, 149
Owl
  Barn, 29, 85, 87, 99, 100, 115, 140, 143
  Barred, 9, 39, 40, 42, 44 (photo)
  Burrowing, 12, 19, 25, 48, 85, 87, 95 (photo), 96, 97, 99, 104, 106, 116, 117, 119, 120, 122, 124, 125, 128, 130, 131, 143
  Eastern Screech-, 2 (photo), 9, 43, 51, 62, 64, 85, 87, 93, 97, 99, 100, 101, 104, 118, 131
  Great Horned, 62, 99, 115, 137
  Long-eared, 43, 45, 51, 53, 85, 96, 100, 101, 104
  Northern Saw-whet, 112, 140
  Short-eared, 43, 52, 72, 73, 97, 99, 100, 124, 128
  Snowy, 9, 18, 122

Padelford, Barbara, 30
Parakeet, Carolina, 7, 12, 15, 16, 17, 32, 34
Partridge, Gray, 16, 45
Parula, Northern, 38, 39, 40, 42, 100, 115
Pathfinder Dam, 75
Patton, Florence, 28
Pawnee (Indian), 8, 9 10, 12, 16, 58
Pawnee County, 50
Pawnee Prairie WMA, 36 (map), 49, 50
Pearse, Arthur, 12, 20
Pelican, American White, 15 (art), 17, 43, 45, 53, 85, 86, 90, 91, 92, 97 (photo), 98, 101, 104, 112, 114, 118, 130
Perkins County, 126, 127, 128
Peterson, Roger Tory, 28
Peterson WMA, 137
Phalarope
  Red, 72
  Red-necked, 99, 100, 112, 118, 119
  Wilson's, 45, 52, 60, 69, 70, 73, 99, 100, 117,
118, 119
Pheasant, Ring-necked, 53, 62, 71
Phelps County, 12, 71, 72, 108
Phoebe
  Eastern, 40 (photo), 44, 45, 55, 62, 81, 85, 87, 97, 104, 130, 136
  Say's, 85, 87, 104, 106, 112, 116, 117, 120, 122, 123, 124, 134, 135, 137 (photo), 140, 143
Pigeon
  Feral, 32
  Passenger, 7, 11, 12, 14, 34
Pike, Zebulon, 15
Pinchot, Gifford, 95
Pine Glen WMA, 107
Pine Ridge, 21, 22, 110, 121, 123, 132, 133, 134, 135, 136, 138, 139, 140
Pine Ridge, Nebraska National Forest, 122, 138
Pintail, Northern, 68, 70, 73, 77, 81, 91, 118
Pintail WMA, 73
Pipit
  American, 52, 73, 92, 119
  Sprague's, 46, 49
Pittman-Robertson Act, 27
Platte County, 63, 66
Platte River, 6, 9, 10, 12, 15, 16, 27, 28, 36 (map), 54, 55, 56, 60 (map), 66, 67, 71, 72, 74, 75, 76, 77, 78, 79, 80, 81
Platte River SP, 54, 55
Platte River Whooping Crane Maintenance Trust, 79
Plover
  American Golden-, 17, 47, 66, 69, 70, 73, 96
  Black-bellied, 17, 52, 69, 70, 73, 115, 118 (photo)
  Mountain, 48, 120, 123 (photo)
  Piping, 16, 17 (photo), 26, 29, 38, 44, 45, 52 55, 56, 64, 68, 72, 77, 78, 81, 96, 102, 104, 112, 113
  Semipalmated, 45, 69, 70, 73, 85
  Snowy, 70, 72, 112 (photo)
Playa wetlands, 65, 66
Plum Creek WMA, 107
Ponca (Indian), 11
Ponca State Park, 37, 38, 43, 44
Ponderosa WMA, 138
Poorwill, Common, 17, 97, 102, 104, 116, 118, 130, 134, 136, 140, 143
Prairie
  Tallgrass, 7, 33 (map), 36 (map), 46, 47 (photo), 48, 49, 50, 51, 55, 58, 78, 120, 138
  Mixed-Grass, 33 (map), 58, 59 (photo), 60, 110 (map), 121 (photo)
  Shortgrass, 120, 123
Prairie-chicken
  Greater, 7, 12, 46, 49, 81, 85, 87, 89, 91, 92, 97, 99, 104, 106, 114, 129
  Lesser, 46, 99, 129, 130
Prairie Wolfe WMA, 62, 64
Pressey, H.E., 61
Pressey WMA, 60 (map), 61
Pritchard, Claremont "Bud," 28, 31
Pritchard, Mary Hanson, 31

Rail
  Black, 90, 91
  King, 91, 115, 116 (photo)
  Virginia, 45, 52, 65, 72, 90, 91, 92, 100, 101, 104, 115, 118, 119, 131
  Yellow, 52, 90, 91
Rainwater Basin, 6, 7, 60 (map), 66, 67 (photo), 68, 69, 70, 71, 72, 73, 80
Rapp, William, 26, 28
Raven, Common, 15
Rawhide Creek, 34
Redhead, 45, 65, 91, 92, 99, 100, 101, 112
Redhead WPA, 73
Red Willow County, 130
Red Willow Reservoir, 60 (map), 82, 87
Redpoll, Common, 122
Redstart, American, 14, 40, 42, 43, 44, 45, 62, 97, 104, 106, 140
Republican River, 82, 84, 126
Richardson County, 11, 17, 21
Ridgway, Robert, 19
Ridgway, J.L., 19
Robin, American, 25, 48
Rock Creek, 110 (map), 126
Rock Creek Fish Hatchery, 131
Rock Creek Lake SRA, 131
Rocky Mountain Bird Observatory, 29, 123
Roosevelt, Theodore, 93, 95, 106
Roosevelt, Franklin D., 31
Rosche, Richard, 96, 100, 108, 111, 115, 118, 119, 134, 138
Rowe, Annette, Sanctuary, 60 (map), 78, 79
Ruff, 70, 71

Sacramento WMA, 60 (map), 71, 72
Saline Wetlands, 52
Salt Creek, 12, 20, 51, 52
Salt Valley, 52, 53
Sanderling, 112, 118
Sandhills, 6, 7, 16, 33 (map), 88, 89, 90 (map), 91, 95, 97, 98, 99, 100, 101, 126
Sandpiper
  Baird's, 45, 70, 73, 96, 97, 99, 112, 115, 118, 119
  Buff-breasted, 53, 70, 73, 96, 112, 115
  Curlew, 72
  Least, 45, 70, 73, 99, 115, 118, 119
  Pectoral, 52, 65, 70, 73, 96, 99, 115
  Semipalmated, 45, 70, 73, 115
  Solitary, 70, 96, 106
  Spotted, 43, 44, 45, 53 (photo), 57, 62, 64, 81 104, 106, 131
  Stilt, 45, 52, 70, 73 (photo), 96, 99, 115, 119
  Upland, 7, 14, 32, 47, 48, 49, 50, 51, 59, 66, 69, 70, 73, 77, 79, 81, 89, 91, 92, 96, 99, 100, 104, 106, 115, 122, 123, 124, 128, 131 (photo)
  Western, 98, 115, 118, 119
  White-rumped, 70, 73, 98, 99, 119, 130
Sandpiper WMA, 73
Sapsucker
  Red-naped, 135
  Yellow-bellied, 43
Sarpy County, 31
Sather, Henry, 27, 30
Saunders County, 51, 52, 66
Say, Thomas, 12
Scaup
  Greater, 53, 100, 111, 112
  Lesser, 31 (stamp), 43, 77, 112, 118
Schildman, George, 27
Schilling, Randall W., WMA, 56
Schramm Park SRA, 36 (map), 54, 55, 56
Scoter
  Black, 43, 52, 53, 111
  Surf, 43, 45, 52, 53, 100, 111
  White-winged, 43, 52, 53, 111, 125
Scotts Bluff County, 72, 108, 113
Scotts Bluff National Monument, 110 (map), 116, 132
Sessions, L., 59, 60
Sharpe, Roger, 12, 15, 16, 18, 28, 31, 144
Sheldon, Mrs. Addison, 25, 61
Shell Creek, 65
Sheridan County, 12, 98

APPENDIX

Acknowledgments

Birding Nebraska contains the combined knowledge of dozens of people who graciously shared information gleaned from years of studying birds in Nebraska. This willingness to share information has a long history in Nebraska bird study and can be traced back to the likes of Myron Swenk and Wilson Tout, to whom encouraging the study of birds was as important as studying birds themselves. It is, after all, in sharing such knowledge and love that the future of the state's avifauna is balanced. The specific contributions of these people are too numerous to cite individually. Several devoted many hours in many ways over several months to the project and deserve special recognition, in particular John Dinan, Jeanine Lackey, Wayne Mollhoff, Ross Silcock and Gerry Steinauer. Our apologies to anyone whose contribution is inadvertently not acknowledged.

Those who contributed regional or site birds lists are Cris Carnine, Kathy Delara, John Dinan, Dean Drawbaugh, Phyllis Drawbaugh, Larry Einemann, Ruth Green, Rocky Hoffmann, Bill Huser, Jan Johnson, Stephen Jones, Joel Jorgenson, Clem Klaphake, Jeanine Lackey, Wayne Mollhoff, Babs Padelford, Loren Padelford, Don Paseka, Janis Paseka, Kevin Poague, Neal Ratzlaff, Ross Silcock, Kent Skaggs, T.J. Walker and Harley Winfrey.

Those who graciously reviewed and commented on portions or all of the text include John Dinan, Steve Dinsmore, Rocky Hoffmann, Mace Hack, Stephen Jones, Joel Jorgensen, Alice Kenitz, Jeanine Lackey, Ted LaGrange, Wayne Mollhoff, Janis Paseka, Mary Lou Pritchard, Richard Rosche, Ross Silcock, Gerry Steinauer, Mark Vrtiska and T.J. Walker.

Valuable information and research was provided by Ruth Green, Betty Grenon, Larry Hutchinson, Paul Johnsgard, Joel Jorgensen, Teresa Kreutzer-Hodson, Betsy McFadden, Cynthia Monroe, Jim Swinehart, Barbara Voeltz and Richard Voeltz.

Birding destinations were selected by Nebraska Game and Parks Commission biologists and wildlife managers, and derived from reports in *The Nebraska Bird Review*. Numerous Commission staff also reviewed the text for accuracy. Those Commission employees are Laurel Badura, Mark Feeney, Jeff Fields, Daylan Figgs, Mace Hack, Lance Hastings, Jeff Hoffman, Wayne Kelly, Ted LaGrange, Chuck Lesiak, Nick Lyman, Michael Morava, Tom Morrison, Tom Motacek, Bob Muduna, Ritch Nelson, Mike Remund, Ben Rutten, Bruce Sackett, Gary Schlichtemeier, Warren Schwanebeck, Jeff Sprock, Clayton Stalling, Chad Taylor, Scott Taylor, Neal VanWinkle, T.J. Walker, Tom Welstead and Scott Wessel.

Federal and private conservation organization staff who provided information on their areas and reviewed text include Jeff Buettner and Mark Peyton, Central Nebraska Public Power and Irrigation District; Gary Garabrandt, Fontenelle Nature Association; Royce Huber, Mark Lindvall, Kathy McPeak, Gene Mack, Jeff Drahota, Brad McKinney and Steve Knode, U.S. Fish and Wildlife Service; Robert Manasek and Lil Morava, National Park Service; Jerry Schumacher, U.S. Forest Service; Al Steuter, Jim Lusinger and Tracey Vodehnal, The Nature Conservancy; and Paul Tebbel and Kent Skaggs, Rowe Sanctuary. Those who contributed in other ways are Kari Andreson, Mark Brogie, Tom Labedz, Marge Seuferer, Sam Wilson and Ruth Wusk.

Jim Omernik and Jeff Comstock deserve acknowledgment for providing the ecoregions maps in digital format. The poster was produced by Chapman, Shannen S., Omernik, James M., Freeouf, Jerry A., Huggins, Donald G., McCauley, James R., Freeman, Craig C., Steinauer, Gerry, Angelo, Robert T., and Schlepp, Richard L., 2001, Ecoregions of Nebraska and Kansas, (color poster with map, descriptive text, summary tables, and photographs): Reston, Virginia, U.S. Geological Survey (map scale 1:1,950,000). Maps adapted for *Birding Nebraska* by Tim Reigert.

A special thanks is due Jim Douglas and the Nebraska Game and Parks Commission's Wildlife Division for contributing personnel time and funding for this issue. Information and Education staff members who diligently applied their talents, skills and attention to detail and accuracy in fashioning the raw materials into this special *NEBRASKAland* issue are Tom White, Doug Carroll and Tim Reigert.

The content and any errors are solely the responsibility of the author.

– Jon Farrar

Birding
Nebraska

Writer and Coordinator: Jon Farrar
Editors: Tom White, Doug Carroll
Art Director: Tim Reigert

NEBRASKALAND MAGAZINE STAFF

Editor: Tom White
Associate Editor: Doug Carroll
Art Director: Tim Reigert
Senior Editors: Jon Farrar, Ken Bouc
Regional Editors: Eric Fowler, Bob Grier, Rocky Hoffmann
Contributing Editors: Michael Forsberg, Tom Keith
Circulation: Donna Robinson

NEBRASKA GAME AND PARKS COMMISSION

Administration

Director: Rex Amack
Assistant Directors: Roger Kuhn, Kirk Nelson
Information and Education Administrator: Ken Bouc
Information and Education Art Director: Steve O'Hare

Board of Commissioners

Chairman: Randall K. Stinnette, Inland
Vice Chairman: Marvin Westcott, Holdrege
2nd Vice Chairman: James Stuart Jr., Lincoln

Bill Grewcock, Omaha
Dr. Mark Pinkerton, Wilber
Bill Zutavern, Dunning
Gary Parker, Columbus

Inside Back Cover: A familar and favorite woodland edge species, brown thrashers are found statewide. Photo by Rod Nabholz.

NEBRASKAland Magazine
Published by the Nebraska Game and Parks Commission